The Carolina Curriculum
for Infants and Toddlers
with Special Needs

The Carolina Curriculum for Infants and Toddlers with Special Needs

Third Edition

By

Nancy M. Johnson-Martin, Ph.D.
Susan M. Attermeier, Ph.D., PT
and
Bonnie J. Hacker, M.H.S., OTR/L

·PAUL·H·
BROOKES
PUBLISHING CO.®

Baltimore • London • Sydney

Paul H. Brookes Publishing Co.
Post Office Box 10624
Baltimore, MD 21285-0624

www.brookespublishing.com

Typeset by Barton Matheson Willse & Worthington, Baltimore, Maryland.
Manufactured in the United States of America by
Edwards Brothers, Inc., Ann Arbor, Michigan.

The case studies in this book are composites based on the authors' experiences. In all instances, names
and identifying details have been changed to protect confidentiality.

The following Carolina Curriculum products can be purchased separately:

The Carolina Curriculum for Infants and Toddlers with Special Needs, Third Edition, Assessment Log
and Developmental Progress Chart (available in English in print, on CD-ROM, or in PDF format
on the web, and available in Spanish in PDF format on the web)

The Carolina Curriculum for Preschoolers with Special Needs, Second Edition

The Carolina Curriculum for Preschoolers with Special Needs, Second Edition, Assessment Log and
Developmental Progress Chart (available in English in print, on CD-ROM, or in PDF format on
the web, and available in Spanish in PDF format on the web)

Please visit http://www.brookespublishing.com/ccupdates for more information on these products. To
order, contact Paul H. Brookes Publishing Co. at the address above, or call 1-800-638-3775 (U.S. and
Canada) or 1-410-337-9580 (worldwide).

Library of Congress Cataloging-in-Publication Data

Johnson-Martin, Nancy, 1934–
    The Carolina curriculum for infants and toddlers with special needs / by Nancy M. Johnson-
Martin, Susan M. Attermeier, and Bonnie J. Hacker.—3rd ed.
        p.   cm.
    Rev. ed. of: The Carolina curriculum for infants and toddlers with special needs / Nancy Johnson-
Martin . . . et al.]. 2nd ed. ©1991.
    Includes bibliographical references (p.   ) and index.
    ISBN 1-55766-653-9 (spiral bound : alk. paper)
    1. Children with disabilities—Education (Preschool)—Curricula—United States. 2. Children with
disabilities—Services for—United States. 3. Children with disabilities—United States—
Development. 4. Infants—United States—Development. I. Attermeier, Susan M., 1942– II. Hacker,
Bonnie J. III. Carolina curriculum for infants and toddlers with special needs. IV. Title.

LC4019.2.J64 2004
371.9'0472—dc22   2004004635

British Library Cataloguing in Publication data are available from the British Library.

Contents

Curriculum Sequences

Personal-Social

Cognition

About the Authors

Nancy M. Johnson-Martin, Ph.D., is a consultant for assessment and early intervention following her retirement from the University of North Carolina at Chapel Hill where she held positions in the Division for Disorders of Development and Learning and in the Frank Porter Graham Child Development Center (now called the Frank Porter Graham Child Development Institute).

Susan M. Attermeier, Ph.D., PT, is a pediatric physical therapist in private practice in Hillsborough, North Carolina. She was previously Assistant Professor in the Division of Physical Therapy at the University of North Carolina at Chapel Hill.

Bonnie J. Hacker, M.H.S., OTR/L, is an occupational therapist with more than 25 years' experience working with children. She holds certifications in Neurodevelopmental Therapy, Southern California Sensory Integration Tests, and Sensory Integration and Praxis Tests. She is currently the director of Emerge—A Child's Place, a pediatric clinic in Durham and Chapel Hill, North Carolina, that provides children with occupational and speech therapy services.

Acknowledgments

This volume would not have been possible without the efforts of those who played a major role in the development of the two earlier versions of this curriculum. Specifically, we recognize Kenneth Jens, Ph.D., who coauthored the first two editions; Karen O'Donnell, Ph.D., and Peggy Ogelsby, Ph.D., who contributed to the chapter on guiding learning in the first edition; Judy Burke, who coordinated the initial field testing of the curriculum in the Infant Treatment Program at the University of North Carolina at Chapel Hill, Division for Disorders of Development and Learning; Sara Carter, CCC-SP, who provided major assistance in the development of the language portions of the second edition; and Barbara Davis Goldman, Ph.D., who contributed much to our thinking about language and cognitive and social skills in young children. We are also indebted to Harrie Chamberlin, Director of the Division for Disorders of Development and Learning, who encouraged us and supported the development of the Infant Treatment Program, and to James Gallagher, Ph.D., who was the director of the Frank Porter Graham Child Development Center and the Carolina Institute for the Early Education of the Handicapped, the umbrella under which the first edition of the curriculum was developed.

We acknowledge and thank those professionals who took time from their busy schedules to review the second edition of the curriculum and make suggestions for improving this revision.

Finally, we thank Bob Johnson for his time and expertise in capturing on film the personalities of our cover children; our families and friends for their support of our endeavors; Heather Shrestha for her encouragement and help in getting us started on this revision; and Mackenzie Lawrence for her wisdom, diligence, patience, and persistence in shepherding us from our first draft to the finished product.

To the children, parents,
and dedicated child care workers who,
for the past 30 years, have come into our lives,
teaching us much of what we know about
human development, courage, determination, adaptability,
and the joy of accomplishment. Without them,
this curriculum would not have been created.

ONE

■ ■ ■

Introduction

There have been many changes in the field of early intervention since the first edition of *The Carolina Curriculum for Handicapped Infants and Infants at Risk* (Johnson-Martin, Jens, & Attermeier) was published in 1986. Following the enactment of the Education of the Handicapped Act Amendments of 1986 (PL 99-457), there was a dramatic expansion of early intervention services in the United States of America. We have progressed from having widely scattered services focused exclusively on the child to having programs in every state that focus on the child as part of a family unit and from having only a few therapists trained to work with young children with special needs to having a variety of personnel specifically educated and trained to work with this population and their families. There are now special educators, speech therapists, occupational therapists, physical therapists, psychologists, nurses, social workers, and nutritionists who are specialists in early intervention. Moreover, these professionals have learned to work together, not only sharing information and expertise but also allowing the boundaries between their roles to blur as appropriate. There has been a shift from professionals providing services primarily in center-based programs to providing services in homes, child care centers, and preschools. Professionals now form partnerships with parents, child care providers, and teachers to develop and implement intervention activities within the daily routines of the children they serve.

At the time the first *Carolina Curriculum* was developed, the field urgently needed materials for children functioning in the birth to 24-month range and for children with significant disabilities who could not be expected to develop evenly across all developmental domains. Thus, that curriculum focused on the birth to 24-month developmental period and tried to accommodate uneven developmental patterns by dividing the skills included in the five basic domains of development (personal-social, cognition, communication, fine motor, and gross motor) into 24 sequences of skills, arranged in an order that promoted building a new skill on the foundation of previously learned skills.

The acceptance of *The Carolina Curriculum for Handicapped Infants and Infants at Risk* encouraged the authors to develop a companion volume, *The Carolina Curriculum for Preschoolers With Special Needs* (CCPSN; Johnson-Martin, Attermeier, & Hacker, 1990), directed toward children in the 24- to 60-month developmental range. An attempt to integrate the infant and preschool curricula was made when the infant curriculum was revised in 1991 (*The Carolina Curriculum for Infants and Toddlers with Special Needs, Second Edition [CCITSN]*; Johnson-Martin, Jens, Attermeier, & Hacker). However, interventionists found it difficult to use either curriculum efficiently with children whose skills were scattered between the two volumes.

This revision of the CCITSN and its companion volume, the second edition of the CCPSN, are designed to provide a guide for working with children who have special needs from birth to 60 months. The infant and toddler curriculum now includes items that cover developmental skills from birth to 36 months, whereas the preschool curriculum includes items to cover developmental skills from 24 to 60 months. The sequence and the item names are identical in both volumes for the 24- to 36-month range so that interventionists can move smoothly from one curriculum to the other.

WHAT IS THE CCITSN APPROACH?

This edition, like previous editions of the CCITSN, links assessment to intervention through hierarchies of developmental tasks that are both relevant to typical routines for young children and pertinent to long-term adaptation—an approach described as "authentic" by Bagnato, Neisworth, and Munson (1997). That is, the intervention is integrated in a meaningful way into the child's life. Because each item on the assessment tool is linked directly to a curriculum item that describes procedures for teaching the assessed skill, readers have a framework for moving smoothly from assessment to intervention. This edition includes the following characteristics:

1. The curriculum is based on typical sequences of development but does not assume that a child will develop at the same rate across domains or even within one domain (e.g., a child may exhibit typical cognitive development along with very delayed motor development, a child may have age-appropriate grammatical structures but have significantly delayed vocabulary). Thus, the curriculum is designed for you to use both with the child who is developing slowly but in a typical pattern and with the child whose pattern of development is markedly atypical due to one or more impairments.

2. The curriculum approaches atypical development in two ways. First, the items in each developmental domain are subdivided into logical teaching sequences (i.e., a sequence in which item order is primarily determined by how one skill builds on another, not only by the mean age levels at which typical children learn the skills). Second, general modifications of the items in each develop-

mental domain are suggested so that you can accommodate a child's particular sensory or motor limitations. Thus, a child with severely delayed motor abilities but potentially average cognitive skills is not held up in progressing through the cognitive domain because he or she cannot do items that require typical motor skills.

3. The curriculum is based on the recognition that many infants and toddlers with serious impairments will never develop typically in spite of intervention efforts. Thus, in treating these children, you must consider teaching atypical but highly adaptive skills that may temporarily or permanently replace typical skills. For example, should a child be unable to talk, it is appropriate for you to teach pointing or another indicator response that will allow him or her to make choices, communicate wishes, and so forth.

4. Although the curriculum is developmental, with items drawn from standard developmental assessment tools, clinical experience, and the observations of Jean Piaget, behavioral theory and methodology underlie item construction. There is also a strong emphasis on developing adaptive functional skills, even if these are not necessarily typical (e.g., moving by scooting on one's buttocks or using a scooter board when crawling would be typical but is not functional).

WHAT IS INCLUDED IN THE CCITSN?

The CCITSN has been designed to provide a systematic approach for developing intervention plans for children with special needs who are functioning within the birth to 36-month developmental range. In this curriculum, you will find

*   A criterion-referenced assessment for determining the child's mastery of important social, cognitive, language, motor, and adaptive skills

*   Suggestions for selecting educational objectives from the assessment

*   Guidelines for developing activities for the individualized family service plan (IFSP) that incorporate the educational objectives

WHAT HAS CHANGED IN THIS REVISION?

The changes in this revision reflect the need to reorganize the sequences to provide a smooth transition to the CCPSN, the recognition of the greater sophistication of many of those who use the curriculum, and a desire to include information not addressed in the previous editions.

Expanded Age Range

As noted previously, this edition of the CCITSN is intended for use with children functioning in the birth to 36-month range; previous editions covered development in the birth to 24-month range.

Reorganization of Sequences

In addition to including sequences for the developmental level from 24 to 36 months, other sequences in the infant and toddler curriculum have been reorganized to smoothly flow into the preschool curriculum. Most notably, in the cognitive area, the items previously included in several Object Permanence sequences are now included in two sequences: 1) Attention & Memory: Visual and 2) Attention & Memory: Auditory. This change was made not only to provide better linkage to the preschool curriculum but also to accommodate current thinking about the nature of object permanence tasks, now often described as "memory and motor tasks" (Agular & Baillargeon, 1999, p. 137). This new description does not diminish the importance of these sequences but assigns them a somewhat different role in cognitive development.

Table 1.1 provides a list of the sequences and the developmental domains under which they are organized in this curriculum. Note that three sequences—Concepts/Vocabulary: Receptive; Concepts/Vocabulary: Expressive; and Attention & Memory: Auditory—are listed as Cognition/Communication. The skills assessed in these sequences are included on almost all tests of cognitive ability and almost all tests of language ability. Thus, they clearly belong in both domains and should be included in both when estimating a summary level of development for those domains.

Items also have been moved to different age levels on the Assessment Log based on the most recent revisions of commonly used tests of development, including the Bayley Scales of Infant Development, Second Edition (Bayley, 1993); the Peabody Developmental Motor Scales, Second Edition (Folio & Fewell, 2000); and the Preschool Language Scale, Fourth Edition (Zimmerman, Steiner, & Pond, 2002).

Greater Reliance on the Expertise of the Curriculum User

When the first edition of the curriculum was developed, it was reasonable to expect that most curriculum users would not only be fairly inexperienced in providing early intervention but also would not have a strong background in the development of young children. Given the rapid growth in professional development and the growing number of experienced interventionists, it seems appropriate to provide somewhat less elementary information and encourage you to make use of your experience and wisdom when using the curriculum. However, we recognize that there will continue to be some inexperienced users and that some interventionists find it effective to provide curriculum items to parents. Thus, the assessment and curriculum items continue to be written simply, and examples are provided as appropriate. It is our intent that people with minimal experience and education in child development can understand and follow the instructions for assessing the skill each item represents and for engaging in activities to promote the development of that skill.

Table 1.1.   Developmental domains and the sequences of the CCITSN

Personal-Social		Communication	
1.	Self-Regulation & Responsibility	13.	Verbal Comprehension
2.	Interpersonal Skills	14.	Conversation Skills
3.	Self-Concept	15.	Grammatical Structure
4-I.	Self-Help: Eating	16.	Imitation: Vocal
4-II.	Self-Help: Dressing		
4-III.	Self-Help: Grooming		
4-IV.	Self-Help: Toileting		
Cognition		**Fine Motor**	
5.	Attention & Memory: Visual/Spatial	17.	Imitation: Motor
6-I.	Visual Perception: Blocks & Puzzles	18.	Grasp & Manipulation
6-II.	Visual Perception: Matching & Sorting	19.	Bilateral Skills
7.	Functional Use of Objects & Symbolic Play	20.	Tool Use
8.	Problem Solving/Reasoning	21.	Visual-Motor Skills
9.	Number Concepts		
Cognition/Communication		**Gross Motor**	
10.	Concepts/Vocabulary: Receptive	22-I.	Upright: Posture & Locomotion
11.	Concepts/Vocabulary: Expressive	22-II.	Upright: Balance
12.	Attention & Memory: Auditory	22-III.	Upright: Ball Play
		22-IV.	Upright: Outdoor Play
		23.	Prone (on Stomach)
		24.	Supine (on Back)

Note: Sequences 10, 11, and 12 overlap the cognition and communication domains and have been separated in this table to show this.

Reduced Emphasis on Specific Adaptations

In the first two editions of the infant and toddler curriculum, specific adaptations for children with visual, hearing, and/or motor impairments were included with every item. This produced considerable redundancy. Due to the growing number of experienced early intervention specialists, we concluded that it would be sufficient to make general suggestions for modifications at the beginning of each sequence, relying on curriculum users to devise specific modifications to meet the needs of the individual children with whom they work.

Omission of Chapter on Motor Development

Given that pediatric physical and occupational therapists can provide specific information about motor development for serving the needs of individual children, we felt a chapter on motor development was no longer necessary. Interventionists who have not had an opportunity to obtain a background in the motor development of young children are encouraged to seek that information from one of the popular books on development, such as *Touchpoints: Your Child's Emotional and Behavioral Development: Birth to 3* (Brazelton, 1992) or *Your Baby and Child: From Birth to Age Five* (Leach, 1997), or from the previous edition of *The Carolina Curriculum for Infants and Toddlers with Special Needs* (Johnson-Martin et al., 1991). However, for information about the needs of a specific child, interventionists without a background in motor development of young children should seek consultation from a physical or occupational therapist.

Increased Emphasis on Functional Activities

When the authors sought critiques from users of the second edition of the infant and toddler curriculum, many suggested increasing the emphasis on functional activities. In part, this concern may be due to a lack of clarity about how a particular skill related to a broader category of skills. For example, one interventionist felt that she spent far too much time teaching a child to remove cloths from objects (the focus of many items in the Object Permanence sequence). The purpose of those items was not to teach a child cloth pulling but to help the child learn to focus attention on an object and remember the object when it could no longer be seen (object permanence). The various ways of hiding the objects challenged the child's attention and memory. These purposes apparently had not been made clear.

In this third edition of the curriculum, the section in each item formerly titled *Use in Daily Routines* is now titled *Daily Routines & Functional Activities* to emphasize the importance of the skill being practiced in a variety of typical, day-to-day situations and to indicate how the skill can be practiced in a way that promotes greater effectiveness in the environment. Greater effectiveness may mean developing greater independence in play, increasing curiosity, using a skill for different functions, and so forth.

Nothing we write, however, is a substitute for you using your own education and experience and taking a long-term perspective. *The purpose of early intervention is to help children master the skills they will need to be prepared for both learning and social adjustment in kindergarten and beyond.* The functional activities or daily routines suggested for some items may be inappropriate for certain children or may be unacceptable in certain ethnic cultures. Thus, you need to consider how the skills you teach infants and toddlers relate to the goals families have for their children and the demands they will meet in school and in their communities. In addition, specific impairments may prevent a child from moving through one or more of the sequences included in the curriculum. When this happens, you need to think about how the sequence relates to parental goals and long-term academic, self-help, and social skills. It may be necessary to try to devise alternative ways for the child to achieve some competence in those areas (e.g., mastering language through the use of a communication board rather than speech). No general curriculum is a substitute for activities and goals informed by a child's unique characteristics.

Emphasis on Emergent Literacy

To encourage interventionists to think of the long-term goal of preparing children for school, this edition of the curriculum attempts to highlight the importance of emergent literacy skills. Since the 1980s, there has been a growing recognition that literacy does not begin with learning to read and write (Notari-Syverson, O'Connor, & Vadasy, 1998). Rather, it begins in the infant, toddler, and preschool years through

- *Print/book awareness:* Reading to children before they can read themselves is highly related to their later ability to read. Parents and families play a primary role by reading books to children, letting children see them reading, and pointing out text in the environment. Awareness of print includes early scribbling, drawing, letter/word formation, and the understanding that written words express ideas.

- *Metalinguistic awareness:* Metalinguistic awareness refers to the ability to reflect on, manipulate, and talk about linguistic forms. At the age level covered in this curriculum, this generally involves an interest in novel sounds and new words and the recognition that a new word shares characteristics with known words (e.g., isolating initial sounds in words, forming rhymes). Children learn these skills through rhyming, singing, and picking out sounds in words.

- *Oral language:* Oral skills related to reading include using words and sentences to describe events, tell a story, carry on a conversation, and express feelings (Notari-Syverson et al., 1998)

Items related to emergent literacy are scattered throughout the curriculum. They include attention to sounds, memory for sequences of sounds, interest in pictures and books, understanding that words stand for specific objects and pictures, speaking words, matching shapes, scribbling, and drawing shapes. Emergent literacy is one of the long-term goals that should be kept foremost in mind when developing intervention programs for children with special needs, whether the program is to be implemented at home or in a preschool.

A checklist of emergent literacy skills is included in the appendix at the end of this chapter. It covers skills learned from infancy through the preschool years (the ages covered by the CCITSN and the CCPSN). Most of these skills are included in one or another of the curriculum sequences. The value of the checklist is not only to help you assess a child's progress in emergent literacy but also to demonstrate the relationship of literacy to specific curriculum items focusing on visual, motor, cognitive, language, or social skills.

References for Parents and Teachers
Regarding Common Conditions Affecting Development

Many children who are served in early intervention programs have unspecified "developmental delays." The lack of a more specific diagnosis is due to both the genuine difficulty of making correct diagnoses in young children whose development is variable and a reluctance of professionals to label a young child. As authors, we also have concerns about labeling young children. Yet, a diagnosis is sometimes helpful to parents and the child in providing access to services that are earmarked for specific conditions. Furthermore, the diagnosis may have an impact on family planning and other important issues.

We encourage those working in early intervention to familiarize themselves with the characteristics of common conditions affecting early development. As you work with a child described as having a developmental delay, it may become apparent that the child does not just have delays but has characteristics that suggest a more specific condition or may simply be very puzzling. If this happens, you may wish to encourage the family to seek further evaluation or professional consultation to better understand the nature of the child's problems, especially if a specific diagnosis would provide access to additional services or support for the family. To help in this process, Appendix A at the end of the book provides a list of common conditions affecting development. Characteristics of each of these conditions, their effects on development, specific tips for interventionists or classroom teachers, and a list of resources are included on the Paul H. Brookes Publishing Co. web site (http://www.brookespublishing.com/ccupdates).

FOR WHOM IS THE CCITSN INTENDED?

This edition of the CCITSN is designed to provide curricular intervention strategies for use with children with impairments who are functioning in the birth to 36-month developmental range. The earlier editions have been used successfully by a variety of interventionists like yourself: educators, psychologists, child care workers, public health nurses, physical and occupational therapists, and speech-language pathologists. These interventionists have worked with children who have a wide range of impairments, from mild to severe. To encourage continued broad usage, a major effort has been made to avoid professional jargon in the wording of the materials. There also has been an effort to alert users to a child's characteristics or responses that require attention from professionals with particular skills (e.g., a physical, occupational, or speech-language therapist).

The CCITSN is appropriate for use in center- and home-based intervention programs. It is anticipated that parents and other caregivers, with professional consultation and guidance, will use the curriculum items in their daily interactions with children who have special needs.

HOW WERE ITEMS CHOSEN FOR THE CCITSN?

The basic content for all three editions of the infant and toddler curriculum was selected in the same manner that it has been selected for most other early intervention curricula. That is, the developmental skills listed on a variety of norm-referenced tests of development were reviewed, and pertinent skills were incorporated into the curriculum (e.g., Bayley, 1993; Bzoch, League, & Brown, 1991; Folio & Fewell, 2000; Rosetti, 1990; Sparrow, Balla, & Cicchetti, 1984; Zimmerman et al., 2002). To these basic items were added items selected from the Ordinal Scales of Psychological Development (Uzgiris & Hunt, 1975), one of the better-known tests of cognitive development based on the theories of Jean Piaget, skills the authors judged to be alternatives for children whose specific disabilities prevent the development of typical skills, skills from The Communicative Intention Inventory (Coggins & Carpenter, 1981) to broaden the focus of the communication section, and a few other skills that were considered to be important by the authors for social development and motivation. Specialists in speech-language pathology, occupational and physical therapy, nursing, psychology, education, and nutrition reviewed the lists of skills and contributed to the final selection process.

WHAT RESEARCH SUPPORTS THE CCITSN?

The first edition of the infant curriculum was developed as a part of a federal grant and was field tested in 22 centers in 11 states serving 150 children, including a number of children with severe physical and/or sensory disabilities.

Data Collected

Usefulness

Reviewers who had no experience with the curriculum completed a rating scale covering the comprehensiveness, understandability, usefulness for preparing an individualized education program (IEP), applicability to children with a broad range of disabling conditions, and ease of monitoring progress (perceived usability). Those participating in the field testing after 6–8 months of using the curriculum (actual usability) completed a similar scale.

Reliability of Use

Local field-test sites were visited bimonthly, and data were collected on how the curriculum was being implemented.

Child Progress

A five-step process examined the effectiveness of the curriculum for promoting developmental change: an initial assessment, a 3-month period of intervention focusing on half of the appropriate sequences, a second assessment, another 3-month period of intervention focusing on the neglected sequences, and a final assessment. This allowed a comparison of a child's progress in those sequences that were the focus of intervention with his or her progress in those sequences that were not the focus of intervention.

Outcomes

The data collected demonstrated that the curriculum users found *The Carolina Curriculum for Handicapped Infants and Infants at Risk* (Johnson-Martin et al., 1986) to be useful, that they used it as intended, and that it promoted developmental progress. Subsequent editions have not had the luxury of further field testing, but the authors have sought and incorporated feedback from interventionists who use the curriculum and scholars in child development and early intervention.

SUMMARY

The first two editions of the CCITSN have been used in a variety of settings to promote developmental progress in young children with special needs. They linked a developmental assessment procedure with curricular activities and provided suggestions for modifying activities to meet the needs of children with specific and severe disabilities. This revision is an attempt to update the curriculum by responding to feedback from users—building on the strengths of the previous editions as well as addressing concerns.

REFERENCES

Agular, A., & Baillargeon, R. (1999). Perseveration and problem solving in infancy. *Advances in Child Development and Behavior, 27,* 135–180.

Bagnato, S.J., Neisworth, J.T., & Munson, S.M. (1997). *LINKing assessment and early intervention: An authentic curriculum-based approach.* Baltimore: Paul H. Brookes Publishing Co.

Bayley, N. (1993). *Bayley Scales of Infant Development* (2nd ed.). San Antonio, TX: Harcourt Brace & Co.

Brazelton, T.B. (1992). *Touchpoints: Your child's emotional and behavioral development: Birth to 3.* Boulder, CO: Perseus Publishing.

Bzoch, K.R., League, R., & Brown, V. (1991). *Receptive Expressive Emergent Language Test* (2nd ed.). Los Angeles: Western Psychological Services.

Coggins, T.E., & Carpenter, R.L. (1981). The Communicative Intention Inventory: A system for observing and coding children's early intentional communication. *Applied Psycholinguistics, 2,* 235–251.

Education of the Handicapped Act Amendments of 1986, PL 99-457, 20 U.S.C. §§ 1400 *et seq.*

Folio, M.R., & Fewell, R. (2000). *Peabody Developmental Motor Scales* (2nd ed.). Los Angeles: Western Psychological Services.

Johnson-Martin, N.M., Attermeier, S.M., & Hacker, B. (1990). *The Carolina Curriculum for Preschoolers with Special Needs.* Baltimore: Paul H. Brookes Publishing Co.

Johnson-Martin, N.M., Jens, K.G., & Attermeier, S.M. (1986). *The Carolina Curriculum for Handicapped Infants and Infants at Risk.* Baltimore: Paul H. Brookes Publishing Co.

Johnson-Martin, N.M., Jens, K.G., Attermeier, S.M., & Hacker, B. (1991). *The Carolina Curriculum for Infants and Toddlers with Special Needs* (2nd ed.). Baltimore: Paul H. Brookes Publishing Co.

Leach, P. (1997). *Your baby and child: From birth to age five.* New York: Alfred A. Knopf.

Notari-Syverson, A., O'Connor, R.E., & Vadasy, P.F. (1998). *Ladders to literacy: A preschool activity book.* Baltimore: Paul H. Brookes Publishing Co.

Rosetti, L. (1990). *The Rosetti Infant-Toddler Language Scale.* East Moline, IL: LinguiSystems.

Sparrow, S.S., Balla, D.A., & Cicchetti, D.V. (1984). *Vineland Adaptive Behavior Scales.* Circle Pines, MN: American Guidance Service.

Uzgiris, I.C., & Hunt, J.M. (1975). *Assessment in Infancy: Ordinal Scales of Psychological Development.* Urbana: University of Illinois Press.

Zimmerman, I.L., Steiner, V.G., & Pond, R.E. (2002). *Preschool Language Scale* (4th ed.). San Antonio, TX: Harcourt Brace & Co.

■ ■ ■

Checklist for
Emergent Literacy Skills

Print/book awareness

____ Handles and plays with books

____ Looks at pages

____ Turns pages

____ Examines pages visually

____ Puts hands on pictures

____ Indicates a particular picture when asked, "Show me . . ."

____ Has favorite pictures or pages

____ Comments on story

____ Orients book correctly (i.e., right side up, opening from right side)

____ Has favorite books, asks to have them read

____ Talks about a story while looking at pictures

____ Points to text while talking

____ Knows that text moves from left to right

____ Reads environmental print and logos

____ Recognizes simple words in text

____ Answers questions about the story

____ Relates story to own life experience

____ Knows names and sounds of letters

____ Makes marks on paper

____ Scribbles

____ Copies lines

____ Copies shapes

____ Copies letters

____ Copies words

____ Pretends to write

____ Uses invented spelling to write short messages

Metalinguistic awareness

____ Uses environmental sounds in play

____ Repeats single sounds when asked to

____ Fills in next line in repeated line story

____ Participates in nursery rhymes

____ Recalls one word from a sentence

____ Understands and produces rhymes

____ Recognizes beginning sounds of a word

____ Blends syllables into words

____ Divides words into syllables

Oral language

____ Uses words

____ Uses sentences

____ Describes an event with a beginning, middle, and end

____ Repeats stories that have been read

____ Has sustained conversations

____ Uses categories to describe objects (e.g., animals, food)

____ Talks about past experiences during play

____ Predicts what might happen

____ Differentiates between real and pretend

____ Describes feelings and motivations

Source: Notari-Syverson, A., O'Connor, R.E., & Vadasy, P.F. (1998). *Ladders to literacy: A preschool activity book.* Baltimore: Paul H. Brookes Publishing Co.

TWO

Guiding Learning

Principles and Suggestions

The goal of the CCITSN is to provide assistance to early intervention personnel, families of children with disabilities, and other caregivers as they strive to optimize children's interactions with their world and the people in it. As O'Donnell and Ogle noted, interventionists and caregivers "have the unique and exciting opportunity to arrange experiences that will allow children to know that what they do, indeed, makes a difference on their surroundings" (as cited in Johnson-Martin, Jens, & Attermeier, 1986, p. 7).

Each item included in this curriculum is based on principles that have been found to be effective in teaching young children. This chapter summarizes the principles that underlie both the way the curriculum activities are written and the intent of the authors as to how the curriculum should be implemented. These basic principles consist of the following:

- Include play
- Follow the child's lead
- Provide choices
- Make consequences count
- Ensure success by breaking tasks into smaller steps
- Provide sameness and change
- Build learning experiences into daily routines
- Use clear language
- Allow quiet time

INCLUDE PLAY

Play is the context in which children do most of their learning. It is critical that parents and interventionists weave intervention activities into children's play, treat their interactions with children as *play* rather than *therapy*, and devise ways that children with significant impairments can play independently. Many activities throughout the curriculum are described as games in an attempt to emphasize this point. We encourage you to also try other activities, either ones that you create yourself or ones that draw from readily available books dedicated to play activities, rhymes, and songs for children functioning in the birth to 36-month range. A few examples are listed in Appendix B at the end of the book.

Play is also critical as a window into a child's cognitive, emotional, and social development. Observing a child's independent play, play with a parent, and play with peers tells us what the child is interested in, what the child is trying to understand, what problem-solving strategies the child uses, how the child handles frustration, and how the child views his or her social world. All of these factors should be considered in devising an appropriate IEP.

Children's impairments affect the ways in which they can play. For example, one of the salient features of childhood autism is stereotypic play or a restricted range of play activities. One approach found to be helpful for these children is the use of *floor time*, as described by Greenspan, Wieder, and Simon (1998). This involves playing with the child on the floor using the toys the child chooses, allowing the child to take the lead in how the toys are used. The adult's role is to help the child expand his or her play themes or activities. For example, if the child is spending his or her time spinning the wheels on a car, the adult may spin wheels on another car, talk about how fast or slow the wheels can go, or model pushing the car across the floor and lifting it to see how the wheels are turning. This may evolve into longer periods of pushing the cars on the floor and episodes of more complex pretend play.

Because so much of a child's early play involves motor manipulations of one sort or another, impairments in motor function may interfere dramatically with play and, consequently, the child's cognitive, language, and social development. Appendix C at the end of the book provides a brief summary of typical play development, suggestions for encouraging play in children whose motor impairments prevent the usual interactions with objects and people, and a case study example.

FOLLOW THE CHILD'S LEAD

From birth, children constantly experiment to see the effects of their actions on their physical and social environments. Their success in creating effects reinforces their motivation for learning and their growing concept of themselves as competent individuals (Jennings & MacTurk, 1995). One of the greatest risks of providing a curriculum for infants and toddlers with special needs is that adults may become too directive, seeking to teach children specific skills on the adults' timetable, thereby reducing children's natural exploration and initiative and often disrupting the joyful social interactions that are a critical aspect of early personal and emotional development.

Therefore, one of the most important principles to remember in developing intervention plans for infants and toddlers (or older children functioning at that developmental level) is to integrate intervention with children's immediate interests and ongoing activities.

When a child has severe or multiple disabilities and participates in few ongoing activities, identifying his or her interests may be difficult. In these situations, the caregiver will have to take a more active and creative role in stimulating the child's attention and interest, modifying materials to provide more intense or varied stimulation. Yet, it remains critical to give the child as much control as possible, even if it is no more than choosing activities by using eye gaze.

PROVIDE CHOICES

In the typical course of development, children begin making choices soon after birth and continue to make choices throughout their lives. Early choices are simple (e.g., whether to look at a toy or at a person, whether to continue sucking or to stop). As children become more capable and more mobile, the available choices increase dramatically. In addition, children become both more consciously aware of making choices and more invested in the choices they make. Making choices is critical to developing a sense of control and mastery. It is also an important aspect of communication (choices communicate desires long before children can talk).

The more severe a child's impairments, the fewer choices there are available. Caregivers often fall into the trap of doing what they think is best for a child without offering alternatives. This may result in a passive child who has little need or desire to communicate. Or, if the child has begun to seek independence, he or she may become highly oppositional if given few opportunities to choose. Regardless of a child's impairments, caregivers should make a conscious effort to provide opportunities for choice throughout the day *and* should respect the child's decisions. For example, at mealtime the caregiver could hold up juice in one hand and a spoonful of eggs in the other. Give the child whichever one he or she looks at or reaches toward. Even if this is accidental and not a "real choice," it is teaching the child that actions make a difference and will lay the foundation for deliberate choices at a later time. *Note:* It is vital that a caregiver accept the child's decision once a choice has been offered. The caregiver, therefore, must offer choices between acceptable alternatives and must not have a preconceived notion about what the right choice for the child is.

Many behavioral problems in the "terrible twos" phase can be avoided by providing choices. If children are asked to choose one of two activities, it is highly unlikely that both options will be rejected, even if neither is generally a preferred activity (e.g., "Would you like to brush your teeth now or put on your pajamas?"). This is especially important to remember when you are trying to help a child learn something that is particularly difficult. Present materials that are related to two or three different intervention activities. Let the child choose one, then the other(s) in turn. You are thereby following the child's lead, giving the child a sense of control, listening to his or her communication, indicating your respect for the child, *and* meeting your desire to have the child work on the difficult task(s).

MAKE CONSEQUENCES COUNT

One of the most fundamental precepts of learning is that behaviors followed by a desirable or interesting event are more likely to be repeated or continued. If a behavior has no discernable effect or is followed by an undesirable event, however, it is less likely to be repeated or continued. Some consequences of our actions are a function of physical laws (e.g., if you shake a rattle, it makes a noise), but many are a function of social interchanges (e.g., if you smile at someone, he or she smiles back at you; if you do a good job, you get a pat on the back). Through their social responses and their control of their children's environments, adults are responsible for providing most of the consequences for young children's behavior.

Guidelines for Making Consequences Effective

Promoting learning through the use of consequences sounds simple, and it is. You must, however, remember some crucial aspects if consequences are to be effectively used.

1. Naturally occurring consequences are the most effective in teaching children about their ability to bring about change in the environment. This is especially true for developmentally young children. Consider the difference between a child who can make a mobile move by pulling a string and another child who receives candy for stacking two blocks. Both children may repeat these activities and, thus, "learn" them. The first child, however, has learned how to affect the physical environment (i.e., move the mobile) and may not only repeat this action but also may experiment with it during other activities throughout the day. The second child has learned to complete a task in order to receive a candy from an adult and may have no interest in the given activity or other objects unless an adult is around to provide a treat. The more serious a child's disability, the more a caregiver may have to set up learning situations so that interesting and desirable events happen when the child interacts with the environment. For example, if a child has severe physical limitations, it may be necessary to select toys that produce effects with minimal movement on the part of the child or to introduce electronic switches that activate toys with minimal action.

2. Social consequences are powerful. From birth, children need attention and will repeat activities that result in adult attention. The adult who learns to attend to the child's desirable actions and ignore the child's undesirable actions will most likely experience fewer behavioral problems. Genuine excitement over a child's accomplishments (e.g., hugging a child when he or she takes the first independent step) is a good supplement for the more intrinsic sense of accomplishment in the child. Clapping, hugging, and other signs of approval are effective consequences but should be used judiciously, primarily to provide support for learning difficult tasks in which the more natural consequences may initially be hard to achieve or appreciate.

3. When the nature of a task makes it necessary to support or replace natural consequences with social consequences, food, or other rewards, reduce this form of reinforcement as soon as there are signs that the child is beginning to respond to the natural consequences of his or her actions.

4. Social consequences are natural consequences when teaching communication skills. Learning to communicate depends on a responsive listener. This begins with attending to the child's eye gaze (e.g., returning a gaze, responding to an object at which the child is looking) and proceeds through turn-taking games to conversations.

5. The same consequences will not be effective for all children. Some children will respond more readily and positively to interactions with toys, whereas others may prefer social exchanges. A few children will respond only to one or two consequences (e.g., food) and will need to be taught to enjoy social consequences and environmental effects. Careful observation is important to determine the best consequences for a given child.

6. Positive consequences are more effective if varied. Like adults, children can become bored with the same consequences, and previously desired events or experiences can become less exciting.

7. A consequence is most effective if it immediately follows the target behavior and is applied consistently. This helps children perceive the relationship between what they do and what happened in the environment. Consistency is particularly important when children are learning something new and when caregivers are providing undesirable consequences (e.g., time-out) for negative behaviors. When trying to get rid of a behavior, the consequence should be employed *every time* the behavior occurs. For example, a child may become confused if he or she was excluded from group activities only some of the times that he or she tried to bite another child.

8. When children begin to understand language, the effectiveness of consequences can be increased by verbally explaining the consequences to them. In this way, children receive an additional clue about the way in which they affect the en-

vironment (e.g., "Push the button and see the television come on," "Give me your hands, and I will pick you up," "Eat lunch, and then we will go outside").

ENSURE SUCCESS BY BREAKING TASKS INTO SMALLER STEPS

To ensure children's continued motivation and interest, it is vital that they experience success. The items in the CCITSN sequences are arranged in order of expected difficulty for most children. Although the procedures for each item will be sufficient for most children, it will be necessary to break down the task into smaller steps in order to ensure success and facilitate learning for some children. Breaking down a task may involve changing materials and/or teaching parts of the task separately. For example, if a child has difficulty releasing blocks so that they balance on one another and the task is to build a three-block tower, you might start with bristle blocks that the child can stick together without being concerned about balance. When the child masters building a bristle block tower, you can then introduce smooth blocks. Creativity in breaking down tasks will be necessary to meet the needs of children with varying abilities.

PROVIDE SAMENESS AND CHANGE

Although it sounds contradictory, children need both sameness and change in their surroundings. Sameness gives children a sense of security. Interventionists and caregivers should provide order and routine in children's lives; this helps children learn that the world is, in part, predictable. Children learn what to expect from specific people and in what order daily routines such as bathing, eating, and dressing occur. Children also learn what to expect from particular toys and may take great pleasure in repeating an activity long after it has become uninteresting or even irritating to adults. Of course, routines are altered sometimes, but a sense of sameness helps children learn to feel safe in their world and to trust their caregivers. Within this secure world children are able to recognize changes and become interested in bringing them about.

BUILD LEARNING EXPERIENCES INTO DAILY ROUTINES

Children learn in all domains of development every day. Although for some children development may be relatively advanced in some areas and more delayed in others, these children have a possibility of learning something new in a number of areas with each activity. Playing Pat-a-cake, for instance, involves gross motor, fine motor, cognitive, and social skills.

Similarly, interventionists and caregivers have the opportunity to encourage learning in every interaction with children, whether it is during a specific time that is set aside for particular activities or during routine caregiving activities. In fact, ample evidence shows that experiences that take place as a part of daily routines are more effective for teaching than those that are isolated in a specific teaching activity (Sandall, 1997). For instance, a child who is learning to improve his or her grasp has many opportunities to practice this skill during the day (e.g., during dressing, eating, bathing, play).

USE CLEAR LANGUAGE

It is important that adults neither talk down to children nor talk over them. This becomes especially critical for children who are developing slowly and remain in the infant-toddler stage of development for a long period of time and children whose impairments affect their ability to communicate effectively.

Do Not Talk Down

Adults should use correctly articulated, adult forms of words (e.g., horse, *not* horsey) to encourage children's language development and support social development. Make language easier to understand by using shorter sentences, expanding them as the child's understanding expands.

Do Not Talk Over

If a child is not talking much, adults are inclined to talk about the child (e.g., report preferences, failings) as if he or she were not present, as if he or she could not hear. This is detrimental both to the child's self-concept and his or her ability to learn language.

Do Talk To

Speak directly to children, looking for other cues of understanding if they are unable to speak. Encourage children to make choices through whatever responses are available to them. Introduce children to others, and let them know they are valued.

ALLOW QUIET TIME

Like adults, all children need time to themselves (i.e., time to play by themselves or time to play with adults without the adults making any demands). Adults can teach a great deal by simply being responsive to children and showing interest and enthusiasm for the children's interests. Use curricular materials, such as those provided in this book, consistently and regularly, but keep in mind that the activities featured in this edition constitute only a few of the important routines that children will do on a daily basis.

SUMMARY

This chapter has focused on facilitating the learning of individual children by building intervention into play and other typical daily activities; being sensitive to the child's developmental level, needs, and desires; providing appropriate consequences; allowing times for quiet and independent play; and using clear language. Yet, these principles are only part of the equation for giving children their best hope for optimal development. The other part of the equation is the safety, security, and stimulation provided by the larger environment. These factors are the focus of the next chapter.

REFERENCES

Greenspan, S.I., Wieder, S., & Simon, R. (1998). *The child with special needs: Encouraging intellectual and emotional growth.* Reading, MA: Perseus Books.

Jennings, K.D., & MacTurk, R.H. (1995). The motivational characteristics of infants and children with physical and sensory impairments. In R.H. MacTurk & G.A. Morgan (Eds.), *Mastery motivation: Origins, conceptualizations, and applications. Vol. 12: Advances in applied developmental psychology* (pp. 147–219). Norwood, NJ: Ablex Publishing Corporation.

Johnson-Martin, N.M., Jens, K.G., & Attermeier, S.M. (1986). *The Carolina Curriculum for Handicapped Infants and Infants at Risk.* Baltimore: Paul H. Brookes Publishing Co.

Sandall, S.R. (1997). Early intervention contexts, content, and methods. In A.H. Widerstrom, B.A. Mowder, & S.R. Sandall (Eds.), *Infant development and risk* (2nd ed., pp. 261–286). Baltimore: Paul H. Brookes Publishing Co.

THREE

■ ■ ■

Environmental Factors Influencing Learning, Development, and Emergent Literacy

This chapter focuses on important factors affecting learning and development that may be overlooked when intervention plans are created for young children. In our work in home and child care centers, we have observed that many parents and child care workers are unaware that the environments they provide for children may not be optimal for promoting the mastery of basic developmental skills or for laying the foundation necessary for acquiring early literacy skills. First, we address factors that are important in the physical environment. Then, we consider the role of music, rhythm, and movement in promoting development. Since the 1960s, there has been increasing recognition of the important role early music exposure plays in promoting the development of language, emotional, cognitive, social, and motor skills (Campbell, 2002; Gardner, 1993; Madaule, 1994). Finally, we address home and school environments and activities that encourage emergent literacy skills.

PREPARING THE PHYSICAL ENVIRONMENT

The environment established at home and in classrooms provides an integral framework for the development of children's cognitive, motor, social, emotional, and language skills. Infants and young children learn best in an environment that offers safety and security, meets children's physical needs, includes areas for different types of play, and provides an appropriate amount of stimulation without being overwhelming.

Offers Safety and Security

Homes and classrooms need to be carefully child proofed. It often helps to get down on the floor and move around the area at toddler height to discover potential hazards. To avoid potential hazards

- Cover electrical outlets and secure any cords.

- Put dangerous materials (e.g., cleaning materials, medicines, scissors) up high and lock them away.

- Cover sharp edges, maintain open areas and pathways through rooms, remove small rugs, and make sure shelving cannot be pulled over. These measures are particularly important for children who are learning how to walk, especially if they have any motor challenges.

Meets Children's Physical Needs

Materials in homes and classrooms need to be physically accessible to children. For an environment that is child friendly

- Keep toys on low shelves to provide easy access.

- Designate certain areas for toys (children need to be able to count on toys being located in predictable places).

- Use furniture that is appropriately sized for children. When sitting at a table, a child's feet should be flat on the floor or supported by a footstool.

- Make sure that equipment (e.g., walkers, standers, wheelchairs) can be placed at play centers easily for children who require assistance.

Includes Areas for Different Types of Play

At home, using different areas for different types of play will likely mean using different rooms in the house or, perhaps, different areas in one or two rooms. A classroom should be divided into zones. Different types of play include quiet/reading, active, art, manipulatives, dramatic play/dress-up, and music.

Quiet/Reading

It is important to have a quiet area where children can go if they are stressed or overwhelmed. At home this may be a corner in the child's bedroom. In a classroom this often can be combined with the book/reading area, which tends to be a quiet, cozy place. Include soft pillows and maybe a beanbag chair. In either place include a variety of sturdy books. A love of books is one of the building blocks for a love of reading. Although you may wish to protect books that you read to the child, he or she should have unfettered access to cloth or board books that have interesting pictures and are not easily damaged.

Active

Although active areas will include outside/playground, there also should be an active area inside, which is especially valuable on inclement weather days. Space will determine what can be used, but some possibilities include a water bed mattress filled with air or water, a small climbing structure with slide, a ball pit, a trampoline, a mat or mattress, and/or a cloth tunnel.

Art

Provide access to a variety of art materials, including paint, markers, play dough, fingerpaint, chalk, collage materials, glue, and a variety of papers. In addition to the structured instruction included within curriculum items, children should be encouraged to explore and interact with art materials in an unstructured, open-ended fashion. The process of learning to engage with these materials is more important than the final product (Kohl, 2002). Avoid making judgment statements about the child's artwork; instead, provide specific observations or feedback. For instance, it is better to say, "I like the way you used the color red here" than to say, "That's a great picture."

Encourage tactile exploration of materials, while being mindful of children who are still mouthing objects. If a child is still mouthing, try art activities using food, such as pudding or whipped cream. Group art activities with such materials are an excellent way to promote social interaction.

Manipulatives

Provide a variety of manipulative toys that encourage children to use their hands and eyes together. Some of these toys involve close-ended play, while others encourage more open-ended, imaginative, and social play. Typically, this area would include the following objects:

- Several different types and sizes of blocks
- A range of puzzles, from those in which each piece has its own hole to simple interlocking puzzles
- Pegs and pegboards
- Shape sorters
- Toy animals and people
- Small vehicles

Dramatic Play/Dress-Up

When children reach the toddler stage of development and begin imitating adult actions with props, it is important to provide a variety of materials to promote the development of imaginative and social play. At home, this area might include simple items, such as children's dishes; a few cooking utensils borrowed from the kitchen;

a doll or stuffed animal; a toy telephone; and some cast-off clothes, hats, and shoes. A few scarves can be used to create a variety of outfits. Many classrooms often include child-size stoves and refrigerators; doll beds; and a variety of dishes, cooking utensils, and toy foods.

Music

Simple rattles, bells, and chime balls will serve to help infants attend to different sounds and rhythms. Materials for older toddlers may include xylophones, toy pianos, drums, and so forth. A tape or CD player with a collection of music is useful for providing musical exposure and setting the tone or mood. Soft, quiet music can be used to calm children for quiet play or naptime. Lively music can be used for movement experiences to help children release pent-up energy.

Provides an Appropriate Amount of Stimulation without Being Overwhelming

Children need to have a variety of sights and sounds to stimulate them but do not learn effectively in an environment that is too cluttered, busy, noisy, or unpredictable. It might be a good idea to limit the number of toys available so that children are not too distracted to play. If the child or classroom has a lot of toys, try rotating them every few weeks. Limiting background noise is also important. Both homes and classrooms need a reasonable degree of quiet and order. A television that is constantly on at home may teach a child to tune out sounds—not only the sounds on the television but also others that are important for learning. Loud and constant noise in a classroom is detrimental. The value of *inside voices/noises* and *outside voices/noises* should be stressed. Speaking in a firm but quiet voice is generally more effective in maintaining an orderly classroom than yelling.

It is important to recognize that individual children may have very different needs in terms of stimulation. Some children may be easygoing and adaptable, others may be highly sensitive or easily overwhelmed, while others may be relatively unresponsive. Often these needs are evident in infancy. Environmental modifications may be necessary for children to function effectively.

- *If the child is easygoing and adaptable:* Provide an interesting and stimulating environment. This child will readily adapt to minor changes in environment and schedule.

- *If the child is highly sensitive or easily overwhelmed:* Tone down the environment. Use neutral colors. Keep lighting low. Indirect, natural lighting is preferable. Avoid visual clutter, such as busy wallpaper or multiple pictures on the wall. Maintain a predictable schedule. Reduce noise level. Play quiet, rhythmic music. A slow drum beat can be soothing. Keep your voice soft and your movements slow and gentle. Use soft, natural clothing and bedding for the child. Sometimes a child like this cannot function in a group of 10–15 other children until he or she has had time to develop coping skills in a less stimulating environment.

- *If the child is relatively unresponsive:* Provide a more stimulating environment. Use bright and contrasting colors. Play music with a lively tempo and variable style and rhythm. Be animated in your movements and voice when interacting with the child. Engage the child in vigorous age-appropriate physical play. Change toys frequently.

Offering an environment that meets children's needs provides a powerful tool for promoting optimal development. It is the foundation on which everything else rests. Whether you are a parent or teacher, creating an environment in which the child feels comfortable and secure and offers diverse and appropriate learning opportunities provides a critical foundation for the child's growth and development.

ENRICHING THE ENVIRONMENT THROUGH MUSIC AND MOVEMENT

Early music experiences contribute to the development of the rhythm and timing that provides a foundation for cognitive and language skills, social interactions, attention, focus, and motor coordination. Music is a powerful tool that connects us to each other and ourselves. Sharing early songs and rhymes provides children with a shared cultural heritage, which is being lost as society has moved toward passive, prepackaged music experiences (Campbell, 2002). Unfortunately, many young parents do not know these simple songs and chants and, therefore, are unable to pass them down to their children. Children with special needs often demonstrate a strong affinity for music. Reluctant children can sometimes be encouraged to participate in more challenging activities through the use of music and singing. Familiar songs (traditional or made up) can be used to ease transitions and establish routines. In the following sections, you will find specific ideas about incorporating different types of music experiences into the child's daily routine.

Rhythm

An infant's earliest rhythmic experience begins in the womb, listening to the mother's heartbeat. That consistent, regular beating tends to be calming and helps organize the infant's movements and behavior. After birth, infants are often comforted by being held close to a parent's chest where they can feel the heartbeat. For children who are a little older, a steady drumbeat often can be used in a similar fashion to help a child settle down and organize his or her behavior. Playing Native American music with a steady drum beat can be very helpful in transitioning children from more active play to rest time.

Singing

Singing is a wonderful way to connect with infants and young children. Infants will typically become quietly attentive and may begin to move their arms or legs in rhythm to your singing. Gentle songs, such as lullabies, will usually calm an irritable infant. As infants become a little older, they often will begin to chime in, initially it may be to the tune of the song without any words, but gradually they will begin to fill in words. Repetitive songs, such as Old MacDonald (Had a Farm), provide natural opportunities for young children to join in singing. Start with the songs you know, but then take advantage of the many children's song books available so that you may offer the child a richer musical experience. Finally, do not hesitate to create your own songs. Most children are enchanted by simple, made-up songs that can accompany routine activities, such as cleaning, getting dressed, or brushing teeth.

Chanting

Simple chants or rhymes provide the rhythm, and often the rhyme, of language to children. They are also good for adults who are less comfortable with singing. Examples include Hickory, Dickory, Dock; Simple Simon; Baa, Baa Black Sheep; This Little Piggy; or Jack and Jill.

Recorded Music

Recorded music can provide a rich variety in music exposure. The music experiences during the first few years of life train children's ears for future music understanding in much the same way that the language(s) we are exposed to train our understanding of speech sounds (Campbell, 2002). It is important, therefore, to expose children to a wide variety of music, including music from different cultures. Look for quality recordings of music, including those that may not have been recorded specifically for children. An excellent source for a large variety of children's music is Music for Little People (1-800-346-4445).

Hand Rhymes

Starting with early favorites such as Pat-a-cake and The Itsy Bitsy Spider, simple hand rhymes help young children learn imitation skills, rhythm, and timing. Initially, you should help the child move through the motions, gradually fading your physical prompts. These activities are often very popular with young children, and many will want to repeat them again and again.

Rhythm Instruments

Collect and/or make a variety of rhythm instruments (e.g., drums, wooden sticks, tambourines, shakers, bells, maracas). A homemade drum might be a box or pot and a wooden spoon. A shaker might be a film canister filled with some rice and secured firmly. Be sure the instruments are safe and sturdy, with nontoxic paint and smooth edges. Let children explore and play with the instruments. Demonstrate ways to use the instruments to create different sounds. Ask the child to imitate you: "Can you play fast . . . or slow? Can you play soft . . . or loud?" Use the instruments to animate the sounds in songs (e.g., shake a maraca for rain). When singing or listening to music, demonstrate how to play an instrument in time with the music. Children may not begin to maintain a rhythm with an instrument until they are older than 2 years.

Movement

Children naturally respond to music, and even young infants will often spontaneously move their bodies to the rhythm. Rock infants in your arms as you sing to them. Bounce them on your knees as you sing a galloping or other movement song. Play music and/or a drum as older children march around the room. Introduce movement songs that involve the whole body, such as If You're Happy and You Know It, Clap Your Hands. Sing songs about stretching up to the sky, down to the ground, and turning around. Use songs to reinforce identification of body parts, such as Head, Shoulders, Knees, and Toes.

   Participation in group music and movement classes is a good way for children to be exposed to a wide variety of music and to experience music in a social environment, sharing the experience with others. Group music and movement classes also provide parents with an expanded repertoire of music to share with their children. Contact the Early Childhood Music and Movement Association (1-360-568-5635) if you need help locating an instructor in your area.

USING THE ENVIRONMENT TO PROMOTE EMERGENT LITERACY

Having a *text-rich* environment and sharing books regularly with children, either by reading or by looking at pictures, are two of the most important factors in developing emergent literacy skills. A text-rich environment is one in which printed materials are in abundance (e.g., newspapers, books, magazines) so that children are exposed to print and have an opportunity to observe adults reading, whether it is the newspaper, a recipe book, instructions for constructing a toy, or print on a computer monitor.

Emergent Literacy in the Home

Reading to a child should be a daily activity, beginning with picture books with bright colors and textures for infants and gradually moving to books with simple stories and/or rhymes for children between 2 and 3 years old. Encourage parents to use the *lap method* for reading to their child. For maximum effectiveness, parents and caregivers should focus on the pleasure of reading, not on teaching the child to read. In a playful way, parents and caregivers can point out pictures and text, elicit questions about the story, and relate the story to events in their child's life. Favorite books can be revisited many times, and new books should be introduced. It is also fun to make a photo album book about the child's day, with photographs depicting the child's activities—waking up, eating, going to school, taking a bath. Pictures of familiar activities and people will hold the child's interest.

Encourage parents and caregivers to model and talk about literacy-related activities. For example, they can show their child how they follow a recipe, read the newspaper, identify favorite store logos, or look at road signs.

If a child's parents have low literacy skills, they are at risk for becoming alienated from the child's educational process (Lewis, 1992). Do everything you can to keep them involved. Point out to parents that they will contribute to their child's ability to read by teaching basics such as orienting the book, moving from left to right, and turning pages. By making up a story to go with the pictures, parents can help their child focus on details and understand that stories have a beginning and an end. Books without text, such as the *Carl the Dog* series, can be used to teach all of these basic concepts. The most important message to the child should be that reading is pleasurable. If a parent wants to improve personal reading and writing abilities, encourage him or her to seek out a local literacy council or community college for free instruction.

Non–English-Speaking Children and Families

If the parents are non–English speakers, strongly encourage them to read to their children in their own language. If necessary, help them construct their own books. Also encourage them to call their child's attention to the text and logos on environmental items such as cereal boxes and canned goods. Reassure them that their most important contribution is to instill awareness of reading as an important and enjoyable activity.

Emergent Literacy Activities in Child Care or Preschool

Provide a text-rich environment with charts, posters, and labels on doors and furniture. When you set up theme-based centers for play, include materials for reading and writing along with other props. For example, a kitchen center can include paper and markers for making shopping lists and simple cookbooks. The block and puzzle area can include alphabet blocks and/or alphabet puzzles. Join the children to help them structure the play and model reading/writing activities. Engage children in conversation about their activities and feelings during playtime and lunch. Avoid the use of television except for specific educational purposes.

Read to children daily, alternating new books with old favorites. As you read to the children, encourage them to visually examine the pages of the book and predict what will happen next. For younger children, repeated line books, such as *Are You My Mother?* or *Brown Bear, Brown Bear,* help develop attention, memory, and prediction.

Reserve a corner of the room for quiet exploration of books. Provide cushions or a small couch for a relaxed atmosphere. Keep in mind that many children also enjoy books with accompanying tapes.

If your class includes non–English-speaking children or children for whom English is a second language, include references to that language and text in that language in your classroom. This serves several purposes. It provides a transition for children who speak another language as well as validates that language. It does the same for these children's parents, providing a signal that they are welcome in the classroom. In addition, it introduces English-speaking children to the fact that other languages exist. To expose children to another language, you could label environmental objects in both English and the other language(s), sing (or listen to) songs in the other language(s), or serve foods familiar to the non–English-speaking children, preferably packaged with labels in their language(s).

Adaptations of Emergent Literacy Materials for Children with Special Needs

You will need to make an extra effort to promote skill acquisition for children who have conditions that limit their ability to readily engage in emergent literacy activities. Speech therapists, occupational and physical therapists, and vision specialists can assist you in constructing materials and selecting appropriate media tools and positioning strategies. These specialists may provide children with an alternative system of reading-related communication consisting of gestures or pictures. Older preschoolers may be provided with a computerized system. Therapists can also assist in selecting literacy software and books on videotape. Although each child is unique, the following ideas can help you get started.

For Children with Motor Impairments

Adapt books by inserting small pieces of adhesive-backed weather stripping on the upper right-hand corner of each page; this will make pages easier for children to turn. You can also cut the pages out of a book and insert them into plastic sleeves in a three-ring binder.

Place strips of male Velcro (the side with plastic bristles) on the outside of the covers of a book. These will keep a book in place on carpet. Lightweight rubber shelf liner is very helpful to hold books on other surfaces.

Make sure that books and writing materials are physically accessible to the children. If a child moves on the floor, place materials on low shelves. Provide adapted writing and drawing materials. Crayons with round tops or fat markers are often helpful. Physical assistance may be necessary to ensure that children with motor impairments participate in group play activities that include emergent literacy activities.

For Children with Visual Impairments

Most children with visual impairments have some degree of vision. Provide brightly colored materials to encourage children with visual impairments to use their residual vision. Experiment with each child to see which colors he or she best perceives.

Vision specialists can provide light boxes to illuminate reading materials. Provide books with tactile features, and teach children to explore the pages with fingers as you tell a story.

For Children with Hearing Impairments

Consult with the child's parents and speech-language therapist regarding communication strategies. Signing and picture systems are commonly used. Learn to use the signs the child understands, and, to the extent practical, teach the other children in the class to use the signs. Parents and/or teachers can construct books that combine text with representations of signs. You can easily make a videotape of an adult reading a story by using signs.

SUMMARY

Chapters 2 and 3 have provided guidelines for facilitating learning and development through your interactions with the child and through providing or facilitating appropriate environments. With this foundation, we are ready to move on to the specifics of how to assess a child and develop an appropriate intervention plan using the CCITSN.

REFERENCES

Campbell, D. (2002). *The Mozart effect for children.* New York: HarperCollins.
Gardner, H. (1993). *Frames of mind: The theory of multiple intelligences.* New York: Basic Books.
Kohl, M. (2002). *First art: Art experiences for toddlers and twos.* Beltsville, MD: Gryphon House.
Lewis, A. (1992). *Helping young urban parents educate themselves and their children.* New York: ERIC Clearinghouse on Urban Education. (ERIC Document Reproduction Service No. ED355314)
Madaule, P. (1994). *When listening comes alive: A guide to effective learning and communication.* Norval, Ontario, Canada: Moulin Publishing.

FOUR

■ ■ ■

Using The Carolina Curriculum

The CCITSN is a systematic curriculum that directly links a skills assessment with activities to promote those skills that have not been mastered. It includes an Assessment Log that has space for multiple assessments to follow the child's progress over time, a Developmental Progress Chart that provides a visual representation of the child's skills in the various domains of development, and curriculum items that describe the necessary materials and procedures for promoting each skill listed in the assessment log. Each item also lists criteria for determining when the child has sufficiently mastered the skill and can move to more advanced skills.

ASSESSMENT

The first step in designing any intervention plan is to carefully assess the child's developmental abilities. For this purpose, the items from this curriculum's 24 sequences have been incorporated into an Assessment Log (which can be found following this chapter), with space for scoring several assessments. (Additional copies of the Assessment Log, along with the Developmental Progress Chart, are available in various formats and may be obtained from Paul H. Brookes Publishing Co., 1-800-638-3775 (U.S. and Canada) or 1-410-337-9580 (worldwide); http://www.brookespublishing.com/ccupdates.) The numbers assigned to the curriculum sequences are not in any way related to the importance of a given sequence. Each of the sequences represents a significant area of development. Thus, it is important that each child be evaluated in all of the sequences appropriate to his or her developmental level. (Some sequences do not begin until the 6- to 9-month level or later; others begin at birth but are "outgrown" within the first year.) It is also important, however, to be sensitive to families' cultural practices in child rearing and respect their beliefs about certain items (e.g., some cultures feel strongly that children not engage in mirror play).

There are four steps in the assessment process, beginning with a period of informal observation and ending with completing a chart that provides a visual representation of the child's skills in each of the 24 sequences included in the curriculum. The goal of the assessment is to determine the skills a child has mastered and the skills that should be the next goals for his or her development.

Please note: Although the completed chart provides a basis for estimating a developmental level for each of the sequences, *it is critical that curriculum users recognize that the curriculum assessment is not a standardized assessment instrument* (unlike the Bayley Scales of Infant Development, for example) and that the age levels are *estimates* based on information from standardized instruments and the literature on infant and toddler development.

Step 1: Preparation

Prior to beginning an assessment, you should be thoroughly familiar with the Assessment Log, be able to recognize the kinds of skills that are included in each sequence, and generally be aware of the relative difficulty of items within each sequence. Most of the items are self-explanatory; however, if it is unclear what you should do to assess a particular skill, turn to the curriculum item associated with it for an explanation.

Note that on the Assessment Log there are four columns to the right of the item descriptions. This is to provide space for recording one child's abilities at four different times (e.g., at the time the child first enters an intervention program and 4, 8, and 12 months later). Enter the date of the current assessment at the top of the first open column.

Assemble the materials needed for the assessment (see list in Table 4.1). The assessment does not require the use of a kit with specific materials. All of the needed items are common children's toys or household objects and can usually be gathered within the child's home or child care setting. (*Note:* Never leave a child unattended with any small items that pose a choking hazard.) Some people find it more convenient to carry a box of toys to do an assessment, but there is often an advantage in using materials that are familiar to the child and his or her caregiver. The familiarity of objects may help the caregiver understand the assessment better and make it easier for the caregiver to integrate the child's intervention activities into typical daily routines.

Step 2: Observation

Select a place for the assessment where the child and the caregiver are comfortable playing together but are free from the distractions of other children, the telephone, and so forth. Assessments often will be done on the floor. Ask the caregiver to play with the child in a typical fashion, using familiar toys or objects (or the materials

Table 4.1.   Assessment materials

The following materials have been found useful when assessing a child with the CCITSN. Feel free to modify the materials as appropriate for the child's impairments and/or the customs of the family, provided you maintain the intent of the item.

Toys with different textures

Bells, rattles, and other noisemaking toys

A variety of small, brightly colored toys, including some that produce interesting sights or sounds with minimal action on the part of the child (e.g., chime ball, busy box, soft squeeze toy)

Several cloths, handkerchief size

Spoon, fork, knife, cup, bottle, bowl, straw, foods usually eaten by the child

Mirror

Crayons

Large and small peg boards and pegs

Fingerpaints, pudding, or whipped cream

Play dough or clay

A variety of containers, some with holes in the lids

A selection of everyday objects (e.g., toothbrush, hairbrush, tissue, shoe, ball)

Items usually found in a housekeeping center (e.g., broom, dustpan, dust cloth, purse, hats, toy cooking utensils)

Dolls, doll furniture, stuffed animals, toy cars, and toy trucks

Blocks of various sizes and colors, including some 1-inch square blocks

A ring stack (rings of graduated sizes that fit on a cone-shaped post)

Balls (3 inch and 8 inch)

Simple form boards and shape sorters with circles, squares, and triangles

Several dowels of different diameters

Gum or candy in wrappers

Small edibles (e.g., cereal)

Pop beads

Large and small beads for stringing

Small jars with lids

Magazines, picture books, and simple storybooks, some with cardboard pages

One or more pull toys or other objects attached to a string

Washable markers, crayons, and paper

Several small wind-up toys, tops, or other toys that must be manipulated in a certain way to get an effect

Toy hammer, Pound-a-Peg, or box into which balls can be driven with a hammer

Wooden inset puzzles appropriate for children between 2 and 3 years

Simple, four- to five-piece puzzles with interconnected pieces

Xylophone with mallet

Cloth strip or clothing with large buttons and buttonholes

Scissors and colored paper that can be cut into shapes

---

you have assembled). This time allows you to determine what activities the child and caregiver enjoy doing together and how the caregiver elicits the child's attention and responses. It also enables you to determine the child's general developmental status. You will find that this brief (15–20 minutes), informal observation period will provide sufficient information to score many of the items in the sequences without further assessment (especially the motor and language items). This time also allows you to establish a comfortable relationship with the child and his or her caregiver.

The convention for scoring the Assessment Log is a *plus* (+) for a skill the child has mastered, a *plus/minus* (+/–) for an inconsistent or emerging skill, and a *minus* (–) for a skill that the child is unable to do. When working with a child with severe motor impairments, it is useful to add an (A) alongside the (+) or (+/–) to indicate that the child accomplished the task with physical assistance (e.g., stabilizing the shoulder so that the child has more control of his or her arms and hands for cognitive and visual-motor activities). The (A) also can be superimposed on the Developmental Progress Chart, which is described in Step 4.

Step 3: Directed Assessment

To complete the assessment, either instruct the caregiver to try particular activities with the child or try them with the child yourself. When a child does not demonstrate a skill, explain the skill you are attempting to assess and ask the caregiver if he or she has ever seen the child demonstrate the skill under other circumstances. If the caregiver reports that the child has shown the skill, you and the caregiver will have to decide together whether the skill is relatively new and not generalized (i.e., is emerging) or whether it has been mastered sufficiently to move on to the next task in the sequence. There are some skills, particularly those in the Personal-Social sequences, which you may rarely have an opportunity to observe because they are most natural and functional in the family setting. For these it will be necessary to rely entirely on the caregiver's report.

The items within each curriculum sequence are listed in the order of their expected development. That is, the skill described in Item a is typically learned before Item b, Item b before c, and so forth. Ideally, if a child is observed to have mastered Item c of a sequence and not Item d, it could be assumed that the child has also mastered Items a and b and will not have mastered Items e and f. A child often practices several related skills at once, however, and there is little consistency as to which skill will emerge first. Furthermore, specific impairments may have different effects on the various skills within a sequence, disrupting the usual pattern of mastery. It is important, therefore, that a sufficient number of items be assessed in each sequence to be certain which skills should be the focus of intervention. As a general rule, continue administering items until the child has passed all at one age span (e.g., 3–6 months) and has not met the criteria at another. (The end of one age span and the beginning of another are indicated by a line extending into the column at the left of the items on the Assessment Log. The age that marks the end of the span is above the line.)

The first time you perform an assessment with the CCITSN, it may seem both confusing and time consuming. With a little practice, however, you should find that the assessment can generally be completed in 60–90 minutes. Although there are many items to be scored, it may take only a few minutes to complete a sequence because the items are closely related and may require the same materials. You also will find that an activity selected to assess a skill in one sequence often will reveal skills in another sequence that you can score when you reach that sequence. For example, you may be assessing a child's ability to match colors (Sequence 6-II, Item 6-IIb) and find that he or she not only is matching them but also identifying them when they are named (Sequence 10, Item 10s). If necessary, it is perfectly acceptable to do the assessment in two or more sessions, depending on the child's state and time constraints.

Step 4: Complete the Developmental Progress Chart

The Developmental Progress Chart can be found at the end of the Assessment Log. Each item in the Assessment Log is represented by a square on the Developmental Progress Chart. Using a highlighter or other colored writing instrument, fill the squares associated with items marked (+). Make a diagonal line through squares associated with items marked (+/–) and color them in halfway. Those marked with a (–) should be left blank. Complete the chart by filling in the squares preceding the age span in which all items were passed (see example in case study on p. 40).

This chart will then represent the child's relative strengths and weaknesses in graphic form. Subsequent assessments can be added to the chart using a marker of another color, demonstrating progress over time.

SELECTING EDUCATIONAL/INTERVENTION OBJECTIVES

Selecting attainment goals or objectives for an IFSP should be a collaborative process between the interventionist and the child's caregiver(s). The next skills to be learned as indicated by the curriculum assessment must be integrated with the caregivers' goals and wishes for the child. The following list outlines the most effective procedure for selecting educational objectives from the curriculum assessment to include in the IFSP:

1. From the Assessment Log, develop a list of the next skills to be learned in each of the major domains of development (personal-social, cognition, communication, fine motor, gross motor). This will give you a list of 16–22 items, depending on the developmental level of the child.

2. Meet with the child's parent(s) or other caregiver(s). Invite them to share their concerns and their long- and short-term goals for the child. Show the caregivers the Developmental Progress Chart and the list of next skills. Discuss the child's strengths and weaknesses as depicted in the chart and how the caregivers' goals relate to the list of next skills.

3. Tell caregivers how they are already working on some of the next skills through their routines of feeding, dressing, and bathing the child. Identify one or two additional next skills that can readily be integrated into these activities.

4. With the caregivers, select several next skills from each of the major domains that will be the focus of the next intervention period. These become the child's *intervention objectives*.

5. Set an approximate date for reassessing the child with the intent of selecting objectives from any sequences omitted during the intervention period just completed.

Coping with Important Differences in Goals

There will be instances in which an interventionist is frustrated because a family has very different goals for a child than those that the interventionist believes are appropriate. For example, it may be quite clear that a 20-month-old child with severe athetoid cerebral palsy has neither the breath control nor the oral-motor control to develop speech as a primary mode of communication in the near future. The professional may feel it is urgent to begin developing the skills that would facilitate the use of an augmentative and alternative communication (AAC) system. Yet, the family may be opposed to any intervention that could be construed as using something other than speech for communication. In such a situation, it is essential that the partnership between caregiver and interventionist not be disrupted. The interventionist should seek ways in which to help the family diligently work on their primary concerns (e.g., obtaining speech therapy), while remaining ready to explore other options when (and if) the caregivers become ready to do so. In the meantime, the interventionist may find that many of the skills that would be helpful in converting to an AAC system can be developed as part of other intervention objectives with which the caregivers are in full agreement (e.g., helping the child develop an accurate touching, pointing, or eye gaze response that will allow him or her to do matching tasks to improve cognitive skills but could also be used later to access an AAC system).

DEVELOPING THE EDUCATION/INTERVENTION PLAN

There are basically two steps to follow in order with move from the list of objectives to an intervention plan: 1) review the relevant curriculum items and 2) combine several curriculum items into one activity or a series of related activities.

Step 1: Review the Relevant Curriculum Items

There is an item in the curriculum corresponding with each item on the Assessment Log, identified by the sequence and the item number (e.g., Sequence 14: Conversation Skills, Item 14a). Identify those curriculum items that go with the objectives you have chosen. Each curriculum item has four sections:

- *Materials:* Most materials listed are toys that are common in homes or can be readily made from simple, inexpensive materials. For many items, particularly those in the Communication domain, no special materials are needed. In such cases, the materials are then described as "None required."

- *Procedures:* This section usually describes an activity that will allow you to assess whether the child can perform the skill being assessed. This activity is also the first step in teaching the skill in a one-to-one situation. It may include two or more activities for teaching the skill and describe ways in which to prompt and reinforce the child's learning.

- *Daily Routines & Functional Activities:* This section serves to 1) ensure that intervention naturally takes place throughout the day, rather than in particular times that are set aside for such intervention, and 2) maximize the likelihood that the skill that is learned by the child will be generalized (i.e., the child will be able to demonstrate the skill in a variety of settings). In some cases, this means providing the child with particular materials when he or she is playing alone or suggesting ways that the caregiver can use the activities to entertain the child during other adult activities. The section also may include suggestions for games or other activities that would incorporate a child's learning objective into an exercise that a small group of children might enjoy.

- *Criterion:* The last section describes the criterion for skill mastery. These are often stated in general terms such as *frequently, several days in a row,* and so forth rather than in precise terms (e.g., three of four trials) because few programs are in a position to keep that kind of data. In the final analysis, the interventionist must use his or her judgment about whether a skill has been sufficiently mastered so that the child can move on to the next skill in the sequence. *Sufficiently mastered* should refer to skill generalization (i.e., the behavior should be observed on more than one occasion and in a variety of different circumstances).

As noted in Chapter 1, the individual items in this edition of the curriculum do not include suggested adaptations for children with impairments in vision, hearing, or motor development. Rather, suggested adaptations are made at the beginning of each sequence. This change was made in response to the fact that there is an endless variety and combination of impairments, and there is no substitute for the creativity of the professional in devising modifications that are appropriate for an individual child.

Step 2: Combine Several Curriculum Items into One Activity or a Series of Related Activities

One curriculum item may cover up to a page in this volume in an attempt to define the skill and provide a variety of suggestions for teaching it. It is not our intent, however, for you to work on each item in isolation. Children develop in a holistic fashion. They learn cognitive, language, and self-help skills while engaging in motor activities and motor skills as they follow their cognitive desire to explore and experiment with the physical world. Thus, curriculum items (intervention objectives) for the child should be embedded in activities that challenge the child in two or more domains.

Assessment

Use the Assessment Log as you gather information from:

Observation

Interview

Parent

Teacher

One-to-one assessment

Fill in Developmental Progress Chart

↓

Select Objectives

Make a list of "next skills"

With parent, select several from each major domain for learning objectives

↓

Intervention Plan

Combine two or more objectives into several specific activities
and/or assign three to five objectives to general activities
(e.g., outdoor play, circle time, mealtime)

Figure 4.1.   Procedure for developing an intervention plan with the CCITSN.

Review the list of objectives and develop four to six activities that combine two or more of these objectives. Use the curriculum items as a guide. An example of combining goals into one activity would be to teach a child to pull to standing (Item 22-Ie) by placing desirable toys out of reach on top of a support. The toys are ones that serve different functions such as a squeaky toy and a pull toy (Item 7j). The ring stacker also invites the child to remove the rings (Item 18q). Three objectives are addressed in this one activity. Five or six items can be readily included in a general activity such as reading, pretend play, outdoor play, or snack time. Figure 4.1 illustrates the process for going from assessment to an intervention plan.

CCITSN IN ACTION

Two case studies follow to demonstrate the process of moving from assessment results to intervention activities, as described within this chapter. The first includes a Developmental Progress Chart to illustrate the child's abilities and lists only the skills chosen as learning objectives. The second omits the chart but lists all of the next skills, starring those chosen as objectives.

Lucia

Lucia is an 11-month-old girl with severe mixed cerebral palsy who has been in the intervention program approximately 1 month. Her neck and trunk are weak. Her arms show very high muscle tone in addition to involuntary movement and are held up and back in all supine (lying on her back) positions. She has a strong asymmetric tonic neck reflex; therefore, she cannot maintain her head in midline or maintain a midline gaze unless she is relaxed and positioned by a caregiver. When placed in a prone position (lying on her stomach), her arms flex tightly, and she is unable to move against gravity. She has no mobility skills and is unable to sit. She can bear weight when standing. Lucia has no self-feeding or independent play skills. She needs to be held and entertained constantly and has no way of providing self-comfort. When shown books, she looks closely at the pictures. When she looks at a cow, she approximates the sound made by a cow. She laughs when her parents do silly games and indicates that she wants more by fussing. She has no way of indicating what she wants to do. When properly relaxed, positioned, and given physical assistance, she shows delight in play and feeding activities. Her parents are very involved with her. Her mother expresses a need to have Lucia do a few things for herself, such as hold a cup and entertain herself for short periods.

Assessment Results

If a child has severe motor impairment, it is important to distinguish between items that are beyond the child's capability or beyond what could be expected at that age and items that can be performed with physical assistance or correct positioning. In Lucia's case, it was clear that her poor motor skills were masking good cognitive, language, and social skills. Items that Lucia could perform with physical assistance (positioning and joint stabilization), therefore, were coded with an (A) on the Developmental Progress Chart shown (Figure 4.2). Items that were inconsistently performed even with physical assistance were coded as (+/–).

Lucia is served at home by an early intervention program. After discussion between Lucia's parents and members of the early intervention team, the following items were selected from the list of potential items to work on. They reflect the priorities of communication, independent play, and participation in feeding.

Personal-Social

1d. Comforts self

1e. Entertains self with toys for short periods of time

4-Il. Chews with rotary/side-to-side action

4-Im. Feeds self with fingers

4-In. Holds and drinks from cup

Cognition

7a. Moves hand to mouth

DEVELOPMENTAL PROGRESS CHART

Child: _Lucia_
Interventionist: _Pat W._

Dates
1. _2/20/04_
2.
3.
4.
● ○ ○ ○ ○

Curriculum Sequence	0–3 Months	3–6 Months	6–9 Months	9–12 Months	12–15 Months
PERSONAL–SOCIAL					
1. Self-Regulation & Responsibility	a b c	d	e	f	l m
2. Interpersonal Skills	a b c	d	f g	h i j k	l m
3. Self-Concept				a b	c
COGNITION					
4-I. Self-Help: Eating	a	b	c d e f	g Ah Ai j k l	m n o
4-II. Self-Help: Dressing				a	b c
4-III. Self-Help: Grooming			a	b	c
4-IV. Self-Help: Toileting					
5. Attention & Memory: Visual/Spatial	a b c d e f	g h Ai i j	k Al Am An	Ao Ap q	r s
6-I. Visual Perception: Blocks & Puzzles					a
6-II. Visual Perception: Matching & Sorting	A a A b	Ac Ad e	Af Ag	Ah Ai	j
7. Functional Use of Objects & Symbolic Play	a b c	Ad Ae f	g h i Aj Ak	Al m	n o p
8. Problem Solving/Reasoning					
9. Number Concepts					
COG/COMM					
10. Concepts/Vocabulary: Receptive	a b c	d e f g	a b c d e	
11. Concepts/Vocabulary: Expressive	a	b c	a b c	a b c d e	k
12. Attention & Memory: Auditory		f g h i j k	h i	Ag	Ah s t
13. Verbal Comprehension	a b c d e	d Ae f	l m n o	Ap q Ar s t
COMM-UNICATION					
14. Conversation Skills	a b	c d e	f g	h i j k l
15. Grammatical Structure	a	Ab Ac	Ad	Ae Af g h
16. Imitation: Vocal	a b Ac Ad	Ae Af Ag Ah Ai	Aj Ak Al Am	o p q	r s t
17. Imitation: Motor	A a b	Ac Ad Ae f Ag	A h	Ai j	k l
FINE MOTOR					
18. Grasp & Manipulation		b	c	d	
19. Bilateral Skills				A a	A b
20. Tool Use				a	a k
21. Visual-Motor Skills	a b	c d e f g h	i j k l	e f g h i	j
GROSS MOTOR					
22-I. Upright: Posture & Locomotion	a b c	d e f g			
22-II. Upright: Balance					
22-III. Upright: Ball Play				m n o p
22-IV. Upright: Outdoor Play					a

Figure 4.2. Sample Developmental Progress Chart.

The Carolina Curriculum for Infants and Toddlers with Special Needs, Third Edition, by Nancy M. Johnson-Martin, Susan M. Attermeier, & Bonnie J. Hacker. © 2004 Paul H. Brookes Publishing Co., Inc. All rights reserved.

  8k.   Plays with a variety of toys to produce effects

Cognition/Communication

  11d.   Uses two or more words to label objects or to name people

Communication

  14k.   Makes requests by directing caregiver's attention

  14s.   Uses words or signs to express wants

  16i.   Imitates familiar two-syllable words with syllable changes

Fine Motor

  18i.   Rakes and scoops small objects (i.e., fingers against palm)

  18m.   Grasps an object, using thumb against index and middle fingers

  19g.   Plays with own feet or toes

Gross Motor

  22-Ia.   Holds head steady when held

  22-Ib.   Holds trunk steady when held at hips

  23c.   Extends head, arms, trunk, and legs in prone position

  24d.   Maintains head in midline position while supine

Intervention Activities

The items selected for initial intervention were used to design a set of activities that would be implemented daily by Lucia's parents. During weekly visits from the early intervention team members, Lucia's progress will be recorded. As she gains skills, the activities will be expanded and made more challenging.

Mealtime

Rock and relax Lucia until she can be comfortably placed in a semi-reclined position. Move her legs so that they are flexed over her abdomen. Gradually move her arms into a flexed position in front of her face. Keep her head in midline (Item 24d). Place some food on a spoon and encourage her to look at it—ask her if she wants some food, and watch her response (Item 14s). Place the spoon between her hands, and assist her in bringing the spoon to her mouth (Item 7a). Ask her if she wants more, and observe her body language to determine her answer (Item 14s). Place harder textured foods in the side of her mouth so she must move her tongue to the side (Item 4-Il). Offer small pieces of dry cereal that she can rake or obtain with a thumb–finger grasp (Items 4-Im, 18i, and 18m). Place a lidded cup in her hands and assist her in drinking from it (Item 4-In). Occasionally bring her feet to her hands and let her play with them (Item 19g), and help her put her fingers in her mouth (Item 1d). As the meal comes to an end, ask her if she wants more or if she's finished. Look for her indication that she's finished (Item 14s).

Storytime

Rock and relax Lucia until she can be placed in a semi-reclined sitting position in your lap. Relax her arms and hold them in front of her. Place two favorite books on her lap, and ask which one she wants to read (Item 14k). Choose the book she looks at or turns toward. As she looks at the pictures, label the pictures for her, then ask her, "What's that?" (Item 11d). Select pictures that can be described with two-syllable words, such as "baby" or "rabbit," and ask her to say the words (Item 16i). From time to time, you can bring Lucia into a more upright position to encourage her to hold up her head and trunk (Items 22-Ia and 22-Ib). Experiment with placing her in a forward slanted position to encourage trunk extension.

Independent Play

Position Lucia tilted back in an adapted chair that provides firmly fitted head and trunk support and holds her arms forward. Place a lap tray on the chair and with Velcro attach three small round switches connected to the following devices:

1. A tape recorder that plays a favorite song

2. A video monitor with a tape of Lucia's caregiver reading a book (The caregiver will focus on each page for 20–30 seconds, pointing out pictures, relating them to Lucia's life, then saying, "Time to turn the page.")

3. A talking doll

   Provide a fourth recordable switch with a message such as "Mommy, I'm finished."

   After ensuring that Lucia can reach and activate all of the switches, show her how to alternate between the activities (Item 8k). Then, start leaving the room for short periods, extending this time to 15–20 minutes at a time (Item 1e).

Summary

As Lucia participates in these activities and begins to experience more control and independence, ongoing attention will be given to expanding her options for feeding, communication, and independent play at her current level of function. Lucia's parents and the early intervention staff will offer a variety of books, music, and games, just as they would to a typical 12-month-old child. At the same time, they will probe for newly emerging cognitive and language skills by assessing Lucia's performance on the first items not passed in each sequence. As these skills emerge, they will be integrated into new activities. Because Lucia can be expected to develop her nonmotor skills at a typical pace, reassessment on the entire curriculum will occur every 3 months.

Derrick

Derrick is 2½ years old and has been diagnosed with autism. He has a history of severe sensory defensiveness and was distressed and irritable for the first 18 months of life. At 18 months, occupational therapy was initiated and his defensiveness was reduced. Derrick became better able to cope with other intervention programs, including speech and education. Derrick now attends an inclusive preschool program three mornings a week with the assistance of a one-to-one aide. He is using a number of single words to label objects and express basic needs and desires. Derrick enjoys looking at books, listening to music, and singing. His independent play skills are limited, and he does not relate to other children. His parents are interested in his learning to play with toys and other children. They continue to work on increasing his communication skills and his ability to be comfortable in a variety of environments.

Assessment Results

Derrick was evaluated using the CCITSN, and a list was made of the first item in each sequence that he had not passed. This list formed the basis of program planning, helping the interventionist determine which skills to target next. In reviewing this list with Derrick's parents, a number of skills were selected based both on the parents' priorities and Derrick's current interest and readiness. An asterisk (*) indicates that the item was chosen as an intervention objective. Activities were then developed that would target several skill areas.

Personal-Social

    *1j.   Puts away toys in correct places

    *2l.   Spontaneously shares with adults

    *3b.   Plays with mirror image

  *4-Ip.   Scoops food from dish with spoon

   4-IIc.   Removes loose clothing

 *4-IIId.   Allows teeth to be brushed

  4-IVa.   Indicates need for soiled diaper or pants to be changed

Cognition

    *5z.   Puts away objects in correct places and notices when they are not in the correct place

   6-Ic.   Imitates building a chair with blocks

    *7k.   Experiments with unfamiliar objects to determine their functions

    *8r.   Solves simple problems without adult assistance

  *10i.   Points to five body parts on request

Cognition/Communication

  *11i.   Meaningfully says "no"

  12o.   Matches objects to their sounds

Communication

  *13j.   Retrieves objects within view on verbal or signed request

14v.   Greets familiar people with appropriate vocalization or sign

16o.   Imitates three-syllable words (or two-word phrases containing three syllables)

Fine Motor

17i.   Imitates activities involving a combination of objects or two actions with one object

18z.   Turns doorknob with forearm rotation

*19n.   Unwraps edible item or other small object

*20d.   Uses hammer to pound in balls

*21d.   Imitates vertical stroke

Gross Motor

*22-Is.   Walks up three stairs, same-step foot placement, without rail

*22-IIf.   Walks 5 feet on balance beam with one foot on the balance beam and the other on the floor

*22-IIId.   Kicks ball 3 feet

*22-IVh.   Climbs vertical ladders

Intervention Activities

Derrick's intervention activities take place at home, at preschool, and in weekly sessions with an occupational therapist. The therapist demonstrates the activities to Derrick's mother and his aide in the preschool and has them keep a weekly diary of his progress.

Mirror Play

Seat Derrick in front of a mirror. Draw his attention to the mirror by tapping on it lightly and saying, "Look, it's Derrick." Bring Derrick's hands to the mirror (Item 3b). Use markers designed for writing on glass to practice drawing vertical lines (Item 21d). Use markers to draw a face on the mirror. Encourage Derrick to point to the facial features on the mirror and then identify the body parts on himself (Item 10i). Try on hats or play glasses while looking at the mirror. Ask Derrick to get hat, glasses, marker, or tissue (to clean off mirror; Item 13j). Show Derrick how to put markers back in the box and return hats and glasses to the dress-up box (Items 1j and 5z).

Mealtime

Place food for Derrick in a scoop dish. Provide physical and verbal prompts as needed to facilitate scooping food with a spoon (Item 4-Ip). Offer some of Derrick's favorite finger foods wrapped in plastic wrap. Show Derrick how to open food (Item 19n). Ask him for a piece of the food (Item 2l). If he does not respond, hold out your hand and ask again. Offer Derrick some of your foods, including at least one that you know he does not like. If he does not spontaneously say no, prompt him to say no, modeling as needed (Item 11i). After eating, brush teeth. If Derrick is resistant, experiment with different types of toothbrushes, including electric, to see what he tolerates the best. Because Derrick enjoys singing, make up a teeth-brushing song that will both relax him and establish a routine (Item 4-IIId). One possibility is to say, "This is the way we brush our teeth, brush our teeth, brush our teeth. This is the way we brush our teeth so early in the morning" (to the tune of Here We Go Round the Mulberry Bush).

Exploratory Play
Collect a few novel toys (e.g., nested barrels, spinning top, Jack-in-the-box, hammering toy [Item 20d], bank with latch), put the toys in a box, and set the box in front of Derrick. Observe what he does, looking for him to explore the toys and figure out how to play or interact with some of them (Items 7k and 8r). If he makes little progress in exploring or playing with the toys, casually demonstrate playing appropriately with one or two of the toys. Pause and wait for Derrick to imitate. If needed, provide physical prompts.

Gymnastics or Outdoor Activities
The therapy room the occupational therapist uses to work with Derrick includes equipment to facilitate gross motor skills being targeted (e.g., balance beam, kick ball, vertical ladder, set of steps). The preschool and a local city park have jungle gyms that offer similar equipment. Try establishing a circuit for Derrick to follow. For example, in the therapy or play room, you might have Derrick climb a ladder or steps to a loft, jump down into pillows, walk a balance beam (one foot on, one off), and then kick a ball (Items 22-Is, 22-IIf, 22-IIId, and 22-IVh). At the school or park, Derrick could climb a ladder to a platform, jump into the sand, go back up the ladder, jump down again, walk a balance beam (or curb), and kick a ball. A picture schedule of these activities may be useful in cuing Derrick to know what he is expected to do next. Either line drawings or actual pictures of the equipment can be attached to a board with Velcro. This way, the order can be changed on subsequent occasions.

Summary
These activities, based on Derrick's current goals, are incorporated into his school, therapy, and home programs. As Derrick participates in these activities, his progress is monitored, and the activities are expanded and/or replaced as needed. When he has achieved an objective, that objective may be replaced by the next skill in that particular sequence, or a "next skill" from a different sequence on the original list. At some point, the complete curriculum assessment should be readministered with new objectives selected and new intervention activities developed. Depending on Derrick's progress, this could be in 3 months, 6 months, or 1 year.

IMPLEMENTING THE INTERVENTION PROGRAM

When the intervention activities have been defined, the intervention process can begin. Each of these activities can generally be described in a few sentences (as in the preceding examples) as a reminder to the caregiver and/or teacher. These reminders may be written on record-keeping forms (see the following Assessing Progress section and example) or simply may be given to a caregiver or teacher as one list or several lists related to where (or when) the intervention procedures should take place.

Assessing Progress

In order to maintain continuity, measure progress, and make program modifications, it is essential to keep careful records for each child. The kinds of records that you need to keep, however, will vary depending on the setting, characteristics, and circumstances of the child's family, caregivers, and teachers, as well as time and other constraints on the assisting professionals.

A Simple Update

At the simplest level, record keeping will consist of entering the date when an item was mastered in the column to the right of the last assessment in the Assessment Log. When the next full assessment takes place, these items will, of course, not have to be reassessed. Teachers can readily update the log in a few minutes each day based on observations in the classroom. Some interventionists who make home visits use the first 15 minutes of one visit per month to assess the child's progress on the current goals in the intervention program, using both caregiver report and direct observations to update the Assessment Log. Other interventionists who work with fairly sophisticated families leave the Assessment Log with the family so that they can fill in the dates that any items have been mastered. Either way, there is an ongoing record and information to indicate a need to revise the activities for the child.

A Weekly Record of Activities

In center-based intervention programs and with certain families in home-based programs, more extensive records will be possible and will provide a clearer picture of a child's progress. One approach is to have a form made up that will detail the child's weekly activities. On this form, the caregiver or interventionist will have to check whether the child had an opportunity to practice the skill and whether he or she was successful. Figure 4.3 is an example of such a form.

Changing Goals in a Timely Fashion

When developmental attainment goals are chosen for the IFSP, it is important to recognize that these are only initial goals. The intent of the CCITSN is for children to work through the sequences, not just on particular items. Thus, as soon as any item is mastered, interventionists should move on to the next item in that sequence without waiting for a new IFSP to be developed.

Name: _Denah_   Week: _3/14–20_

Location: _Home_

Situation	Goal	Opportunity to Observe					Date Mastered
		M	T	W	Th	F	
Child on back (diapering, playing)	Visually tracks, circle	−	+	−			
	Turns head to search for sound	+	+	+			3/16
	Feet in air for play	+	−	+			
On back or sitting supported	Alternates gaze at toys in hands	−	−	−			
	Plays with toys placed in hands	+	+	−			
	Both hands on toy at midline	+	−	+			
	Repeats acts that produce effects	+	+	+			3/16
Mealtimes and other social situations	Anticipates events in games	−	+/−	+			
	Acts differently: family versus stranger		−				
	Smiles reciprocally	+	−	+			
	Laughs	−	−	−			
	Repeats sounds imitated	+	+	−			
	Turns to name being called	−	+	−			
	Vocalizes consonant-vowel combination	+	+	+			3/16
Mealtime	Munches food	+/−	+/−	+			
Bath/ dressing	Holds trunk steady when held at hips	−	+	+			

Figure 4.3. Sample weekly record for child learning objectives of the IFSP. A + indicates successful completion, a +/− indicates an inconsistent or emerging skill, and a − indicates a skill the child is unable to do.

THE ROLE OF THE CCITSN
IN THE ASSESSMENT AND IFSP PROCESS

The provision of Part H of the Education of the Handicapped Act Amendments of 1986 (PL 99-457) and Part C of the 1997 Amendments to the Individuals with Disabilities Education Act (IDEA; PL 105-17) require that each child with special needs have a multidisciplinary assessment. Although the CCITSN covers the domains that are generally evaluated in a multidisciplinary assessment, it cannot be substituted for a multidisciplinary assessment. Individual professionals are required to assess attributes of the child beyond the scope of this curriculum. For example, the physical, occupational, and speech therapists will need to look at motor patterns, praxis, articulation, and other characteristics that are not part of a developmental curriculum.

Likewise, the CCITSN is not a substitute for standardized assessment instruments and cannot be used to determine eligibility in states where standardized test scores are required for eligibility determination.

Part C of IDEA also requires that IFSPs be developed for each child younger than 3 years who is receiving early intervention services. (Part B, section 619, leaves IFSPs to the discretion of local education authorities for preschool children between 3 and 5 years.) An IFSP must include an assessment of family strengths and needs as well as an assessment of the child's strengths and needs. The assessment of the child's strengths and needs and the development of appropriate intervention activities for the child are the contributions of the CCITSN to the IFSP process. The Developmental Progress Chart highlights strengths and weaknesses by providing approximate age levels for the items within each sequence. The curriculum items indicate ways that the skills included in the assessment can be taught.

It should be noted, however, that the age levels attributed to the items in each sequence are rough approximations based on other tests and developmental literature. As a criterion-referenced assessment, the CCITSN assessment is not designed to provide a single developmental level for each of the major development domains. Yet, such age levels are a requirement of many local programs. Although we prefer users to focus on systematic intervention goals rather than developmental age levels, we recognize that, in order to avoid overtesting a child, some users may need to estimate domain age levels from the curriculum assessment.

Using the Developmental Progress
Chart to Estimate Developmental Levels

We suggest the following procedures if you wish to report age levels in the broad domains:

1. Look on the lefthand side of the Developmental Progress Chart to identify which sequences are included in each of the broad development domains: personal-social, cognition, communication, fine motor, and gross motor. Three

sequences are included in both the cognition and communication domains because they are critical to both.

2. Examine the child's performance in each of the sequences included in a domain. In most cases, you will find that they cluster around one of the age levels listed on the chart (e.g., 6–9 months). This gives you the best estimate of a *developmental age* for that domain.

3. If instead of a range you must have only 1 month listed, you can estimate that by looking at the percentage of items in that age range that the child has passed (e.g., almost all passed in the 6- to 9-month range would be considered the 9-month level, about half would be the 8-month level, a quarter the 7-month level, and any fewer the 6-month level). It is important to recognize, however, that this is only an estimate. It is not a score based on a standardized test. It is also important to recognize that although standardized tests may provide more accurate age levels (because they are based on larger and more representative samples), these, too, are *estimates*. Age scores represent the mean age at which a sample of children attained a certain score or passed a particular item on the test. An age score of 24 months does not mean that the typical 2-year-old will have that score. Rather, it means that within a group of children, some achieved that score at 18 months whereas others did not achieve it until 30 months, but the average of their ages was 24 months. Age scores are much less reliable (less stable) indicators of a child's developmental status than are standardized scores (e.g., IQ scores, Developmental Quotients) that indicate how a child compares with other children of the same age.

4. If the child's skills are widely scattered within a domain, it is not reasonable to give one age level for that domain. Instead, indicate a range and provide an explanation. For example, a child with autism might have vocal imitation skills near the 36-month level, expressive vocabulary skills around the 24-month level, and conversation and verbal comprehension skills near the 9-month level. In such cases, it is not reasonable to assign one age level. Rather, language skills should be described as being widely scattered from 9 to 36 months, with strong verbal imitation skills but with significant and atypical delays in the pragmatic understanding and use of language.

USING THE CCITSN IN CONJUNCTION WITH THE CCPSN

Although the CCITSN and the CCPSN now have a 12-month overlap, there will still be children who have such scattered skills that they cannot be fully accommodated by either curriculum alone. It is possible, however, to move smoothly from one curriculum to the other because the sequences have the same numbers and labels, and the items listed in the 24- to 36-month range are identical in the two curricula. You will need to be alert, though, to the fact that the letters assigned to these items are different in the two curricula (e.g., a sequence in the CCITSN with items labeled r, s, t, and u in the 30- to 36-month age range may have the same items labeled a, b, c, and d in the 30- to 36-month age range of the CCPSN).

USING THE CCITSN WITH OLDER CHILDREN

Although the CCITSN has been designed primarily for use with infants and toddlers, the original field testing did include some older individuals with severe and multiple disabilities. Interventionists who want to use the CCITSN with these groups will need to make appropriate adaptations to the items and materials that are used. Generally, the sequences can be maintained, but the overriding concern should be to teach behaviors that are adaptive for the individual. For example, it is appropriate to use blocks when teaching matching to a young child. With a teenager or preteen, however, it would be more beneficial to construct a prevocational task using tableware or different-size envelopes.

SUMMARY

With a little practice following the guidelines provided in this chapter, you will be ready to observe and assess a child with confidence in one, two, or more sessions as your time, the environmental conditions, and the child's state require. Just remember that the curriculum assessment is not a standardized test. It is an attempt to understand what a child knows and can do *now*. Following the assessment, you will have a list of the next skills the child needs to master so that you can discuss these with the child's caregivers and decide together on appropriate educational objectives. In the sequences that follow are the curriculum items that make suggestions for teaching each of the skills listed in the Assessment Log. Identify those that match the objectives you have chosen. You are free to make modification in the activities suggested to suit the needs of an individual child or educational setting. On the basis of the case examples in this chapter (Lucia and Derrick), you also should be able to combine the activities suggested in several items into one activity or situation so that a child is working on several educational objectives at once. This is the natural way to learn. Think about it. We rarely learn any skill in isolation from other skills. Most of what we learn and do in our daily lives involves some combination of language, motor, social, and cognitive skills. You are ready. Dive in!

REFERENCES

Bayley, N. (1993). *Bayley Scales of Infant Development* (2nd ed.). San Antonio, TX: Harcourt Brace & Co.

Education of the Handicapped Act Amendments of 1986, PL 99-457, 20 U.S.C. §§ 1400 *et seq.*

Individuals with Disabilities Education Act (IDEA) Amendments of 1997, PL 105-17, 20 U.S.C. §§ 1400 *et seq.*

Assessment Log and
Developmental Progress Chart

■ ■ ■

The Carolina Curriculum
for Infants and Toddlers
with Special Needs

THIRD EDITION

■ ■ ■

Assessment Log
and Developmental
Progress Chart

■ ■ ■

Child's name: _____

Child's date of birth: _____

Family's name and address: _____

_____

Name of person(s) completing form: _____

_____

DIRECTIONS:

Assessment Log: Insert the date of your assessment at the top of the column and insert a + in the box for each mastered item, a +/– for an inconsistent or emerging skill, and a – for a skill the child is unable to do. When working with a child with severe motor impairments, it is useful to add an A alongside the + or +/– to indicate that the child accomplished the task with physical assistance.

Developmental Progress Chart: Each item on the Assessment Log is represented by a square on the Developmental Progress Chart. Using a highlighter or other colored writing instrument, fill in the squares associated with items marked with a +. Make a diagonal line through squares associated with items marked with a +/– and color them in halfway. Those marked with a – should be left blank. Complete the chart by filling in the squares preceding the age span in which all items were passed. When working with a child with severe motor impairments, it is useful to add an A to the box to indicate that the child accomplished the task with physical assistance.

ASSESSMENT LOG

Age (months)	Curriculum Sequences	Date: ___	Date: ___	Date: ___	Date: ___	Notes:
Personal–Social						
	1. Self-Regulation & Responsibility					
0–3	a. Stops crying when sees or touches bottle or breast					
	b. Can be comforted by being spoken to, held, or rocked					
	c. Calms when swaddled					
3–6	d. Comforts self					
6–9	e. Entertains self with toys for short periods of time					
9–12	f. Moves away from the primary caregiver who is in same room					
12–15	g. Moves partially out of the primary caregiver's sight for short periods of play					
	h. Gets toys to play with from a box or shelf of toys					
15–18	i. Plays alone with toys for 15 minutes					
18–21	j. Puts away toys in correct places					
	k. Explores					
21–24	l. Tolerates being taken into a variety of environments					
24–30	m. Avoids common dangers					
	n. Plays comfortably in a small group of children					
30–36	o. Knows what toys can and cannot do and uses them appropriately					
	2. Interpersonal Skills					
0–3	a. Smiles to auditory and tactile stimulation					
	b. Smiles reciprocally					
	c. Smiles at familiar person					
3–6	d. Laughs					
	e. Tries to attract attention by making sounds, smiling, making eye contact, or using body language					
6–9	f. Responds differently to family members and strangers					
	g. Participates in simple games					
	h. Repeats activity that elicits laughter from observer(s)					

Age (months)		Curriculum Sequences	Date: ___	Date: ___	Date: ___	Date: ___	Notes:
9–12	i.	Shows an interest in other children—tries to attract their attention through eye gaze, smiles, and vocalizations					
	j.	Initiates playing games					
	k.	Laughs or smiles at adults who are engaging in unexpected behaviors					
12–15	l.	Spontaneously shares with adults					
	m.	Shows affection					
15–18	n.	Tries to please others					
	o.	Plays alongside other children (some exchange of toys)					
	p.	Plays simple interactive games with other children					
18–21	q.	Helps with simple household tasks					
	r.	Approaches peer or adult to initiate play					
21–24	s.	Responds appropriately to social contact made by familiar adults					
	t.	Tries to comfort others in distress					
	u.	Spontaneously shares with peers, often briefly					
	v.	Tries to help by running errands on request or anticipating what is needed					
24–30	w.	Negotiates with peers about toys (may trade)					
	x.	Shows awareness of social standards (e.g., wants clothes changed when dirty, brings broken toys to be fixed)					
30–36	y.	Works collaboratively toward a goal with peers					
	z.	Expresses affection and/or preference for some peers					
	aa.	Expresses regret when another child is hurt or experiences unpleasantness					
	bb.	Requests permission					

3. Self-Concept

Age (months)		Curriculum Sequences	Date:	Date:	Date:	Date:	Notes:
9–12	a.	Responds to name					
	b.	Plays with mirror image					
12–15	c.	Makes choices					
15–18	d.	Recognizes self and others in mirror					
	e.	Says "no" or otherwise indicates refusal					

Age (months)		Curriculum Sequences	Date: ___	Date: ___	Date: ___	Date: ___	Notes:
18–21	f.	Expresses feelings of interest, pleasure, surprise, excitement, warning, and complaint (four or more)					
	g.	Resists attempts from others to assist with feeding					
	h.	Identifies objects as "mine"					
	i.	Competes with peers for toys					
21–24	j.	"Performs" for others					
	k.	Asks for snacks or drinks					
	l.	Shows determination/persistence in choosing or continuing activities					
	m.	Distinguishes and names self in photographs					
24–30	n.	Shows pride in achievements					
	o.	Makes positive statements about self					
	p.	Knows age (tells or holds up fingers)					
30–36	q.	Tells own first name					
	r.	Answers correctly when asked if he or she is a boy or a girl					
	s.	Is selective about what tasks he or she will and will not try (recognizes limitations)					
	t.	Shows guilt or shame over accidents or prohibited behavior					

4-I. Self-Help: Eating

Age (months)		Curriculum Sequences	Date:	Date:	Date:	Date:	Notes:
0–3	a.	Smoothly sucks from nipple					
	b.	Infrequently "roots" toward food or objects					
3–6	c.	Infrequently bites down on spoon					
	d.	Infrequently gags (only when appropriate)					
	e.	Munches food (chewing up and down)					
	f.	Uses purposeful tongue movements					
	g.	Pulls food off spoon with lips					
6–9	h.	Holds own bottle (omit for breast-fed infants)					
	i.	Assists in drinking from cup that is held by adult					
	j.	Eats junior or mashed table food without gagging					
	k.	Cleans lower lip with teeth					
	l.	Chews with rotary/side-to-side action					
9–12	m.	Feeds self with fingers					
12–15	n.	Holds and drinks from cup					

Age (months)		Curriculum Sequences	Date: ___	Date: ___	Date: ___	Date: ___	Notes:
	o.	Brings spoon to mouth and eats food off of it					
15–18	p.	Scoops food from dish with spoon					
	q.	Chews well					
	r.	No longer uses bottle or breast					
18–21	s.	Feeds self without spilling (with almost no help)					
	t.	Drinks from straw					
21–24	u.	Feeds self meal with spoon and cup as main utensils					
	v.	Distinguishes between edible and nonedible substances					
24–30	w.	Begins to use fork					
	x.	Drinks from small glass held with one hand					
	y.	Gets drink unassisted (turns tap on and off)					
30–36	z.	Pours liquid from one container into another					

4-II. Self-Help: Dressing

Age (months)		Curriculum Sequences					
9–12	a.	Cooperates in dressing and undressing					
	b.	Partially pulls shirt over head					
12–15	c.	Removes loose clothing					
15–18	d.	Unties shoes or hat as an act of undressing					
18–21	e.	Unfastens clothing zipper that has a large pull tab					
	f.	Puts on hat					
21–24	g.	Removes simple clothing (e.g., open shirt or jacket, stretch pants)					
24–30	h.	Removes shoes					
	i.	Removes coat					
	j.	Puts on simple clothing (e.g., pants, shoes, socks)					
30–36	k.	Puts on all clothing unaided, except for fasteners					
	l.	Undoes fasteners (e.g., large buttons, snaps, shoelaces)					

4-III. Self-Help: Grooming

Age (months)		Curriculum Sequences					
6–9	a.	Enjoys playing in water					
9–12	b.	Does not drool					
12–15	c.	Cooperates in washing and drying hands					
15–18	d.	Allows teeth to be brushed					
18–21	e.	Allows nose to be wiped					

The Carolina Curriculum for Infants and Toddlers with Special Needs, Third Edition, by Nancy M. Johnson-Martin, Susan M. Attermeier, & Bonnie J. Hacker. © 2004 Paul H. Brookes Publishing Co., Inc. All rights reserved.

Age (months)		Curriculum Sequences	Date: ___	Date: ___	Date: ___	Date: ___	Notes:
21–24	f.	Washes own hands					
	g.	Wipes nose if given a tissue					
24–30	h.	Dries hands					
30–36	i.	Brushes teeth with assistance					
	j.	Washes self with washcloth					

4-IV. Self-Help: Toileting

Age (months)		Curriculum Sequences					
15–18	a.	Indicates need for soiled diaper or pants to be changed					
18–21	b.	Cooperates with diaper changing					
21–24	c.	Stays dry for 2- to 3-hour periods during the day					
24–30	d.	Urinates when placed on toilet					
	e.	Has bowel movement when placed on toilet					
30–36	f.	Usually indicates need to toilet (rarely has bowel accidents)					
	g.	Uses toilet by self, except for cleaning after bowel movement					

Cognition

5. Attention & Memory: Visual/Spatial

Age (months)		Curriculum Sequences					
0–3	a.	Visually fixates for at least 3 seconds					
	b.	Visually tracks object horizontally (from side to side)					
	c.	Visually tracks object vertically (from head to stomach)					
	d.	Visually tracks object in a circle					
	e.	Gaze lingers where object or person disappears					
	f.	Shows anticipation of regularly occurring events in everyday care					
3–6	g.	Pulls cloth from face					
	h.	Pulls cloth from caregiver's face					
	i.	Retrieves object partially hidden under a cover					
	j.	Anticipates frequently occurring events in familiar games after two or three trials					
6–9	k.	Anticipates frequently occurring events in familiar games on first trial					
	l.	Retrieves object fully hidden under a cover					
	m.	Finds toy hidden under one of two covers, alternately					

Age (months)		Curriculum Sequences	Date: ___	Date: ___	Date: ___	Date: ___	Notes:
	n.	Finds toy hidden under three superimposed covers					
9–12	o.	Finds toy after seeing it covered and removed in two places and left covered in a third					
	p.	Finds toy under (or in) one of two containers after containers are reversed					
	q.	Remembers location of objects that are put down for a few minutes					
12–15	r.	While sitting on a caregiver's lap, attends to picture book for at least 5 minutes, patting the pictures or otherwise indicating interest					
	s.	Reacts to a change in familiar game and/or reacts when objects vanish or do not function in usual ways					
15–18	t.	Finds object after it is covered in two places and has not seen where it was left					
	u.	Finds object after seeing it covered in three places and has not seen where it was left (systematic search)					
	v.	Recognizes familiar toys, people (in addition to family members and regular caregivers), and places					
18–21	w.	Recognizes own and others' clothing, toys, and personal belongings					
	x.	Retrieves own toys from usual locations					
	y.	Retrieves household (or classroom) objects from usual locations on request (signed or spoken)					
	z.	Puts away objects in correct places and notices when they are not in the correct place					
21–24	aa.	Acts out parts of rhymes or songs independently					
24–30	bb.	Points to hand that is hiding a toy (both when toy remains in that hand and when toy is transferred to the other hand, out of sight)					
	cc.	Recognizes the covers of several books and labels them					
	dd.	Recognizes familiar signs					
	ee.	Identifies (points to) object or picture shown briefly and shown again in an array of three					
30–36	ff.	Identifies (points to) object or picture shown briefly and shown again in an array of four					
	gg.	Tells the name of object or picture shown briefly in a group of two and then hidden					
	hh.	Remembers incidental information					

Age (months)		Curriculum Sequences	Date: ___	Date: ___	Date: ___	Date: ___	Notes:
	6-I.	**Visual Perception: Blocks & Puzzles**					
12–15	a.	Places large round form in form board					
15–18	b.	Places large square form in form board					
	c.	Imitates building a chair with blocks					
	d.	Places round and square forms in form board when they are simultaneously presented					
18–21	e.	Places large triangular form in form board					
21–24	f.	Places round, square, and triangular forms in form board when they are simultaneously presented					
	g.	Completes simple puzzles					
	h.	Places correct forms in shape sorter					
24–30	i.	Places round, square, and triangular forms in reversed form board					
	j.	Imitates block train					
30–36	k.	Puts together two-piece puzzles					
	l.	Imitates block building					
	m.	Imitates block bridge					
	n.	Puts together puzzle with four or five interconnected pieces					
	6-II.	**Visual Perception: Matching & Sorting**					
24–30	a.	Sorts by size (big and little)					
	b.	Matches primary colors					
	c.	Sorts by shape					
30–36	d.	Sorts by two characteristics					
	7.	**Functional Use of Objects & Symbolic Play**					
0–3	a.	Moves hand to mouth					
	b.	Explores objects with mouth					
3–6	c.	Plays with (e.g., shakes, bangs) toys placed in hand					
	d.	Commonly performs four or more activities with objects					
	e.	Responds differently to a different toy in a group of similar toys					
6–9	f.	Demonstrates appropriate activities with toys that have obviously different properties					
	g.	Combines two objects in a functional manner					

Age (months)		Curriculum Sequences	Date: ___	Date: ___	Date: ___	Date: ___	Notes:
9–12	h.	Orients materials appropriately (e.g., turns cup right side up, places cars on wheels)					
	i.	Manipulates books by looking, patting, pointing, or turning pages (may use as a hinge)					
12–15	j.	Plays spontaneously with a variety of objects, demonstrating their functions					
15–18	k.	Experiments with unfamiliar objects to determine their functions					
18–21	l.	Spontaneously engages in adult activities with props					
21–24	m.	Engages in adult role play (e.g., cooks, hammers, talks on play telephone)					
	n.	Pretends that objects are something other than what they are (e.g., blocks are food)					
24–30	o.	Talks to dolls or animals and/or makes them interact with one another					
30–36	p.	Assumes different roles in fantasy play					
	q.	Represents more complex events in play					
	r.	Uses different voices for different people in play					

8. Problem Solving/Reasoning

Age (months)							
0–3	a.	Shifts attention (i.e., visual fixation, body orientation) from one object to another					
	b.	Looks for or reaches toward objects within sight that touch the body					
	c.	Repeats activites that produce interesting results					
3–6	d.	Plays with toys placed in hands					
	e.	Persists in efforts to obtain an object or create an effect					
	f.	Repeats activities that elicit interesting reactions from others					
6–9	g.	Looks for or reaches toward objects that make a noise while falling from view					
	h.	Looks for or reaches toward objects that fall quietly from view					
	i.	Looks or moves in correct direction for objects that fall and roll or bounce to a new location					
	j.	Overcomes obstacles to get toys					
	k.	Plays with a variety of toys to produce effects					

Age (months)		Curriculum Sequences	Date: ___	Date: ___	Date: ___	Date: ___	Notes:
9–12	l.	Increases rate of usual activity with toy when it stops working or tries another activity to make toy work					
	m.	Retrieves toys from container when they have been dropped through a hole in the top of container					
12–15	n.	Reaches object from behind a barrier					
	o.	Pulls string to get object from behind a barrier					
	p.	Moves self around a barrier to get object					
15–18	q.	Uses adults to solve problems					
	r.	Solves simple problems without adult assistance					
18–21	s.	Retrieves familiar objects from usual locations in another room on request					
	t.	Puts away objects in correct places					
21–24	u.	Uses tools to solve problems					
	v.	Independently plays with toys that require pushing buttons, pulling strings, and/or operating switches to get effects					
24–30	w.	Experiments with cause and effect when playing					
	x.	Independently nests four containers, or stacks rings or blocks of graduated sizes					
	y.	Comments that something is not working when expected effects are not produced					
30–36	z.	Independently explores objects to determine their functions and/or shows other people how they work					
	aa.	Answers at least one "why do" question correctly					

9. Number Concepts

Age (months)			Date:	Date:	Date:	Date:	Notes:
21–24	a.	Understands "more" as an addition to some existing amount					
24–30	b.	Selects "just one"					
	c.	Points and recites at least three numbers in correct sequence when asked to count objects					
30–36	d.	Correctly answers "how many" for one and two objects					
	e.	Gives/selects two and three objects					
	f.	Follows instructions including "all," "none," and "not any"					

Age (months)	Curriculum Sequences	Date: ___	Date: ___	Date: ___	Date: ___	Notes:
Cognition/Communication						
10. Concepts/Vocabulary: Receptive						
9–12	a. Points to three objects or people on request					
	b. Shows shoes, other clothing, or object on request					
12–15	c. Points to most common objects on request					
15–18	d. Points to three pictures of animals or objects on request					
	e. Points to three body parts on request					
18–21	f. Sorts objects/pictures into simple categories (e.g., dogs, cats, houses, chairs) when given an example					
	g. Follows directions to indicate an understanding of "you," "me," "your," and "my"					
	h. Points to 15 or more pictures of animals and/or common objects on request					
	i. Points to five body parts on request					
21–24	j. Selects "big" and "little" when given a choice between two objects/pictures					
	k. Selects examples of two or more inclusive categories (e.g., animals, toys, food)					
	l. Points to or shows three or more of the following: tongue, chin, neck, shoulder, knee, elbow, ankle					
24–30	m. Selects pictures of actions (e.g., eating)					
	n. Follows directions including "in," "out," "on," and "off"					
	o. Selects a similar object/picture when shown a sample and asked to find "another one"					
	p. Selects objects/pictures that are "the same" or "like this"					
	q. Selects "biggest" and "littlest" (or "smallest") from a group of three objects/pictures					
30–36	r. Selects objects/pictures to indicate an understanding of at least two relative concepts or comparisons					
	s. Points to five or more colors on request					
	t. Selects objects and pictures to indicate which are square and which are round					
	u. Selects objects by usage					
	v. Understands part–whole relationships (e.g., the tail of the dog)					

Age (months)		Curriculum Sequences	Date: ___	Date: ___	Date: ___	Date: ___	Notes:
	11.	**Concepts/Vocabulary: Expressive**					
6–9	a.	Vocalizes repetitive consonant–vowel combinations					
9–12	b.	Uses two or more gestures associated with verbal concepts (e.g., "all gone," "so big," "more," "bye-bye")					
	c.	Uses one or more exclamations					
12–15	d.	Uses two or more words to label objects or to name people					
	e.	Says "bye-bye" (or equivalent) at appropriate times					
15–18	f.	Uses seven or more words to label objects or people					
	g.	Labels two or more pictures					
18–21	h.	Appropriately uses 15 or more words					
	i.	Meaningfully says "no"					
21–24	j.	Names most common objects					
	k.	Names objects touched or handled but not seen					
24–30	l.	Names six or more pictures of common objects					
	m.	Uses at least 50 different words					
	n.	Names eight or more line drawings of common objects					
	o.	Uses "other" or "another" to refer to additional or similar objects					
30–36	p.	Names most pictures and line drawings of familiar objects					
	q.	Listens carefully to new words (may ask for repetition)					
	r.	Repeats new words to self					
	12.	**Attention & Memory: Auditory**					
0–3	a.	Quiets when presented with noise					
	b.	Visually searches for sound					
	c.	Turns head and searches for or reaches toward sound at ear level while on back					
3–6	d.	Turns head or reaches toward sound at ear level while sitting					
	e.	Turns head toward sound and looks or reaches directly when sound is at shoulder level					
	f.	Responds differently to a new sound					
	g.	Looks or reaches directly toward a noisemaker when sound is to the side at waist level					

Age (months)		Curriculum Sequences	Date: ___	Date: ___	Date: ___	Date: ___	Notes:
6–9	h.	Turns head back and forth or reaches to either side for two sounds					
	i.	Anticipates frequently occurring events in familiar games involving sounds after two or three trials					
9–12	j.	Anticipates frequently occurring events in familiar games involving sounds on first trial					
12–15	k.	Actively searches for source of sound when sound is not visible					
15–18	l.	Shows recognition of a few familiar sounds					
	m.	Makes sounds associated with pictures or objects					
18–21	n.	Attends to stories, repeating words and/or sounds					
	o.	Matches objects to their sounds					
21–24	p.	Identifies objects, people, and events by their sounds					
	q.	Anticipates parts of rhymes or songs					
24–30	r.	Joins in saying nursery rhymes (repeats parts of them)					
	s.	Says or sings at least two nursery rhymes or songs in a group with an adult					
30–36	t.	Independently says or acts out parts of rhymes or songs					
	u.	Notices and reacts to changes in familiar rhymes, songs, or stories					

Communication

13. Verbal Comprehension

Age (months)		Curriculum Sequences	Date:	Date:	Date:	Date:	Notes:
0–3	a.	Appropriately reacts to tone of voice and/or some facial expressions					
3–6	b.	Turns to the direction from which name is being called					
	c.	Stops activity when name is called					
6–9	d.	Does previously learned task on verbal or gestural cue					
	e.	Responds with correct gestures to "up" and "bye-bye"					
	f.	Responds to "no" (briefly stops activity)					
9–12	g.	Responds to "give me" (spoken or signed)					
12–15	h.	Follows two or more simple commands (one object, one action), spoken or signed					
	i.	Appropriately indicates "yes" or "no" in response to questions					

Age (months)		Curriculum Sequences	Date: ___	Date: ___	Date: ___	Date: ___	Notes:
15–18	j.	Retrieves objects within view on verbal or signed request					
18–21	k.	Understands "look"					
21–24	l.	Understands words used to inhibit actions (e.g., "wait," "stop," "get down," "my turn")					
	m.	Follows commands in familiar contexts					
24–30	n.	Follows two-part related commands in novel contexts					
30–36	o.	Follows three-part commands (three objects and one action, three actions and one object, or three objects related by activity)					

14. Conversation Skills

Age (months)		Curriculum Sequences	Date:	Date:	Date:	Date:	Notes:
0–3	a.	Smiles to person who is talking and/or gesturing					
	b.	Provides consistent signals for states of hunger, distress, and pleasure					
	c.	Protests by vocalizing disapproval of actions and/or events					
	d.	Vocalizes five or more consonant and vowel sounds					
	e.	Laughs					
3–6	f.	Repeats vocalizations and/or gestures that elicit reactions					
	g.	Indicates interest in toy or object through eye gaze, reaching, or vocalization					
	h.	Requests continued action of familiar toy, song, or activity by body movements, eye contact, and/or vocalizations					
	i.	Waits for adult to take a turn					
	j.	Begins to coordinate looking with listening					
	k.	Makes requests by directing caregiver's attention					
6–9	l.	Indicates "no more" and "I don't like this" by vocalization, turning, or pushing away					
	m.	Notices and vocalizes when primary caregiver prepares to leave					
	n.	Uses eye gaze to select another person as partner for a communication exchange					
	o.	Changes pitch/volume to signify intensity of desires					
9–12	p.	Raises arms to be picked up					

Age (months)		Curriculum Sequences	Date: ___	Date: ___	Date: ___	Date: ___	Notes:
	q.	Indicates desire to "get down" or "get out" in some consistent fashion other than fussing or crying					
	r.	Plays reciprocal games (e.g., Peek-a-boo, clapping, taking turns making sounds)					
12–15	s.	Uses words or signs to express wants					
	t.	Seeks adult's assistance in exploring the environment by vocalizing, pointing, or using other communicative signals					
15–18	u.	Uses inflection patterns when vocalizing (or uses gestures as if signing)					
	v.	Greets familiar people with an appropriate vocalization or sign					
	w.	Directs caregiver to provide information through pointing, a questioning look, vocal inflection, and/or words					
18–21	x.	Says (or signs) "no" to protest when something is taken away					
	y.	Experiments with two-word utterances or two-sign gestures to achieve specific goals					
21–24	z.	Spontaneously says (or signs) familiar greetings and farewells at appropriate times					
	aa.	Says (or signs) "yes" and "no" to indicate desires or preferences					
	bb.	Spontaneously uses words (or signs) in pretend play					
	cc.	Uses words or signs to request actions					
	dd.	Answers simple questions with a verbal response, gesture, or sign					
24–30	ee.	Asks simple questions with a vocalization or gesture					
	ff.	Asks yes/no questions with appropriate inflection					
	gg.	Requests assistance					
	hh.	Uses word or sign combinations to describe remote events					
30–36	ii.	Comments on appearance or disappearance of objects or people					
	jj.	Sustains conversation for several turns					
	kk.	Reads books to others by making multiple-word utterances					
	ll.	Responds appropriately to "where" and "why" questions					

Age (months)		Curriculum Sequences	Date: ___	Date: ___	Date: ___	Date: ___	Notes:
	15.	**Grammatical Structure**					
18–21	a.	Uses inflection patterns in a sentence with one or two understandable words (or mixes recognizable signs with gestures)					
21–24	b.	Uses two-word utterances to indicate possession and action (e.g., "Mommy's sock," "my doll," "eat cookie")					
24–30	c.	Uses two-word utterances to indicate nonexistence and recurrence					
	d.	Uses two-word utterances to indicate specificity and characteristics					
	e.	Uses "-s" on the ends of some words to form plurals					
	f.	Uses auxiliary verbs, usually shortened (e.g., "gonna," "wanna," "hafta")					
30–36	g.	Uses "-ing" on verbs					
	h.	Uses negative terms					
	i.	Uses personal pronouns					
	j.	Uses prepositional phrases					
	k.	Uses three-word phrases to specify, to indicate rejection, and/or to describe					
	16.	**Imitation: Vocal**					
0–3	a.	Quiets to voice					
	b.	Looks at person who is talking					
3–6	c.	Repeats sounds just made when imitated by caregiver					
	d.	Shifts sounds (imitates sounds in repertoire when made by caregiver)					
	e.	Imitates inflection					
6–9	f.	Experiments with making own mouth move like that of an adult					
	g.	Attempts to match new sounds					
9–12	h.	Imitates familiar two-syllable words without syllable changes					
	i.	Imitates familiar two-syllable words with syllable changes					
12–15	j.	Imitates most novel one-syllable words					
	k.	Imitates a variety of novel two-syllable words					
	l.	Imitates familiar words overheard in conversation or from books					

The Carolina Curriculum for Infants and Toddlers with Special Needs, Third Edition, by Nancy M. Johnson-Martin, Susan M. Attermeier, & Bonnie J. Hacker. © 2004 Paul H. Brookes Publishing Co., Inc. All rights reserved.

Age (months)	Curriculum Sequences	Date: ___	Date: ___	Date: ___	Date: ___	Notes:
15–18	m. Imitates the vocalizations others use for environmental sounds					
18–21	n. Imitates two-word phrases or sentences					
21–24	o. Imitates three-syllable words (or two-word phrases containing three syllables)					
24–30	p. Repeats novel two-word or two-number sequence					
30–36	q. Repeats three-word sentences					

Fine Motor

17. Imitation: Motor

Age (months)	Curriculum Sequences	Date:	Date:	Date:	Date:	Notes:
0–3	a. Looks at caregiver and makes facial movements when caregiver is talking or making noises					
3–6	b. Continues movement if it is imitated by caregiver					
	c. Imitates an activity in repertoire after observing caregiver doing that activity					
6–9	d. Imitates unfamiliar movements					
9–12	e. Imitates simple gestures, such as signaling "bye-bye" or "no"					
	f. Imitates frequently observed actions with objects (e.g., stirs with spoon)					
12–15	g. Imitates actions related to the function of objects					
	h. Imitates gestures or signs caregiver commonly uses					
15–18	i. Imitates activities involving a combination of objects or two actions with one object					
	j. Imitates activities involving a combination of objects several hours after observing actions					
18–21	k. Incorporates sequence of imitated adult activities into solitary play					
21–24	l. Attempts to solve problems (including activating toys) by imitating adult actions					
24–30	m. Imitates postures or actions that do not involve props					
30–36	n. Imitates sequence of two unrelated motor acts					

18. Grasp & Manipulation

Age (months)	Curriculum Sequences	Date:	Date:	Date:	Date:	Notes:
0–3	a. Actively moves arm after seeing or hearing an object					
	b. Looks to one side at hand or toy					
	c. Brings toy and hand into visual field and looks at them when toy is placed in hand					

Age (months)		Curriculum Sequences	Date: ___	Date: ___	Date: ___	Date: ___	Notes:
	d.	Watches hands at midline (actively moves and watches results)					
3–6	e.	Bats at object at chest level					
	f.	Grasps object that is placed in hand (i.e., not reflexive grasp)					
	g.	Reaches out and grasps objects near body					
	h.	Displays extended reach and grasp					
	i.	Rakes and scoops small objects (i.e., fingers against palm)					
6–9	j.	Reaches out for toys and picks them up when toys are in visual field					
	k.	Manipulates objects with hands and fingers					
	l.	Releases one object to take another					
	m.	Grasps an object, using thumb against index and middle fingers					
	n.	Uses inferior pincer grasp (i.e., thumb against side of index finger)					
9–12	o.	Uses index finger to poke					
	p.	Uses neat pincer grasp (i.e., thumb against tip of index finger)					
	q.	Removes objects from holders (e.g., rings from post, pegs from holes)					
12–15	r.	Releases objects into container					
	s.	Imitates building two-block tower					
	t.	Grasps two small objects with one hand					
15–18	u.	Places round pegs in holes					
	v.	Imitates building three- to four-block tower					
18–21	w.	Pokes or plays with play dough					
	x.	Turns pages one at a time					
21–24	y.	Imitates building six- to eight-block tower					
24–30	z.	Turns doorknob with forearm rotation					
	aa.	Puts small object through small hole in container					
30–36	bb.	Builds tower of 8–10 blocks					

19. Bilateral Skills

0–3	a.	Raises both hands when object is presented (hands partially open)					

Age (months)		Curriculum Sequences	Date: ___	Date: ___	Date: ___	Date: ___	Notes:
	b.	Looks at or manipulates toy placed in hands at midline					
3–6	c.	Brings hands together at midline					
	d.	Places both hands on toy at midline					
	e.	Transfers objects from hand to hand					
	f.	Glances from one toy to another when a toy is placed in each hand, or alternatively plays with the toys					
	g.	Plays with own feet or toes					
6–9	h.	Claps hands					
9–12	i.	Uses both hands to perform the same action					
	j.	Plays with toys at midline (one hand holds the toy and the other manipulates it)					
12–15	k.	Pulls apart pop beads					
	l.	Holds dowel in one hand and places ring over it					
15–18	m.	Puts dowel through hole in piece of cardboard					
	n.	Unwraps edible item or other small object					
18–21	o.	Unscrews small lids					
21–24	p.	Puts loose pop beads together					
	q.	Strings three large beads					
24–30	r.	Demonstrates hand preference (typically in eating)					
30–36	s.	Unbuttons large buttons					
	t.	Strings small beads					
	u.	Screws on lids					

20. Tool Use

Age (months)		Curriculum Sequences	Date:	Date:	Date:	Date:	Notes:
9–12	a.	Pulls string to obtain object or make effect					
12–15	b.	Hits drum with stick					
15–18	c.	Uses stick to obtain object					
18–21	d.	Uses hammer to pound in balls					
21–24	e.	Uses mallet to play xylophone keys					
24–30	f.	Holds bowl and stirs					
	g.	Uses hammer to pound pegs in pounding bench					
30–36	h.	Transfers material with spoon					
	i.	Spreads with knife					
	j.	Cuts with edge of fork					

Age (months)		Curriculum Sequences	Date: ___	Date: ___	Date: ___	Date: ___	Notes:
	21.	**Visual-Motor Skills**					
12–15	a.	Marks paper with writing implement					
15–18	b.	Scribbles spontaneously					
18–21	c.	Fingerpaints with whole hand					
21–24	d.	Imitates vertical stroke					
	e.	Imitates shifting from scribble to stroke and back					
24–30	f.	Imitates horizontal stroke					
	g.	Pretends to write					
30–36	h.	Copies a circle with a circular scribble					
	i.	Snips with scissors					
	j.	Makes continuous cuts across paper					

Gross Motor

Age (months)		**22-I. Upright: Posture & Locomotion**					
0–3	a.	Holds head steady when held					
3–6	b.	Holds trunk steady when held at hips					
6–9	c.	Moves to sitting position from stomach or all-fours position					
	d.	Sits alone					
9–12	e.	Pulls self to standing position					
	f.	Steps sideways holding a support					
	g.	Stoops to pick up toy while holding a support					
	h.	Removes hands from support and stands independently					
	i.	Takes independent steps					
12–15	j.	Moves from hands and knees to hands and feet to standing					
	k.	Squats down to retrieve object					
15–18	l.	Walks sideways					
	m.	Walks backward at least 5 feet					
	n.	Walks up three stairs, same-step foot placement, with rail					
	o.	Walks down three stairs, same-step foot placement, with rail					
18–21	p.	Maintains a squatting position in play					

Age (months)		Curriculum Sequences	Date: ___	Date: ___	Date: ___	Date: ___	Notes:
	q.	Runs stiffly					
	r.	Jumps on floor					
	s.	Walks up three stairs, same-step foot placement, without rail					
21–24	t.	Jumps off stair					
24–30	u.	Walks backward 10 feet					
	v.	Walks on all types of surfaces without falling					
	w.	Uses heel–toe pattern (arms free to carry objects)					
	x.	Takes three to four steps on tiptoes					
	y.	Runs at least 10 feet without falling					
	z.	Jumps down from 8-inch height (one foot leading)					
	aa.	Walks up three stairs, alternate pattern, with rail					
30–36	bb.	Walks at least 20 feet on tiptoes					
	cc.	Avoids obstacles when running					
	dd.	Walks up three stairs, alternate pattern, without rail					
	ee.	Walks down three stairs, same-step foot placement, without rail					
	ff.	Jumps over 2-inch hurdle					
	gg.	Jumps down from 16-inch to 18-inch height (one foot leading)					
	hh.	Broad jumps 4 inches to 14 inches					

22-II. Upright: Balance

Age (months)		Curriculum Sequences	Date:	Date:	Date:	Date:	Notes:
15–18	a.	Stands on one foot while hands are held					
18–21	b.	Lifts one leg momentarily					
21–24	c.	Rises onto tiptoes momentarily					
	d.	Stands on one leg with stable posture (1–2 seconds)					
24–30	e.	Stands sideways with both feet on balance beam with stable posture					
	f.	Walks 5 feet on balance beam with one foot on the balance beam and the other on the floor					
	g.	Walks along 10-foot line, following the general direction of the line					
30–36	h.	Stands with stable posture on one leg with hands on hips and opposite knee bent (1–2 seconds)					
	i.	Walks three steps on balance beam and maintains balance					

Age (months)		Curriculum Sequences	Date: ___	Date: ___	Date: ___	Date: ___	Notes:
	j.	Walks along 10-foot line, keeping feet on the line and maintaining balance					

22-III. Upright: Ball Play

15–18	a.	Rolls ball back and forth with an adult					
	b.	Tries to kick ball					
	c.	Hurls ball 3 feet					
18–21	d.	Kicks ball 3 feet					
21–24	e.	Throws 8-inch ball to an adult who is 5 feet away					
24–30	f.	Throws 3-inch ball to an adult who is 7 feet away					
	g.	Throws 3-inch ball to an adult who is 9 feet away					
30–36	h.	Catches 8-inch ball with arms in front of body from an adult who is 5 feet away					
	i.	Kicks ball 4–6 feet					

22-IV. Upright: Outdoor Play

12–15	a.	Explores play area with supervision					
15–18	b.	Enjoys swinging and sliding					
18–21	c.	Climbs on low equipment					
21–24	d.	Climbs slanted ladder					
	e.	Uses slide independently					
24–30	f.	Runs on playground, pausing at surface changes					
	g.	Climbs on low jungle gym bars and will drop several inches to the ground					
	h.	Climbs vertical ladders					
30–36	i.	Walks on movable surfaces using some hand support					

23. Prone (on Stomach)

0–3	a.	Lifts head, freeing nose (arms and legs flexed)					
	b.	Lifts head to 45-degree angle (arms and legs partially flexed)					
3–6	c.	Extends head, arms, trunk, and legs in prone position					
	d.	Bears weight on elbows in prone position					
	e.	Rolls from stomach to back					
	f.	Reaches while supported on one elbow					
	g.	Supports self on hands with arms extended and head at 90 degrees					

Age (months)		Curriculum Sequences	Date: ___	Date: ___	Date: ___	Date: ___	Notes:
	h.	Pivots in prone position					
6–9	i.	Pulls forward in prone position					
	j.	Pulls self to hands and knees					
	k.	Rocks forward and backward while on hands and knees					
	l.	Plays with toys in asymmetrical half-sitting position					
9–12	m.	Moves forward (creeps) while on hands and knees					
	n.	Raises one hand high while on hands and knees					
12–15	o.	Creeps up stairs					
	p.	Creeps down stairs, backwards					

24. Supine (on Back)

Age (months)		Curriculum Sequences	Date	Date	Date	Date	Notes
0–3	a.	Turns head from side to side in response to auditory or visual stimuli					
	b.	Bends and straightens arms and legs					
	c.	Brings hands to mouth					
	d.	Maintains head in midline position while supine					
3–6	e.	Reaches out with arm while supine					
	f.	Holds feet in air for play					
	g.	Rolls from back to stomach					

DEVELOPMENTAL PROGRESS CHART

Child: _____
Interventionist: _____

Dates
1. _____
2. _____
3. _____
4. _____

	Curriculum Sequence	0–3 Months	3–6 Months	6–9 Months	9–12 Months	12–15 Months
PERSONAL–SOCIAL	1. Self-Regulation & Responsibility	a b c	d	e f g h	f i j k	g h l m
	2. Interpersonal Skills	a b c	d e	f g h	i j k	l m
	3. Self-Concept				a b	c
	4-I. Self Help: Eating	a b	c d e f g	h i j k l	m	n o
	4-II. Self-Help: Dressing			a	b	c
	4-III. Self-Help: Grooming					c
	4-IV. Self-Help: Toileting					
COGNITION	5. Attention & Memory: Visual/Spatial	a b c d e f	g h i j	k l m n	o p q	r s
	6-I. Visual Perception: Blocks & Puzzles				h i	a
	6-II. Visual Perception: Matching & Sorting				l m	j
	7. Functional Use of Objects & Symbolic Play	a b	c d	f g	h	
	8. Problem Solving/Reasoning	a b c	d e f	g h i j k	a b	n o p
	9. Number Concepts					
COG/COMM	10. Concepts/Vocabulary: Receptive				a b	c
	11. Concepts/Vocabulary: Expressive	a b c	d e f g	a	b c	d e
COMMUNICATION	12. Attention & Memory: Auditory	a	d e f g	h i	j	k
	13. Verbal Comprehension	a b c d e	b c	d e f	g	h i
	14. Conversation Skills	a b		l m n o	p q r	r s t
	15. Grammatical Structure		f g h i j k			
FINE MOTOR	16. Imitation: Vocal	a b	c d e	f g	h i	j k l
	17. Imitation: Motor	a	b c	d	e f	g h
	18. Grasp & Manipulation	a b c d	e f g h i	j k l m n	o p q	r s t
	19. Bilateral Skills	a b	c d e f g	h	i j	k l
	20. Tool Use				a	b
	21. Visual-Motor Skills					a
GROSS MOTOR	22-I. Upright: Posture & Locomotion	a	b	c	e f g h i	j k
	22-II. Upright: Balance			d		
	22-III. Upright: Ball Play					
	22-IV. Upright: Outdoor Play					
	23. Prone (on Stomach)	a b	c d e f g h	i j k l	m n	o
	24. Supine (on Back)	a b c d	e f g			o p

	Curriculum Sequence	15–18 Months	18–21 Months	21–24 Months	24–30 Months	30–36 Months
PERSONAL-SOCIAL	1. Self-Regulation & Responsibility	n	j	s t u v	m l n	o
	2. Interpersonal Skills	i o p	q r		w x	y z aa bb
	3. Self-Concept	d e	f g h i k	j k l m	n o p	q r s t
	4-I. Self-Help: Eating	p q r	s t	u v	w x y	z
	4-II. Self-Help: Dressing	d	e f	g	h i j	k l
	4-III. Self-Help: Grooming	d	e	f g	h	i j
	4-IV. Self-Help: Toileting	a	b	c	d e	f g
COGNITION	5. Attention & Memory: Visual/Spatial	t u v	w x y z	aa	bb cc dd ee	ff gg hh
	6-I. Visual Perception: Blocks & Puzzles	b c d	e	f g h	i j	k l m n
	6-II. Visual Perception: Matching & Sorting				a b c	d
	7. Functional Use of Objects & Symbolic Play	k	l	m n	o	p q r
	8. Problem Solving/Reasoning	q r	s t	u v	w x y	z aa
	9. Number Concepts			a	b c	d e f
COMM/COG	10. Concepts/Vocabulary: Receptive	d	f g h i	j k l	m n o p q	r s t u v
	11. Concepts/Vocabulary: Expressive	f g	h i	j k	l m n o	p q r
	12. Attention & Memory: Auditory	l m	n o	p q	r s	t u
	13. Verbal Comprehension		k	l m	n	o
COMMUNICATION	14. Conversation Skills	u v w	x y	z aa bb cc dd	ee ff gg hh	ii jj kk ll
	15. Grammatical Structure		a	b	c d e f	g h i j k
	16. Imitation: Vocal	m	n	o	p	q
	17. Imitation: Motor	i j	k	l	m	n
FINE MOTOR	18. Grasp & Manipulation	u v	w x	y	z aa	bb
	19. Bilateral Skills	m n	o	p q	r s	t u
	20. Tool Use	c	d	e	f g	h i j
	21. Visual-Motor Skills	b	c	d	f g	h i j
GROSS MOTOR	22-I. Upright: Posture & Locomotion	l m n o	p q r s	t	u v w x y z aa	bb cc dd ee ff gg hh
	22-II. Upright: Balance	a		c d	e f g	h i j
	22-III. Upright: Ball Play	a b c	d	e	f g	
	22-IV. Upright: Outdoor Play	b	c	d e	f g	h
	23. Prone (on Stomach)					i
	24. Supine (on Back)					

Curriculum
Sequences

■ ■ ■

1
Self-Regulation
& Responsibility

Young infants are dependent on their caregivers to provide a safe and secure environment and establish interactions that are responsive to the infants' needs. Successfully meeting these needs facilitates the infants' ability to develop self-regulation skills. During the first year of life, infants learn to organize basic physiological states (e.g., wake–sleep cycles, hunger, satiety, elimination) and how to calm and comfort themselves. An infant's early regulatory development provides a critical foundation for successful adaptation to the world. The ability to self-regulate also provides a foundation for the infant to feel secure in his or her environment, establish relationships with others, initiate communication, and develop purposeful and organized play behavior. This first sequence highlights some of the milestones demonstrated by children who are developing adequate self-regulation. Children with regulatory difficulties may demonstrate difficulties in multiple areas, including disruption of physiological processes (e.g., sleeping, eating, feeding, elimination), behavioral organization, mood, attention and focus, sensory processing, social interactions, and achievement of developmental milestones (DeGangi, Sickel, Kaplan, & Weiner, 1997; DeGangi, 2000; Greenspan, 1992; Greenspan & Salmon, 1995).

The infant begins to develop self-control at the age of 18 months (DeGangi, 2000). As a result, it becomes increasingly important for children to be allowed to initiate and direct their own activities. This aspect of development is often overlooked, with too much emphasis placed on adult-directed learning. In fact, self-initiated activity is sometimes regarded negatively and considered to be a nuisance in intervention programs rather than a necessary component of active learning.

Although not stressed in the items themselves, it should be recognized that learning to deal with rules is a part of self-direction. While encouraging independence, curiosity, and exploration, the caregiver should also provide firm boundaries with clear consequences for transgressing them.

The skills listed in this sequence are felt to be important developmental milestones during the first 3 years of life. The age that a child acquires many of the skills is highly variable based on the child's temperament and experience. As a result, some children may demonstrate certain skills, such as tolerating different environments or playing comfortably in a small group of children, much earlier or later than indicated.

ADAPTATIONS

Children with Motor Impairments

Several items in this sequence require motor responses to facilitate active exploration and self-initiated movement away from the caregiver. If children with motor impairments are unable to make these responses, the focus will have to be on helping the children comfortably separate from their primary caregiver and make choices between adult-determined activities. For example, a child may be shown two pictures, one of an indoor play area and the other of a swing, and asked if he or she wants to play inside or go outside and swing. The child chooses his or her next activity by pointing to or looking at one of the pictures.

Children with Visual Impairments

Children with visual impairments tend to be slower to develop self-reliance and independence. Caregivers need to be careful not to step in too quickly to rescue a child, thereby allowing him or her the opportunity to develop his or her own strategies. Verbal cues will be very important in teaching the child how to help him- or herself. Maintain a consistent environment with toys neatly organized and kept in the same place so that the child can learn to find the toys on his or her own. Furniture should also remain in consistent places with clear paths that are easy to negotiate.

Children with Hearing Impairments

When speaking to children with hearing impairments, make sure that they are looking directly at you. If a child has a significant hearing impairment, it is helpful to begin pairing manual signs with speech to facilitate his or her understanding of instructions. Demonstrate expected activities for the child to imitate.

1. SELF-REGULATION AND RESPONSIBILITY

a.   Stops crying when sees or touches bottle or breast
b.   Can be comforted by being spoken to, held, or rocked
c.   Calms when swaddled
d.   Comforts self
e.   Entertains self with toys for short periods of time
f.   Moves away from the primary caregiver who is in same room
g.   Moves partially out of the primary caregiver's sight for short periods of play
h.   Gets toys to play with from a box or shelf of toys
i.   Plays alone with toys for 15 minutes
j.   Puts away toys in correct places
k.   Explores
l.   Tolerates being taken into a variety of environments
m.   Avoids common dangers
n.   Plays comfortably in a small group of children
o.   Knows what toys can and cannot do and uses them appropriately

■ ■ ■

1a. Stops crying when sees or touches bottle or breast

MATERIALS   Infant's bottle or mother's breast (at feeding time)

PROCEDURES

Give the child ample time to see the bottle or breast before feeding begins. Observe to see if the child quiets when he sees that he is about to be fed. Try to get the child's attention by briefly presenting the bottle or breast in his line of sight before beginning to feed child.

DAILY ROUTINES & FUNCTIONAL ACTIVITIES

Be sure that anyone feeding the infant follows the same routine. Let the child see the bottle before allowing him to drink.

   Note: This item is primarily important because it helps the child establish connections between his communicating a need (i.e., through crying), a person responding to that need, and the child's changing his communication (i.e., through ceasing to cry).

CRITERION   The child usually stops crying upon seeing or touching the bottle or breast.

■ ■ ■

1b. Can be comforted by being spoken to, held, or rocked

MATERIALS   None required

PROCEDURES

When a child shows distress and is crying, first try to comfort her by leaning over and talking softly to her.

If the child does not quiet in response to talking, touch her gently while speaking softly.

If the child is still showing distress, pick her up and hold her gently, but try to hold her arms close to her sides so that she does not thrash around.

If the child is still not comforted, rock her while holding her. Try different positions for holding the child to find the one most helpful to her: at your shoulder, on your lap with her head nestled against your stomach or breast, cuddled in your arms, and so forth.

DAILY ROUTINES & FUNCTIONAL ACTIVITIES

It is important to comfort a child fairly quickly when you notice that the child is distressed. This teaches the child that help is available and will come soon. It is also important, however, to give attention to the child when she is doing something other than crying or she may learn that the only way to get attention is to cry.

The steps toward comforting the child noted in the Procedures section offer minimal assistance to the child at first in order to allow her to assist in comforting herself.

CRITERION   The child usually can be comforted in a reasonable period of time (e.g., 5 minutes).

■ ■ ■

1c. Calms when swaddled

MATERIALS   A small blanket

PROCEDURES

When a child shows distress and crying, particularly if he is tired or seems overwhelmed, wrap him snuggly in a small blanket, swaddling his entire body (except head). The goal of this item is for the child to begin learning to calm himself with assistance from an adult.

Briefly talk or sing to the child in soft soothing tones and gently rock him in your arms before laying him in his crib or infant seat. Most infants will calm down and go to sleep in a short period of time. If the child continues to cry, try patting him rhythmically.

DAILY ROUTINES & FUNCTIONAL ACTIVITIES

Swaddling can be used on a daily basis. Infants often quickly become accustomed to being wrapped and will quickly calm down.

Note: Although swaddling is very effective for many children, this item does not need to be mastered before moving on to the next step. The goal of many of these early self-regulation items is for the adult and child to discover what is effective for a particular child and for the child to learn to calm and organize himself with little adult intervention.

CRITERION   After swaddling, the child calms and possibly goes to sleep within a short period of time.

■ ■ ■

1d. Comforts self

MATERIALS   None required (unless child finds a particular toy or item soothing)

PROCEDURES

When the child is fussy but not hungry, wait a couple of minutes before responding in order to give her the opportunity to comfort herself. The oral stimulation provided by rhythmical sucking is calming to most infants. Many infants learn to soothe themselves by bringing their hands to their mouths to suck on the fist or fingers. Other children prefer sucking on a pacifier or blanket and will learn to bring these to their mouth.

If the child does not spontaneously attempt to soothe herself in these ways, you may want to physically prompt bringing her hand to her mouth, or you may want to give her a pacifier or blanket.

DAILY ROUTINES & FUNCTIONAL ACTIVITIES

Be sure to have the preferred material for self-calming readily available for the infant. You may also want to explore visual and/or auditory input to see what the child responds to. A slowly moving mobile over the crib or soft music, particularly with a regular beat, may provide the input a child needs to soothe herself.

CRITERION   *When fussy, the child is able to soothe herself within a few minutes at least half of the time.*

■ ■ ■

1e. Entertains self with toys for short periods of time

MATERIALS   A variety of toys or objects that will be selected by the child for play

PROCEDURES

Set up an area with a few toys or objects that are interesting to the child. Be sure that he is comfortable, with adequate support for sitting, if needed. Start the child playing and then become involved in another activity in the same room (e.g., reading, writing notes). If he does not continue to play with toys, help redirect him to another toy.

DAILY ROUTINES & FUNCTIONAL ACTIVITIES

Provide several opportunities throughout the day for the child to play with toys. Be sure toys are within easy reach. Look for toys that have a high interest for the child. Children often demonstrate preferences at this age for certain toys.

CRITERION   *The child plays alone (for at least 5 minutes) several times a week.*

■ ■ ■

1f. Moves away from the primary caregiver who is in same room

MATERIALS   A variety of toys or objects with which the child likes to play

PROCEDURES

Set up the room so that there are interesting and enticing activities or toys in various parts of the room that are away from where the primary caregiver and child are located.

Engage the primary caregiver in conversation, while basically leaving the child alone but close to the interesting and enticing new toys or activities. Watch the child. If she does not move to engage in play activities, have another adult or child begin to interact with the objects and/or encourage the child to join in the fun.

DAILY ROUTINES & FUNCTIONAL ACTIVITIES

Make toys available in a corner of a room where you are working or relaxing and encourage play there. Teachers can do the same in a classroom setting.

CRITERION   The child moves away from the primary caregiver to play when attractive toys are available in another location.

■ ■ ■

1g. Moves partially out of the primary caregiver's sight for short periods of play

MATERIALS   A variety of toys or objects with which the child likes to play

PROCEDURES

Set up an area nearby but away from your immediate presence (e.g., just inside the doorway to another room, in an alcove, on the other side of a room divider) that contains something of interest to the child. The adult should become involved in an activity of his own interest (e.g., reading, talking with someone, cooking).

If the child does not move to engage in the activity that was set up away from you, point out the items that are available for him to play with, or have another adult or child play with the toys in the nearby area and entice the child to join in the fun. Be sure to keep an eye on the child from a distance to ensure his safety.

DAILY ROUTINES & FUNCTIONAL ACTIVITIES

The child will be torn between wanting to be close to the caregiver and wanting to play with his favorite toys or objects that are now in different locations. Be sure to encourage the child to move toward the new play areas and to reinforce playing when it occurs alone for a few minutes at a time.

CRITERION   The child moves partially out of the caregiver's sight for short periods of play.

■ ■ ■

1h. Gets toys to play with from a box or shelf of toys

MATERIALS   A variety of toys that are regularly kept in a toy box or on a special shelf that the child can reach

PROCEDURES

Make the child aware that toys are always available in a given place (e.g., the toy box, a shelf). When she is unoccupied or begins to cling, guide her to where the toys are kept. Encourage the child to make a choice from among the toys, and then move away when she selects one.

If the child continues to seek interaction, encourage another choice of toys, asking, "Are you finished with the [toy]?" "Now what would you like, the [toy]?" As soon as the child begins to play alone, be sure to offer her verbal praise and reassurance that you are nearby.

DAILY ROUTINES & FUNCTIONAL ACTIVITIES

This item is most readily done as part of typical daily activities. It can be encouraged at home or in any caregiving environment. It requires only that toys be picked up and kept in given places.

CRITERION   *The child gets toys by himself to play with, from a box or shelf where they are regularly kept.*

■ ■ ■

1i. Plays alone with toys for 15 minutes

MATERIALS   A variety of toys or objects that will be selected by the child for play

PROCEDURES

Set up an area with a few toys or objects that are interesting to the child. Be sure that he is comfortable (e.g., in a supported position if needed). Give the child opportunities to play with these toys alone in this selected place, and be sure to check on him every few minutes. Start the child playing and then withdraw to the next room or become involved in another activity in the same room (e.g., reading, writing notes).

Check on him and offer verbal reinforcement for "good playing" every few minutes. Be careful to reinforce his playing only when it is actually occurring, so that the child does not merely sit idle. If he is found to be idle or stressed, help him to redirect to another activity or temporarily move the child back into your proximity.

Note: If self-stimulatory behaviors are observed during free play, search for more responsive and interesting toys and, if necessary, increase adult interaction. The adult should give attention after a short period of non–self-stimulatory behavior, rather than at the point that the self-stimulating behaviors occur.

DAILY ROUTINES & FUNCTIONAL ACTIVITIES

Provide several opportunities throughout the day for the child to play with toys. In the home, it is helpful to have a basket of toys available in several different rooms of the house. In addition, have a bag packed with a few toys so that the child will have something to play with on outings.

CRITERION   *The child plays alone for 15 or more minutes, several times per week.*

■ ■ ■

1j. Puts away toys in correct places

MATERIALS   None required

PROCEDURES

Whenever they are not in use, keep the child's toys and other items in specific locations in the home or at the group care program. Have the child observe you putting away items and removing them from their location for play. Frequently talk to the child about the location of items as you put them away (e.g., "The ball goes on the bottom shelf").

Ask the child to help you pick up and put away items that were used. Observe where the child puts the items. If she does not place them in the correct locations, say something such as, "Oops, I think you got the ball in with the blocks. Can you put it over there in that tub with the other balls?"

It helps to group like objects together (e.g., all of the balls go in the basket, the blocks go in the box, the trucks go on the shelf).

DAILY ROUTINES & FUNCTIONAL ACTIVITIES

It may be helpful to have pictures designating the correct placement of toys attached to shelves and storage areas. This is particularly important in a group care setting. Locate toy storage near where the child uses particular toys. For instance, keep bookshelves in the bedroom, paper and crayons near the dining room table, and dolls and trains in the play room.

Note: If many toys are in sight, the child may be disorganized by so many stimuli. It will help if you organize the task (e.g., "Let's see if we can pick up all the blocks first. I will help you. Let's see how many blocks we can find"). Praise the child for helping you and in her presence tell others about what a good helper she was. It may be helpful to use a cleanup song to signal that it is time to clean up and help the child move into the rhythm of cleaning up.

CRITERION   *The child puts away familiar toys in their correct places.*

■ ■ ■

1k. Explores

MATERIALS   A variety of natural environments

PROCEDURES

After child-proofing the house, encourage the child to explore by placing his favorite toys in unfamiliar places or by putting particularly interesting new toys or materials in corners, under tables, in accessible drawers, or in other places that the child usually does not go.

At first, show the child the object and where you are placing it. Later, simply place it so that it is partially visible and will invite exploration. Take the child with you when you shop, visit friends, or go into a new room or area. If the child can move about, encourage him to investigate the new environment. If necessary, help the child explore a new environment; however, fade your presence as soon as possible.

Note: Be sure to be alert to potential hazards before allowing the child the freedom to explore.

DAILY ROUTINES & FUNCTIONAL ACTIVITIES

Children can be allowed to explore, with guidance, in public buildings, shopping malls, parks, and many other places other than the home. (Exploring can be encouraged anywhere, but be very alert to potential sources of danger. In public places, a young child should never be out of your sight or more than a couple of steps away.)

CRITERION   *The child explores his environment, both at home and away from home.*

■ ■ ■

1l. Tolerates being taken into a variety of environments

MATERIALS   Different environments (e.g., playground, preschool, restaurant, grocery store, mall)

PROCEDURES

Plan outings to a variety of environments, starting with those that are less overwhelming. Note the child's reaction to the various settings. The goal is for the child to be relaxed and comfortable in a variety of environments and to transition smoothly to different places.

If the child becomes stressed or overwhelmed, start slowly. Go places that are relatively quiet, and stay only a short period of time. Allow the child to become comfortable at one place, having her visit it repeatedly before adding a second.

Note: There is a wide variety in children's temperaments and adaptability. For many children, this item will not cause any problems; however, for a small group of children, dealing with new and different places can be extremely overwhelming.

DAILY ROUTINES & FUNCTIONAL ACTIVITIES

Include the child in everyday life experiences that are developmentally appropriate. Expose the child to both indoor and outdoor settings and to those with both familiar and unfamiliar people. Children who have experienced a variety of environments and experiences are more likely than those who have been sheltered to make a smooth transition to school.

CRITERION   *The child remains happy and relaxed when taken into a variety of environments.*

■ ■ ■

1m. Avoids common dangers
(e.g., broken glass, high places, busy streets, big animals)

MATERIALS   None required

PROCEDURES

Talk to the child about being careful as you do activities together. For example, as you ap-proach a street during a walk say, "We have to be careful that no cars are coming. Look both ways. Do you see a car coming? No? Okay, now we can cross the street."

Be sure to always give reasons for prohibitions (e.g., "I don't want you to do that *be-cause* you might fall and get hurt"; "Some dogs are friendly, some are not. *Because* we don't know that dog, we won't try to pet him").

If the child starts to do something dangerous, calmly but firmly stop him and explain why he must not do that. If the child persists, a consequence (e.g., time-out) is in order. It is important to communicate to the child that you expect him to be responsible and that you notice and comment when he is responsible.

Don't always stop the child before he has a chance to decide on an appropriate ac-tion. For example, if you (or the child) break something made of glass, don't immediately pick up the child. Wait to see if he starts to approach it. If the child moves away, says "uh-oh," or takes other appropriate action, say, "That's good thinking. Leave it there, and I will clean it up so you won't get hurt."

DAILY ROUTINES & FUNCTIONAL ACTIVITIES

In a group setting, take time to reinforce rules of safety. You may want to devote a few min-utes every week to a quick review of safety rules at school (e.g., "What do we do in the hall? Do we run? No, we walk. Sam, why don't we run? Because we might fall and get hurt").

Note: Some children are, by nature, highly active and impulsive. They are much more likely to do dangerous things without thinking about them. It is especially impor-tant to be vigilant to keep these children safe. It is also important to remain calm, to con-tinue telling them the reasons for rules, and to be very attentive to them when they do manage to obey the rules.

CRITERION   *The child avoids common dangers most of the time—that is, you do not have to stop the child and retrieve him from a bad situation more than once a week.*

■ ■ ■

1n. Plays comfortably in a small group of children

MATERIALS   None required

PROCEDURES

Start with a small group of two or three other children, for short periods of time. If the child is hesitant, it may help to have a parent stay close by and for the child to bring a favorite toy with her. At this stage, the child is not likely to play with the other children. The goal is that the child is comfortable being around other children and is able to engage in parallel (near, but separate) play.

Note: Children without siblings may find this more challenging at first than children with siblings.

DAILY ROUTINES & FUNCTIONAL ACTIVITIES

If the child is not in a group care setting, the parents may want to consider weekly involvement in a small playgroup or a mother's morning out program. Or, consider exchanging child care with a friend who has a child of similar age.

CRITERION   *The child is comfortable playing in a small group of children for at least 30 minutes on several different occasions.*

1o. Knows what toys can and cannot do and uses them appropriately

MATERIALS   A general assortment of appropriate playthings

PROCEDURES

When the child gets a new toy or visits another child who has different toys than the ones at home, take time to show the child what the toy is used for and how it works. Talk about it as you show the child.

The child may be curious and experiment with other ways to use the toy. Or, he may be unable to use the toy in the way intended and will try to do something inappropriate with it. Do not interfere unless the experimentation is clearly inappropriate or dangerous (e.g., throwing something breakable, trying to pull the toy apart). At those times, say something such as, "That toy is not for throwing. It will break. You see, it works like this." Help the child use it appropriately.

If a toy is not age appropriate for the child, remove it and interest him in another toy.

DAILY ROUTINES & FUNCTIONAL ACTIVITIES

As you go about your daily activities, you may want to involve the child in simple tasks, showing him how different things work. This is a good opportunity to teach practical skills, such as sweeping with a small broom, putting groceries away, or putting money in a piggy bank.

CRITERION   *The child almost always knows what toys can and cannot do and uses them appropriately. The child may experiment with new toys but will be careful. He does not break the toy or do something highly inappropriate with it in his experimentation.*

REFERENCES

DeGangi, G. (2000). *Pediatric disorders of regulation in affect and behavior: A therapist's guide to assessment and treatment.* San Diego: Academic Press.

DeGangi, G., Sickel, R.Z., Kaplan, E.P., & Weiner, A.S. (1997). Mother-infant interactions in infants with disorders of self-regulation. *Physical and Occupational Therapy in Pediatrics, 17*(1), 17–39.

Greenspan, S.I. (1992). Reconsidering the diagnosis and treatment of very young children with autistic spectrum or pervasive developmental disorder. *Zero to Three Bulletin, 13,* 1–9.

Greenspan, S.I., & Salmon, J. (1995). *The challenging child: Understanding, raising, and enjoying five "difficult" types of children.* New York: Perseus Publishing.

Interpersonal Skills

Most of human learning and development takes place within a social context. Children's social responses to their caregivers not only provide information about what children are thinking, feeling, and learning but also reward the caregivers for the time and energy they devote to the children. When a child has an impairment that interferes with his or her ability to smile, laugh, and otherwise positively interact, caregivers and peers may begin to pay less attention to the child, and the child, in turn, may further reduce his or her efforts to interact, further reducing the likelihood of positive social experiences.

In developing an intervention plan for a young child, the interaction between the caregiver and the child must be a primary focus. In the birth to 12-month developmental period, it may be necessary to *orchestrate* interactions so that both the child and the caregiver are rewarded for their efforts. Such orchestration may be necessary, for example, when a child has a condition such as hypotonia that causes the child to be unusually slow to respond to an overture on the part of the caregiver. Often in these situations, because the child takes so long to respond, many caregivers will repeat the overture because they feel the child has not noticed what they did. Unfortunately, however, this repetition can come just as the child is finally getting organized to make a response, and thereby disrupts the child's thought process. In this case the interventionist should coach the caregiver to slow down (e.g., silently count to 10 before making a second attempt to attract the child's attention). Often this simple changing of pace will lead to reciprocal interactions that are more satisfying to both parties.

Another situation that requires orchestration is one in which it is difficult to "read" a child's responses. That is, the child's impairments prevent him or her from mutual eye gaze, smiling, laughing, or gesturing like his or her peers, and the caregiver is missing the feedback necessary to maintain a satisfying interaction. In the case of severe visual impairments, it may be necessary to help caregivers learn to "read" subtle hand movements for indications of interest and involvement. In the case of severe motor impairments, it may be necessary to help caregivers identify facial expressions (e.g., grimaces) that are the functional equivalent of smiles even though they may not look like other children's smiles.

During the 12- to 36-month developmental period, the emphasis shifts to helping children initiate social interactions and respond to social overtures of peers and a broader range of adults.

ADAPTATIONS

Children with Motor Impairments

If a child has very limited movement and motor control, you will need to be sensitive to subtle cues of social engagement, especially eye gaze and smiles. Seek help from the child's occupational and/or physical therapist to find optimal positioning for the child to observe other children and to participate in group activities.

Children with severe motor impairments may be able to operate toys by using switches. Such toys can be effective in engaging other children's attention and interest and can provide opportunities for sharing, turn taking, and other social interactions.

Children with Visual Impairments

Children with severe visual impairments will learn to respond socially to auditory and tactile stimuli. Earliest responses to caregivers may be subtle hand movements rather than smiles. Watch for these and other body language responses for cues indicating a desire to be picked up or to receive attention.

Children with severe visual impairments will probably be especially sensitive to sound and to nuances of approval and disapproval in the voices of those who provide care. It is even more critical than with other children to talk to these children frequently and to be alert to what you may be communicating by tone or volume of voice.

Children with severe visual impairments will need special help in learning to interact with other children. They may need physical guidance to hand things to someone else or to play simple games. Peers without visual impairments may have to be coached in ways to play with children with visual impairments.

Children with Hearing Impairments

Children with significant hearing impairments may miss many social cues. It may be necessary to use touch to get attention. Choose activities for interaction that involve a lot of tactile stimulation and motor actions. For example, interact around action rhymes, such as This Little Piggy or Pat-a-cake; play turn-taking games that involve patting, tickling, or rubbing one another's hands or arms; read books with textures to be felt or flaps that can be lifted. Good social interactions may also be obtained by bouncing the child on a large ball, swinging the child, and so forth.

2. INTERPERSONAL SKILLS

a. Smiles to auditory and tactile stimulation

b. Smiles reciprocally

c. Smiles at familiar person

d. Laughs

e. Tries to attract attention by making sounds, smiling, making eye contact, or using body language

f. Responds differently to family members and strangers

g. Participates in simple games

h. Repeats activity that elicits laughter from observer(s)

i. Shows an interest in other children—tries to attract their attention through eye gaze, smiles, and vocalizations

j. Initiates playing games

k. Laughs or smiles at adults who are engaging in unexpected behaviors

l. Spontaneously shares with adults

m. Shows affection

n. Tries to please others

o. Plays alongside other children (some exchange of toys)

p. Plays simple interactive games with other children

q. Helps with simple household tasks

r. Approaches peer or adult to initiate play

s. Responds appropriately to social contact made by familiar adults

t. Tries to comfort others in distress

u. Spontaneously shares with peers, often briefly

v. Tries to help by running errands on request or anticipating what is needed

w. Negotiates with peers about toys (may trade)

x. Shows awareness of social standards

y. Works collaboratively toward a goal with peers

z. Expresses affection and/or preference for some peers

aa. Expresses regret when another child is hurt or experiences unpleasantness

bb. Requests permission

■ ■ ■

2a. Smiles to auditory and tactile stimulation
2b. Smiles reciprocally
2c. Smiles at familiar person
2d. Laughs

MATERIALS   None required

PROCEDURES

Lean over the child or hold her so that you are looking directly at her. Try to establish eye contact. Talk to her, making a variety of sounds. Pat or rub her. Observe her reactions.

When the child has begun to smile to auditory and/or tactile stimulation, try looking at her and smiling without talking or patting her. Observe for a few minutes. If she does not smile, begin talking and providing tactile stimulation.

When the child has begun to smile in response to your smiling, try approaching her with a neutral look. If she does not smile in recognition begin talking and smiling and providing tactile stimulation.

Listen for the child's first laughs. These are often in response to gentle tickling or other tactile stimulation. When the child begins to smile or laugh, make it clear to her by the change in your tone of voice, a hug, a bounce, and so forth, that you have noticed and like her response. Also, take note of what you were doing that seemed to promote the smiling and/or laughing.

DAILY ROUTINES & FUNCTIONAL ACTIVITIES

A child's first smiles appear to be responses to internal events and physical stimuli rather than responses to social events. It is your smiling at the child and your response to the child when she smiles that creates a social interaction and lays the groundwork for social smiles.

In all caregiving activities, it is important to provide physical contact (e.g., holding, stroking) and to talk to the child and to smile often. Try to maintain eye contact with the child (even if her diagnosis is "cortically blind," because sometimes these children begin to respond to visual stimuli as they mature).

Watch briefly for the child to smile when she sees or hears you or any other person, before offering any tactile stimulation or picking her up.

Play with the child, making funny noises, tickling her, blowing on her stomach, and so forth. Do this as part of your typical caregiving routine as well as during special play times during the day.

Note: Ensure that the child has a small number of primary caregivers who regularly interact with her and who consistently reinforce social responses.

CRITERION 2a   *The child smiles to auditory and/or tactile stimulation on a regular basis.*

CRITERION 2b   *The child smiles in response to a person smiling at her (without tactile stimulation or sounds other than a greeting) on a regular basis.*

CRITERION 2c   The child frequently smiles to the appearance or voice of a familiar person (without tactile stimulation, the other person smiling first, or being picked up). This should happen at least once a day over several days.

CRITERION 2d   The child frequently laughs in response to tactile, auditory, and/or social stimuli.

■ ■ ■

2e. Tries to attract attention by making sounds, smiling, making eye contact, or using body language

MATERIALS   None required

PROCEDURES

The behavior of trying to attract attention is most easily observed in natural settings, particularly in situations in which adults are interacting with one another and a child might feel that he is being ignored. The child may look to adults as they speak, wave his hands, or vocalize. When one of the adults looks at the child, the child is likely to smile. You can try to set this up artificially to evaluate the child's response by recruiting the child's parent or other caregiver to converse with you and deliberately ignore the child. Observe the child's reactions. Does he use some method of attracting attention other than fussing?

When the child does try to attract attention in a social way, reinforce him by smiling back and giving him your full attention for a few minutes.

DAILY ROUTINES & FUNCTIONAL ACTIVITIES

Respond to the child's social overtures throughout the day. It is not necessary to attend to him all of the time, but do acknowledge his wish to be recognized. You can provide attention by talking to him while you go about other activities.

CRITERION   The child tries to get the attention of others by repeating sounds, smiles, eye gaze, or motions.

■ ■ ■

2f. Responds differently to family members and strangers

MATERIALS   None required

PROCEDURES

Parents or other caregivers are usually able to tell you whether a child is reacting differently to family members and strangers. Their observations can be credited for the assessment. If you wish to observe this behavior directly you will need to recruit one or more family members and someone the child does not know to come into the room at separate times so that you can observe the child's reactions. You cannot teach this skill, but you can try to ensure that the child has daily experiences that will help her acquire the ability to distinguish family members from strangers.

DAILY ROUTINES & FUNCTIONAL ACTIVITIES

At home, have the child present for family activities. Everyone in the family should spend time in face-to-face contact with the child, holding, touching, and/or talking to her. Watch the child for signs of recognition of family members (usually smiles). Then, pay careful attention to what the child does when an unfamiliar person visits the home or when the child is approached by an unfamiliar person away from home. Indications of knowing the difference between family members and strangers may be in facial expression (e.g., smiling at family and "studying" strangers), in activity level (e.g., excitement or quieting), or in other behaviors. Children tend to have their own unique ways of responding.

Note: If the child is in a group care environment, it is important that the environment provides a consistent setting in which a limited number of people provide primary care. The child may learn to respond differently to strangers who visit the child care setting, but it is more likely that she will simply begin responding differently to the group care provider and the family member who picks her up (or drops her off).

CRITERION   The child regularly responds differently to family members and strangers (or to family members and child care providers). It should be possible for two adults to agree on the response differences that were observed.

■ ■ ■

2g. Participates in simple games

MATERIALS   None required

PROCEDURES

Play Peek-a-boo with the child. Also try finger plays such as Here Comes a Little Bug (i.e., "walk" your fingers up the child's arm to his chin and then tickle him) and This Little Piggy (i.e., touching the toes).

Once the child has begun to smile during games, try to get him to become more actively involved. For example, when you play the Peek-a-boo game, wait a few seconds to see if the child will try to pull off the cover or if he looks to one side to anticipate your reappearance.

DAILY ROUTINES & FUNCTIONAL ACTIVITIES

Playing simple games is one of the best ways to entertain a child while you are changing his diapers, dressing him, or trying to keep him occupied while you do something else. Stop other games part way through to see if the child will try to get you to continue them to completion.

CRITERION   The child laughs during social interactions and tries to participate in the game by taking turns, anticipating an event, or indicating he wants you to continue playing.

■ ■ ■

2h. Repeats activity that elicits laughter from observer(s)

MATERIALS   None required

PROCEDURES

It is natural to laugh at things young children do. After you laugh, watch the child to see if she repeats the activity. If she does it again, combine your laughter with clapping or some other gesture to indicate pleasure with what the child has done. If the child does not spontaneously repeat an activity when you laugh at her, try to get the child to do it again by imitating what she just did.

DAILY ROUTINES & FUNCTIONAL ACTIVITIES

There should be numerous opportunities during the course of daily activities to observe how the child reacts when someone laughs at what she does.

CRITERION   The child frequently repeats activities that elicit laughter from observer(s).

■ ■ ■

2i. Shows an interest in other children—tries to attract their attention through eye gaze, smiles, and vocalizations

MATERIALS   None required

PROCEDURES

Take the child to a place where there are other children. Observe whether he behaves differently than when alone. For example, does the child watch the other children's activities intently, or does he attempt to attract their attention through vocalization, eye gaze, or other appropriate behaviors?

DAILY ROUTINES & FUNCTIONAL ACTIVITIES

Try to provide the child with many opportunities to be around both children and adults. Observe the way the child responds around each group. Does he show special interest in a child or a group of children? Does he try to get the attention of the children as much or more than the attention of adults? Young children will often stop fussing if placed on the edge of a group of playing children, will watch children quietly for much longer periods of time than if left with adults who are not directly interacting with them, will show more excitement (e.g., body movement, vocalization) when a child approaches, and so forth.

CRITERION   The child demonstrates an interest in other children by watching them intently, quieting when placed near them, trying to get their attention, and so forth. Two adults should agree on the responses that were observed.

■ ■ ■

2j. Initiates playing games

MATERIALS   None required

PROCEDURES

Sit with the child in a position you frequently use for playing a particular game. Wait to see if she will try to initiate the game. For example, if you have played Pat-a-cake with her sitting on your lap, does she try to start the game by holding your hands and patting them together? If she does not initiate the game, start it and then stop to see if she will try to get you to continue.

You can increase the likelihood of the child initiating social play by responding quickly and regularly to any of her efforts to draw you into play. Stopping to play for even 30 seconds will make her more likely to initiate playing games in the future.

DAILY ROUTINES & FUNCTIONAL ACTIVITIES

In the course of your daily routine, watch for the child's efforts to start games that you have previously played with her. When getting dressed or undressed, the child may present her feet (e.g., hoping to play This Little Piggy) or try to get on your foot when you are sitting cross-legged (e.g., for a ride on your foot). She may duck her head under something to start Peek-a-boo or start a turn-taking game by imitating something you have done and looking at you to let you know it is now your turn.

CRITERION   *The child seeks social play several times a day.*

■ ■ ■

2k. Laughs or smiles at adults who are engaging in unexpected behaviors

MATERIALS   None required

PROCEDURES

Play with the child using familiar toys, letting him take the lead in what you do. Then try to do something unexpected or silly and observe his response. For example, try to put a shoe on the doll's hand or stand the doll on her head in a chair. If the child laughs, laugh with him and, if it seems appropriate, repeat the silly act. If the child looks puzzled or troubled by what you have done, say something like "Silly me, look what I did," and laugh.

DAILY ROUTINES & FUNCTIONAL ACTIVITIES

As you go through your daily routines, occasionally surprise the child by doing something you would not typically do. For example, prepare the child's bottle or cup, but pretend to drink it yourself; when the music comes on the radio, stop what you are doing and dance around vigorously; put your hat on upside down; or try to put a glove on your foot. Try not to laugh yourself until you see what the child is going to do.

Some time later, try a different silly behavior and observe the child's reactions.

Note: It is important not to do the same silly behaviors often or they will cease to be unexpected and may no longer be funny.

CRITERION   The child laughs or smiles at adults who are engaging in unexpected behaviors on several occasions.

■ ■ ■

2l. Spontaneously shares with adults

MATERIALS   Two different kinds of cereals that child can manipulate (e.g., Cheerios), blocks or other toys

PROCEDURES

Prepare two small servings of two different kinds of cereals. Give one bowl to the child and keep one for yourself. Taste a piece of your cereal and say, "This is good. Would you like a piece of this?" Give her a piece and wait a little to see if she will offer you a piece of hers. If she does not, ask her if you might have a piece of hers. If she says no, ask her if she would like another piece of yours.

Use a similar procedure with two piles of blocks or groups of other toys. Offer to share yours. Wait long enough so that the child has a chance to offer items to you without being asked for them, but do ask and extend your hand for items if they are not offered. Be sure to say "thank you" each time the child gives you an item. Also, offer items to her in return.

DAILY ROUTINES & FUNCTIONAL ACTIVITIES

Sharing, like many behaviors, is most readily learned by imitation. It often begins by the caregiver sharing food with the child and the child then imitating by offering some of her food to the caregiver. Sharing can be encouraged by regularly asking the child "Would you like some?" when you are having a snack or eating a meal. Soon after sharing with her, give her a cracker (or some other finger food) and ask, "May I have some?" as you lean forward toward her. If the child pulls it away, it is important to respect her wish to keep the cracker for herself. However, continue modeling sharing by giving her some portion of what you have and occasionally asking her to share with you.

CRITERION   The child spontaneously shares, without prompting, especially when a sharing game has been initiated.

■ ■ ■

2m. Shows affection

MATERIALS   None required

PROCEDURES

Freely show affection for the child in whatever manner is appropriate for his culture. For example, smile at him, pat him gently, hug and kiss him on occasion, and tell him that you care for him.

After a kiss, put your cheek close to the child's mouth and ask for a kiss. If necessary, press your cheek against his lips and then act pleased and kiss the child again. Likewise, place the child's arms around your neck and ask for a hug. Help the child hug you, if necessary. Respond to the child with another hug and/or a kiss.

DAILY ROUTINES & FUNCTIONAL ACTIVITIES

Express affection to the child throughout the day. Let the child know that you like to have a hug or kiss.

Note: There are family and personal differences regarding the type and amount of affection that is demonstrated. These should be respected when implementing this item. The goal is to help the child learn to give and receive affection in whatever form fits the family's preferences.

CRITERION   *The child shows affection via hugs and kisses, or another reliable behavior, to familiar adults and peers.*

■ ■ ■

2n. Tries to please others

MATERIALS   None required

PROCEDURES

One of the strongest needs of a child is for attention. A child will want to please others if she receives more positive attention (e.g., praise, hugs, smiles) for good behavior than negative attention (e.g., frowns, yells) for bad behaviors. Thus, the best way to encourage a child to try to please others is to focus attention on her behaviors and activities that please you.

Watch for these signs that the child is trying to please you or others:

- She does an activity that has gotten a positive response earlier in the day or on previous days.
- She looks to you or other caregivers for approval after doing a task.
- She looks to an adult for approval or disapproval before starting to do a questionable activity.

Always naturally and positively respond to these overtures by the child.

DAILY ROUTINES & FUNCTIONAL ACTIVITIES

Encourage all of the adults in the child's environment to focus on attending to behaviors they like rather than behaviors they do not like. That is, encourage them to praise and encourage the child when she is behaving appropriately and to ignore minor negative behaviors.

CRITERION   *The child tries to please others by doing actions that she has done in the past or by looking for approval. This behavior should be indefinitely nurtured.*

■ ■ ■

2o. Plays alongside other children (some exchange of toys) 2

MATERIALS   Any toys attractive to the child

PROCEDURES

Arrange an opportunity for the child to be with one or more other children, and provide each child with a set of toys that are somewhat different. This will encourage an interest in the other children's toys and possible exchange of toys.

WATCH FOR

- Different behaviors from what you usually see when the child plays alone (e.g., longer or shorter attention span, more looking around)

- Positive responses to being with other children (e.g., trying to attract their attention, handing them toys)

- Play that is not disruptive in the presence of other children (except for occasional, but not deliberately hostile, "toy snatching")

If the child does not play with other children or shows no interest in the other children, sit with the child and try to facilitate play and interaction by showing the child what to do with one of the toys, handing a toy to another child, and so forth.

DAILY ROUTINES & FUNCTIONAL ACTIVITIES

Provide the child with many opportunities to be with other children. Recruit some older and more competent children to play with the child for brief periods.

Note: Deliberately disruptive behavior should be dealt with by momentarily removing the child from the situation for a few minutes, reintroducing him, and then observing him carefully to see if the disruption recurs. If it does, you need to determine the behavior's function. Is it a reaction to another child? If so, try to assess the appropriateness of the behavior of both children relative to the situation. Is it general discomfort in any group setting? If so, try to introduce the child to a setting with just one other child. Is it primarily a bid for adult attention? If so, it may be helpful for the adult to try to engage that child and another in a joint activity. If nondisruptive behavior cannot be sustained without constant adult attention, it may be necessary to seek the help of a psychologist in setting up a behavior management program.

CRITERION   *The child plays alongside other children for periods of at least 10 minutes, with occasional sharing of toys.*

■ ■ ■

2p. Plays simple interactive games with other children

MATERIALS   None required

PROCEDURES

The most common interactive games that young children play are some form of chasing each other. Ask one child to try to catch another child. If one child is crawling, encourage the other to crawl as well. Children particularly enjoy going around some object where they are out of each other's sight for a few seconds at a time. One can encourage variations on this by giving the children toys on strings that they can pull, either side-by-side or chasing each other.

DAILY ROUTINES & FUNCTIONAL ACTIVITIES

The goal of this item is for the child to play interactively rather than just alongside other children. Often this begins with the child playing with an older sibling or another older child whom she can imitate or follow. If there are no siblings in the home and the child is not attending a child care program, explore other options in the community for interactions with other children (e.g., mother's morning out programs or other playgroups, infant-toddler activities sponsored by various groups, or activities at public parks and recreation departments).

CRITERION   The child engages in interactive play (including turn taking) with one or more other children on several occasions.

■ ■ ■

2q. Helps with simple household tasks

MATERIALS   None required

PROCEDURES

When you have been playing with the child, tell him that it is time to pick up. Begin putting away toys, and encourage him to put away some, too. Give the child a cloth, and ask him to clean off the table. Ask him to take some trash to the trashcan. Always thank the child for helping.

DAILY ROUTINES & FUNCTIONAL ACTIVITIES

When doing routine jobs in the house or yard, try to think of ways in which the child can provide help. For example, when cleaning up after meals, let the child try to wipe off his own tray or the table. Let the child have a few dishes in a pan to wash. Ask the child to drop his dirty clothes in the hamper. Or, give him a cloth with which to dust while you are dusting.

Remember to always thank the child for helping. Praise the effort rather than the efficiency of the job. As the child's skills improve, he will be able to help more and more.

CRITERION   The child tries to help with several different household tasks on various occasions.

■ ■ ■

2r. Approaches peer or adult to initiate play

2

MATERIALS   None required

PROCEDURES

Watch for the child to seek interactions that will result in play (e.g., bringing toys to share, taking your hand to lead you to a play activity). These are the child's early attempts to determine what and with whom she wants to play. Reinforce this activity by asking, "Do you want to [activity]?" or "Shall we play with the [toy]?" Then allow the child to direct the sharing/ playing roles of the two of you for a few minutes.

DAILY ROUTINES & FUNCTIONAL ACTIVITIES

Also watch the child in situations in which she is with other children. If she does not try to initiate interactions with other children, lead her to another child, and try to include her in that child's activity. Choose the play partner with care so that it will be a successful experience for the child (i.e., choose a child who generally gets along well with other children and welcomes them into play).

Note: It is particularly important to allow the child to take the lead in play that she has initiated with you. Too much direction on the part of an adult will discourage the child's sense of competence and exploration. This is not so important when the child is with other children. Less competent children learn by modeling their behavior on that of those who are more competent.

CRITERION   The child approaches a peer or an adult to initiate play at least once a day.

■ ■ ■

2s. Responds appropriately
to social contact made by familiar adults

MATERIALS   None required

PROCEDURES

Always demonstrate appropriate greetings and interactions with other adults and with children. Greet the child and use "please" and "thank you" during your interactions with him. Say "goodbye" when you leave. Prompt him to say these words if he does not.

DAILY ROUTINES & FUNCTIONAL ACTIVITIES

Give the child opportunities to interact with friends and visitors. Prompt the child to say "hello," "goodbye," "please," "thank you," and so forth (or give "high fives" or whatever else is culturally appropriate) at the appropriate times, but do not insist that he speak if he is reluctant. Be sure to notice when he does greet people appropriately, and let him know you liked what he did.

CRITERION   The child responds appropriately to social contact made by familiar adults on most occasions (e.g., says "hello," gives "high fives," says or waves "goodbye," says "thank you," answers or asks questions).

■ ■ ■

2t. Tries to comfort others in distress

MATERIALS   None required

PROCEDURES

Comfort the child whenever she is distressed. Demonstrate comforting other people in natural ways when they show distress (e.g., kissing hurt places, patting or hugging a crying person). Request this kind of attention from the child (e.g., ask the child to "kiss it better" when you hurt your finger). In pretend play, suggest that the child comfort a hurt doll or stuffed animal.

DAILY ROUTINES & FUNCTIONAL ACTIVITIES

Seeing others care for the feelings and needs of the people around them should be a part of the child's daily experience. In a group setting, encourage children to comfort one another when they bump themselves, fall down, and the like during the day. Reinforce them for doing this. Show that you appreciate the fact that they are showing concern for others.

CRITERION   The child tries to comfort others in distress on several separate occasions.

■ ■ ■

2u. Spontaneously shares with peers, often briefly

MATERIALS   Any toys or objects with which the child enjoys playing (e.g., a telephone, dishes, tools, objects that are better used with two people)

PROCEDURES

Select another child to join you and the child you are working with for play. Observe how they play together. If there is no spontaneous sharing, suggest activities for the children that will encourage sharing. Prompt sharing if necessary and indicate pleasure when either of the children shares.

DAILY ROUTINES & FUNCTIONAL ACTIVITIES

Spontaneously sharing with peers is a natural activity whenever two children are playing together. Pretend kitchens and meal preparation items, building blocks, car and truck games, dolls and dresses, and sand or water activities all facilitate sharing.

When playing with dishes, pretend foods, clothes, and so forth, the child may take an item to another child and give it to or set it near the child, whether it is actually accepted or not. Reinforce the child for doing this (e.g., "Good sharing!" "Is [child's name] having lunch with you?" "Are you letting [child's name] help you with the dishes?").

Children frequently use a great deal of verbal jargon while doing this kind of sharing, especially as they give objects and, later, retrieve them. Thus, this offers a chance to work on early communication skills. Sharing can be facilitated by suggesting that "[peer] might like to play" or by guiding the child to share items and then commenting that others like such sharing. Don't forget to reinforce sharing when it is observed.

CRITERION   *The child gives objects to peers while playing, without being prompted to do so.*

■ ■ ■

2v. Tries to help by running errands on request or anticipating what is needed

MATERIALS   None required

PROCEDURES

Play with the child in a natural way. Look for opportunities to request that he get something for you.

Do some activity that will require help. For example, begin gathering blocks or other toys in your hands until there are so many you cannot pick up another one without dropping one. Observe whether the child spontaneously tries to help you. If not, ask him for help. Always praise the child for being helpful.

DAILY ROUTINES & FUNCTIONAL ACTIVITIES

The two best ways to encourage helpfulness in a child is to demonstrate being helpful to others and to reward the child's efforts at helpfulness with praise, hugs, and so forth. As you go about daily activities at home or in a group care setting, look for ways to have the child help (e.g., fetching a diaper or a bottle for a younger child, putting napkins on the table for lunch, taking the paper to someone to read).

Watch for times the child anticipates a need before you have made a request (e.g., running to get a bottle if an infant is crying; going to get a tool when someone is trying to fix something, even if it is the wrong tool). Let the child know how much you appreciate his help.

CRITERION   *The child runs simple errands or fetches things in anticipation of needs on a daily basis.*

■ ■ ■

2w. Negotiates with peers about toys (may trade)

MATERIALS   None required

PROCEDURES

Recruit another child to play with the child who has special needs. Have a variety of toys for them, but be sure to have only one of several toys that are highly prized by most children (e.g., one riding toy, one pair of tongs, one paint brush and easel). As they play, observe how they share and how they handle a situation where they both want the same toy. Prompt taking turns and trading toys as appropriate. Comment on sharing and cooperation, letting the children know you appreciate it.

DAILY ROUTINES & FUNCTIONAL ACTIVITIES

Demonstrate to the child how to negotiate with peers by having the children take turns or trade toys whenever a conflict arises. Emphasize using words to solve problems rather than grabbing, hitting, or other physical means. Notice when children share and play cooperatively. Comment on it.

CRITERION   The child negotiates with peers and/or siblings about toys several times a day over several days.

■ ■ ■

2x. Shows awareness of social standards (e.g., wants clothes changed when dirty, brings broken toys to be fixed)

MATERIALS   None required

PROCEDURES

As you play with the child, watch for signs that the child is aware of social standards. If there are few opportunities to observe this, you may create some by deliberately including a broken toy in the materials you are using for play, by spilling some of your drink, by giving the child some paper object that is fragile and likely to be damaged, and so forth. Observe the child's reactions. If she shows distress, acknowledge her distress but treat the event in a matter-of-fact manner (e.g., "I know you did not mean to do that. Let's fix it").

DAILY ROUTINES & FUNCTIONAL ACTIVITIES

A child learns social standards by observing the adults and other children around her. Encourage this learning by talking to the child about why you do things (e.g., "That dress has gotten pretty dirty. Let's change it before we go to the store"; "Oops, you spilled your milk. Let's clean it up"; "That's broken. Let's see if we can fix it"; "Oh, dear, you tore Danny's paper. Tell him you are sorry").

CRITERION   The child shows awareness of several different social standards, such as a desire for clean clothes, the need to repair items that are broken, the necessity of saying "I'm sorry" when having an accident, and so forth.

■ ■ ■

2y. Works collaboratively toward a goal with peers

MATERIALS   None required

PROCEDURES

Recruit one or two other children to play with the child. Suggest a project for them to do together. Some possible projects are to build a train out of chairs and pretend to go for a ride, to construct a block building, or to make roads for cars by placing blocks end to end. If you are doing block activities, provide each of the children with a pile of blocks, making it more likely that all children will participate. If any child plays independently with his blocks, tell him that all of the blocks are needed to make a really big house (or long road). Praise the children when they cooperate with one another in the task.

DAILY ROUTINES & FUNCTIONAL ACTIVITIES

Provide experiences for the child to interact with other children at home, in religious schools, in child care, or in other settings. If he does not spontaneously join into collaborative play, recruit another child to play with you and him. Select materials that especially encourage collaboration, such as blocks or other construction materials. Participate as much as necessary to get them started and then gradually withdraw. If conflicts occur, encourage compromise. Comment on how well the children work together and what they accomplish together.

CRITERION   The child works collaboratively toward a goal with one or more peers on several occasions.

■ ■ ■

2z. Expresses affection and/or preference for some peers

MATERIALS   None required

PROCEDURES

Children learn to express affection by experiencing affection from their families and other caregivers. Freely express affection for the child in whatever manner is appropriate for her culture. For example, smile at her, pat her gently, hug and kiss her on occasion, and tell her that you care for her. Also, express affection for others in the child's presence.

DAILY ROUTINES & FUNCTIONAL ACTIVITIES

In group settings, give the children kisses, hugs, pats, or other culturally appropriate indications of affection. Encourage the children to help each other and comfort each other when they are hurt. Use group time to encourage older children to talk about what things people do to let them know they are loved.

CRITERION   *The child expresses affection and/or preference for some peers. This should be a common occurrence, although frequently it will vary according to the opportunities available. Some sign of affection or preference should be seen each time the child is with other children.*

■ ■ ■

2aa. Expresses regret when another child is hurt or experiences unpleasantness

MATERIALS   None required

PROCEDURES

Model being sensitive to other people's misfortunes. Help the child when he gets hurt, be sympathetic when he is frustrated or unhappy, and help him find solutions to problems. Encourage the child to help other family members (e.g., "Johnny hurt his finger. Come help me kiss it and make it better").

Engage the child in pretend play with dolls, animals, or puppets that involves one character caring for another when hurt.

Always let the child know you appreciate it when he is sympathetic to another child.

DAILY ROUTINES & FUNCTIONAL ACTIVITIES

Observe the child both in family settings and in a variety of settings where he is with other children. Watch for him to show sympathy for someone who is distressed. If the child does not do this spontaneously, model the behavior, and prompt him to comfort or help the person in distress.

CRITERION   *The child expresses regret when another child is hurt or experiences unpleasantness, five or more times. At this level, the child need not spontaneously try to help the child but should either tell the adult to help or will help when asked by the adult.*

■ ■ ■

2bb. Requests permission (e.g., "Johnny go out?" "I turn it?")

MATERIALS   None required

PROCEDURES

Divide up a group of toys or other objects between you and the child. Label them as yours and hers. After a few minutes, ask the child if you can play with (or use) one of her objects for a few minutes. Play with it momentarily and then return it. Identify an object in your group that is particularly interesting and do something with it. If the child reaches for it but does not ask permission to use it, say "Do you want my [object]? Ask me for it nicely." If necessary tell her to ask, "Please, may I have it?" You can do a similar activity using snack foods, with a different kind for each of you.

DAILY ROUTINES & FUNCTIONAL ACTIVITIES

Always request permission to use the personal property of the child and others around you. Listen for the child to begin asking permission to do activities. Respond positively to these requests. If the requests cannot be granted, tell the child why not and, if appropriate, when they can be granted (e.g., "You can't go outside now. It's too rainy. We'll go out when the rain stops").

CRITERION   The child requests permission from an adult or child several times without being prompted.

3
Self-Concept

A person's sense of self (self-concept) includes a sense of identity (e.g., who you are, how competent you are, how you appear to others, where you fit into the family and community) and feelings or value judgments about that identity. The period of infancy is crucial for laying the foundation for a sense of competence and worth (Turner, 1994). It is especially important that young children feel valued by their caregivers and peers in order for young children to value themselves. When young children feel good about themselves they are often more enthusiastic about trying challenging tasks and are usually able to cope with failure.

This sequence includes the components of a healthy self-concept. However, caregivers must provide the affection and enthusiasm that will make the curriculum activities effective. Children are quick to pick up on adult attitudes and feelings. If the adult values and accepts the child with special needs, siblings and other children will be likely to do so as well.

Note: It is important to recognize that some aspects of a healthy self-concept may provide special challenges to caregivers. These include the child making undesirable choices, refusing to follow commands, showing determination in pursuing a goal, becoming possessive about toys and other objects, and competing with peers for toys or attention. These behaviors, which blossom in the 18- to 30-month developmental range, are what define the "terrible twos." Although these behaviors can be irritating and may last longer in a child who is developing slowly, they should be valued as important indicators of the child's growing sense of independence. Caregivers can help children channel their growing sense of independence into socially acceptable behavior by having consistent rules, giving the child frequent opportunities to choose between acceptable alternatives (rather than just telling him or her what to do), and focusing on teaching the child favorable behaviors. In all activities, the child should experience more success than failure and more positive than negative feedback from his or her caregivers and peers.

ADAPTATIONS

Children with Motor Impairments

It is difficult for children with severe motor impairments to develop the sense of competence that arises from becoming independent and being able to compete with peers. The challenge for caregivers is to identify activities in which the child can have success. Adaptive equipment, including communication devices and toys, operated with switches may be helpful. Seek the guidance of the child's therapists.

Children with Visual Impairments

The items that involve looking in mirrors and at photographs should be omitted for children with severe visual impairments. These children will learn to identify themselves and others in different ways, such as by the sound of voices, by smell, or, in some cases, by the general outline and colors of skin and hair. Few other adaptations are needed beyond helping the child locate and identify objects by touch, smell, and sound so that he or she can make choices.

Children with Hearing Impairments

For children with severe hearing impairments, consult a communication specialist about appropriate aids for communication, such as using signs or a communication device.

3. SELF-CONCEPT

a.   Responds to name

b.   Plays with mirror image

c.   Makes choices

d.   Recognizes self and others in mirror

e.   Says "no" or otherwise indicates refusal

f.   Expresses feelings of interest, pleasure, surprise, excitement, warning, and complaint (four or more)

g.   Resists attempts from others to assist with feeding

h.   Identifies objects as "mine"

i.   Competes with peers for toys

j.   "Performs" for others

k.   Asks for snacks or drinks

l.   Shows determination/persistence in choosing or continuing activities

m.   Distinguishes and names self in photographs

n.   Shows pride in achievements

o.   Makes positive statements about self

p.   Knows age (tells or holds up fingers)

q.   Tells own first name

r.   Answers correctly when asked if he or she is a boy or a girl

s.   Is selective about what tasks he or she will and will not try (recognizes limitations)

t.   Shows guilt or shame over accidents or prohibited behavior

■ ■ ■

3a. Responds to name

MATERIALS   None required

PROCEDURES

When the child is playing, say his name. If he does not respond, say his name a little louder. If there is still no response, say his name while touching him on the shoulder or arm to get his attention. When he does respond to his name, smile and talk to him.

Once the child has begun responding when you say his name, check his recognition of his name by saying other words at a similar volume.

DAILY ROUTINES & FUNCTIONAL ACTIVITIES

Use the child's name frequently while interacting with him. Until he has learned to recognize his name, it is better to use his name and yours rather than to use the pronouns that are usual in speech to older children and adults (e.g., "David is Mommy's big boy" rather than "You are my big boy").

Call the child's name as you begin to pick him up or when you first enter the room. At first, he may turn and look at you regardless of the sound you make. Gradually, however, he should react differently to his own name than to other words or sounds.

Try saying the child's name when he is occupied with some activity to see if he will stop and look at you, even momentarily.

CRITERION   The child usually turns to look at the speaker when his name is called or gives some other consistent sign of recognition.

■ ■ ■

3b. Plays with mirror image

MATERIALS   Unbreakable hand mirror, toys with mirrors, or mirror mounted on the wall

PROCEDURES

Sit with the child on your lap facing away from you. Hold the mirror in front of her so that she sees her own face and not yours. Observe her reactions. At first, children tend to study their mirror images quietly. Then they begin to pat them playfully, smile, and/or laugh.

DAILY ROUTINES & FUNCTIONAL ACTIVITIES

Children tend to love mirrors. Some crib gyms or busy boxes have mirrors attached. If the child has one of these, observe the changes in her responses to her mirror image over time.

When you carry the child past a wall mirror in the house or in other environments, make a point of moving the child back and forth in front of the mirror so that she sees herself for a few minutes and then does not see herself. Note changes in her reactions to her reflection.

CRITERION   On several occasions the child plays with her mirror image for several minutes, patting, mouthing, smiling, laughing, or otherwise behaving in a playful manner.

■ ■ ■

3c. Makes choices (e.g., has preferred toys, foods)

MATERIALS   Toys or food, including preferred items

PROCEDURES

Play with the child and/or feed him one of his meals. Give him opportunities to make choices. Hold up two toys and ask, "Which one do you want?" Give him the toy he reaches for (or looks at steadily), naming it as you give it to him.

Try pairing what appears to be a preferred toy with a variety of other toys to see if the child has any consistent pattern of preferences.

When feeding the child, give him a taste of two or three different foods that make up the meal. When you try to give second bites, does he turn his head away for some and open his mouth for others? If not, try holding up his milk and a spoon of food and asking which one he wants. Give him the one he reaches for (or looks at, if reaching is difficult).

When the child seems to have made a choice, comment on it (e.g., "Oh, you want the cookie? Is it good?" "You don't like spinach? Let's try some peaches").

DAILY ROUTINES & FUNCTIONAL ACTIVITIES

Throughout the day, observe what the child does to let you know what he likes and does not like. Does he turn away when certain foods are presented and open his mouth eagerly for others? Does he have a particular toy, blanket, or other object that he wants to take to bed with him or that he wants to hold when upset? Does he show a preference for a certain person when he is hurt but another when he wants to play? If you hold out two foods (e.g., a cookie and an apple), will he look at both but then reach toward one?

Note: Recognizing and honoring a child's preferences is not the same as "spoiling" him. A responsible adult must decide what is good for the child and not allow him to do things or have things that are harmful. The caregiver, however, should give the child many opportunities to make choices among acceptable things and activities.

CRITERION   The child regularly makes choices among toys, foods, and/or people, demonstrating clear preferences.

■ ■ ■

3d. Recognizes self and others in mirror

MATERIALS   Unbreakable hand mirror, toys with mirrors, or mirror mounted on the wall

PROCEDURES

Sit with the child on your lap facing away from you. Hold the mirror in front of her so that she sees her own face and not yours. Observe her reactions. Then tilt the mirror so that the child can see both herself and you. Observe her reactions again. At first, children tend to study their mirror images quietly. Then they begin to pat them playfully, smile, and/or laugh. These behaviors, however, do not suggest self-recognition. Self-recognition becomes apparent when the child experiments more extensively with the image by moving her head back and forth, making faces, blowing bubbles, and so forth. If the child looks up at you and then back at the mirror when you are reflected in the mirror, it is likely that she is recognizing both you and herself in the mirror.

DAILY ROUTINES & FUNCTIONAL ACTIVITIES

Children tend to love mirrors. Some crib gyms or busy boxes have mirrors attached. If the child has one of these, observe the changes in her responses to her mirror image over time.

When you carry the child past a wall mirror in the house or in other environments, make a point of moving the child back and forth in front of the mirror so that she sees herself for a few minutes and then does not see herself. Note changes in her reactions to her reflection.

CRITERION   The child shows recognition of herself and others in mirrors by experimenting with different facial expressions or behaviors when she sees herself and by looking back and forth between the mirror and another person when she sees that person in the mirror.

■ ■ ■

3e. Says "no" or otherwise indicates refusal

MATERIALS   None required

PROCEDURES

Children learn to say "no" because other people say "no" to them, usually in attempts to inhibit behavior. When a child first begins to say or indicate "no" by a sign or shake of the head, it is usually to refuse something being offered to him. It is important to honor these refusals by not insisting that he take what is offered or do what the adult has asked him to do. By recognizing the child's preferences, you are teaching him that he is an effective person who can exert some control over his environment.

You may be able to elicit refusals by offering the child something you are fairly sure he does not want, but it is more effective to simply observe what he does as you and others interact with him throughout the day.

DAILY ROUTINES & FUNCTIONAL ACTIVITIES

Although you cannot honor all of the child's refusals throughout the day, it is important to honor those that are not detrimental to the child or to the people around him. In cases where it is necessary that the child do something he is trying to avoid (e.g., taking a nap, taking medicine, having his nose cleaned) it is important to communicate your recognition of his wishes but the necessity of going against those wishes (tell him you are sorry and you know he doesn't like the activity, then state the reason he must do it). He may not really comprehend the words, but he will get the message that he has control over some things and not others.

CRITERION   *The child refuses foods or activities by saying "no," shaking his head, or using some other consistent method.*

■ ■ ■

3f. Expresses feelings of interest, pleasure, surprise, excitement, warning, and complaint (four or more)

MATERIALS   None required

PROCEDURES

One cannot teach a child to feel. The goal of this item is for the child to *express* her feelings. In order to encourage this expression, the caregiver should make an effort to understand what the child is feeling and then respond appropriately to that feeling. It is important for children to learn that they are acceptable people and that their feelings are valid, regardless of how they feel. Some ways to help children express their feelings include the following:

• Look for indications of feelings in the child's behavior, and then respond by labeling the feeling that you think the child is experiencing and identifying the reasons for the feeling (e.g., "You seem very *excited* about going to see grandma. I'm excited, too"; "I know you're *angry* because Johnny took the truck, but I can't let you hit him").

- Share your own feelings (e.g., "I'm crying because I'm *sad* that . . .," "I'm *angry* because . . .," "I'm *excited* because . . .").
- Call the child's attention to other people's feelings and how they express them. Make it clear that all feelings are natural but that one is not allowed to act on negative feelings in a way that harms other people (e.g., "I know he's angry, but we do not allow hitting, so he must go to time-out").
- When you read stories to the child, talk about how the characters feel.

DAILY ROUTINES & FUNCTIONAL ACTIVITIES

Observe the child in a variety of settings to determine whether she explores feelings in ways that others can identify them.

CRITERION   *The child expresses feelings in a way that regular caregivers can identify them. The child must express at least four of the six feelings listed.*

■ ■ ■

3g. Resists attempts from others to assist with feeding

MATERIALS   Typical mealtime food and utensils

PROCEDURES

Allow the child to help hold the spoon when you are feeding him, and let him try to use it on his own. Provide finger foods when he is able to chew and swallow them. After you have been giving him some independence for a while, try to feed him and observe his reactions.

DAILY ROUTINES & FUNCTIONAL ACTIVITIES

During all snacks and meals allow the child as much independence as possible. Do not insist on helping if he resists. If you cannot tolerate the mess the child makes with a spoon, try to give him most of his meal in a form he can pick up with his fingers.

CRITERION   *The child tries to eat independently and resists others' efforts to help him.*

■ ■ ■

3h. Identifies objects as "mine"

MATERIALS   None required

PROCEDURES

Before beginning to play with the child, take off your shoes and the child's shoes. Set them aside for a few minutes. Then point to your shoe and say, "Whose shoe is that?" If she does not reply or replies incorrectly say, "That shoe is mine. See, it goes on my foot.

Now, whose shoe is that?" (pointing to the child's shoe). If she does not replay say, "That is your shoe. It's [child's name] shoe."

Use the same procedure for other articles of clothing or other objects where the ownership should be clear to the child.

DAILY ROUTINES & FUNCTIONAL ACTIVITIES

Ensure that the child has at least a few objects that belong only to her and that she has a consistent place for her belongings. At home, the child may have a room or a bed and shelf in a room she shares with others. At a group care center, she should have a "cubby" or another area designated as hers.

When you are going about your daily activities with the child, identify items that belong to one person or another and the ones that belong to the family or the school. For example, when cleaning up you can say, "This is your car. Please put it in your room" or, "This is Mary's coat. Where does that go?"

Watch for the child to begin identifying objects as "mine," or claiming ownership by placing them with her things or holding them tightly in her arms.

Note: Most young children will go through a phase of identifying any object that they want as their own. Although this may be aggravating, it is an indication of the child's growing sense of herself as an important person. Acknowledge the child's desire for the object but also identify the true owner.

CRITERION   The child regularly identifies objects as "mine," either verbally or through putting them in her pockets or with her things. It is not necessary that her statement of ownership be accurate.

■ ■ ■

3i. Competes with peers for toys

MATERIALS   A variety of toys

PROCEDURES

Arrange a play time for the child with one or two other children. Look for signs that he is competing with other children for toys. This may involve asking another child for a toy, snatching a toy from another child, watching for another child to put down a toy and then quickly taking it, running to get on a riding toy before someone else can reach it, gathering a group of toys in front of himself so that others cannot get them, or other similar behaviors. You may need to intervene to prevent fights over toys and reinforce the ideas of taking turns and sharing.

If the child makes no attempt to try to get toys for himself, prompt him to ask for a turn with a toy that seems to capture his interest.

DAILY ROUTINES & FUNCTIONAL ACTIVITIES

Observe the child in a variety of settings with other children to determine whether he is beginning to compete for toys.

Note: Competition for toys is a healthy and typical developmental stage. Some children will try to hoard all of the available toys for themselves. This is not a cause for alarm or punishment but provides an opportunity to begin to teach the child the concepts of following rules, sharing, and taking turns. If the child is hoarding, you can make a rule that no child may have more than two toys at one time and must choose which two it will be. For teaching turn taking, it is sometimes helpful to have a kitchen timer so that you can easily enforce a rule that the child may play with the toy for 5 minutes but then must allow another child to have it for 5 minutes.

CRITERION   The child frequently competes for toys, trying to make sure he has access to some of them.

3

■ ■ ■

3j. "Performs" for others

MATERIALS   None required

PROCEDURES

When you are working with the child on skills such as singing a song, reciting a nursery rhyme, dancing, and so forth, praise her and ask her to show someone else how well she does it. Choose an "audience" that is familiar to her (e.g., parent, grandparent, sibling). Do not insist that she perform if she is resistant. You may prepare her better for performing by simply calling someone over while she is in the process of doing something. Their praise is likely to make her more comfortable "performing" at another time.

DAILY ROUTINES & FUNCTIONAL ACTIVITIES

Young children like to please adults and to "show off" for them. They will do this spontaneously, as well as on request at times. They like, and should be encouraged, to sing songs, say short nursery rhymes, do tricks, and generally show that they are developing skills and competencies of which they are proud. When children "perform," be sure to show excitement and to praise and applaud their efforts.

CRITERION   The child "performs" for others, either spontaneously or on request, on several separate occasions.

■ ■ ■

3k. Asks for snacks or drinks

MATERIALS   Foods and drinks typically provided as snacks

PROCEDURES

Before you begin to play with the child, put snacks (e.g., fruit, cereal) out of the child's reach but within view. Do not offer the snacks to the child; rather, wait for him to clearly indicate that he wants the snack and/or drink. If he does not make a request, do not give him the snack. If he points or whines, try to get him to make a verbal (or signed) request, saying it for him so that he can imitate if necessary.

DAILY ROUTINES & FUNCTIONAL ACTIVITIES

Throughout the day, be attentive to the child's attempts to request a drink or a snack. Be sure to respond to appropriate verbal or gestural communication from the child, but do not respond to whining, tugging at your clothes, or other inappropriate behaviors that a child might use to get something he wants.

CRITERION   *The child asks for snacks or drinks once a day.*

■ ■ ■

31. Shows determination/persistence in choosing or continuing activities

MATERIALS   None required

PROCEDURES

Observe the child's activities for signs of determination and persistence. Some indications of these characteristics are

- The child stays with a toy for an extended period of time, repeating the same activity.
- The child protests when you take her away from a toy or activity for meals or bedtime.
- The child is adamant about a choice she has made and rejects a substitute.
- The child expresses frustration and abandons a task when it is difficult, but she returns to it repeatedly at later times until she masters it.

DAILY ROUTINES & FUNCTIONAL ACTIVITIES

Observe the child throughout the day as she selects and plays with toys. Watch for the signs of determination and persistence listed in the Procedures section. If the child becomes frustrated because a toy does not work or because she cannot do something she wishes to do, provide enough help to ensure success, but do not provide more help than she needs.

Note: Although persistence and determination are important characteristics for a child to develop, they may create conflict with peers and caregivers. It is important to affirm the child's determination but, at the same time, set appropriate limits (e.g., "I understand that you want to keep playing with your blocks, but it's bedtime. You can play with them in the morning. Do you want to put them back in the box or leave them right here?"). Providing the child with a choice related to what she is determined to do will often decrease resistance to ending the task.

Some impairments lead children to perseverate, choosing or continuing one activity to the exclusion of all others. This should, of course, be discouraged.

CRITERION   *The child regularly shows determination and persistence in choosing or continuing activities.*

■ ■ ■

3m. Distinguishes and names self in photographs

MATERIALS   Photographs of the child and other people whom he knows

PROCEDURES

Look through a photograph album with the child, pointing to the pictures and identifying the people in them. Ask the child if he can find himself and others. At another time, just look through the book with the child to see if he will name himself and others spontaneously. Repeat these two steps until he does name them spontaneously.

DAILY ROUTINES & FUNCTIONAL ACTIVITIES

Have a place in which photographs, including one or more of the child, are displayed (e.g., on a shelf, on the refrigerator door). As you pass them with the child, point them out to him. Begin waiting to name the pictures to see if the child will identify them himself.

CRITERION   The child regularly identifies photographs of himself and says or signs his name.

■ ■ ■

3n. Shows pride in achievements

MATERIALS   None required

PROCEDURES

Show excitement and praise a child for her accomplishments (e.g., clap your hands, hug her, and say, "You made a beautiful picture. We'll hang it on the wall"). Praise the child and show off her accomplishments to other children or adults. Watch for the child to bring accomplishments to you for approval, to show them to others, and to repeat an accomplishment over and over.

DAILY ROUTINES & FUNCTIONAL ACTIVITIES

Encourage everyone in the child's environment to notice and reinforce the child's accomplishments, regardless of how small they are.

CRITERION   The child regularly shows pride in her accomplishments by bringing them to the attention of others, repeating a difficult task several times after the first mastery, or by other means.

■ ■ ■

3o. Makes positive statements about self

MATERIALS   None required

PROCEDURES

When you are interacting with the child, comment on the things he does well and how hard he tries. Be as specific as possible (e.g., "You are such a good helper"; "I like the way you are sharing"; "You look so handsome in that sweater"; "You're so smart to get that puzzle together").

Also, make positive statements about the child to other children and adults in the child's presence.

Listen for the child to begin making positive statements about himself (e.g., "I big," "I run fast") Let him know you accept and appreciate such statements (e.g., smile, nod, verbally agree with him).

DAILY ROUTINES & FUNCTIONAL ACTIVITIES

Comment on the child's good behaviors throughout the day. Children will think positively about themselves and be more likely to make positive statements about themselves if they hear adults saying positive statements about them. If a child misbehaves and needs to be away from the group for a short period, focus on the deed (e.g., "We do not hit. Tell [child] you are sorry, and sit over here for a few minutes until you are ready to play again" or "None of us like to hear you scream. You must stay in your room until you stop screaming"). As soon as possible after a child is reprimanded, look for something good to comment on. It is important for him to hear more positive than negative statements.

CRITERION   On several occasions the child makes a positive statement about himself.

■ ■ ■

3p. Knows age (tells or holds up fingers)

MATERIALS   None required

PROCEDURES

Ask the child, "How old are you?" If she does not reply or replies incorrectly, tell her age and help her hold up the correct number of fingers, counting them for her. Ask the same question every few days until she begins to answer correctly.

DAILY ROUTINES & FUNCTIONAL ACTIVITIES

Make a point of talking about age at the celebration of the child's birthday and at the celebrations of birthdays for family members and friends. Although the child will have no real concept of the meaning of the numbers associated with birthdays, she will learn that age is a part of who a person is and will be more prepared to answer the frequently asked question, "How old are you?"

Occasionally ask the child how old she is and then prompt her so that she answers appropriately. When someone else asks her, "How old are you?" wait for her to answer on her own. If she does not, prompt her by saying the age and showing the correct number of fingers.

CRITERION   On several occasions the child states the correct number or holds up the correct number of fingers in response to the question, "How old are you?"

■ ■ ■

3q. Tells own first name

MATERIALS   Puppets or dolls

PROCEDURES

Play make-believe with the child. Have a doll, puppet, or animal approach the child and say, "My name is Juanita. What is your name?" If the child does not answer, ask him if he is [some name other than his]. If he does not give his name, say, "Oh you must be [correct name]." Repeat with another doll, puppet, or animal until he readily says his name.

DAILY ROUTINES & FUNCTIONAL ACTIVITIES

Frequently address the child by his name. When someone asks the child his name, prompt the child to answer (e.g., "Tell Mrs. Liu your name," "Tell her your name is Billy").

If the child is in a group, you can introduce "Mr. Mix-up" during circle time. He can be a puppet, an animal, or a doll. He always gets information wrong and must be corrected. For example, he will say to Mary, "Oh, I remember you. You are Lachandra." All of the children will probably laugh and then you can say for him, "You're not Lachandra. Well then, who are you?" Alternate Mr. Mix-up's getting names incorrect with getting other information incorrect. It is a good way to get children to listen and think about what they have heard.

CRITERION   The child will tell his first name when asked, "What is your name?" or "Who are you?" or the equivalent on several occasions without prompting by an adult.

■ ■ ■

3r. Answers correctly
when asked if he or she is a boy or a girl

MATERIALS   Several dolls, some dressed as boys and some dressed as girls

PROCEDURES

Play with the child, giving roles to the dolls (e.g., daddy, little boy, mommy, little girl) Give the child instructions that involve having a boy or a girl doll do something (e.g., "Let the boy sit in the chair"). Let the child give you instructions as well. After a few minutes of play, ask the child, "Are you a boy or a girl?" If she does not reply, say, "Are you a girl?" Regardless of her answer ask, "Are you a boy?"

DAILY ROUTINES & FUNCTIONAL ACTIVITIES

Use the designation boy or girl when you praise or talk to the child about herself. (e.g., "You are a big girl," "What a pretty girl you are today," "That's Mama's smart girl"). Similarly, identify other members of the family or other children in a group care setting. Occasionally, playfully ask the child, "Are you a girl?" "Am I a girl?" "Is Daddy a girl?" Correct the child's errors.

If a number of children are present, you can ask the girls to do one activity and the boys to do another as a way of seeing how well the child identifies her own gender.

CRITERION   *The child answers correctly the questions, "Are you a boy?" and "Are you a girl?" on two or more days.*

■ ■ ■

3s. Is selective about what tasks he or she will and will not try (recognizes limitations)

MATERIALS   A variety of puzzles (ranging from very easy to very difficult), other toys/tasks that vary in difficulty

PROCEDURES

Tell the child this is puzzle day. Give him a puzzle to do that you are sure will be easy for him. Praise his accomplishment and then present a harder puzzle to him. Continue increasing the difficulty of the task, and observe the child's reactions. Does he lose interest as the task becomes too difficult to master readily? Does he request help? Does he refuse to try when the puzzle is far beyond his capabilities?

DAILY ROUTINES & FUNCTIONAL ACTIVITIES

In the course of daily activities, observe how the child reacts when encountering a new and challenging activity. Does he initially seem excited but on finding it difficult leave it for another activity? Does he ask you for help? On another day, will he ignore it and go back to a more familiar activity on which he has previously had success?

Note: The goal of this item is for the child to recognize that he has limitations and that there are some tasks that are too difficult to accomplish without help. A child with a healthy self-concept will choose activities that are a little challenging but can be mastered. He will either avoid or ask for help on tasks that are too difficult for his current skills.

CRITERION   *On several occasions the child demonstrates recognition that some tasks are too difficult for him by avoiding them or seeking help.*

■ ■ ■

3t. Shows guilt or shame over accidents or prohibited behavior

MATERIALS   None required

PROCEDURES

The goal of this item is *not* to teach a child to experience guilt or shame. Such emotions develop naturally in a child from experiencing caregiver disapproval and punishment for particular acts. The goal of this item *is* to prompt caregivers to be alert to signs that the child is beginning to experience these emotions and to respond appropriately. Guilt and shame are important indicators that the child is developing a conscience; that is, she is be-ginning to incorporate the behavioral standards proscribed by her caregivers.

There should be simple but consistent rules for the child, regardless of her disability. Generally accepted rules include prohibitions against deliberately breaking things, wast-ing materials (e.g., pulling all of the toilet paper off the roll, squeezing out all of the toothpaste), and harming other people or their belongings. The child will probably learn that breaking these rules results in disapproval and undesirable consequences (e.g., time-out) before she is able to inhibit her impulses to engage in them. Thus, as soon as the child sees what she has done, she may expect disapproval or punishment and try to "hide the evidence," clean up, or go to another location, hoping that whatever she did will not be associated with her. All of these behaviors are signs that the child is experiencing guilt or shame.

When such events occur, it is important for caregivers to react calmly, acknowledge that the child has done something she should not have done, and provide appropriate consequences, such as finishing the clean up, apologizing, going to time-out for a few minutes, and so forth. It is important, however, to focus on the deed and the natural con-sequences of that deed (e.g., "You broke Jim's truck. You must tell him you are sorry and help me try to fix it") and not attribute evil intent or generalized behavior characteristics to the child (e.g., *do not* say, "What a naughty girl you are" or "You are mean"). Regularly hearing such negative adjectives may cause them to become a part of the child's image of herself and lead to further unacceptable behaviors.

DAILY ROUTINES & FUNCTIONAL ACTIVITIES

Encourage everyone involved with the child's care to provide consistent rules and conse-quences for breaking those rules. Stress the importance of expecting appropriate behav-ior from the child, regardless of her disabling conditions.

CRITERION   The child shows guilt or shame by hiding messes she has made, bringing some-thing that is broken to a caregiver while looking distressed, "trying to look innocent" when caught doing a prohibited activity, or other similar behaviors.

REFERENCE

Turner, P. (1994). *Child development and early education.* Boston: Allyn & Bacon.

4-1
Self-Help: Eating

I t is important to encourage young children, with or without disabilities, to be as independent as possible in self-care activities. As children move into child care and school settings, they are expected to independently complete as many self-care skills as they can. Furthermore, independence in self-help skills contributes to a child's sense of self-competence and is part of the process of separation from dependence on the child's parents. This sequence of items is directed toward the establishment of appropriate feeding patterns and, later, the development of independent eating. Beginning feeders usually will be very messy. It is helpful to use a full bib and place a large plastic mat under the child's high chair.

Children with developmental disabilities may demonstrate a variety of feeding difficulties that require intervention from an occupational or speech-language therapist. Difficulties may include

1. Poor oral-motor control that can lead to difficulty coordinating chewing and swallowing

2. Excessive drooling

3. Oral defensiveness that results in avoidance of many textures of food

4. Poor control of hands and arms, making utensil use poor

ADAPTATIONS

Children with Motor Impairments

When working with children who have physical disabilities, it will be important to frequently seek consultation and assistance from a person knowledgeable about oral-motor problems (e.g., communication disorders specialist, physical therapist, occupational therapist) who can assist in establishing the best possible program for developing feeding/eating skills during the child's first year. You should not feed children while they are lying down or while their heads are tipped back. Use of a hard plastic spoon with a small bowl or a coated bowl is useful for children with a bite reflex.

When working on the development of self-feeding skills, it may be necessary to use adaptive equipment to facilitate self-feeding. An occupational therapist should be able to offer suggestions on how to adapt eating utensils for each child.

Children with Visual Impairments

Encourage children with visual impairments to use their fingers to explore food and utensils. Colorful foods and good lighting may help children who have some functional vision. Be consistent about where you place food on a child's tray or table (i.e., always place the cup in the same place), and encourage the child to do the same.

Children with Hearing Impairments

Children with hearing impairments need few adaptations when developing eating skills. Be sure to pair speech with demonstrations when needed.

4-I. SELF-HELP: EATING

a. Smoothly sucks from nipple

b. Infrequently "roots" toward food or objects

c. Infrequently bites down on spoon

d. Infrequently gags (only when appropriate)

e. Munches food (chewing up and down)

f. Uses purposeful tongue movements

g. Pulls food off spoon with lips

h. Holds own bottle (omit for breast-fed infants)

i. Assists in drinking from cup that is held by adult

j. Eats junior or mashed table food without gagging

k. Cleans lower lip with teeth

l. Chews with rotary/side-to-side action

m. Feeds self with fingers

n. Holds and drinks from cup

o. Brings spoon to mouth and eats food off of it

p. Scoops food from dish with spoon

q. Chews well

r. No longer uses bottle or breast

s. Feeds self without spilling (with almost no help)

t. Drinks from straw

u. Feeds self meal with spoon and cup as main utensils

v. Distinguishes between edible and nonedible substances

w. Begins to use fork

x. Drinks from small glass held with one hand

y. Gets drink unassisted (turns tap on and off)

z. Pours liquid from one container into another

■ ■ ■

4-Ia. Smoothly sucks from nipple

MATERIALS   Infant's bottle or mother's breast at feeding time

PROCEDURES

Get the child's attention by making sure that she sees the breast or bottle before feeding begins. Help her adjust to a comfortable position and angle for sucking. Closely observe, especially while very young, to make sure the child obtains good grasp of the nipple.

Note: No child should be given a bottle while lying on her back, particularly if mobility is limited. Not only is choking more likely, but if the child's oral-motor function is abnormal, liquid may flow into the ear canals, causing infection. A child should be able to smoothly suck and swallow within a few days after birth.

Because sucking problems are often early signs of neurological problems, they frequently mean that professional assistance is needed. Arrange for a physical therapist, occupational therapist, speech therapist, or pediatrician to see the child if a feeding problem exists.

DAILY ROUTINES & FUNCTIONAL ACTIVITIES

If the infant is having difficulty latching on, a lactation coach may be helpful. If the mother's milk is slow to come in, the infant may need supplementation to breast feeding. If the infant is using a bottle, some experimentation with different types of nipples may be needed to find the type that best suits the infant.

CRITERION   *The child is able to take liquids from a bottle or the breast without choking, withdrawing, or becoming tense.*

■ ■ ■

4-Ib. Infrequently "roots" toward food or objects

MATERIALS   None required

PROCEDURES

Touch the child lightly on the cheek and see if he turns his head as if to find and suck on your finger. This movement is called the "rooting reflex." It is present at birth and should begin to disappear by 3–4 months. It appears to be inhibited by hand-to-mouth activity, so if the child is bringing his hands to his mouth, no further intervention should be necessary.

You may also touch around the child's mouth with your fingers, using first a firm and then a light touch. Do this several times a day. The rooting reflex will always be more easily elicited when the child is hungry than when he is sleepy or upset. Assessment should be done with the infant alert and midway between feedings.

Note: Some children cannot tolerate being touched around the mouth without arching their backs or becoming irritable. If this is the case, you should seek the advice of a physical, occupational, or speech therapist.

DAILY ROUTINES & FUNCTIONAL ACTIVITIES

Encourage the child to bring his hands to his mouth, particularly if he has an active rooting reflex. Experiment with putting the child in several positions to see which increases the probability of hand-to-mouth activity (often sidelying is best). Then you may physically guide the child's hand to his mouth and prompt mouthing by placing a good-tasting substance on his hands.

CRITERION   *The child does not automatically turn his head in response to his cheek being touched.*

■ ■ ■

4-Ic. Infrequently bites down on spoon

MATERIALS   Baby food, small spoon

PROCEDURES

Place a small amount of baby food on a spoon and put it on the child's tongue, touching the bottom gum. Wait to see if the child's jaws close tightly. This is called a "bite reflex."

4-I

A typically developing infant will be able to open her mouth immediately. Inability to do so is a likely sign of neurological problems and indicates the need for consultation with and/or intervention by a therapist.

The bite reflex typically fades as the child begins to eat solid foods. Some techniques to use if the bite reflex is too strong include the following:

• Rub the gums with your finger prior to feeding.

• Use a smaller spoon.

• Use baby foods that encourage munching and chewing.

Note: If a child has a strong bite reflex, never place your fingers into her mouth. If a child is biting down hard on something and cannot release it, wait a few seconds for the child to relax and release her bite. If the child does not release her bite, press your fingers on the muscles at the back of the jaw. Do not pull the spoon from the child's mouth. This increases the bite reflex and could damage her mouth.

DAILY ROUTINES & FUNCTIONAL ACTIVITIES

A strong bite reflex is something to watch for at feeding times. You also can rub the child's gums with your finger while holding her, allowing the child to take small amounts of desired foods (e.g., jam, apple sauce) from your fingertip while you do this.

CRITERION   The child does not bite down on a spoon or tightly hold it in her mouth.

■ ■ ■

4-Id. Infrequently gags (only when appropriate)

MATERIALS   Baby foods, small spoon

PROCEDURES

Gradually introduce different tastes and textures of pureed or strained foods. If gagging occurs, choose foods with very smooth textures. When the child tolerates those foods, gradually work up to more textured foods. Adding small amounts of baby cereal to strained foods will increase their texture and stimulate tolerance for textured foods.

One technique that may reduce gagging is "tongue walking" (i.e., pressing firmly on the tongue with the tip of a small spoon, working from the front to the middle of the tongue). Be sure to hold the child as upright as possible and to provide good head support while feeding.

Note: If a child frequently gags beyond 6 months of age or if he never gags on food in the back of the mouth before 6 months of age, consult a therapist.

DAILY ROUTINES & FUNCTIONAL ACTIVITIES

Eating should be a pleasant routine. Have several foods available and change between less and more textured ones while feeding.

CRITERION   The child eats strained foods including cereal without gagging.

■ ■ ■

4-Ie. Munches food (chewing up and down)

MATERIALS   Strained baby foods, infant cereals, small spoon

PROCEDURES

Place food in the child's mouth and observe her reaction. If the child pushes it out with her tongue, try placing the next spoonful in the side of her mouth. Pushing food out of the mouth with the tongue may be reflexive at first and is not necessarily a rejection of the food that is being offered.

Watch for the child to start moving her jaws up and down while using the tongue to mash food against the roof of her mouth. If the child does not, you may be able to prompt with gentle assistance to her jaw.

Note: If a child persists in pushing food out of her mouth beyond 6 months of age or has not developed a munching pattern, consult a therapist.

DAILY ROUTINES & FUNCTIONAL ACTIVITIES

Offer the child pureed foods at least twice a day. Experiment with different foods so that the child gains experience with foods offering slightly different textures. You can use a baby food grinder to puree soft table foods.

CRITERION   The child chews with an up and down motion with food in her mouth.

■ ■ ■

4-If. Uses purposeful tongue movements

MATERIALS   Regular meals, sticky foods (e.g., oatmeal), small spoon

PROCEDURES

Observe the child eating. Notice if the child moves his tongue to touch the food at the sides and the top of his mouth or if he pulls the tongue back while either eating or babbling. If you are not readily seeing tongue movement, try placing small amounts of sticky foods, such as oatmeal or jam, on the roof of the child's mouth, near the front, and between the cheek and gums. Observe the child's use of his tongue to retrieve these foods.

If you note that the child is having difficulty with this activity, work on it for only a few minutes at each feeding, placing preferred foods at the front of the mouth so as to require tongue action for retrieval.

Note: Peanut butter is often used to promote tongue mobility but must be used very cautiously. Because it does not readily dissolve, there is some danger of aspiration.

DAILY ROUTINES & FUNCTIONAL ACTIVITIES

Begin to routinely include food that is slightly thicker in order to require more tongue movement from the infant. Avoid dumping the food onto the middle of the child's tongue. Instead, try to place it to the side or front of the mouth.

CRITERION   The child moves his tongue both to the side and to the top of his mouth.

■ ■ ■

4-Ig. Pulls food off spoon with lips

MATERIALS   Foods child routinely eats, small spoon

PROCEDURES

Place a spoonful of food in the child's mouth, touching the lower lip only. Do not scrape the food off against the upper lip. Watch for the child to move her upper lip toward the spoon to clean it off, move the spoon up a little, if necessary, to help the child get the food.

If there is no lip movement, try alternately touching the top and bottom lips with the spoon, waiting for lip closure. Use this method with the child's favorite sticky foods (e.g., fruit, pudding). If that proves unsuccessful, try touching just above the child's lip with your finger, putting light pressure on the spoon with her upper lip.

Note: If a strong bite reflex is present, it may be triggered by the spoon touching the teeth. If this is a problem, use a very small spoon and avoid the teeth, pressing the spoon firmly on the front of the tongue. Pay special attention to keeping the child as relaxed as possible.

DAILY ROUTINES & FUNCTIONAL ACTIVITIES

Everyday feeding provides opportunities for this spoon-feeding activity. It also encourages the child to be active in the feeding process. Let the child take the food from the spoon, rather than giving it to her.

CRITERION   The child uses her lips to clean food off of a spoon.

■ ■ ■

4-Ih. Holds own bottle (omit for breast-fed infants)

MATERIALS   Bottles (a small "preemie" bottle or one made to fit an infant's hands, if the child cannot handle a regular bottle)

PROCEDURES

Present the child with a bottle by placing the nipple in his mouth while you continue to hold it. Once the child is comfortably sucking on the bottle, gently place his hands on the bottle. Over time, the child will take a firmer grip on the bottle.

Hold the bottle a few inches from the child's mouth, and wait to see if he will reach out for it. As these reaching skills improve, gradually release your hold on the bottle. Occasionally check to see that the child hasn't dropped the bottle.

Note: Do not put a child in bed with his bottle. Let the child drink first and then go to bed. Bottle drinking in bed is associated with both an increase in middle-ear infection and tooth decay.

DAILY ROUTINES & FUNCTIONAL ACTIVITIES

You and the child will both enjoy his first steps toward independent feeding. Be sure to regularly check to see if the child needs help with retrieving a bottle that was dropped.

CRITERION   *The child holds her bottle alone while drinking.*

■ ■ ■

4-Ii. Assists in drinking from cup that is held by adult

MATERIALS   Preferred liquids (avoid sugared beverages), several kinds of cups and small juice glasses, plastic cup with a weighted bottom, plastic cup with one side cut out so that the top does not hit the child's nose

PROCEDURES

Start with a small amount of liquid in a cup. Bring the cup to the child's mouth and tip it slightly, waiting for the child to actively cooperate by closing her lips around the cup. Hold the cup about an inch away from the child's mouth, and wait for her to lean toward the cup.

It may be helpful to start teaching cup drinking by using thicker liquids (e.g., milk, a light mixture of milk and cereal), which are easier for the child to handle.

Note: Closed cups with spouts are not very helpful in teaching the head and lip control that is needed for drinking from a cup.

DAILY ROUTINES & FUNCTIONAL ACTIVITIES

Begin incorporating cup drinking into the child's snack and mealtime routine. A small paper cup is sometimes helpful, as it can be shaped to the child's mouth. Children with a strong bite reflex will need to use a sturdy plastic cup.

CRITERION   *The child leans toward a cup and drinks without excessive spilling or choking.*

■ ■ ■

4-Ij. Eats junior or mashed table food without gagging

MATERIALS   Both smooth and textured foods (e.g., infant and junior baby foods, graham crackers, special infant crackers)

PROCEDURES

Offer child foods with a variety of textures. Try to offer foods of at least two, or even three, different consistencies at any given meal. At 6–7 months of age, the child should be able to tolerate textures in foods without gagging. If he rejects textures or gags, very gradually increase texture (e.g., adding a little baby cereal or wheat germ to strained foods and allowing adjustment to that before moving on to junior foods).

Note: If the gag reflex remains strong enough so that the child cannot tolerate junior foods after 9 months of age, seek professional help.

DAILY ROUTINES & FUNCTIONAL ACTIVITIES

Change the foods that you feed the child daily so that he will develop an acceptance of a wide range of tastes and textures. Children are more likely to accept new foods when they are hungry, so it is helpful to offer new foods at the beginning of the meal. Do not let the child fill up on juice or milk before eating.

CRITERION   The child eats junior or mashed foods at every meal without gagging.

■ ■ ■

4-Ik. Cleans lower lip with teeth

MATERIALS   Usual, semi-solid foods (e.g., baby foods; mashed, well-cooked regular foods)

PROCEDURES

Look for "lip cleaning" to spontaneously occur as the child is eating and when food sticks to her lower lip. Do not routinely wipe off the child's mouth after every bite. If the child is not starting to use her teeth to clean food off her lower lip, place favored sticky foods on the lip so that the child will have to retrieve them in order to get the taste. It may help to gently touch the lower lip with the spoon.

Note: If the child has an oral-motor problem that makes cleaning the lower lip very difficult, don't work on it too persistently. Try it just once or twice so that eating remains an enjoyable activity.

DAILY ROUTINES & FUNCTIONAL ACTIVITIES

When feeding the child, do not routinely wipe her mouth after every bite. Give her an opportunity to use her teeth to clean her lips.

CRITERION   The child spontaneously and routinely cleans her lower lip during meals.

■ ■ ■

4-Il. Chews with rotary/side-to-side action

MATERIALS   A variety of textured foods (e.g., junior baby foods, mashed table foods, baby sausages and meats, rice, mashed spaghetti)

PROCEDURES

Observe the child's response to textured foods and watch for adult-like chewing movements (i.e., rotary/side-to-side movements of the jaw). Frequently, just the stimulation of textured foods in the mouth is enough to trigger those movements and no further intervention is needed. If the movements are not occurring, however, try placing some of the child's favorite foods on one side of his mouth between the cheek and teeth.

DAILY ROUTINES & FUNCTIONAL ACTIVITIES

Continue to increase the variety of foods you feed the child, offering different tastes and textures. Start to include more table foods in the child's diet, starting with soft foods that can be mashed with a fork.

CRITERION   The child spontaneously and consistently shows rotary jaw movements when chewing textured foods.

■ ■ ■

4-Im. Feeds self with fingers

MATERIALS   A variety of foods such as oatmeal, pudding, cereal bits, bread sticks, or crackers

PROCEDURES

Introduce the idea of self-feeding by placing sticky foods, such as oatmeal or corn syrup, on the child's fingers so that she can lick them off.

Provide a bowl of pudding so that the child can place a hand in it and lick off the food. Progress to foods that are easy to grasp and do not require finger release to place in the mouth (e.g., bread stick, cracker). When the child is proficient with these foods, gradually move to smaller items (e.g., cereal bits) that require release to place in mouth. As in all feeding items, new skills should be presented gradually.

DAILY ROUTINES & FUNCTIONAL ACTIVITIES

Finger feeding can be quite messy at first. Prepare for the mess by putting a large bib or clothes that can be soiled on the child. Model finger feeding by putting your finger in the food (e.g., pudding) and then eating the food from your finger.

CRITERION   The child picks up and eats small bits or amounts of food without help.

■ ■ ■

4-In. Holds and drinks from cup

MATERIALS   Plastic, easily held cup

PROCEDURES

Fill the child's cup approximately one third full with liquid, and give it to the child when
he is thirsty. If the child cannot hold a cup and bring it to his mouth to drink, help him
by placing both of his hands on the cup and bringing it to his mouth to drink. Gradually
reduce your assistance.

Note: Many different types of cups are available on the market. Experiment to see
which type of cup the child uses most easily (e.g., a cup with one or two handles, a cup
with big or small handles, a cup with the rim cut out on the side).

DAILY ROUTINES & FUNCTIONAL ACTIVITIES

Give the child plenty of opportunities to drink from a cup during meals, while pretend
playing, and when he wants a drink during the day. When drinking at the table, try to use
a cup without a lid. If using a sippy cup at other times during the day, use one that has
a straw that goes to the bottom of the cup so that the child will be discouraged from tip-
ping his head far back while drinking.

CRITERION   The child drinks from a cup without help.

■ ■ ■

4-Io. Brings spoon to mouth and eats food off of it

MATERIALS   Small spoon, bowl, a variety of foods that can be easily scooped

PROCEDURES

Place a bowl with food in it in front of the child. Fill the spoon and help the child grasp
it. Tell the child "Eat your food." If the child is unable to successfully bring the spoon to
her mouth, try gently elevating her elbow with your hand. If more assistance is needed,
put your arm under the child's arm, and place your hand gently on top of her wrist while
standing or sitting behind her. In this manner, you can assist the child with added support and wrist guidance.

At first, help the child to get food into her mouth. Then, assist only to the point that
the spoon is several inches from the child's mouth, letting her complete the task on her
own. Gradually reduce all help until the child can do this skill on her own.

DAILY ROUTINES & FUNCTIONAL ACTIVITIES

Many children try to reach for a spoon as they are being fed. Give the child one spoon
while you use a second one. Encourage the child to feed herself, regardless of how messy
it is at first. It may help to scoop the food at first for or with the child, and then let the
child bring the spoon independently to her mouth. Do not tire the child by insisting that

she feed herself all of every meal at first. In the beginning, encourage the child to feed herself when eating preferred foods and those that stick easily to the spoon.

CRITERION   The child brings the spoon to her mouth and puts food in without help. Help getting food onto the spoon may be provided.

■ ■ ■

4-Ip. Scoops food from dish with spoon

MATERIALS   Small spoon, dish, a variety of foods that are easy to scoop

PROCEDURES

Place a bowl of food in front of the child. Have the child grasp a spoon, and encourage him to eat. If the child brings the spoon to his mouth but does not successfully scoop food onto the spoon, show the child how to scoop food. If necessary, physically assist the child to scoop food, but decrease your assistance as quickly as possible.

Be sure to give the child plenty of time and opportunity to practice scooping. Start with foods that adhere well to the spoon (e.g., pudding, mashed potatoes, mashed bananas).

DAILY ROUTINES & FUNCTIONAL ACTIVITIES

Offer the child the opportunity to feed himself at least twice a day. Allow extra time, as the child will not be very efficient at first. It is a good idea to put a plastic cover on the floor underneath the child to make clean-up easier. Scoop bowls that have a suction ring and one edge of the bowl higher to facilitate successful scooping are recommended and usually can be found wherever baby equipment is sold. A spoon with a large, short handle and a small bowl will also encourage success.

CRITERION   The child scoops food from a dish with a spoon without assistance.

■ ■ ■

4-Iq. Chews well

MATERIALS   A variety of foods

PROCEDURES

Give the child the opportunity to eat a variety of foods that have small lumps, different or unusual textures, and various consistencies.

Once the child begins to chew, try to encourage more mature chewing by giving the child different solids between her back teeth. Try foods such as long strips of hard cheese, semicooked carrots, and so forth. If necessary, hold one end, while letting the child chew the other end. Move food to different places in the child's mouth to stimulate a combination of vertical, horizontal, and rotary jaw movements. Repeat this activity at each meal if the child does not protest.

DAILY ROUTINES & FUNCTIONAL ACTIVITIES

Offer foods that require some chewing at least twice daily. Vary the foods you offer. At this point, the child can typically eat many table foods. The use of prepared infant/toddler foods can be gradually discontinued.

CRITERION   *The child chews a typical variety of foods.*

■ ■ ■

4-Ir. No longer uses bottle or breast

MATERIALS   Bottle or cup

PROCEDURES

As the child learns to drink from a cup (Item 4-In), gradually reduce the quantity of liquid given in a bottle or the time spent nursing. Substitute other cuddling behaviors for the time that was typically spent holding the child for bottle or breast feeding.

Note: There is considerable variance in the age at which children are weaned. In the United States, many physicians and dentists recommend weaning from the bottle at or shortly after 12 months of age, although individual practices vary. In some cultures, children are not weaned until they are considerably older.

DAILY ROUTINES & FUNCTIONAL ACTIVITIES

Some parents find it helpful initially to limit nursing or to use a bottle during certain times of the day. Once-common practice is to allow the child to nurse or drink from a bottle only in the evening, while having the child drink from a cup during the day for all snacks and meals. At this point, the evening drinking provides more comfort than nutritional support. Pair it with other comfort activities, such as rocking, reading, or singing, then fade the nursing or bottle use while continuing the other comfort activities.

CRITERION   *The child no longer drinks from a bottle or the breast.*

■ ■ ■

4-Is. Feeds self without spilling (with almost no help)

MATERIALS   Small spoon, dish, a variety of foods that are easy to scoop

PROCEDURES

Place food in a bowl or scoop dish and place spoon in bowl or on table. Encourage the child to self-feed. If the child has mastered Item 4-Ip, he will typically develop greater proficiency with practice. Although it is often much faster to feed the child, allowing him the time to feed himself will gradually increase his competence.

DAILY ROUTINES & FUNCTIONAL ACTIVITIES

Allow the child to begin each meal feeding himself. If he tires or if there is a particularly messy food, provide assistance as needed. Temperamental differences play a significant role in the establishment of independent feeding. Some children strongly assert their independence, wanting no help eating, while other children are happy being fed by a caregiver and must be encouraged to develop greater independence.

CRITERION   The child feeds himself with a spoon without much spilling.

■ ■ ■

4-It. Drinks from straw

MATERIALS   Straw, cup with liquid (optional: juice box)

PROCEDURES

Show the child how you drink from a straw. Then, without the straw in your mouth, demonstrate the sucking motion, making a small inhalation sound as you do so. Hold a cup and straw in front of the child, placing the end of the straw in the child's mouth and encouraging her to drink. A juice box is handy for teaching straw drinking because you can squeeze the juice box, which forces the liquid to the top of the straw and makes it much easier for the child to experience initial success. Earlier use of a sippy cup with an internal straw that goes to the bottom of the cup may facilitate acquisition of straw drinking.

Straw drinking promotes good lip closure and tends to provide a calming, regulatory effect. It is a valuable skill for children with severe motor impairments who may not be able to pick up and drink from a cup.

DAILY ROUTINES & FUNCTIONAL ACTIVITIES

Give the child frequent opportunities to practice straw drinking. Use a straw during mealtimes and when the child wants a drink during the day. Once the child is successful with straw drinking, using a straw makes drinking "on the go" an easier and less messy activity.

CRITERION   The child is able to drink from a straw independently.

■ ■ ■

4-Iu. Feeds self meal with spoon and cup as main utensils

MATERIALS   Small spoon, dish, cup appropriate for children

PROCEDURES

Place food on the child's dish and serve it to the child, putting a spoon next to the plate and a cup of milk, water, or juice near it also. Encourage the child to eat his meal while you do the same. If the child loses interest or begins to play, prompt appropriate eating behavior, but resist feeding the child. Let him eat independently.

DAILY ROUTINES & FUNCTIONAL ACTIVITIES

Prepare food so that it is easy for the child to eat independently, and place a small amount of each food on the child's plate. It may be helpful to use a child-size spoon and cup to facilitate independence.

CRITERION   The child feeds himself a complete meal.

■ ■ ■

4-I

4-Iv. Distinguishes between edible and nonedible substances

MATERIALS   Edible items (i.e., foods), nonedible items (i.e., nonfood objects)

PROCEDURES

Observe whether the child mouths nonedible items in her play. If she does, remove them and provide her something else with which to play.

Offer the child two similar items (i.e., one edible item and one nonedible item). Praise the child when she eats the edible item and plays with the nonedible one. If the child still insists on putting the nonedible item in her mouth, make a face and verbally tell her to take it out. Get the child to imitate you. If necessary, remove the nonedible item.

DAILY ROUTINES & FUNCTIONAL ACTIVITIES

Observe the child's behavior when she plays alone. Ask the child to remove nonedible items from her mouth as necessary. Some children have a high need for oral stimulation. You may want to identify one or two specific items that are okay for the child to chew on (e.g., chewy tube). Consult with an occupational therapist if mouthing or chewing on toys is a persistent issue beyond the age of 2 years.

CRITERION   The child distinguishes between familiar edible and nonedible substances and does not attempt to eat nonedible items.

■ ■ ■

4-Iw. Begins to use fork

MATERIALS   Fork, plate, easily speared food (e.g., cut-up pancakes, scrambled eggs, casseroles)

PROCEDURES

Place plate with food on it and a fork in front of the child. Show him how to stab food with the fork and place it in his mouth. Tell the child that it is now his turn to eat with the fork. If the child does not pick up the fork, place it in his hand (if child has demonstrated a hand preference, use that hand; otherwise, place it in either hand). At this age, most children will hold a fork in a gross grasp with forearm pronated (i.e., palm down). Give the child physical assistance as needed to stab the food and to bring it to his mouth. Decrease your physical assistance as quickly as possible.

DAILY ROUTINES & FUNCTIONAL ACTIVITIES

Practice is important; let the child feed himself with a fork for a number of consecutive meals once he is successful. Be sure to serve the child foods that are easy to eat with a fork.

CRITERION   The child eats some foods with a fork.

■ ■ ■

4-Ix. Drinks from small glass held with one hand

MATERIALS   Small glass or cup (e.g., juice size), liquid that the child enjoys

PROCEDURES

Fill a small glass about one third of the way full. Place it in front of the child at a time when she is likely to be thirsty (e.g., meal or snack time). Encourage the child to pick up the cup and to take a drink. If needed, place the cup in the child's hand and help her to bring it to her mouth. Children often learn to pick up a cup and to bring it to their mouths before they learn to set the cup back on the table. It may be necessary to catch the child's hand as she removes the cup from her mouth to help the child guide the cup to the table and set it down. Pair this with a verbal command (e.g., "Put the cup on the table"). Then fade the physical prompt while still using the verbal command.

DAILY ROUTINES & FUNCTIONAL ACTIVITIES

Mealtimes are typically the best opportunity to practice independent cup drinking. Use small cups with no lids for all liquids given at mealtimes. Away from home or child care, it is often more practical to use a cup with a lid and straw.

CRITERION   The child drinks from a small glass held with one hand.

■ ■ ■

4-Iy. Gets drink unassisted (turns tap on and off)

MATERIALS   Accessible sink (e.g., child size or standard with sturdy step stool), small cup

PROCEDURES

Show the child how to turn on the cold water tap, to fill up a cup, and then to turn off the water. Have the child practice this activity, providing any assistance needed. Children who have difficulty turning on the tap may need practice with activities in the Fine Motor Skills: Manipulation sequence. Before children are allowed to get a drink independently, the hot water tap should be deactivated or the water temperature reduced to avoid accidental burns. As the child demonstrates success, fade any verbal or physical cues that you may have been using.

DAILY ROUTINES & FUNCTIONAL ACTIVITIES

Allow the child to obtain his own drink as appropriate. It may be helpful to provide a small step stool in front of the sink to facilitate independence.

CRITERION   *The child gets a drink of water unassisted, turning tap on and off.*

■ ■ ■

4-I

4-Iz. Pours liquid from one container into another

MATERIALS   Small pitcher with liquid, cup

PROCEDURES

Place a pitcher with liquid and a cup in front of the child. Show her how to pour liquid into the cup. Usually, children will need to hold the pitcher handle in one hand and support it from underneath with the other hand as they pour. At first, only put the amount of liquid in the pitcher that will fit in the cup. Later, the child can learn to stop pouring before the cup is full. When older, the child can hold the pitcher with one hand and the cup with the other.

DAILY ROUTINES & FUNCTIONAL ACTIVITIES

Allow the child to pour her own liquid from a small pitcher at meal and snack time. Practice pouring skills by pouring sand or beans from one container into another.

CRITERION   *The child pours liquid from one container into another.*

4-II
Self-Help: Dressing

The dressing and undressing activities presented in this sequence are intended to promote as much independence as possible on the part of a young child. While it often seems easier and certainly faster to do everything for a child, keep in mind that you want the child to do as much for him- or herself as possible. Regular opportunities for practice will build the child's competence. Dressing and undressing skills require some degree of motor facility. It may be helpful to address the development of fine and gross motor skills to provide a foundation for the skills needed in dressing.

ADAPTATIONS

Children with Motor Impairments

If a child with motor impairments tends to be stiff while dressing, you may need to engage in activities that are relaxing before this can be accomplished.

Be creative in selecting types of clothing for children with motor difficulties. You may need to make some clothing adaptations (e.g., using Velcro closures rather than buttons or snaps) for children with significant motor impairments. Loose-fitting clothing may promote independence, as it is often easier to put on, especially for children with increased muscle tone or limited range of motion.

A child with severe motor impairments may always have extreme limitations, perhaps to the point of only being able to cooperate in the dressing process. When assisting a child in the dressing process, it is very important to talk to him or her about what is happening. Make comments about the clothing's color, how nice a given article of clothing may look on the child, and so forth, in order to engage the child cognitively in the dressing task, even if he or she does not actively participate.

Children with Visual Impairments

When dressing children with visual impairments, be sure to talk about everything that is being done, and be gentle in your approach with the clothes. It is frightening to have something pulled over your head or to have your arm pulled when you don't expect it.

Children with Hearing Impairments

Children with hearing impairments need few adaptations when developing dressing skills. Be sure to pair speech with demonstration when needed.

4-II. SELF-HELP: DRESSING

a. Cooperates in dressing and undressing

b. Partially pulls shirt over head

c. Removes loose clothing

d. Unties shoes or hat as an act of undressing

e. Unfastens clothing zipper that has a large pull tab

f. Puts on hat

g. Removes simple clothing

h. Removes shoes

i. Removes coat

j. Puts on simple clothing

k. Puts on all clothing unaided, except for fasteners

l. Undoes fasteners

■ ■ ■

4-IIa. Cooperates in dressing and undressing (e.g., holds arm out for sleeve, holds foot out for shoe)

MATERIALS   Clothing that is loose and easy to put on or pull off

PROCEDURES

While dressing the child, name his body parts as you touch them. Encourage the child to move the named body part (e.g., arm, leg).

Place the child's arm or leg partially in or out of a garment, and encourage him to assist you during dressing or undressing (e.g., "Push your leg through here," "Pull your arm out!"). You can play Peek-a-boo when pulling a shirt over the child's head. Encourage and help him to finish pulling off the shirt.

DAILY ROUTINES & FUNCTIONAL ACTIVITIES

A child can have an aversion to dressing if shirts are pulled roughly over his head or if dressing is hurried. Talk to the child about what is being done. Allow plenty of time and try to get the child involved in helping you. Make it fun!

CRITERION   The child cooperates in both dressing and undressing.

■ ■ ■

4-IIb. Partially pulls shirt over head

MATERIALS   Shirts, undershirts

PROCEDURES

The first step in learning to remove clothing is to learn to pull things off that are already partially removed (e.g., a shirt pulled to the top of the head, socks pulled to the middle of the foot). Help the child to grasp partially removed shirts and to finish pulling them off. As the child demonstrates success, reduce your assistance.

DAILY ROUTINES & FUNCTIONAL ACTIVITIES

Make a game of this activity. Play Peek-a-boo when pulling a shirt over the child's head. Encourage and help her to finish pulling the shirt off. Whenever dressing or undressing the child, give her the opportunity to help (e.g., with jackets, caps, pajamas).

CRITERION   The child removes shirts that have been partially removed by an adult.

■ ■ ■

4-IIc. Removes loose clothing (e.g., socks, mittens, hats, untied shoes)

MATERIALS   Socks, mittens, hats, shoes

PROCEDURES

Draw the child's attention to what you are doing when you undress him by both talking about the process and encouraging him to participate.

Start the process of removing clothing and have the child finish (e.g., pull shoe partially off foot and then have the child remove the article of clothing the rest of the way). Assist the child through the process, and gradually fade your assistance. Use different articles of clothing.

DAILY ROUTINES & FUNCTIONAL ACTIVITIES

Make a game of this activity. Play Peek-a-boo when pulling a hat over the child's head. Encourage him to pull the hat off of his head. Whenever dressing or undressing the child, give him the opportunity to help (e.g., with hats, socks, mittens, pajamas).

CRITERION   The child removes loose clothing without assistance.

■ ■ ■

4-IId. Unties shoes or hat as an act of undressing

MATERIALS   Shoes with laces, hat with ties, mirror

PROCEDURES

When you undress the child, describe what you are doing. As you untie the child's shoes, say, for example, "Now, let's untie your shoes and take them off." Have the child watch as you untie her shoes.

After the child has watched you untie her shoes, put your hands over hers, and lightly guide her through the process of pulling the ends of the shoestrings to untie them.

You can use this same process with a hat that has ties; however, it will help to untie the hat in front of a mirror to make the process visual to the child.

DAILY ROUTINES & FUNCTIONAL ACTIVITIES

Incorporate this as a routine part of undressing, encouraging the child to be as independent as possible. You can also tell the child to untie your shoes. Wrap presents with a simple bow so that the child can pull the ends and untie it. This can be done as part of a pretend game.

CRITERION   The child unties her shoes or hat as an act of undressing.

4-II

■ ■ ■

4-IIe. Unfastens clothing zipper that has a large pull tab

MATERIALS   If the child's clothing has small zipper tabs, attach key tags to them to make them easier to grasp.

PROCEDURES

Show the child how to unfasten his coat or pants. Zip up the zipper and then ask the child to unzip it. If the child cannot or does not grasp the pull tab on the zipper, assist him by placing the metal tab in his hand. If the child cannot maintain his grasp, an adaptation to the pull tab may be necessary (e.g., key tag attached to it). If grasp is maintained, but the child does not unzip, then assist him by helping to start the motion. Physically assist only as much as necessary, fading support as quickly as possible. You may need to hold the bottom of the coat for the child to be successful.

DAILY ROUTINES & FUNCTIONAL ACTIVITIES

A dressing doll may be helpful for practicing zipping skills. If the pull tab on the child's clothing is difficult to grasp, you can securely tie a key tag to the pull tab.

CRITERION   The child unzips his own clothing.

■ ■ ■

4-IIf. Puts on hat

MATERIALS   Hats that are easy to put on and take off

PROCEDURES

Give the child a hat. While saying "Put the hat on your head," make the movement of placing a hat on your head with your hand. Put a hat on the child's head, remove it, and say, "You put it on."

Provide a box of hats from which the child can choose a hat; use a mirror so that she can see the hat she has put on.

DAILY ROUTINES & FUNCTIONAL ACTIVITIES

Playing dress-up is a fun activity for young children to play. Encourage the child to put on hats as part of play activities. Provide different kinds and shapes of hats.

CRITERION   The child puts on a hat without assistance.

■ ■ ■

4-IIg. Removes simple clothing (e.g., open shirt or jacket, stretch pants)

MATERIALS   Loose-fitting shirts, jackets, and pants with an elastic waistband

PROCEDURES

When a shirt has been opened in front, let the child take it off. Show him how to use one hand to pull the shirt from the other arm. Cue this behavior by saying, "Take your shirt off" and touching the proper place to begin.

Physically prompt the child to pull down pants, hooking his thumbs over the edge of the waistband. Have the child pull them down to his knees and then sit on the floor or a small bench to finish removing.

If the child has difficulty, offer verbal encouragement and provide physical assistance to get the process started. Help only as much as is necessary.

DAILY ROUTINES & FUNCTIONAL ACTIVITIES

Dressing and undressing will occur at several natural times throughout the day. Encourage the child to do as much as possible alone. Praise him for independence in this activity.

CRITERION   The child removes simple articles of clothing (e.g., shirt, jacket, stretch pants) without assistance.

■ ■ ■

4-IIh. Removes shoes

MATERIALS   Shoes that are easy to remove

PROCEDURES

Tell the child to remove her shoes, ideally at a natural time (e.g., before nap). If the child has difficulty, slip one of the shoes off of her heel, and ask the child to finish removing the shoe. Repeat this process with the other shoe. Assist the child as needed in removing her shoes, then gradually fade assistance. If the child has difficulty, start with loose-fitting shoes such as slippers or moccasins.

DAILY ROUTINES & FUNCTIONAL ACTIVITIES

Provide a variety of shoes and boots for dress-up. Large shoes will offer easy practice removing shoes.

CRITERION   The child independently removes her shoes.

■ ■ ■

4-IIi. Removes coat

4-II

MATERIALS   Coat that the child typically wears (should fit the child or be slightly large)

PROCEDURES

Ask the child to remove his coat, ideally at a natural time (e.g., when coming into the classroom). Undo any fasteners if the child is not able to undo them yet. If the child has difficulty, slip the coat down slightly past his shoulders, and ask the child to finish removing it. If the child still has difficulty, help him remove one arm and then ask him to finish taking off the coat. Gradually fade your assistance.

DAILY ROUTINES & FUNCTIONAL ACTIVITIES

In the classroom, provide hooks marked with the child's picture and name. Encourage each child to remove his or her coat and hang it on the proper hook.

CRITERION   The child independently removes his coat.

■ ■ ■

4-IIj. Puts on simple clothing (e.g., pants, shoes, socks)

MATERIALS   Pants with an elastic waistband, tube socks, slip-on shoes

PROCEDURES

Place an article of clothing in front of the child, and ask her to put it on. If the child does not know how to put on a piece of clothing, teach the child by sitting behind her and providing physical assistance. Give simple verbal descriptions as you help the child (e.g., "First put one leg in, now the other leg, now pull your pants up"). Teach the child by initially putting on the clothing halfway and then asking her to finish (e.g., roll up a sock, place it over the toes, and ask the child to finish pulling on the sock). Gradually fade your assistance.

DAILY ROUTINES & FUNCTIONAL ACTIVITIES

Children like to play dress-up with adult clothes and simple costumes. Provide a variety of shoes, shirts, skirts, scarves, and hats.

CRITERION   The child independently puts on simple clothing (e.g., pants, shoes, socks).

■ ■ ■

4-IIk. Puts on all clothing unaided, except for fasteners

MATERIALS Simple, loose-fitting clothing (e.g., shirt, dress, sweater)

PROCEDURES

Place an article of clothing in front of the child, and ask him to put it on. If the child does not know how to do this, teach the child by sitting behind him and providing physical assistance. Provide simple verbal descriptions as you help the child put on the clothing (e.g., "First put the shirt over your head, now put one arm in one sleeve, now the other arm in the other sleeve"). Have the child do as much of the process as possible, gradually fading your assistance (e.g., the child may be able to pull a shirt over his head, but may need help getting his arms in).

DAILY ROUTINES & FUNCTIONAL ACTIVITIES

Provide loose-fitting dress-up clothing for children to wear in pretend games. Have them practice trying them on.

CRITERION *The child independently puts on all clothing (e.g., shirt, dress, sweater).*

■ ■ ■

4-Ill. Undoes fasteners (e.g., large buttons, snaps, shoelaces)

MATERIALS Dressing doll; dressing boards with large, easy-to-handle fasteners; clothing

PROCEDURES

Present child with a dressing doll or board. Tell the child to unbutton the buttons. If she does not know how to approach this task, slowly demonstrate it two or three times. Then, offer physical assistance. The child should hold and lightly pull cloth next to the hole with one hand and grasp the button and push it through the hole with the other hand. It often will be easier for the child to learn this activity on a buttoning board first, where the buttons can be seen easily, before learning to unbutton the clothing she is wearing. Repeat the procedure with other types of fasteners.

DAILY ROUTINES & FUNCTIONAL ACTIVITIES

Play dress-up with very simple clothing that has easy-to-handle fasteners. At this age, the goal is for children to undo fasteners and to remove clothing independently. In another year, the focus will be on independently fastening the clothing.

Buttoning boards that have a surprise picture hidden under the material can be fun to use with a group of children so that they can then share what they found.

CRITERION *The child independently undoes fasteners (e.g., large buttons, snaps, shoelaces).*

4-III
Self-Help: Grooming

Although very young children are dependent on their caregivers for grooming activities, it is important to establish the foundations for habits that will serve children well throughout their lifetimes. Grooming activities are important not only for health preservation—learning to adequately wash hands and brush teeth, for example, will help reduce disease—but also for social acceptance. That is, a child with or without special needs who appears clean and well groomed will find it easier to fit in and be accepted. Finally, good grooming can contribute to a sense of pride and positive self-esteem.

ADAPTATIONS

Children with Motor Impairments

If a child has physical disabilities that require him or her to be dependent on others for grooming and personal hygiene, it is important for those people to talk to the child about the grooming activities as they take place. The young child with a motor limitation should not feel that someone is doing something *to* him or her, but that someone is engaging in important activities *with* him or her for very specific benefits. An occupational or physical therapist can provide consultation regarding optimal positioning for various activities.

Children with Visual Impairments

Talk to children with visual impairments about what you are doing. Keep supplies consistently in the same place (e.g., have a specific place on the sink for soap and toothpaste), and keep bath toys in a container that is always in the same place and within the child's reach.

Children with Hearing Impairments

Children with hearing impairments will need few adaptations when developing grooming skills. Be sure to pair speech with demonstrations when necessary. Most children will learn these skills from daily practice.

4-III. SELF-HELP: GROOMING

a. Enjoys playing in water

b. Does not drool

c. Cooperates in washing and drying hands

d. Allows teeth to be brushed

e. Allows nose to be wiped

f. Washes own hands

g. Wipes nose if given a tissue

h. Dries hands

i. Brushes teeth with assistance

j. Washes self with washcloth

■ ■ ■

4-IIIa. Enjoys playing in water

MATERIALS   A plastic dishpan or any similar container that will hold 2–3 inches of water; objects the child can play with in the water

PROCEDURES

Put water in a pan and then give the child two or three objects that she can play with in the water (e.g., a small cup, a figure-shaped sponge, toys that float). Encourage the child to play and to get her hands into the water. Gently splash the water.

DAILY ROUTINES & FUNCTIONAL ACTIVITIES

Encourage play with a variety of floating bath toys. If the child has difficulty maintaining balance sitting in the bathtub, try placing a plastic laundry basket in the tub and then sitting the child in the basket.

CRITERION   The child plays with a pan of water when presented with the opportunity.

■ ■ ■

4-IIIb. Does not drool

MATERIALS   None required

PROCEDURES

Observe the child throughout the course of the day. You should rarely observe drooling, as children are expected to know how to coordinate swallowing and lip closure in order to handle their own saliva. Persistent drooling may be a sign of other developmental difficulties and may indicate the need for a referral to a physician or therapist.

DAILY ROUTINES & FUNCTIONAL ACTIVITIES

If the child does drool, try to keep his chin as dry as possible to maintain his tactile aware-ness of what being dry feels like. It is better to pat the chin and mouth dry rather than wiping. It is typical for children to drool when they are teething.

CRITERION   *The child rarely drools throughout the course of the day.*

■ ■ ■

4-IIIc. Cooperates in washing and drying hands

MATERIALS   Soap and water, something to stand on so that the child can comfortably get her hands into a sink

PROCEDURES

Provide opportunities for the child to wash her hands before meals and snacks, when com-ing in from outdoor play, and at other times throughout the day. Put water in a sink or basin and demonstrate by washing your hands next to the child. At the same time, en-courage the child to put her hands in the water to also wash. Liquid or foaming soap may be easier than a bar of soap for a child who is learning to wash her hands.

DAILY ROUTINES & FUNCTIONAL ACTIVITIES

If the child is reluctant to wash her hands, try having her engage in a messy activity (e.g., fingerpainting) at first. Then, tell her it is time to wash the paint off of her hands, and point out how the water makes her hands clean. It is sometimes helpful to create songs about daily routines that let the child know that it is time to do an activity and what to expect. Develop your own words to familiar songs (e.g., "This is the way we wash our hands, wash our hands, wash our hands. This is the way we wash our hands before we eat our lunch" [sung to the tune of Here We Go Round the Mulberry Bush]).

Let the child help open the drain to let the water out and get a towel to dry her hands.

CRITERION   *The child does not resist involvement in washing and drying hands.*

■ ■ ■

4-IIId. Allows teeth to be brushed

MATERIALS   Toothbrush, a comfortable place to stand in front of a sink and mirror

PROCEDURES

Place the child in front of a mirror and tell him it is time to brush his teeth. Show the child the toothbrush and how you put toothpaste on it. Tell the child to open his mouth, and proceed to brush his teeth (if the child does not open his mouth, try to gently open his mouth manually and brush). Try to make the experience pleasant. If the child is extremely resistant to contact in or around his mouth, consult an occupational therapist.

Note: Be sure to use a soft child's toothbrush and children's toothpaste when beginning. You may even have to put a little toothpaste on your finger and "brush" with it before using an actual brush. Use a pleasant-tasting toothpaste designed for children.

DAILY ROUTINES & FUNCTIONAL ACTIVITIES

Encourage the child to practice brushing a favorite doll or stuffed animal's teeth. A puppet with a mouth that opens and has teeth works well to help children learn about brushing teeth. Develop a tooth-brushing song.

CRITERION   *The child allows his teeth to be brushed at least once a day.*

■ ■ ■

4-IIIe. Allows nose to be wiped

MATERIALS   Soft tissues

PROCEDURES

When the child has a runny nose (or any other time you feel appropriate), tell her it is time to wipe her nose. Bring tissue to her nose, wiping quickly and firmly. It is common for some children to be resistant to this necessary task. It may be helpful for you to hold your arm around the child's shoulders, cradling her head against your elbow to provide stability. Regular washing of the child's face with a washcloth may help the child to tolerate the wiping of her nose with the tissue.

DAILY ROUTINES & FUNCTIONAL ACTIVITIES

If the child's nose needs to be wiped frequently, consider using tissues with lotion in them. Encourage the child to play at wiping a doll or stuffed animal's nose, your nose, and so forth.

CRITERION   *The child allows her nose to be wiped by an adult with minimal resistance.*

■ ■ ■

4-IIIf. Washes own hands

MATERIALS   Soap and water

PROCEDURES

Model hand washing for the child (e.g., get hands wet, rub on soap, then rinse hands). Tell the child to wash his hands. Provide verbal cues as needed. Give physical assistance only if the child is resistant or is having difficulty. Gradually but regularly decrease your assistance. It is generally better to stand behind the child when giving physical assistance, and then gradually fade your help. Liquid soap may be easier than a bar of soap for a child who is learning to wash his hands.

DAILY ROUTINES & FUNCTIONAL ACTIVITIES

It is easy to arrange opportunities for hand washing by first providing opportunities for the child to get his hands dirty. Playing with fingerpaints, sand, or other messy substances will get hands dirty enough for you to suggest that they need to be washed.

Opportunities to wash dolls, doll clothes, or plastic dishes also provides good practice.

CRITERION   *The child independently washes his hands.*

■ ■ ■

4-IIIg. Wipes nose if given a tissue

MATERIALS   Soft tissues

PROCEDURES

When the child has a runny nose or sneezes, tell her to wipe her nose, and hand her a tissue. If the child makes no attempt to wipe her nose, physically assist her to do so. Gradually withdraw assistance on further trials. You may also demonstrate how to gently blow the nose. Encourage the child to imitate.

DAILY ROUTINES & FUNCTIONAL ACTIVITIES

If the child's nose needs to be wiped frequently, consider using tissues with lotion in them. Encourage the child to play at wiping a doll or stuffed animal's nose, your nose, and so forth.

CRITERION   *The child wipes her own nose when given a tissue and told to do so.*

■ ■ ■

4-IIIh. Dries hands

MATERIALS   Water, towel

PROCEDURES

Hand the child a towel, and ask him to dry his hands. Show the child how to rub the towel over the front and back of his hands. It may be easier for the child to use a small, lightweight towel, such as a dishtowel or a washcloth, at first. Also, show the child how to dry his hands by using part of a towel that is hanging up. Give the child physical assistance as needed, then gradually fade your assistance.

DAILY ROUTINES & FUNCTIONAL ACTIVITIES

Incorporate hand washing and drying as a routine procedure before and after each meal or snack, after any messy play, and after toileting.

CRITERION   *The child independently dries his hands.*

■ ■ ■

4-IIIi. Brushes teeth with assistance

MATERIALS   Toothbrush, a comfortable place to stand in front of a sink and mirror

PROCEDURES

Place the child in front of a mirror, and tell her it is time to brush her teeth. Show the child the toothbrush and how you put toothpaste on it. Hand the child the toothbrush, and tell her to brush her teeth. It may be helpful to demonstrate brushing your own teeth at the same time. Provide physical assistance as needed. At this stage, the child is only expected to make some contact with her teeth using the toothbrush. An adult will then need to complete the tooth brushing to make sure that all teeth are brushed adequately.

DAILY ROUTINES & FUNCTIONAL ACTIVITIES

Establish tooth brushing as a routine practice after each meal. Encourage the child to practice brushing a favorite doll or stuffed animal's teeth. A puppet with a mouth that opens and has teeth works well to help children learn about brushing teeth.

CRITERION   The child holds the toothbrush and brushes at least some teeth independently most of the time.

4-III

■ ■ ■

4-IIIj. Washes self with washcloth

MATERIALS   Two washcloths (or washcloth puppets), soap, water

PROCEDURES

During bath time, give the child one washcloth while you use the other. Show the child how to rub soap on the washcloth and then rub the washcloth on his body. Provide physical assistance as needed. Encourage him to hold the washcloth in the right hand to wash his left arm and then switch the cloth to his left hand to wash his right arm. Use of a washcloth puppet may be both easier and more enticing. This item is designed to begin teaching the child how to wash himself; however, the adult will still need to provide follow-up.

DAILY ROUTINES & FUNCTIONAL ACTIVITIES

Provide the child with a small cloth or sponge to wash play dishes or wipe table. Encourage the child to wash a baby doll with a washcloth.

CRITERION   The child holds washcloth and attempts to wash himself during bath time.

4-IV
Self-Help: Toileting

The typical timetable for achieving toilet training is highly variable, with some children being fully trained by 2 years, while others are not trained until 3–3½ years. Boys are often somewhat older than girls before they have the physical maturation for toilet training. Nighttime wetting may persist throughout the preschool period in some children.

4-IV

Children with developmental disabilities are often delayed in toilet training. A developmental psychologist can be helpful in establishing a toilet training program for an older child who is still in diapers. Note that with some conditions such as spina bifida, toilet training may not be an appropriate goal due to the child's lack of bowel and bladder sensation and control.

ADAPTATIONS

Children with Motor Impairments

Children with motor impairments may need adaptive equipment for toileting. An occupational or physical therapist can assist in determining what would be useful.

Children with Visual Impairments

Children with low vision will probably need few adaptations in learning toileting skills, although young boys may need extra instruction to learn to urinate into the toilet in a standing position. For children with little or no vision, it will be important to allow them to feel the toilet and discuss it. Be sure to teach the child that the toilet is not water to play in.

Children with Hearing Impairments

It is important for children with hearing impairments to establish a way to communicate the need to go to the bathroom. Depending on the child's developmental, motor, and hearing abilities, this may be accomplished through the use of formal sign, a gesture, or spoken language. Everyone who works with the child needs to be aware of how the child communicates the need to toilet.

4-IV. SELF-HELP: TOILETING

a. Indicates need for soiled diaper or pants to be changed

b. Cooperates with diaper changing

c. Stays dry for 2- to 3-hour periods during the day

d. Urinates when placed on toilet

e. Has bowel movement when placed on toilet

f. Usually indicates need to toilet (rarely has bowel accidents)

g. Uses toilet by self, except for cleaning after bowel movement

■ ■ ■

4-IVa. Indicates need for soiled diaper or pants to be changed

MATERIALS   Cloth or disposable diapers

PROCEDURES

Some time after the child is 1 year old, he will typically begin to give clear signals when his diaper is messy. Watch for these signs (e.g., vocalizations, pointing, walking with a wide gait) and ask, "Do you have dirty pants? Do you want me to change your diaper?"

Check to see if the child's diaper is soiled. If it is, talk to the child about changing it as you go through the process. Talk about taking the dirty diaper and clothes off and putting a clean diaper on.

Note: If you are consistently checking and finding that a child's pants are not wet or messy, look carefully at the cues, either verbal or behavioral, to which you are responding. You may need to work to help the child give clearer signals or to be more discerning in picking up cues that the child is offering.

DAILY ROUTINES & FUNCTIONAL ACTIVITIES

It is helpful for everyone working with the child to follow a similar routine. The goal is to increase the child's awareness of the need for his diaper to be changed. It is important not to let the child remain in wet or messy pants for any length of time. You want the child to associate dry, clean pants with comfort and wet or messy pants with the need to be changed.

CRITERION   The child clearly indicates a need to have a soiled diaper or pants changed. This can be done either verbally or nonverbally.

■ ■ ■

4-IVb. Cooperates with diaper changing

MATERIALS   Cloth or disposable diapers

PROCEDURES

When it is time to change the child's diaper, tell her that her diaper is wet or messy and that she needs a clean diaper. The child can actively participate in the diaper changing by bringing the diaper to you, going to the changing table, and climbing up on the changing table if a stool is available. The child is then expected to lie fairly still while her diaper is being changed. Give verbal prompts and provide distractions as needed.

DAILY ROUTINES & FUNCTIONAL ACTIVITIES

Cooperating during a diaper change is often a challenge for mobile toddlers who want to be on the go. It may help to have a favorite toy or book available to hand the child while you change her diaper. For children very resistant to lying down, an alternative is to change the diaper while they are standing up. This requires the child to stand fairly still during the diaper change.

CRITERION   The child cooperates with diaper changing both by actively preparing for the diaper change and by remaining relatively still during the change.

4-IVc. Stays dry for 2- to 3-hour periods during the day

MATERIALS   Cloth or disposable diapers

PROCEDURES

This is not a skill that can be taught, but rather indicates physiological readiness to begin toilet training. Check the child's diaper every 2–3 hours to determine how often the child is wetting his diaper. Having a clear idea of when the child urinates, particularly if there is any predictable schedule, will assist in beginning toilet training.

DAILY ROUTINES & FUNCTIONAL ACTIVITIES

Check the child every 2–3 hours throughout the day. This is also important in making sure that the child is dry most of the time so that he doesn't become comfortable being wet (see 4-IVa).

CRITERION   The child stays dry for 2- to 3-hour periods during the day.

4-IVd. Urinates when placed on toilet

MATERIALS   Child-size toilet or potty chair

PROCEDURES

A child is generally ready to begin toilet training when her diapers are dry for 2–3 hours at a time. At regular periods throughout the day, place the child on the potty chair or toilet, and tell her that it is time to go to the bathroom (using whatever terminology is descriptive and customary in your family or setting). It is important to use an appropriate size potty chair for the child so that her feet rest comfortably on the floor. Some children may be able to use an adaptive seat on a regular toilet if you place a step stool in front of the toilet to aid in getting on the toilet and to provide secure footing while sitting on the toilet. Give positive reinforcement when the child is successful. In addition to the natural times for toileting, it is important to pay attention to a child's physical or verbal cues that she might need to go to the bathroom. By taking her at these times, the child will begin to associate the physical signs with the need to use the toilet. Encourage the child to tell you when she needs to go to the bathroom. Both boys and girls usually first learn to urinate sitting down.

DAILY ROUTINES & FUNCTIONAL ACTIVITIES

It can be very helpful to use a doll that can wet to demonstrate urinating on the toilet. The modeling effect of other children using the toilet will be helpful for a child who is just beginning to toilet train.

CRITERION   *The child frequently urinates when placed on toilet.*

4-IV

■ ■ ■

4-IVe. Has bowel movement when placed on toilet

MATERIALS   Child-size toilet or potty chair

PROCEDURES

A child is generally ready to begin bowel training when bowel movements occur at a predictable time during the day. Often, this occurs in the first hour after a meal. Also, most children give some indication through body language or facial expression when they are ready to have a bowel movement. Place the child on the toilet when you see any indication of the need to go or at the time the child typically goes. Be prepared to spend some time waiting for the child to go. It may be helpful to have books available to read to him while he is sitting on the toilet.

DAILY ROUTINES & FUNCTIONAL ACTIVITIES

You may find it useful to use various resources (e.g., *Everyone Poops* by Taro Gomi) for children who are reticent to use the toilet. It is sometimes helpful to dump the contents of a dirty diaper in the potty in front of the child, telling him that that is where it belongs.

CRITERION   *The child has a bowel movement when placed on toilet.*

■ ■ ■

4-IVf. Usually indicates need to toilet (rarely has bowel accidents)

MATERIALS   Child-size toilet or potty chair

PROCEDURES

This item is an extension of items 4-IVd and 4-IVe, with the child demonstrating increased awareness of the need to go to the bathroom. Check with the child periodically throughout the day, asking, "Do you need to go to the bathroom?" Watch for nonverbal cues and give feedback to the child: "It looks like you need to go to the bathroom." Then take the child to the bathroom. Give positive reinforcement when she is successful. A psychologist can be helpful in developing a program for children who are resistant to toilet training.

DAILY ROUTINES & FUNCTIONAL ACTIVITIES

Be sure that everyone working with the child is aware that the child is toilet training and is alert to the child's verbal and nonverbal cues that she may need to go to the bathroom. Be sure the child has ready access to a toilet. If traveling, it is often helpful to take a potty chair with you.

CRITERION   *The child usually indicates the need to toilet and rarely has bowel accidents.*

■ ■ ■

4-IVg. Uses toilet by self, except for cleaning after bowel movement

MATERIALS   Child-size toilet or potty chair, pants that are easy to remove

PROCEDURES

After the child is having some regular success in toileting, keep him in training pants and easy-to-pull-down outer pants. When the child is not rushed to go to the toilet, encourage him to pull down his own pants. After using the toilet, hand him several pieces of toilet tissue and ask him to wipe himself. Children usually need assistance in wiping after bowel movements for some time. When finished, encourage the child to pull his pants up and then wash his hands. Gradually fade any physical assistance you have been giving. When the child is demonstrating some independence, encourage him to go to the bathroom alone, having you come in when he is finished to assist with cleanup.

DAILY ROUTINES & FUNCTIONAL ACTIVITIES

Continue to be alert to the child's verbal and nonverbal cues that he may need to go to the bathroom. Children sometimes become absorbed in playing and ignore their body signals. Be sure that the child has ready access to a toilet that he can use independently. In group settings, the ability to go to the toilet by oneself is often reinforced by observing other children's independence who have already achieved this step.

CRITERION   *The child uses the toilet by himself, except cleaning after bowel movement.*

5
Attention & Memory: Visual/Spatial

T he focus of this sequence is to develop children's abilities to attend to visual stimuli, remember those stimuli, and act on the basis of those memories. Up to the 12-month level, this sequence primarily consists of visual tracking and items related to immediate memory. After the 12-month level, there is a mixture of items focusing on attention span, memory and motor games, and long-term memory.

ADAPTATIONS

Children with Motor Impairments

Many of the items in this sequence must be modified for children with significant motor impairments. If a child is unable to reach and grasp, it may be necessary to rely entirely on eye gaze to determine if he or she knows where an object is after you have hidden it, where objects are located in the room, and where objects should be put away. (See Appendix D at the end of the book for suggestions to set up a simple eye-gaze system using an object board.)

If the child is unable to carry an object while scooting or walking, you may need to decrease your requests for the child to retrieve objects or, in cases where the child moves well but cannot carry, provide a special piece of equipment to allow him or her to transport objects. Always work closely with the child's physical and occupational therapists when developing modifications for these items.

Children with Visual Impairments

The primary adaptations for children with visual impairments involve using objects and pictures that are large and especially colorful or bright and working in well-lit places (unless checking to see if the child follows a light). It is helpful to seek advice from the child's ophthalmologist or vision specialist in order to choose the most appropriate toys and pictures.

In some cases it is helpful to choose objects for the child that are not only interesting visually but also make noises in order to reinforce the child to look for them. As the child becomes more attentive visually, objects without sounds can be introduced.

If a child has a significant visual impairment, it will be difficult for him or her to learn locations of objects, especially if the child moves during instruction. It is important to teach the child at an early age to search for objects by passing his or her hands over the floor, table, or other surface. It is especially important to keep the physical environment consistent so that objects can be found in the same places. Emphasize tactile information to help the child identify locations—for example, attach sandpaper to a container for blocks, soft fabric to a container for stuffed animals, and so forth. It is also helpful to have containers of distinctly different sizes and shapes.

Note: The early visual tracking items in this sequence should be worked on even if a child has been described as cortically blind and is making no responses. In many cases the child's nervous system has not matured to the point that the child can attend to the sight. Given time and stimulation, that attention may develop. An early consultant to this curriculum project stated, "Do not assume that a child cannot see unless both eyes have been removed." Also, be aware that some children with visual impairments will not fixate at the midline, but rather to one side or the other.

Children with Hearing Impairments

Beyond using gestures and signs (if the child is being taught signs) to communicate with the child about what he or she is to do, few adaptations to the items in this sequence are needed for children with hearing impairments.

5. ATTENTION & MEMORY: VISUAL/SPATIAL

a   Visually fixates for at least 3 seconds

b.   Visually tracks object horizontally (from side to side)

c.   Visually tracks object vertically (from head to stomach)

d.   Visually tracks object in a circle

e.   Gaze lingers where object or person disappears

f.   Shows anticipation of regularly occurring events in everyday care

g.   Pulls cloth from face

h.   Pulls cloth from caregiver's face

i.   Retrieves object partially hidden under a cover

j.   Anticipates frequently occurring events in familiar games after two or three trials

k.   Anticipates frequently occurring events in familiar games on first trial

l.   Retrieves object fully hidden under a cover

m.   Finds toy hidden under one of two covers, alternately

n.   Finds toy hidden under three superimposed covers

o.   Finds toy after seeing it covered and removed in two places and left covered in a third

p.   Finds toy under (or in) one of two containers after containers are reversed

q.   Remembers location of objects that are put down for a few minutes

r.   While sitting on a caregiver's lap, attends to picture book for at least 5 minutes, patting the pictures or otherwise indicating interest

s.   Reacts to a change in familiar game and/or reacts when objects vanish or do not function in usual ways

t.   Finds object after it is covered in two places and has not seen where it was left

u   Finds object after seeing it covered in three places and has not seen where it was left (systematic search)

v.   Recognizes familiar toys, people (in addition to family members and regular caregivers), and places

w.   Recognizes own and others' clothing, toys, and personal belongings

x.   Retrieves own toys from usual locations

y.   Retrieves household (or classroom) objects from usual locations on request (signed or spoken)

z.   Puts away objects in correct places and notices when they are not in the correct place

aa.   Acts out parts of rhymes or songs independently

bb.   Points to hand that is hiding a toy (both when toy remains in that hand and when toy is transferred to the other hand, out of sight)

cc.   Recognizes the covers of several books and labels them

dd.   Recognizes familiar signs

ee.   Identifies (points to) object or picture shown briefly and shown again in an array of three

ff.   Identifies (points to) object or picture shown briefly and shown again in an array of four

gg.   Tells the name of object or picture shown briefly in a group of two and then hidden

hh.   Remembers incidental information

■ ■ ■

5a. Visually fixates for at least 3 seconds

MATERIALS   A variety of interesting objects (e.g., silver ball, red pom-pom, red flashlight, small checkerboard, bull's eye drawn on a card)

PROCEDURES

Hold object 6–10 inches from the child's eyes, wiggling it gently to attract the child's attention. Repeat with a different object.

Note: Sometimes it is very difficult to get certain infants with disabilities to look at anything. Usually, such infants respond best to something very bright and shiny, such as a large ornament that reflects images. Some infants will only respond to a bright light in a darkened room. Experiment to find what objects and what degree of room light get the best responses.

DAILY ROUTINES & FUNCTIONAL ACTIVITIES

Keep the toys you plan to use near the changing table, and work on this activity every time you change the child's diaper.

CRITERION   *The child looks at an object for at least 3 seconds several times a day on several different days.*

■ ■ ■

5b. Visually tracks object horizontally (from side to side)
5c. Visually tracks object vertically (from head to stomach)
5d. Visually tracks object in a circle

MATERIALS   A variety of toys for which the child has shown preference

PROCEDURES

Present an object at midline, about 12 inches from the child's face. When the child looks at it, move it slowly to one side and then to the other side (e.g., 5–8 inches to either side). Do this three or four times using additional objects. Wait 1–2 minutes as you talk to the child. Then choose the object to which she responded best, attract the child's attention at midline eye level, and move the object vertically (to the level of the child's chest and then back to the height of her forehead). Repeat several times.

When the child begins to track both horizontally and vertically, try to get her to track an object in a circle. While the child is attending to the object at midline, move it slowly to one side and then move it in a circle a little larger than the child's face.

If the child does not track at all, try one of the following suggestions until she begins to do so:

- Vary the distance of the objects from the child's eyes
- Use noisy objects
- Vary the illumination of the room and the brightness of the object.

DAILY ROUTINES & FUNCTIONAL ACTIVITIES

Identify one or more daily care activities (e.g., diaper changes, playtime before or after meals) that are appropriate for practicing visual tracking. Keep the materials near the place(s) where the event(s) occur so that it will be easy to remember to practice the tracking each time the child is there.

CRITERION 5b   The child visually tracks at least three different objects from one side of her visual field to the other, crossing the midline smoothly several times a day on several different days.

CRITERION 5c   The child visually tracks at least three different objects at midline from chest level to forehead level and back again several times a day on several different days.

CRITERION 5d   The child tracks at least three different objects through a full circle several times a day on several different days.

■ ■ ■

5e. Gaze lingers where object or person disappears

MATERIALS   A variety of bright, shiny objects for which the child has previously shown a preference

PROCEDURES

Present an object in front of the child at midline, and move it slowly to the left and then to the right. Let the object drop from sight at the child's right. As it drops, talk about it (e.g., "Where's the ball? Where did it go?").

Wait 5 seconds and make the object reappear at the same place while you comment on its reappearance (e.g., "Here it is!"). When the child looks at the object or at the place it disappeared, bring it closer for him to inspect. Help the child touch the object, make a noise with it, or otherwise enjoy it.

Repeat the same procedure, dropping the toy on the child's opposite side. Vary the side where the object disappears randomly as you continue this activity.

Make this activity as much fun as possible. On some trials, substitute yourself for the object, making this a kind of Peek-a-boo game.

DAILY ROUTINES & FUNCTIONAL ACTIVITIES

It is easy to do this activity at any time that you stop to attend to the child. Just do it once or twice and then go on to something else. If other children are around, teach them to play this kind of Peek-a-boo game with the child.

CRITERION   The child's gaze lingers for 3 or more seconds at the point at which the object or person disappeared from sight. This should occur several times a day on several different days.

■ ■ ■

5f. Shows anticipation of regularly occurring events in everyday care

MATERIALS   None required

PROCEDURES

The most important way to "teach" this item is to provide a consistent environment for the child. It should be consistent in terms of the people providing most of the care and the settings in which the care is provided. Routines should be established in diapering, eating, bathing, bedtime, and so forth. After routines have been established, begin to watch for signs that the child is anticipating the next part of the routine. For example, when the child is hungry, does she stop crying when the sounds of food preparation are heard? Or, does she get excited when hearing the bath water being drawn?

DAILY ROUTINES & FUNCTIONAL ACTIVITIES

Ask others who care for the child to note any indications that the child anticipates events that occur regularly.

CRITERION   The child shows anticipation of two or more regularly occurring events in everyday care. These should be observed on several occasions, and at least two different people should be able to agree that the child's behavior indicates anticipation.

■ ■ ■

5g. Pulls cloth from face
5h. Pulls cloth from caregiver's face

MATERIALS   A soft cloth, diaper, towel, or scarf

PROCEDURES

When the child is looking at you, play Peek-a-boo by putting a cloth over his face (leave mouth uncovered). Say, "Where's [child's name]?" Pause to allow the child the opportunity to remove the cloth on his own. If he does not remove it and say "Peek-a-boo" (or whatever is commonly used in the child's community), continue the game through several trials. Attend to any movements that suggest he is attempting to remove the cloth. Assist his movements. Decrease your help as the child is able to do it more independently.

Once the child is pulling a cloth from his own face, begin covering your face, making sure the cover is within easy reach of the child. Say, "Where's [your name]?" If the child does not pull the cloth off, you should pull it off and say "Peek-a-boo." If he seems to be trying to pull it off but cannot, assist him, reducing assistance as he becomes more competent.

DAILY ROUTINES & FUNCTIONAL ACTIVITIES

Peek-a-boo games are usually one of a child's favorite activities and are a good way to keep him occupied when shopping, waiting in line, sitting in the doctor's office, and so forth.

Note: Some children are afraid of having a cloth placed on their faces. You may have to gradually introduce the cloth by initially placing it on only part of the face or body, or by using a relatively sheer cloth that allows the child to still see his surroundings.

CRITERION 5g   *The child completely removes a cloth placed over his face in a Peek-a-boo game. This should be done consistently several times a day on a number of different days.*

CRITERION 5h   *The child completely removes a cloth that is placed over an adult's face in a Peek-a-boo game, several times a day on a number of different days.*

5

■ ■ ■

5i. Retrieves object partially hidden under a cover

MATERIALS   A variety of toys or objects, including toys the child has shown a preference for (e.g., car keys, small rubber doll, brightly colored beads, small car); various covers (e.g., cloths, cushions, scarves, boxes, cups)

PROCEDURES

Show an object to the child and, as she reaches for it, cover more than half of the object with a cover. If the child removes the cover, note whether she simply plays with the cover or retrieves the object.

If the child seems to show no interest in the object after it is partially covered, say, "Where's the [object]? Oh, there it is!" as you cover and uncover it several times. Then, partially cover it again and wait for a response. If there is still no response, try another object, perhaps a favorite toy or a piece of cookie.

As soon as the child begins to uncover partially hidden objects, vary the game by completely hiding the objects (following the same procedures).

If the child does not remove a cover but tries to do so, assist her with the task, then gradually decrease your help as she is better able to do it herself.

DAILY ROUTINES & FUNCTIONAL ACTIVITIES

Watch for times the child retrieves objects from under covers in self-directed activities (e.g., when she covers and uncovers objects herself, retrieves an object when something has fallen on it).

Note: Experiment with the kind of objects that you hide and the covers you use. Some children will only look for food, an object that makes noise, or a favorite toy. Likewise, some covers are easier to remove than others. It is important, however, to try to increase both the variety of objects the child will look for and the variety of the covers.

Sometimes, children will remove covers to play with the covers, showing no interest in the object that was hidden. Similarly, some learn to pull a cloth off of a toy in order to get praise from an adult, rather than to retrieve the object. Observe the child's behavior carefully, and do not move on to the next item until it is clear she is remembering and searching for the object beneath the cover, rather than playing with the cover or removing the cover for adult praise.

CRITERION   *The child retrieves a toy partially hidden under a cover several times a day on a number of different days.*

■ ■ ■

5j. Anticipates frequently occurring events in familiar games (e.g., nursery rhymes) after two or three trials

5k. Anticipates frequently occurring events in familiar games on first trial

MATERIALS   None required

PROCEDURES

Play games with the child that involve rhymes with actions or simply repeated words with actions, such as This Little Piggy or Pat-a-cake. When the child is accustomed to the game and enjoying it, wait a few seconds before a critical line of the saying and observe the child. Does he say "wee, wee," for example, or touch a toe for the last little piggy or give some sign that he is expecting his arms to be raised when you say, "Toss it in the oven"?

Also note whether this anticipation occurs only after you have repeated the game several times or the first time you play a familiar game on a given day.

DAILY ROUTINES & FUNCTIONAL ACTIVITIES

Play games with the child several times a day. For example, when bathing or dressing the child, you can play This Little Piggy with his toes, or play Here Comes a Little Bug (walk your fingers up the child's arm while you say "Here comes a little bug, it's going to get you" and then tickle the child gently). Most bookstores have a collection of books with rhyming games for children. See the suggested readings list at the end of the book. Use these or try others of your choice.

Note: Children generally enjoy games that include touching or tickling, and it is easy to observe their anticipation as they prepare for the tickle or the touch. Some children, however, do not enjoy either touch or tickle. In these cases, you can play other games that rely on interesting sounds for their effects.

CRITERION 5j   *The child shows anticipation of an event in one (or more) familiar game(s) after it is played two or three times in sequence. This should be observed on a number of occasions over a period of several days.*

CRITERION 5k   *On several different days, the child shows anticipation of an event in one (or more) familiar game(s) the first time it is played (i.e., the child remembers it from a previous day or a previous period of time in the same day).*

■ ■ ■

5l. Retrieves object fully hidden under a cover

5m. Finds toy hidden under one of two covers, alternately

5n. Finds toy hidden under three superimposed covers

5o. Finds toy after seeing it covered and removed in two places and left covered in a third

MATERIALS   A variety of interesting toys; various covers (e.g., cloths, nesting cups, boxes)

5

PROCEDURES

Proceed as in Item 5i (Retrieves an object partially hidden under a cover). When the child regularly uncovers a fully hidden toy, introduce a second cover a few inches away from the first. Take the toy and hide it under the second similar cover while the child watches.

If the child looks under the cover where she previously found the toy, say, "Oops, where is it?" Encourage the child to remove the other cover. If she does not, do it for the child to show her where it is.

Repeat this procedure. Do not simply alternate sides but randomly vary the side on which the toy is hidden.

Once the child is successful at finding the object under two covers, introduce a third cover. When you are sure she is watching, place the object under one of the three covers, and ask the child to find it. Repeat, placing the object under the covers randomly.

After the child becomes successful in finding objects hidden under one of three covers, try hiding the toy under all three at the same time. For example, take the toy and place it under a cup, then place a box over the cup, and finally a scarf over the box. If you choose to use three cloths instead of a variety of covers, be sure to secure the bottom two with your fingers so that the child cannot remove all of the cloths at once. The point of this game is for the child to retain her memory and interest in the toy as well as her motivation to get it for as long as it takes to remove the three covers individually.

While the three covers are present, hide the toy under one cover, remove it and let the child see it, place it under the second cover, and remove it and place it under the third. Ask the child to find it. If she is incorrect, show her where it is and try again.

Note: If using scarves or cloths, be sure to bunch them up so that the shape of the toy is not visible.

DAILY ROUTINES & FUNCTIONAL ACTIVITIES

Look for opportunities to observe the child search for objects during the course of the day. Does she go on to another object or activity as soon as a toy is dropped or has rolled away? Does she show persistence in searching for something dropped and out of sight? Help the child focus attention by saying, "Where is it? Where did it go?"

CRITERION 5l   The child uncovers a fully hidden toy on several occasions.

CRITERION 5m   When two covers are present, the child consistently finds the toy under the correct cover (three or four consecutive correct trials) on several different days.

CRITERION 5n   The child retrieves the toy hidden under three covers, removing the covers individually two or three times on several different days.

CRITERION 5o   On several different occasions, the child finds a toy after seeing it covered and removed in two places and left in a third.

■ ■ ■

5p. Finds toy under (or in) one
of two containers after containers are reversed

MATERIALS   Toys or other interesting objects, several pairs of identical containers (e.g., cups, boxes, opaque food storage containers)

PROCEDURES

Place one pair of containers in front of the child. Call his attention to a toy or other object, and place it under one of the containers (or inside if the containers have lids). Then, reverse the position of the containers. Ask the child to find the object. If he selects the incorrect container, tell him to look under the other one. Repeat, randomly placing the object in either the left or right container.

If the child always reaches with both hands and lifts up both containers, use containers with lids so that the child needs to use two hands to expose the toy.

DAILY ROUTINES & FUNCTIONAL ACTIVITIES

This kind of hiding game is primarily functional as a way of entertaining a child for a short period of time while, at the same time, helping develop his attention and memory. It can be done with materials found in kitchen cupboards as well as with toys and special containers.

CRITERION   The child finds the hidden object in the reversed container on three consecutive trials on several different days.

■ ■ ■

5q. Remembers location of objects that are put down for a few minutes

MATERIALS   A few interesting toys

PROCEDURES

Give the child an object to play with. When she drops it or puts it down, call her name or otherwise distract her so that she turns her head away from where the object is. Observe what she does. Does she turn back to look for the object where she dropped it (or put it down) and then pick it up? Does she seem to forget the toy? Does she pick up the toy after a short period of time but react to it as if it were something she had not seen before?

   If the child does not look for the dropped toy, say, "Where is the [toy]"? If she does not look, point to it, pick it up, and hand it to her again.

DAILY ROUTINES & FUNCTIONAL ACTIVITIES

During the course of the day, observe what the child does when she puts the object down and turns away momentarily or drops it out of sight. Does she retrieve the object? If she picks up the object again, does she seem to pick it up because it again came into view or does the child turn to the right location and pick up the toy as if expecting to find it there?

CRITERION   On several occasions, the child demonstrates that she remembers the location of an object that was put down for a few minutes by deliberately retrieving the object or indicating where it is in response to a question.

5

■ ■ ■

5r. While sitting on a caregiver's lap, attends to picture book for at least 5 minutes, patting the pictures or otherwise indicating interest

MATERIALS   Simple picture books, including those with textures that encourage patting, flaps that can be lifted to show something underneath, or other characteristics that encourage the child to interact with the book

PROCEDURES

Hold the child on your lap, show him a book, and talk about what you see. If he does not pat a picture spontaneously, place his hand on the picture and talk about it. Let him manipulate the book. Try to keep him involved with it for 5 or more minutes.

DAILY ROUTINES & FUNCTIONAL ACTIVITIES

Try to read to the child for a few minutes every day. At this level, the child will not comprehend a story so much as enjoy interesting pictures and the close interaction with the caregiver. It increases the child's attention if the caregiver speaks with animation and makes sounds appropriate to the pictures (e.g., "choo-choo" for a train, "moo" for a cow, "roar" for a lion). For books with flaps to lift, it is useful to act surprised by what is there in order to reinforce the child's sense of curiosity.

CRITERION   *The child attends to a picture book for at least 5 minutes, patting the pictures or otherwise showing interest on several different days.*

■ ▧ ▨

5s. Reacts to a change in familiar game and/or reacts when objects vanish or do not function in usual ways

MATERIALS   None required

PROCEDURES

Once a child is showing anticipation of events in games or the household routine, begin checking her understanding by deliberately doing something wrong. For example, instead of giving the child her bottle, begin to feed a doll or pretend to drink it yourself. Or, you might try to do This Little Piggy on the child's fingers instead of her toes.

Play simple games with the child to challenge her understanding of what typically happens. The following are some examples:

1. Place a small toy in one hand and show it to the child. Place your hands behind you, and move the object from the one hand to the other. Bring your hands out, still in fists, and let her open each one to look for the toy. Do this several times, sometimes leaving the toy in the same hand and at other times transferring it. Then, leave the toy behind you in your pocket, under a cushion, or someplace else out of sight. Observe what the child does when the toy is not in either hand.

2. Give the child one or two small toys to drop into a container. Shake them up and let the child take them out. Do this a couple of times. Then remove the toys from the container as you shake it (without letting the child see what you are doing). Give the child the empty container and observe what she does.

3. Play with a wind-up toy that has an on/off switch, regularly presenting it to the child with the switch on after you have wound it. Then, wind it, and present it with the switch off.

Observe the child's reactions. Laughter, a look of puzzlement, trying to correct what you are doing, or fussing may be indicators that the child understands that something is wrong. Respond appropriately to what the child does. For example, laugh at yourself if you've deliberately changed a routine and then do it the way the child expects it to be done.

DAILY ROUTINES & FUNCTIONAL ACTIVITIES

The activities described in the procedures section are good ways to entertain a child when you have some down time (e.g., while you are waiting for someone, when standing in line). They are also good to use as a distraction when the child becomes fussy.

CRITERION   The child reacts to a change in a familiar game or routine, reacts to the disappearance of objects, and/or reacts to items that cease to function in expected ways. This should be observed to occur in two or three different situations and on several different days.

■ ■ ■

5t. Finds object after it is covered in two places and has not seen where it was left

5u. Finds object after seeing it covered in three places and has not seen where it was left (systematic search)

MATERIALS   A variety of covers, various toys/objects small enough to be hidden in your hand or a small box

PROCEDURES

Place two covers on the table. Show the child a small toy in your hand. Close your hand around the toy, and place your hand under the cover on the child's left. Remove your hand, with the toy still hidden, and place your hand under the other cover and leave the toy there.

  If the child does not look for the toy, demonstrate looking under each cover, saying, "Where did the [toy] go? Here it is!"

  Repeat, varying the side on which you leave the toy.

  After the child can find the toy with two covers present, introduce a third cover and follow the same procedure. Vary the sequence of placing the toy under the covers. For example, on one trial, go from left to right; on another, from right to left; and on another, place the toy first under the right cover, then under the left, and then leave it under the center cover.

  Note: When the child does not see you hide the toy, there is no way of knowing where it is. The object of this item is not for the child to guess right every time but to recognize that if the toy is not under one of the covers, it is under another. Make the errors a part of the game by laughing and saying, "I fooled you that time."

  When three covers are present, the important element is that the child engage in a systematic search. It does not matter in what sequence the child lifts the covers, but each should be lifted only once as he searches for the toy. In this way he must not only maintain attention on the toy but also must remember where he has looked previously.

  Take turns with the child, letting him hide the toy from you. Model a systematic search saying something like, "It's not there, I just looked there. Maybe it is here."

DAILY ROUTINES & FUNCTIONAL ACTIVITIES

Play a variety of hiding games with the child when you are just trying to entertain him. For example, try putting a toy or a cracker in one hand, placing your hands behind your back and then bringing them back out. Let the child open the hand he thinks the object is in. Another time, transfer the toy from one hand to the other or drop it in your pocket to see how the child searches for it.

CRITERION 5t   *On at least three different occasions, the child looks under a second cover to find a toy when he fails to find it under the first. This should be done without adult prompts or encouragement.*

CRITERION 5u   *The child finds the object after systematically searching under three covers (lifting each cover no more than one time), on at least three different occasions.*

■ ■ ■

5v. Recognizes familiar toys, people (in addition to family members and regular caregivers), and places

MATERIALS   None required

PROCEDURES

Interact with the child using a consistent set of toys over several days (or treatment sessions). Select one or two of the toys she prefers, and add them to a collection of different toys. When you sit down to play with the child, let her look through the toys you have brought. Watch for signs that she recognizes the toys that you and she previously used for play. For example, she may immediately pick out those toys and play with them before exploring the others, or she may smile broadly when picking up one of them.

DAILY ROUTINES & FUNCTIONAL ACTIVITIES

The best way to help a child learn to recognize things that are familiar is to provide a consistent and predictable environment. For example, the child will learn more effectively if she has only a few toys present to play with at one time, if there are relatively few people providing her primary care, and so forth. Observe the child carefully when something or someone new is introduced and when there is a reunion with someone or something familiar. Watch for signs that the child recognizes people, toys, or places. Signs of recognition may include smiling, saying a name, reaching for a person, going to a place in a room where a special toy has been kept for her visits, and so forth.

If the child is not showing signs of recognition of familiar people or things, make an effort to increase her attention to people, places, and objects in the environment. When shopping, point to and name things that are like the ones at home. Point to and name places to which you take the child (e.g., fast-food shops, grocery stores). Go with the child to explore the outdoors, talk about what you see, hand items to the child, and help her look, feel, smell, and listen to them. Put away an item that the child has played with every day. Bring it out again several days later, but present it with one or two other objects or toys that have continued to be around. Observe the child's responses.

CRITERION   *The child demonstrates recognition of familiar toys, people, and places. The child must show recognition of at least five different toys, people and/or places, and more than one adult should have observed these signs of recognition.*

■ ■ ■

5w. Recognizes own
and others' clothing, toys, and personal belongings

MATERIALS   None required

PROCEDURES

Collect a group of objects from the child's home or child care, some of which belong to the child and some of which belong to two or three other people (e.g., siblings, parents, other children). Tell the child you are going to put all of his things in one pile, all that belong to [other person] in another, and all that belong to [other person] in another. Hold up each object and ask, "Is this yours?" or "Whose is this?" If he does not identify the owner, tell him whom the object belongs to, and place it in its proper pile.

Another time, you may let the child go through the objects independently to see if he spontaneously names the owners.

DAILY ROUTINES & FUNCTIONAL ACTIVITIES

Throughout the day, make a point of identifying the ownership of objects within the child's environment. It is important that the child learn that some objects belong to everyone in the family or group care setting, while others belong to specific people. When dressing the child, talk about his clothing. You can teach a child many other basic concepts in the context of talking about personal belongings. For example, "They're Daddy's shoes. Look how big they are. See your little shoe," or "Susie's coat is blue, Lachandra's is green, and you have a red coat."

Periodically check on the child's knowledge of ownership by asking questions or giving instructions (e.g., "Bring me Daddy's hat," "Take this to Sarah's room," "Where is your coat?"). Correct errors by gently suggesting that the child made a mistake (e.g., "Uh-oh, that's not your coat. That is Derrick's coat. Your coat is right there [pointing]. Please bring it to me").

You can also check on the child's knowledge by "tricking" him (e.g., start to put his coat on yourself, start to put your shoes on him, mix up other articles that have clear ownership). Watch for the child's reactions. If the child does not laugh or do something to indicate that he knows this is wrong, say, "Oops, what did I do? I started to put Johnny's coat on you. Let's give it to Johnny. Can you help me find your coat?" Make this a joking and fun exchange.

CRITERION   *The child recognizes his own and others' clothing, toys, and personal belongings. That is, the child should be able to identify ownership of at least eight different items, no more than half of which belong to himself.*

■ ■ ■

5x. Retrieves own toys from usual locations

5y. Retrieves household (or classroom) objects from usual locations on request (signed or spoken)

5z. Puts away objects in correct places and notices when they are not in the correct place

MATERIALS   None required

PROCEDURES

Work with the child in a familiar environment. Ask her to get specific toy of hers for you to play with. If she does not, lead her to where the toys are, and help her pick it up and bring it back to the area where you are playing together. Always thank and praise the child when she follows an instruction correctly.

Also ask the child to get some familiar item for you (e.g., the broom, the dustpan, the "cleanup sponge," the box for the cars). If she does not, lead her to it and prompt her to take it to where you are playing together.

When you finish your activities together, tell the child it is time to clean up. Observe where she puts the toys or other objects as she is cleaning up. If she puts one in an incorrect place, remove it, tell her it does not belong there, show her where it does belong, and give it back to her so that she can place it there.

Always thank and praise the child both for following these instructions correctly and for trying to follow them, even if she makes errors.

DAILY ROUTINES & FUNCTIONAL ACTIVITIES

Store the child's toys in consistent locations, and have the child assist with cleanup. Observe the child to see if she deliberately goes to get a particular toy from its usual location. For example, the child might be playing with a train engine, then go back to her room to get a train car to go with the engine, or she might find a block, then go retrieve a box of blocks to use with it.

Throughout the day, involve the child in your activities. Especially encourage the child to help you with various tasks. Ask the child to go get items for you that are within her reach. If the child returns without the item you requested or acts confused, make the request again, specifying the exact location of the item. If the child still does not retrieve the item, take her with you to find the item. Talk about where it is and then let the child carry it back to your task location. It is important to act pleased and praise the child when she is able to respond to your requests. It is even more important that you not be critical or negative when the child does not locate the object you requested. By giving the child additional instructions or by going with her to find the object and then letting her carry it to the task location, you will be ensuring that she will feel successful and willing to try another time.

Similarly, give the child objects to return to the place they belong. Provide help as needed and praise the child for being such a good helper to you.

CRITERION 5x   *The child retrieves her own toys from usual locations either on her own or in response to a request. This should be observed for three or more toys, and care should be taken to determine that the child wanted a particular toy and knew where it was rather than just picking up whatever was handy.*

CRITERION 5y   *The child retrieves household (or classroom) objects from usual locations on a daily basis when requested (signed or spoken) to do so.*

CRITERION 5z   *The child puts away objects in their correct place. Objects should include most of the child's belongings as well as five or six that do not belong to her. The child should put the objects away without the adult's assistance but not necessarily without the adult's request.*

■ ■ ■

5aa. Acts out parts of rhymes or songs independently

MATERIALS   None required

PROCEDURES

Frequently read action rhymes or sing action songs to the child (e.g., The Itsy, Bitsy Spider, The Wheels on the Bus, Little Jack Horner, Two Little Blackbirds). After the child is imitating your actions well, begin to wait slightly before you do the actions to see if the child will do them without your model.

DAILY ROUTINES & FUNCTIONAL ACTIVITIES

Singing songs or saying rhymes is a good way to keep a child entertained when you are riding in the car, waiting in a doctor's office, or waiting for other events. Singing songs is also an important part of a group care schedule. The children learn from one another as well as from the adult.

CRITERION   *The child acts out parts of two or more rhymes or songs independently. The adult may say or sing all of the words, but the child must do a good approximation of at least one of the movements associated with the song at the appropriate time without an adult concurrently modeling the movements.*

■ ■ ■

5bb. Points to hand that is hiding a toy (both when toy remains in that hand and when toy is transferred to the other hand, out of sight)

MATERIALS   Several small toys that can be enclosed completely in your hand

PROCEDURES

Show the child a small toy in your hand. Put both hands behind you momentarily. Bring them back out with they toy completely hidden in the same hand and ask, "Which hand is [the toy] in?" After the child points, open the hand so that he can see if he was correct.

If he is not correct, open the other hand and let him see the toy. Repeat the activity. Alternate hands so that the child does not always find the toy in the same hand.

When the child routinely points to the correct hand, transfer the toy on some occasions from one hand to the other behind your back. See if the child will then point to the other hand. If he does not, show it to him. Repeat.

Let the child be the one who hides the toy in his hand. Make errors sometimes so that the child can have the fun of fooling you.

DAILY ROUTINES & FUNCTIONAL ACTIVITIES

Use this game to entertain the child while the two of you are waiting in line at the grocery store or in a similar situation. Teach older children to play the game with the child.

In a group setting, encourage children to play this game with each other.

CRITERION   *The child regularly selects the hand in which the toy was hidden (when the toy is left there), and he finds the toy when the adult has passed it to the other hand out of the sight of the child.*

■ ■ ■

5cc. Recognizes the covers of several books and labels them

MATERIALS   Nine or ten sturdy storybooks with large, colorful pictures

PROCEDURES

Gather together four or five books, some that you have frequently read to the child and some that are new. Allow her to look through them and select the book she wants you to read to her. Listen for her to say something that identifies a familiar book (it need not be the title of the book; it can be something associated with the content). If she does not label the books spontaneously as she looks through them, ask her to find a particular one (e.g., "Where's the book about Spot?"). If she does not find it, show it to her.

DAILY ROUTINES & FUNCTIONAL ACTIVITIES

Spend time each day looking at books with the child. Give the child a choice between two or three books for you to read to her. If the child will sit still, read the story as written. If she is too active to sit still that long, abbreviate the story, making it fit with the pictures. To maintain her interest, read with animation. Use different voices for different characters or different sounds for different animals.

Have the books available to the child on a low shelf so that she can explore them by herself. Watch for the child to begin looking through the books to find a specific one for you to read and for her to say something that identifies the book.

CRITERION   *The child looks through books to find the cover of a favorite book and labels it. She should be able to identify and label at least three different books.*

■ ■ ■

5dd. Recognizes familiar signs
(e.g., restaurants, traffic lights, stop signs, labels on food)

MATERIALS   Magazines with pictures containing familiar signs, labels (or parts of labels) from food or juice containers (not a label with pictures of the contents, but a label with words and/or a logo). Depending on the child's experience, some possible examples are the top half of a Cheerios box or other cereal boxes (with the name of the cereal and the color of the box evident but no picture of a bowl of cereal); Kool-Aid packages; and labels from various kinds of juice, chips, or cracker packages.

PROCEDURES

Look through a magazine with the child and ask, "What's that?" when you see an advertisement that shows a familiar logo.

Collect a group of labels that should be familiar to the child. Glue them into a notebook, and leaf through the pages with the child. Ask what each one is. If he does not know, tell him. See if he remembers the next time you look through the book.

DAILY ROUTINES & FUNCTIONAL ACTIVITIES

5

When preparing the child a snack or a meal, show him the labels of the packages you are using. Similarly, when you are shopping with the child, show him the things you are taking off of the shelves and name them for him.

When driving in the car, point out stop signs and signs of stores or fast-food places you visit frequently.

Watch and listen for the child to point at one of the food labels or signs saying something that indicates he recognizes the sign, whether it is a brand name or something that the child associates with that name. For example, the child would get credit for saying "McDonald's" when he sees the arches, but he also would get credit for saying "fries."

CRITERION   The child recognizes and labels five different familiar signs.

■ ■ ■

5ee. Identifies (points to) object
or picture shown briefly and shown again in an array of three

5ff. Identifies (points to) object
or picture shown briefly and shown again in an array of four

MATERIALS   Eight to ten pairs of identical pictures (e.g., pictures cut from magazines, cards from Animal Lotto, cards from Memory Game), eight to ten pairs of identical objects

PROCEDURES

Play a game with the child in which you place three objects or pictures in front of her, and cover them with a box, a piece of paper, or a cloth. Then show the child an object/picture that matches one of the three objects/pictures that are covered in front of her. Take that picture/object away and remove the cover from the three objects/pictures in front of her and ask, "Where's the one we just saw?" If the child makes an incorrect choice, show her the picture/object again. Have her point to the one just like it. Hide it again, and ask the child to point to the one that was just shown. Then try with a different set of objects/pictures. Occasionally, let her play the part of the "teacher" if she wishes to do so.

At the beginning, select three objects/pictures that are very different from one another (e.g., car, horse, and spoon). Gradually make the task more difficult by selecting objects or pictures that are similar or in the same class (e.g., knife, fork, and spoon; horse, dog, and cat).

When the child is doing well with choosing among three objects/pictures, begin using four, following the same procedure.

This game also can be played by pairs of children, having the children take turns being the person who shows the objects/pictures to be remembered and being the person who finds them.

DAILY ROUTINES & FUNCTIONAL ACTIVITIES

Look for opportunities throughout the day to challenge the child to remember something she has seen (e.g., "What was that animal that ran across the street, a cat or a dog?"). Or, if you are driving or out for a walk, point out the stop sign. When another comes into view, ask the child if she can find another stop sign like the one she saw previously.

CRITERION 5ee   *The child finds an object or picture shown briefly in a group of three on at least five consecutive trials (different objects/pictures each trial).*

CRITERION 5ff   *The child finds an object or picture shown briefly in a group of four on at least five consecutive trials (different objects/pictures each trial).*

■ ■ ■

5gg. Tells the name of object or picture shown briefly in a group of two and then hidden

MATERIALS   A collection of interesting objects and pictures

PROCEDURES

Play a game in which you show the child two familiar objects or pictures briefly. Then, put one object/picture behind your back, under a box, or somewhere else out of sight. Leave the other one in sight and ask the child, "What did I hide?" If he answers incorrectly, bring out the object/picture and show him, saying, "This is what I hid. What is it?" Then try again with another two objects/pictures. You should also let the child be the one to hide something and have you tell what is hidden.

This activity can be done with a group of children taking turns being the one to hide an object/picture.

DAILY ROUTINES & FUNCTIONAL ACTIVITIES

Look for opportunities throughout the day to check the child's memory of something he looks at only briefly. For example, if you meet some familiar person while shopping, ask the child a minute or so later whom it was that he just saw.

CRITERION   The child names one object or picture shown briefly in a group of two that is then hidden. He should be able to do this on several different occasions, rarely making errors.

■ ■ ■

5hh. Remembers incidental information (e.g., "What did you see at the zoo?")

MATERIALS   None required

PROCEDURES

Talk to the child about what she is doing or what she has seen or done, and always act very interested in what she has to say. Take her for a walk outdoors, and point out things you see along the way. When you return, ask her to tell another person what she saw or what happened. Prompt her if she has difficulty.

DAILY ROUTINES & FUNCTIONAL ACTIVITIES

When the child goes with one parent or caregiver to do something, another parent or caregiver should ask, "What did you see?" or, "What happened?" when the child returns. If the child is unable to recall what she saw, the adult who was present with the child should prompt her with leading questions (e.g., "Did you see a fire truck?").

In a group setting, plan brief field trips for the children or invite someone in to show them something interesting. Afterward, talk about the experience to see what the children recall. Begin with very general questions, such as "What did we see at the fire station?" Then, ask more specific questions to help the children remember more of their experiences.

CRITERION   On at least three occasions, the child remembers and tells about two or more objects, events, or experiences when asked a general question about a recent occurrence.

6-1
Visual Perception: Blocks & Puzzles

6-1

These activities require children to interpret and organize information about form and space. In learning about form and space, it is very helpful for children to learn about moving their own bodies through space and around obstacles (e.g., furniture) in everyday life. Refining this knowledge through manipulation of objects and learning how to relate objects to each other further develops concepts of form and space. Developing these skills provides a foundation for later developing academic skills. Math, particularly geometry, is dependent on a good understanding of form and space—that pieces can be put together to create a whole and that different shapes have different relationships to each other. Reading and writing require an understanding of space that is organized from top to bottom and left to right. Even before they have labels for these concepts, children learn to hold a book right side up and to turn pages moving from the front to the back of the book. It is important that classic children's toys, such as blocks and puzzles, be made readily available to young children. They need both structured experiences, in which building ideas and assembly are demonstrated, and unstructured exploration, in which they will achieve greater mastery over space. Provide a variety of puzzles and building materials, including large cardboard boxes, that can be used as pretend houses, trains, and so forth.

ADAPTATIONS

Children with significant motor and visual impairments may have greater difficulty understanding spatial concepts due to their limited opportunities for experiencing space (e.g., climbing under, over, and around objects). Be sure to include ways to help these children physically experience space in order to lay the foundation for developing better spatial perception.

Children with Motor Impairments

Some children with severe motor impairments will not be able to place forms in boards or shape sorters. Forms with a large knob handle may be easier for children with motor impairments to place, or these children may be able to indicate through eye gaze where the shape belongs. For this sequence, it is helpful to have a form board or shape sorter with openings arranged in a single row.

Blocks with Velcro may be helpful for children with poorly controlled hand and/or arm movements. Also, try various sizes and weights of blocks to see what works best for the children.

Children with Visual Impairments

Help children with visual impairments feel the various objects. Describe them in terms of shape, size, and texture. Use materials with interesting textures. For block designs, a model that has been glued together may be helpful.

Due to the heavy emphasis on visual information in this sequence, these activities are less appropriate for young children with severe visual impairments. Although activities can be modified with tactile cues provided, it is likely that children with visual impairments would achieve these at an older age.

Children with Hearing Impairments

Children with hearing impairments will require no adaptations to these items because the items are strongly visually based. Be sure to accompany any verbal instructions with demonstrations as needed.

6-I. VISUAL PERCEPTION: BLOCKS & PUZZLES

a.   Places large round form in form board

b.   Places large square form in form board

c.   Imitates building a chair with blocks

d.   Places round and square forms in form board when they are simultaneously presented

e.   Places large triangular form in form board

f.   Places round, square, and triangular forms in form board when they are simultaneously presented

g.   Completes simple puzzles

h.   Places correct forms in shape sorter

i.   Places round, square, and triangular forms in reversed form board

j.   Imitates block train

k.   Puts together two-piece puzzles

l.   Imitates block building

m.   Imitates block bridge

n.   Puts together puzzle with four or five interconnected pieces

6-I

■ ■ ■

6-Ia. Places large round form in form board

MATERIALS   A large round form, a form board with one large round cutout

PROCEDURES

Present the form board and the round form to the child. Tell the child to put the shape in the hole. If the child does it correctly, praise him. If the child has difficulty, demonstrate placing the form and then ask him to try it. If necessary, physically help the child put the form in the hole. Encourage the child to use his fingers to feel the round shape of the object and the cutout in the form board. Gradually fade your assistance.

Note: If available form boards have several shapes in them, leave the other shapes in while working with the round one. The other shapes may be initially taped in place to avoid confusion.

DAILY ROUTINES & FUNCTIONAL ACTIVITIES

Make a simple shape box by cutting a round hole in the plastic lid of a container. Have the child drop round beads through the hole.

CRITERION   The child puts a large round form in a form board on several different occasions. Using trial and error is acceptable.

■ ■ ■

6-Ib. Places large square form in form board

MATERIALS   A large square form, a form board with one large square cutout

PROCEDURES

Present the form board and the square form to the child. Tell her to put the shape in the hole. If the child does it correctly, praise her. If she has difficulty with the task, demonstrate how to do it by placing the form in the board, and then ask her to try it. If necessary, physically help the child put the form in the hole. Encourage the child to use her fingers to feel the square shape of the object and the cutout in the form board. Gradually fade your assistance.

DAILY ROUTINES & FUNCTIONAL ACTIVITIES

Make a simple shape box by cutting a square hole in the plastic lid of a container. Have the child drop square blocks through the hole.

CRITERION   *The child puts a large square form in a form board on several different occasions. Using trial and error is acceptable.*

■ ■ ■

6-Ic. Imitates building a chair with blocks

MATERIALS   Six blocks of identical size (approximately 1 inch), a small doll

PROCEDURES

Place the blocks in front of the child. Tell the child you are going to make a chair with the blocks. Take two blocks and stack them, then place the third block in front of the stack. Show the child how to sit a small doll on the chair. Tell the child to build his own chair for the doll. Demonstrate the process several times and physically assist the child, if necessary.

DAILY ROUTINES & FUNCTIONAL ACTIVITIES

Have blocks readily available to the child. Build other simple block patterns (e.g., towers, rows of blocks) to keep the child's interest in playing with the blocks. The goal of this item is to promote motor skills, imitation, and eye–hand coordination.

CRITERION   *The child builds a chair with three blocks on several different occasions.*

■ ■ ■

6-Id. Places round and square forms
in form board when they are simultaneously presented

MATERIALS   Round and square forms, a form board with a round hole and a square hole

PROCEDURES

Present a form board to the child with both the round and the square forms in place. Remove the shapes (or tell the child to). Encourage the child to feel the shapes of the forms and holes. Tell her to put the forms in the holes.

If the child has difficulty with the task, demonstrate how to do it and then place the blocks near the correct holes and tell the child to try the task again. If necessary, physically guide the child's hand in placing the objects in the correct holes.

DAILY ROUTINES & FUNCTIONAL ACTIVITIES

Keep a simple shape box available on a low shelf so that the child can play with it frequently.

CRITERION   The child places both a round and a square form in a form board on several different occasions. Using trial and error is acceptable.

■ ■ ■

6-Ie. Places large triangular form in form board

MATERIALS   A triangular form, a form board with one triangular cutout

PROCEDURES

Present a form board to the child with the triangular form already in place. Remove the shape (or tell the child to do so). Encourage the child to feel the shape of the form and the cutout. Tell him to put the form in the hole.

6-I

If the child has difficulty with the task, demonstrate how to do it and then place the blocks near the correct holes and tell the child to try the task again. If necessary, physically guide the child's hand in placing the objects in the correct holes.

DAILY ROUTINES & FUNCTIONAL ACTIVITIES

Keep a simple shape box available on a low shelf so that the child can play with it frequently.

CRITERION   The child places a triangular form in a form board on several different occasions. Using trial and error is acceptable.

■ ■ ■

6-If. Places round, square, and triangular forms in form board when they are simultaneously presented

MATERIALS   Round, square, and triangular forms; form board that has round, square, and triangular cutouts

PROCEDURES

Present a form board to the child with round, square, and triangular forms in place. Remove the shapes one at a time and place them on a table directly below the matching opening in the form board. Tell the child to put the shapes back into the form board.

If she has difficulty with the task, demonstrate how to do it and then place the blocks near the correct holes and tell her to try the task again. If necessary, physically guide the child's hand in placing the objects in the correct holes. Gradually reduce your help, praising the child's effort in placing the forms without help.

After the child has been successful with placing the forms, mix the arrangement of the forms in front of the child, and tell her to put them in again.

DAILY ROUTINES & FUNCTIONAL ACTIVITIES

Keep a simple shape box available on a low shelf so that the child can play with it frequently. A shape sorter with sound effects may provide greater motivation for the child with little interest in this type of activity.

CRITERION   *The child places round, square, and triangular forms correctly in a form board on several different occasions. Using trial and error is acceptable.*

■ ■ ■

6-Ig. Completes simple puzzles

MATERIALS   Large, simple puzzles with four to five independent pieces

PROCEDURES

Place a completed puzzle in front of the child. Draw his attention to the pictures in the puzzle. While the child watches, remove pieces. Tell the child to put the puzzle back together.

If the child has difficulty with the task, place all of the pieces in the puzzle except one. Help the child put the last piece in. When the child is able to place one piece correctly, leave two pieces out, and so forth. Provide physical prompting as needed. Remind the child to turn or rotate puzzle pieces, if needed, in order to make them fit.

When the child learns to complete that puzzle, change to another puzzle. When the child has had success with a number of puzzles with four to five pieces, gradually increase the complexity of the puzzles that are offered.

Note: Puzzles come in a large variety of sizes, ranging from simple to difficult. Start with picture puzzles of familiar objects with pieces that are easy to manipulate. Puzzles with a matching picture under the puzzle piece provide a valuable visual cue for the child just beginning to assemble puzzles.

DAILY ROUTINES & FUNCTIONAL ACTIVITIES

Store puzzles where the child can easily reach them on his own. Because it is important to offer the child a variety of simple puzzles, be sure to rotate the puzzles that you make available to the child. Once a child has mastered a puzzle, it no longer provides a learning challenge. In some communities, the public library may have children's puzzles available for check out.

CRITERION   *The child completes two different simple puzzles. Using trial and error is acceptable.*

6-Ih. Places correct forms in shape sorter

MATERIALS   Shape sorter (form box or ball) with at least six different shapes

PROCEDURES

Present the child with shape sorter and matching shapes. Tell her to put the objects in the correct holes. If the child has difficulty with the task, demonstrate how to place the shapes in, and then tell the child to try the task again.

If necessary, physically assist the child at first by holding the shape sorter so that most holes are covered by your hands, or tape paper over several holes. Gradually allow the child to have more forms, and leave more holes open.

Note: It is important for the child to correct her own efforts when possible. At this stage, many children do the task by trial and error rather than by good form discrimination. Give assistance primarily when the child is frustrated.

DAILY ROUTINES & FUNCTIONAL ACTIVITIES

Store the shape sorter where child can get it to play on her own. Offer two or three different styles of shape sorters to encourage generalization of skills.

CRITERION   *The child places five to six different shapes in a shape sorter on several different occasions. Using trial and error is acceptable.*

6-I

6-Ii. Places round, square, and triangular forms in reversed form board

MATERIALS   Round, square, and triangular forms; a form board that has round, square, and triangular cutouts

PROCEDURES

Present the child with a form board that has various shapes already in place. Remove the shapes one at a time, and place them on a table below the matching opening in the form board. Rotate the board 180 degrees, and place it in front of the child (i.e., above the shapes). Tell the child to put the shapes back into the form board. If the child has difficulty in doing this, demonstrate it for him. Encourage the child to look carefully. Use appropriate word labels. For instance, when the child is holding the round shape, say, "You have a circle. Put it in the circle (round) hole. Where does the circle go?"

DAILY ROUTINES & FUNCTIONAL ACTIVITIES

Keep a simple shape box or puzzle on a low shelf so that the child can play with it frequently.

CRITERION   *The child places round, square, and triangular forms in correct holes when the form board is reversed. Using trial and error is acceptable.*

■ ■ ■

6-Ij. Imitates block train

MATERIALS   Ten 1-inch blocks

PROCEDURES

Place 10 blocks on the table in front of the child. Tell the child that you are going to make a train with the blocks. Align four of the blocks in a straight line. Place a fifth block on top of the first block. Push the train that you have created with the blocks along the table while making a train sound. Then tell the child to use the rest of the blocks to make a train like yours. Leave your train in sight but out of reach. Demonstrate this activity several times, and give the child physical assistance, if necessary.

DAILY ROUTINES & FUNCTIONAL ACTIVITIES

At playtime, help the child use large wooden or cardboard blocks to make trains as well as other vehicles. Reinforce language and spatial concepts by making and talking about trains of different sizes and lengths.

CRITERION   *The child imitates a block train on several different occasions.*

■ ■ ■

6-Ik. Puts together two-piece puzzles

MATERIALS   Simple pictures on cardboard (some cut in half diagonally, others cut in half vertically)

PROCEDURES

Make several puzzles by gluing clear, simple pictures on square pieces of cardboard, each about 6 inches by 6 inches, then cut the board in half, either vertically or diagonally. (Allow the child to help select and glue the pictures. If the cardboard is lightweight, the child may be able to cut the puzzle herself.) Place one of the pictures in front of the child, and correctly put it together. Then, take the picture apart, partially rotating pieces. Ask the child to put the puzzle back together. Encourage her to focus on the picture to be completed (i.e., "Can you fix the car? Try to put it back together"). If the child has difficulty, show her how to put the puzzle together, then take it apart for her to do again. If she is unsuccessful, try putting one half in the correct orientation, and tell her to finish the puzzle. Physically assist her if needed.

DAILY ROUTINES & FUNCTIONAL ACTIVITIES

Provide regular opportunities for the child to play with these puzzles. You may be able to find some simple two- or three-piece commercially made puzzles that are designed for toddlers.

CRITERION   *The child is able to correctly put together two different two-piece puzzles. Using trial and error is acceptable.*

■ ■ ■

6-Il. Imitates block building

MATERIALS   Ten 1-inch blocks

PROCEDURES

Place 10 blocks on a table in front of the child. Tell the child that you are going to make a building with the blocks. Align four of the blocks horizontally and place a fifth block on top of the second block. Then ask the child to use the rest of the blocks to make a building like yours. Leave your building in sight but out of reach. Demonstrate the activity several times and give physical assistance if necessary.

DAILY ROUTINES & FUNCTIONAL ACTIVITIES

Encourage children to use blocks of various shapes and sizes to make buildings that include both horizontal and vertical parts.

CRITERION   *The child imitates a block building.*

■ ■ ■

6-Im. Imitates block bridge

6-I

MATERIALS   1-inch blocks

PROCEDURES

Place blocks on the table in front of the child. Tell the child that you are going to make a bridge with the blocks. Place two blocks on the table with a small space between them. Place a third block on top of the two blocks, forming a bridge. With a pencil, demonstrate going under the bridge to draw the child's attention to the open gap. Then ask the child to make a bridge like yours. Leave your bridge in sight but out of reach. Remind the child that a car needs to be able to pass under the bridge, so he should leave a space between the bottom two blocks. Demonstrate this activity several times and give physical assistance if necessary.

DAILY ROUTINES & FUNCTIONAL ACTIVITIES

Help the children build a network of roads and bridges with large wooden blocks for small cars to drive on, over, and under.

CRITERION   *The child imitates a three-block bridge.*

■ ■ ■

6-In. Puts together puzzle with four or five interconnected pieces

MATERIALS   Several puzzles with four or five pieces that interconnect

PROCEDURES

Give the child an assembled puzzle. Encourage her to look at the picture and tell you what it is. Ask the child to remove the pieces. Then tell her to put the puzzle back together. If she has difficulty, put in some of the pieces, and ask her to put in the last one or two pieces. Remind the child to turn or rotate puzzle pieces, if needed, in order to make them fit. When the child learns to complete one puzzle, try a different one. Allow the child to have success with a number of four- and five-piece puzzles before moving to more complex ones.

DAILY ROUTINES & FUNCTIONAL ACTIVITIES

Store puzzles where the child can easily reach them on her own. Because it is important to offer the child a variety of puzzles, be sure to rotate the puzzles you make available to the child. Once a child has mastered a puzzle, it no longer provides a learning challenge. In some communities, the public library may have children's puzzles available for check out.

CRITERION   *The child is able to put together several different puzzles with four or five interconnected pieces. Using trial and error is acceptable.*

6-II
Visual Perception: Matching & Sorting

Before children can know that a square is a square, that a circle is a circle, or that an "A" is an "A," they must be able to distinguish a square from a circle and an "A" from a "B," and so forth. In addition, they must develop a concept of "squareness," "roundness," and "A-ness" so that size, color, or other characteristics do not interfere with the understanding of a particular shape. Early experiences with form boards and simple puzzles help children develop these discrimination and conceptual skills. At first, children approach the task of completing a form board in a purely trial-and-error manner. Gradually, they begin to see the relationship between the shape of the block and the shape of the hole and become more efficient in completing the boards. These experiences lay the groundwork for the ability to match, sort, and draw conclusions on the basis of visual characteristics. This sequence is separated from sequence 6-I (Visual Perception: Blocks & Puzzles) because the tasks in this sequence require fewer motor skills and are more cognitive in nature.

6-II

The Visual Perception sequence is divided into two categories because many children progress at very different rates through the visual perception tasks with significant motor requirements and the visual perception tasks with minimal motor requirements. It is important to be able to document this difference as it may suggest a need for specific intervention (e.g., occupational therapy for motor planning problems) or for modifications in the child's curriculum.

ADAPTATIONS

Children with Motor Impairments

It is usually easier for children with mild to moderate motor impairments to match and sort than it is to complete puzzles or block patterns. For sorting, materials can be modified to be easier to pick up by attaching a large knob handle, or boxes can be attached to the edge of a table so that the child can simply push an object in the box rather than have to pick up the object.

Children with severe motor impairments may need to indicate through a gross pointing response or eye gaze which picture or object is the correct match or where a picture/object should be placed in a sorting task.

Children with Visual Impairments

Many children with visual impairments need no modifications beyond having materials with brighter colors and/or with greater contrast to the background. Children with severe visual impairments, however, may need to learn to match and sort using different characteristics than some included in this sequence. They can be taught to sort by size and shape by feeling the objects. They are unlikely to be able to sort by color. Sorting by texture would be more adaptive.

Children with Hearing Impairments

Children with hearing impairments will require no adaptations to these items as the items are strongly visually based. Be sure to accompany any verbal instruction with demonstrations as necessary.

6-II. VISUAL PERCEPTION: MATCHING & SORTING

a. Sorts by size (big and little)
b. Matches primary colors
c. Sorts by shape
d. Sorts by two characteristics

■ ■ ■

6-IIa. Sorts by size (big and little)

MATERIALS   Similar toys that are of distinctly different sizes (e.g., large and small cars, large and small stuffed animals)

PROCEDURES

Use the terms "big" and "little" frequently as you talk about or show objects to the child. Occasionally, collect some toys together, and tell the child that you want her to place the toys in two piles—one pile for the big toys and one pile for the little toys. Put an example of each item in the two locations. If there is a toy of intermediate size, talk about the fact that maybe it is a big object because it is much larger than the smallest one but that it might also be a little object because it is littler than the biggest one. Let the child decide where it should go.

DAILY ROUTINES & FUNCTIONAL ACTIVITIES

When cleaning up or sorting laundry, get the child to help by sorting clothing according to size (e.g., "Daddy's big socks go here, and your little socks go there").

CRITERION   Given examples, the child sorts big and little objects

6-II

■ ■ ■

6-IIb. Matches primary colors

MATERIALS   Objects and containers in primary colors

PROCEDURES

Present the child with a red container filled with red objects (e.g., blocks) and a blue container filled with blue objects. Dump them out and mix up the objects. One at a time, begin putting them back into the proper-colored containers, each time saying the color name and holding the object in front of the container to show the child how it matches. Then hand an object to the child, and observe where he puts it.

Or, create two piles of objects that are different colors (e.g., a pile of blue objects and a pile of yellow objects). Then, as you pick up another object to add to the pile, identify each object by color, and place it in the appropriate pile. If the child begins placing the objects in the correct pile but then makes an error, ask, "Oops, does that go there?" and help the child correct the error. If the child begins by randomly putting the objects in the container, however, let him finish, then dump out the objects, and demonstrate the process again. If the child still does not match the objects by color, wait until another day and try two other primary colors or black and white.

When the child easily sorts two colors at a time, add a third, perhaps reducing the number of items of each color to avoid having too many objects for the child to sort.

Note: A child who is colorblind may be able only to match black and white or a dark color and yellow. If you observe that the child is regularly successful with these combinations but not with any of the others, continue to name colors, but do not keep repeating this activity. Refer the child to an eye specialist.

DAILY ROUTINES & FUNCTIONAL ACTIVITIES

Talk to the child about different colors or objects throughout the day. Point out what colors he is wearing. Find objects in the environment that match what he is wearing, and point out that they are the same color. When getting dressed, show him an object of a specific color, and ask him to find a shirt that matches. Sort socks into matching piles.

CRITERION   The child matches primary colors on several occasions.

■ ■ ■

6-IIc. Sorts by shape

MATERIALS   Several matching sets of circles, squares, and triangles (these items should be the same size and color). Paper shapes can be used.

PROCEDURES

Place a circle and a square in front of the child. Using a second set of shapes, show her how to match the shapes, placing the shapes directly on top of the matching items. Say the name of the shape as you place the item. For example, "Here is a circle. It is just like your circle, so I am going to place it on top." It may help the child understand the concept more easily if you have several identical items of each shape to match. When the child is successful at matching two shapes, try three.

DAILY ROUTINES & FUNCTIONAL ACTIVITIES

Pretend that you are cooking with the child. All of the circles (cookies) go on one plate, all of the squares (toast) go on another, and so forth.

CRITERION   Given examples, the child sorts three basic shapes on several occasions.

■ ■ ■

6-IId. Sorts by two characteristics

MATERIALS   Several matching sets of circles in two different sizes and three primary colors. Paper shapes can be used.

PROCEDURES

Place a large and small circle of two different colors in front of the child. Using a second set of shapes, show him how to match the size and color, placing the shape directly on top of its matching item. Point out the characteristics of the item as you consider where to place it. For example, say, "Here is a big blue circle." Hold it next to each shape it does not match, and comment on why it does not belong there (e.g., "This is a circle, but it is a small circle, so it does not match"). After you have demonstrated matching each shape, hand the shapes to the child, one at a time, and ask him to match them. Provide physical prompts and verbal cues as needed.

DAILY ROUTINES & FUNCTIONAL ACTIVITIES

Encourage the child to sort other objects using two characteristics as the guideline. Help him sort cars or stuffed animals by size and color. Have the child help with laundry, putting all the big blue towels in one pile and all of the small blue washcloths in another.

CRITERION   Given examples, the child sorts objects by two characteristics on several different occasions.

6-II

7

Functional Use of Objects & Symbolic Play

L earning to use objects in adaptive and socially appropriate ways lays the foundation for many aspects of problem solving, role taking, and other forms of imaginative play. Sometime between the 8- and 12-month developmental period, children shift from categorizing objects primarily on the basis of form to developing categories based on function. This is an important step in cognitive development (Madde, Oates, & Cohen, 1993). Typically, children spend a great deal of time manipulating objects in order to understand their properties and potential uses.

The items in this sequence are designed to help children develop appropriate ways to interact with objects, play constructively within any constraints imposed by their impairments, and move from a simple understanding of object function to imaginative play in which one object can stand for another.

Although suggestions for adaptations are included below for children with motor, visual, or hearing impairments, further modifications will undoubtedly be necessary for children with multiple and/or severe disabilities. For example, for some children with severe disabilities, the only available mode of teaching may be to simply demonstrate appropriate object usage repeatedly and then check for learning by abruptly shifting to inappropriate usage and watching for signs of amusement, surprise, or dismay. It is especially important to keep daily records of such efforts to teach and to assess the child's learning because "reading" the signals of these children is difficult. Their ability to understand is often underestimated, however. Good records may be the best evidence available to document their capabilities.

ADAPTATIONS

Children with Motor Impairments

When working with children with motor impairments, always consult a physical or occupational therapist to help determine the best positions for a child so that he or she has optimal use of his or her hands, and choose toys that are responsive to whatever motor capabilities the child has.

More preparation (e.g., relaxation exercises) and/or physical assistance may be necessary for children with severe motor impairments to interact with objects.

If a child's impairment is too severe to allow him or her to pick up toys and perform different activities with them, it is important to try to teach the child the function of objects by demonstration. For example, squeak three squeaky toys and then try to squeak a rattle. Act surprised that it does not squeak and say, "What else could I do with it? I think I'll shake it." Talk about the characteristics of the toys as you play with them, whether you think the child can understand or not. Look for indications of surprise or pleasure when you do the wrong activity with a toy—this will let you know that the child understands the appropriate activity.

Children with Visual Impairments

Select toys that have a high contrast in color, brightness, shape, and/or texture for children with visual impairments. Also, include toys that make different noises when the child does an appropriate action with it (e.g., a bell that rings when shaken, a car that clangs when pushed, a ball that chimes when rolled). Shutting your eyes and exploring toys on your own may help you to identify the most appropriate toys for visually impaired children.

It will be necessary to help children with severe visual impairments "see" by having them feel objects and experience the objects' functions as you demonstrate. For example, help a child find his or her bowl on the table with one hand and his or her spoon with the other. Talk about the objects (what they are) and their functions (e.g., "We need to put the spoon in the bowl in order to get the food out"). Guide the child's hand with the spoon to the bowl, and help the child eat. Later, give the child an empty bowl and a spoon. Help him or her locate both objects and observe what the child does with them.

Although it will take more time to do so, be sure to include the child in daily activities. Talk about what you are doing, and help the child experience the activity by hand over hand assistance, if necessary.

Children with Hearing Impairments

In order for children with hearing impairments to hear toys that make noise, be sure that the toys are loud enough or at the proper frequencies. Look for toys that make different visual displays (e.g., cradle gym, busy box) when different activities are done with them. If a child with a hearing impairment is learning to sign as well as to speak, try to make the dolls, puppets, or animals make simple signs as you engage in pretend play with them (e.g., When you say, "This bear is hungry," move the bear's paw to its mouth).

7. FUNCTIONAL USE OF OBJECTS & SYMBOLIC PLAY

a. Moves hand to mouth

b. Explores objects with mouth

c. Plays with (e.g., shakes, bangs) toys placed in hand

d. Commonly performs four or more activities with objects

e. Responds differently to a different toy in a group of similar toys

f. Demonstrates appropriate activities with toys that have obviously different properties

g. Combines two objects in a functional manner

h. Orients materials appropriately

i. Manipulates books by looking, patting, pointing, or turning pages (may use as a hinge)

j. Plays spontaneously with a variety of objects, demonstrating their functions

k. Experiments with unfamiliar objects to determine their functions

l. Spontaneously engages in adult activities with props

m. Engages in adult role play

n. Pretends that objects are something other than what they are

o. Talks to dolls or animals and/or makes them interact with one another

p. Assumes different roles in fantasy play

q. Represents more complex events in play

r. Uses different voices for different people in play

■ ■ ■

7a. Moves hand to mouth

MATERIALS   Sticky substances (e.g., jelly, syrup) that the child enjoys tasting

PROCEDURES

Watch for hand-to-mouth movement. The movement already may be spontaneously occurring. If it does not occur or is infrequent (e.g., three to four times per day), put a small amount of something sweet or good tasting on the back of the child's hand (e.g., on the knuckle below the index finger, wherever it will be easiest for the child to suck it off). Grasp the child's elbow gently, and use it to move the child's hand to his mouth. Hold it there until he has a chance to taste the substance on it. Talk to the child in a soothing tone.

Release the child's elbow, put more sweet substance on his hand, and observe. If the child does not take his hand to his mouth, repeat the above procedure several times, giving as little assistance as necessary.

DAILY ROUTINES & FUNCTIONAL ACTIVITIES

Watch throughout the day for hand-to-mouth movement. If the child's muscles are tight, try to relax him and help him get his hand to his mouth. Help him do this several times a day.

Note: As soon as hand-to-mouth movement is established, toys should be introduced and other activities encouraged. Hand-to-mouth activity is an important part of body awareness and exploration but can become a powerful self-stimulating behavior in children with disabilities if not modified with more advanced behaviors.

Some children develop a bite reflex and will clamp down on anything touching their teeth. Do not work on this item if the child demonstrates this behavior. Seek assistance on this item from a speech-language pathologist, physical therapist, or occupational therapist.

It may be helpful to work on this activity just before feedings or when the child gets fussy and you are holding him. Mouthing the hands is usually a source of comfort to a child.

CRITERION   The child frequently moves his hand to his mouth spontaneously.

■ ■ ■

7b. Explores objects with mouth

MATERIALS   A variety of small objects appropriate for holding and mouthing (e.g., teething toys, rattles; texture, temperature, and taste of these objects may be varied to increase the probability of mouthing)

PROCEDURES

Place a toy in the child's hand and observe. If the child does not carry it to her mouth in a reasonable amount of time, gently grasp the child's elbow and guide the hand and object toward her mouth.

If the child withdraws from the toy, try a different one. Talk in a soothing voice to the child as you try to help her explore the object with her mouth.

If the child drops the toy and puts her hand in her mouth, try other toys to see if some are easier for the child to grasp than others. Or, physically assist by keeping your hand over the child's hand and helping guide the toy to her mouth.

DAILY ROUTINES & FUNCTIONAL ACTIVITIES

Whenever you are holding the child on your lap, place objects in her hands, and help her take them to her mouth if she does not do it spontaneously.

Note: Mouthing is usually the first way infants explore the properties of objects. Mouthing also helps children develop oral-motor skills. A child with impairments, however, may get "stuck" at this level of development. Be sure to move on to the next items in this sequence as soon as the child is able to easily mouth toys.

Observe the child carefully. Some behaviors suggest abnormal reactions that require the help of a specialist (e.g., occupational or physical therapist). For example, you may need the help of a specialist if

- The child seems to get objects to her mouth but then draws back suddenly when they get near her face, usually dropping the object
- The child drops the object and extends her arm away from her body as she turns her head to look at the object.

CRITERION   *The child explores most objects with her mouth when the objects are placed in her hands.*

■ ■ ■

7c. Plays with (e.g., shakes, bangs) toys placed in hand

MATERIALS   A variety of small toys that produce sounds or a visual display when shaken or dropped

PROCEDURES

Hold a rattle or bell out in front of the child and shake it. If the child does not spontaneously take it, place it in his hands.

If the child does not attempt to shake the toy, place your hand over his hand, help shake the toy, and then release the child's hand. If he still does not attempt to shake the object, assist by jiggling his arm at the elbow. Repeat with other toys.

Also, try banging an object on a table or another surface to make the noise. Physically assist the child to bang an object, if necessary.

DAILY ROUTINES & FUNCTIONAL ACTIVITIES

Present the child with a rattle or bell several times throughout the day (e.g., when the child is lying in a crib, when he is on the floor, when he is seated in a swing or chair). Physically assist him to shake the object if he does not do it spontaneously.

CRITERION   *The child spontaneously shakes or bangs several different objects.*

■ ■ ■

7d. Commonly performs four or more activities with objects

MATERIALS   A variety of small toys that reinforce particular behaviors (e.g., squeaky toys that respond to patting, rattles that respond to shaking or waving, textured toys that invite rubbing, hard toys that make a noise when they are banged, soft toys that make no noise when hit against a surface, balls or toys with wheels that roll when pushed)

PROCEDURES

Present toys, one at a time, to the child and observe what she does with each. If the child performs only one or two activities with the objects (e.g., only mouthing and shaking), demonstrate another activity, and physically assist the child to do it (e.g., wave, pat, bang, push).

DAILY ROUTINES & FUNCTIONAL ACTIVITIES

Keep a variety of toys in different parts of the house or room where you care for the child. Give her a toy to play with while you change her diaper, when she is quietly seated and comfortable after eating, or when she is lying on the floor or in a playpen. Observe what she does with different kinds of toys. Show her different things she can do with the toys. Physically prompt her to do these actions if she does not try them spontaneously.

CRITERION   *The child spontaneously performs four different activities with toys throughout the course of a day (e.g., mouthing, shaking, banging, patting, rubbing, deliberately pushing, throwing, dropping).*

■ ■ ■

7e. Responds differently
to a different toy in a group of similar toys

MATERIALS   A collection of toys and safe household items (e.g., plastic or metal jar lids)

PROCEDURES

Select a group of three or four similar objects (e.g., blocks) and one different object (e.g., a ball). Give the objects to the child, and observe his play for 2–3 minutes. Watch for changes in activity when the child handles the toy that is different. For example, the child may always begin exploration by shaking the toy. When the blocks and the ball make no noise, he may try other activities such as banging. When the ball does not make a noise when hit on the table, he may then try some other activity or simply spend more time examining or feeling the toy that is different.

    If the child does not respond to the differences in the toys, demonstrate what you can do with the toys, and talk to the child about them.

DAILY ROUTINES & FUNCTIONAL ACTIVITIES

Keeping a box of lids in the kitchen to entertain the child while you are preparing a meal is an easy way to observe the child's exploration of the differences in objects. Metal lids, plastic jar lids, and the lids to plastic food containers all look different, feel different, and make different sounds when dropped.

CRITERION   *The child responds differently to the different object in several sets of objects, either when the adult is presenting the toys or when the child is exploring objects independently.*

■ ■ ■

7f. Demonstrates appropriate activities
with toys that have obviously different properties

MATERIALS   A collection of toys that usually elicit different responses (e.g., squeaky toys to be patted or squeezed, balls to be rolled, various shapes and textures to be felt, rattles and bells to be shaken, cars to be pushed, a mirror to be looked into)

PROCEDURES

Present the child with one toy at a time, allowing her to play with it as long as she is interested in it. Try to present toys in a sequence to maximize differences (e.g., follow a squeaky toy with a mirror or a car). Note what the child does with each toy.

If the child does not change activities when you change the toy, demonstrate an appropriate use of each toy before handing it to her. Physically assist her in such appropriate use if she does not imitate the demonstration.

DAILY ROUTINES & FUNCTIONAL ACTIVITIES

Make sure that there are a variety of interesting toys within the child's reach or range of exploration. Observe the child's play during the times you are not directly interacting with her to see if she does different things with toys that have obviously different characteristics.

Note: Although it is important to have a variety of toys available, there should not be too many in any one area where the child plays. Limit the number of toys around the child at any one time to no more than five. Having too many toys is often distracting to a child, making it difficult for her to attend to any one of them.

CRITERION   The child engages in appropriate activities with most familiar toys (or, if her motor impairment is too severe, she can indicate an understanding of appropriate toy usage).

■ ■ ■

7g. Combines two objects in a functional manner

MATERIALS   A collection of objects familiar to the child that have a functional relationship (e.g., spoon and bowl, fork and plate, blocks and a container to put them in, "pound-a-peg" and hammer, dowel and "donut block")

7

PROCEDURES

Present the child with two objects that have some functional relationship. Observe him. If the child does not spontaneously combine the objects in some functional way, demonstrate how it is done. Physically prompt the response if necessary. Try the same procedure with other pairs of objects.

DAILY ROUTINES & FUNCTIONAL ACTIVITIES

Maintain several boxes around the house or play areas that contain materials that are functionally related to each other. Give them to the child to explore as you engage in your daily routines. Note whether the child combines objects in a way that indicates some understanding of function.

CRITERION   The child spontaneously combines several sets of objects appropriately. The combinations should be in different classes of objects. For example, if the child puts many different kinds of objects into many different kinds of containers, this is still only one example of combining objects. The child would have to demonstrate one or two other kinds of combinations to pass this item.

■ ■ ■

7h. Orients materials appropriately
(e.g., turns cup right side up, places cars on wheels)

MATERIALS   Various containers, cars, and other toys that need to be in a particular orientation in order to be used in the typical manner

PROCEDURES

Place several cars and two or three cups in front of the child. Have one cup and one car oriented properly. Place the other cars and cups upside down or on their sides. Observe what the child does. If she does not orient them properly, point to one and say, "That's not right. It needs to go this way" (orienting it properly). Point to another and say, "That one is not right either. Can you fix it?" Repeat the procedure with another group of toys.

DAILY ROUTINES & FUNCTIONAL ACTIVITIES

Most children learn the appropriate orientation of objects simply by observing how they are used. For example, a caregiver sets a cup upright on the table and then pours milk into it. Some children with impairments, however, may not pay much attention to these events, and it is important to emphasize them in order for these children to learn the relationship between an object's orientation and its function.

To emphasize this, place a cup or glass upside down on the table, get ready to pour liquid into it and say, "Oops, that won't work. Let's turn it over." Turn it over and then pour. Or, present a container (e.g., can, cup) that is upside down along with some blocks. If the child does not turn the container over to put the blocks in it, do it for her and drop a block in.

CRITERION   The child properly orients at least two different objects without an adult's help on several different days.

■ ■ ■

7i. Manipulates books by looking, patting,
pointing, or turning pages (may use as a hinge)

MATERIALS   Sturdy picture books

PROCEDURES

Hold the child on your lap and read to him (i.e., hold the book in front of him, talk about what you see, point to pictures, turn pages, and so forth). Lift up the corner of the page and encourage the child to turn it.

Let the child hold the book and see what he does with it. Does he do any of the things that one typically does with a book? Does he turn a page (or the cover) back and forth (as a hinge), pat it, point to it, or vocalize while looking at it? Repeat this activity frequently.

DAILY ROUTINES & FUNCTIONAL ACTIVITIES

Some time should be spent each day holding the child and looking at books with him. Cloth books or books with lift-up flaps are particularly good for very young children because the children cannot tear the books.

Note: Young children often look at books upside down. Turn a book upright only if you are trying to read to the child. Otherwise do not correct him. At this stage of development, it is irrelevant to the child whether a picture is right side up or upside down.

CRITERION   *The child holds a book, pats it, points to it, manipulates it as a hinge, vocalizes to it, or does another activity closely associated with looking at books. This should happen on several different days.*

■ ■ ■

7j. Plays spontaneously with a variety of objects, demonstrating their functions

7k. Experiments with unfamiliar objects to determine their functions

MATERIALS   A collection of objects that demonstrate many functions (e.g., hairbrushes, washcloths, squeaky toys, cups, spoons, dolls, whistles, pull toys)

PROCEDURES

Present the child with three or four familiar objects, and observe what she does with each one. If the child does not use the object for its intended purpose, say, "What else can we do with that?" Model an appropriate use of the object and encourage the child to imitate. For example, if she bangs the hairbrush on the table, show her how to brush her own hair or a doll's hair.

Present the child with a novel object and observe what she does with it. Does she explore different things that might be done with it? For example, she might pull it if it has a string, manipulate moving parts, or move her hands all over it to feel it. Does she then decide on some action that "works" and repeat it. Does she hand it to you indicating she wants you to show her how it works? If so, show the child the function of the object.

DAILY ROUTINES & FUNCTIONAL ACTIVITIES

Observe the child's play with objects throughout the day. Note whether she uses objects according to their functions. Also note how she explores novel objects such as a new toy or some household object she encounters as she explores the environment. (The television remote is one of the first items an exploring child is apt to pick up.)

CRITERION 7j   *The child spontaneously plays with a variety of objects, demonstrating their functions.*

CRITERION 7k   *On several different occasions, when presented with an unfamiliar object, the child tries several activities with it in an attempt to determine its function or requests a demonstration.*

7

■ ■ ■

7l. Spontaneously engages in adult activities with props

7m. Engages in adult role play
(e.g., cooks, hammers, talks on play telephone)

MATERIALS   Objects typically found in the home or in the pretend play center in a class-room (e.g., child-size broom, mop, adult hat, mirror, dust cloth, playhouse, dolls, toy animals, play telephone, old purses and/or briefcases)

PROCEDURES

Set out five or six of the objects described in the materials section, placing them randomly around a small area where you will interact with the child. Talk to him as he explores the objects, and observe what he does with them. Does he use any of the props in the way he would have seen an adult use them? If not, show him how to use each one. Try the same exercise later with a different group of props.

   As the child plays with the props, try to engage him in some pretend play. For example, ring the toy telephone, answer it, and then say, "It's [name of someone the child knows]. She wants to talk to you." Hand him the telephone, and observe what he does. Does he alternate talking with listening as though having a conversation? If you have placed toy dishes out, suggest that he fix you some supper. Observe if he goes through a two- or three-step routine, such as getting a plate, pretending to scoop something on it, and giving it to you.

DAILY ROUTINES & FUNCTIONAL ACTIVITIES

As you go about your everyday activities, make a point of talking about what you are doing, and give the child a chance to try as well. For example, if you are sweeping, talk about sweeping up the dirt, show the child the pile, and discuss how you clean it up. Give the child a small broom so that he can "work" alongside you. Or, if you're using a hammer to build something, give the child a small hammer or wooden mallet and a piece of wood so that he can pretend to hammer. Or, ask the child to help you clean up spills by handing him a cloth to use while you use another.

   Let the child play with adult materials that are safe or small toy replicas of those materials (e.g., tools, pots, pans, dishes, play telephones). If he does not automatically use these objects for pretend play, encourage him to do so by demonstrating an activity and handing him the materials to imitate you (e.g., pretend to pour something from a bottle into a pan, bang a toy hammer on a piece of wood, talk on the telephone).

   Observe the child's spontaneous play. Does the child try to clean up when something has spilled, although you have not suggested it? Does he get the broom out of the pantry and try to sweep? Does he hug a doll or stuffed animal? If such activities rarely or never occur, select an object, and show the child what to do with it, providing physical assistance to get him started. Watch to see if that activity spontaneously occurs again later in the day or in the next few days. Repeat with other objects.

CRITERION 7l   *The child spontaneously engages in several adult activities with props. That is, the child does the activities without having just seen the adult do the same activity. This activity should be observed to occur several different times.*

CRITERION 7m   *On several occasions, the child engages in more advanced adult role play such as having conversations on the telephone (i.e., alternating listening and talking, saying "good-bye"), laying out play dishes as though setting the table for several people, or attempting to fix something by trying to place a screwdriver into a screw.*

■ ■ ■

7n. Pretends that objects are something other than what they are (e.g., blocks are food)

MATERIALS   Toy dishes, blocks, beads, play dough, sandbox or sand table

PROCEDURES

Provide simple materials for the child that will encourage pretend play. Model pretend play for the child. For example, help the child make hamburgers, hotdogs, or cookies with play dough and then pretend to eat them. Place a block in the child's hand, and tell her it is a cookie. Ask her to take it to Mr. Bear because Mr. Bear is hungry. Make a circle of blocks, label it a fence, and put some toy animals inside.

Gradually reduce the suggestions you make, and watch for the child to set up the pretend play. Follow her lead.

DAILY ROUTINES & FUNCTIONAL ACTIVITIES

Respond to the child's attempts to involve you in pretend play throughout the day. If she presents you with a mud pie, pretend to eat it. If she puts her legs over a broom or over a push toy with a long handle and begins to run, ask her if she is riding a horse.

7

CRITERION   *On several occasions the child pretends that an object is something else without the adult first suggesting it.*

■ ■ ■

7o. Talks to dolls or animals and/or makes them interact with one another

MATERIALS   A variety of toys that stimulate imaginative play (e.g., dolls, doll bed, bottles, small dishes, cars, trucks, toy animals, puppets, doll clothing)

PROCEDURES

Place a puppet on each hand, and make the puppets talk to each other (or stand two stuffed animals up and provide them with a brief conversation, e.g., "Hello, Mr. Bear. What do you want for dinner?" "I would like some ice cream," "Okay, Let me get you some"). Then, give the child one of the puppets or animals, and try to get him to speak for it as you play together.

Try giving the child two animals or puppets while you have one. Observe to see if he will have the two interact with each other as well as with the animal you have.

DAILY ROUTINES & FUNCTIONAL ACTIVITIES

Frequently play pretend with the child. Hug and kiss a baby doll or toy animal, take one for a ride in a car or truck, talk for it, and so forth. Encourage the child to participate (e.g., "The poor bear is hungry. Can you feed him some supper?" "Oh, dear. The bear fell down. He is crying. Boo hoo").

Pretend play is a good way to play with a child when you have time to devote yourself to the play, but it is also an excellent way to entertain a child when you are busy doing something else. You can encourage the child to take dolls or animals on trips, to get the one that is lonely and needs some company, and so forth.

Watch for the child's spontaneous use of fantasy play in which he talks to animals or dolls or has the animals or dolls interact with one another.

Note: Some adults are uncomfortable with little boys playing with dolls. If this is true for a family you are working with, encourage the family to use stuffed animals or male action figures in pretend play with the child. Fantasy play usually begins as an imitation of the actions of adults and the ways they interact with children and one another.

CRITERION   On several occasions, the child spontaneously engages in imaginative play during which he talks to toy animals or dolls or has the animals/dolls interact with one another (animals fighting one another is common fantasy play for some children).

■ ■ ■

7p. Assumes different roles in fantasy play

7q. Represents more complex events in play (e.g., plays doctor with doll or animal, shops using a wagon as a shopping cart)

MATERIALS   Dolls, stuffed animals, wagons or other wheel toys, empty food boxes, play dishes and utensils, pencils and paper, a collection of old shoes and hats or other cast-off adult items that the child could use for play

PROCEDURES

Play with the child, modeling different roles. For example, pretend to be a baby and have the child feed you or otherwise take care of you. You can also suggest a different role for the child (e.g., "Let's pretend you're Mommy and you're going off to work. What do you need?").

Encourage more complex fantasy play by modeling this kind of play for the child and participating with her if she tries to involve you (e.g., take the role of the storekeeper if the child comes and says she is shopping). Occasionally make suggestions without actually structuring the play for the child (e.g., "This bear has hurt its leg. It needs a doctor," or "I see you have your wagon. Are you going shopping today?").

DAILY ROUTINES & FUNCTIONAL ACTIVITIES

Participate in the child's pretend play when she tries to involve you. When other children are present, encourage them to play together with the dress-up clothes and toys. If the children do not spontaneously assume roles, suggest some ("Who would like to be the Mommy? Who wants to be the Daddy?").

CRITERION 7p   Child assumes at least three different roles in play. This may be done sponta-neously or in response to a suggestion from someone else, but the child must indicate some un-derstanding of each role by the use of different props or by different behaviors (e.g., sucking a bottle or crying for baby, putting on a hat for Daddy, using a stethoscope for doctor).

CRITERION 7q   On at least three occasions, the child spontaneously represents complex events in fantasy play (e.g., assumes a role and follows through a sequence of activities, such as pre-tending to cook and then serve a meal; using a wagon as a shopping cart, pretending to buy food, taking the food home, and putting it away; saying that a truck is broken, pretending a block is a tool, repairing the truck, and then having it run again).

■ ■ ■

7r. Uses different voices for different people in play

MATERIALS   Dolls, puppets, stuffed animals, or other toys that facilitate role playing

PROCEDURES

When you are engaging in pretend play with the child, use a different voice for each role you assume. For example, use a high-pitched voice and "baby talk" when you are the baby, use a low-pitched voice when you are the daddy, and use a big roaring voice if you speak for a lion.

7

Listen to the child as he takes different roles. Is he also changing voices?

DAILY ROUTINES & FUNCTIONAL ACTIVITIES

When you read to the child, use different voices for the different characters. When the child becomes familiar with a story, let the child tell it to you as he looks at the pictures. Listen to see if the child also uses different voices for the different characters.

Observe the child's spontaneous play and the times he looks at books. Does he use different voices for different characters?

CRITERION   The child alters his voice to portray the role of a puppet, doll, or story character on several occasions.

REFERENCE

Madde, K.L., Oates, L.M., & Cohen, L.B. (1993). Developmental changes in infants' attention to function and form function correlations. *Cognitive Development, 8,* 189–209.

8
Problem Solving/Reasoning

I nfants aptly have been described as "scientists in the crib" (Gopnik, Meltzoff, & Kuhl, 1999). Infants are born with a desire to know, to experiment, and to master the problems they encounter daily. Their experience with solving concrete problems through their own actions lays the foundation for their later ability to form verbal hypotheses and reason about both physical and social events. In addition, successful problem-solving experiences are critical for developing a sense of competence and maintaining motivation for learning (Hauser-Cram & Shonkoff, 1995).

The purpose of this sequence is to help children become aware of their world, be curious, observe the effects they have on the objects around them, and, as language emerges, be able to discuss perceptions and conclusions with adults. Another goal is to help children develop both confidence and pleasure in their efforts to understand the world around them.

Children with conditions that make exploration and manipulation difficult may need extra help and practice, not only to find solutions to problems but also to maintain their motivation to solve them. Each time a child masters a problem-solving situation, the child's desire for mastery is reinforced, and he or she can then tackle the next difficult task with some confidence. It is important that adults give enough help so that the child does not experience repeated failures; however, it is equally important that adults not solve problems for a child too quickly, which interferes with the child's experience of mastery.

ADAPTATIONS

Children with Motor Impairments

To the extent possible, adapt materials to suit the capabilities of children with motor impairments. For example, it may be easier for children to pick up a string if it is attached to a ring, a spool, or some other object that the child can grasp. You should consult a child's physical and/or occupational therapist for advice about how to maximize the child's interactions with the environment.

When a problem naturally occurs for a child with motor impairments, try to think of a way that the child might solve the problem using his or her specific capabilities, rather than trying to teach the child to solve the problem in the typical manner. You should demonstrate that solution for the child.

Be creative when devising tasks for children with severe motor impairments so that the tasks will challenge but not overwhelm the children's motor capabilities. For a child with severe motor impairments, it is critical to search for any behaviors that are, or can be shaped to become, voluntary. These behaviors can then be used either to signal an adult for help or to activate toys or other objects (with electronic switches, if necessary). We have found that the pleasure usually demonstrated by the child the first time the child recognizes that he or she is in control of what is happening justifies whatever effort was necessary to get the child to that point. Furthermore, the foundation has been set for the child to operate a communication board or other device, should this become necessary.

Expose children with motor impairments to other children who solve problems in the environment. Talk about what the other children are doing. Encourage the other children to place their toys in front of the child with motor impairments and show him or her how they work.

Children with Visual Impairments

Choose materials for children with visual impairments that will challenge both residual vision and tactile and motor capacities but will also provide enough sound or other effects to maintain interest.

It may be necessary to teach children with visual impairments to explore objects with their hands and to use whatever residual vision they have. Likewise, you should help children learn to use tactile information to identify barriers (e.g., doors, furniture, other items they encounter when trying to find toys or move from place to place) and possible ways to overcome them. Provide both hand-over-hand help and verbal feedback as necessary. Children with visual impairments may need to rely more heavily on verbal information about the location of objects in space than do children with better vision.

Helping children with visual impairments learn to solve the problems of mobility within the home or group care environment may provide activities that are good functional substitutes for some of the items included in this sequence, such as items 8j, 8m, 8n, and 8o. All of these items require visual-spatial skills and are not functional for a child with severe visual impairments. More functional is learning to use auditory and tactile cues to solve spatial problems, such as locating and negotiating stairs and doors, getting on furniture or play equipment, and opening containers.

Children with Hearing Impairments

No adaptations are required for children with hearing impairments other than selecting toys that are visually interesting and/or make especially loud noises.

8. PROBLEM SOLVING/REASONING

a.   Shifts attention (i.e., visual fixation, body orientation) from one object to another

b.   Looks for or reaches toward objects within sight that touch the body

c.   Repeats activities that produce interesting results

d.   Plays with toys placed in hands

e.   Persists in efforts to obtain an object or create an effect

f.   Repeats activities that elicit interesting reactions from others

g.   Looks for or reaches toward objects that make a noise while falling from view

h.   Looks for or reaches toward objects that fall quietly from view

i.   Looks or moves in correct direction for objects that fall and roll or bounce to a new location

j.   Overcomes obstacles to get toys

k.   Plays with a variety of toys to produce effects

l.   Increases rate of usual activity with toy when it stops working or tries another activity to make toy work

m.   Retrieves toys from container when they have been dropped through a hole in the top of container

n.   Reaches object from behind a barrier

o.   Pulls string to get object from behind a barrier

p.   Moves self around a barrier to get object

q.   Uses adults to solve problems

r.   Solves simple problems without adult assistance

s.   Retrieves familiar objects from usual locations in another room on request

t.   Puts away objects in correct places

u.   Uses tools to solve problems

v.   Independently plays with toys that require pushing buttons, pulling strings, and/or operating switches to get effects

w.   Experiments with cause and effect when playing

x.   Independently nests four containers, or stacks rings or blocks of graduated sizes

y.   Comments that something is not working when expected effects are not produced

z.   Independently explores objects to determine their functions and/or shows other people how they work

aa.   Answers at least one "why do" question correctly

8

■ ■ ■

8a. Shifts attention (i.e., visual fixation, body orientation) from one object to another

MATERIALS   A variety of brightly colored toys of different sizes, shapes, and textures, including some that make noise

PROCEDURES

Present a toy to the child at eye level, holding it about 10–14 inches from her face and 6–8 inches to the left or right of midline. When the child's attention is fixed on the object, present a second object at the same distance on the opposite side. Alternate shaking or wiggling the two objects for 20 seconds.

Observe whether the child shifts her attention from one object to another (indicated by moving eyes back and forth or moving head from side to side).

Perform one or more of the following activities after every trial in which the child fails to shift her attention between the two objects until the response is achieved:

* Alternate moving the items into the midline and closer to the child to attract her attention and then move them back to their original position and try to attract attention to them, one after the other.

* Present an item on either side, removing one as you present the other.

Note: Change the toys frequently in order to maintain the child's interest. Make notes regarding which toys the child seems to prefer. Use these preferences in selecting toys for future teaching sessions.

DAILY ROUTINES & FUNCTIONAL ACTIVITIES

Try this item during diaper changes or at other times when you usually play with the child. It sometimes helps to keep a couple of small toys in your pockets so that you will be ready whenever a situation to play arises.

CRITERION   The child shifts her attention (i.e., visual fixation, body orientation) from one object to another and back again as the objects are alternately jiggled or waved.

■ ■ ■

8b. Looks for or reaches toward objects within sight that touch the body

MATERIALS   A variety of toys of different sizes, shapes, and textures, including some that make noise

PROCEDURES

Observe where the child is looking, and touch his body with one of the objects that are well within his line of vision.

Note whether the child looks at the toy. Talk about the toy, wiggle it, and place it in the child's hand (or allow the child to take it if he reaches for it).

Touch the child's body with a different toy in another area outside of his direct line of vision, but where he could easily see (e.g., on the hand, on the leg). Observe to see if the child looks. Again, talk about the toy, wiggle it, or place it in the child's hands.

Perform one or more of the following activities after every trial in which the child fails to look or reach for the object until the response is achieved:

- Choose a different object and touch the child.

- Gently rub the child's skin with the object or apply slightly more pressure as you touch him with the toy.

- Attract the child's attention to the object at eye level. Then move it slowly to the place where it touched the child, trying to keep the child's gaze on the object. Touch him with the toy again.

- Physically guide the child's hand to the object.

Note: Be sure that the child has tactile sensitivity in the areas that are being stimulated. Avoid multiple trials of this item at one time. A child may habituate (i.e., cease to notice the stimulus) if he is touched in the same place several times in a row.

Also, avoid light touching or rubbing in areas where the child is known to be tactilely defensive (i.e., withdraws or cries when touched). For a child who is tactilely defensive, it helps if he sees the object as it touches him. In addition, firm pressure is less likely to provoke a negative reaction than is light pressure.

DAILY ROUTINES & FUNCTIONAL ACTIVITIES

Try this item once or twice each time you change the child's diaper or have other opportunities to play with the child for a few minutes.

CRITERION   On three or more occasions, the child looks for or reaches toward objects that touch him within easy sight.

8

■ ■ ■

8c. Repeats activities that produce interesting results

MATERIALS   A variety of "responsive" toys (e.g., crib mobiles, bells, squeaky toys made of very soft rubber)

PROCEDURES

Provide the child with a variety of toys that respond to very simple movements on the part of the child. Place them so that the child can contact them.

If the child does not seem to repeat activities that produce noises or sights, tie a bell to her wrist or ankle with brightly colored ribbon for 15-minute periods, three or more times a day. Observe the child carefully during this time to determine if she moves more with the bell on or off. To be sure of the effect, record the number of times she moves the wrist or ankle in the 3 minutes prior to attaching the bell, and compare that number with the number of times she moves it in the 3 minutes after the bell has been attached (allowing 3 minutes immediately after the bell is attached for the child to discover that movement produces sound).

If the child does not spontaneously move her limb that has the bell attached in the first minute, physically assist movement several times. Observe again to see if the child spontaneously moves.

Another approach is to attach one end of a string to the child's wrist or ankle and the other end of the string to a mobile or other easily seen toy in her crib so that limb movement causes the toy to move. Leave the string attached for no more than 10–15 minutes. Observe to see if the child moves more when the string is attached to the toy or when is the string is not attached. *Do not leave the child unattended if you have attached a limb to a toy with a string.*

DAILY ROUTINES & FUNCTIONAL ACTIVITIES

As you go about your daily routines, be sure that there are responsive toys available to the child. Children are often kept satisfied for a longer period of time when they have a variety of toys within reach to look at, hear, and feel. Responsive toys will usually interest the child the longer than nonresponsive toys.

CRITERION   The child repeats an activity three or more times to produce an interesting result.

■ ■ ■

8d. Plays with toys placed in hands

MATERIALS   A variety of small toys that the child can grasp easily and that create different effects (e.g., different sounds or movements) when manipulated

PROCEDURES

Place the child in whatever position allows him the greatest use of his hands while maintaining his visual attention to them (e.g., reclined in an infant seat or carrier). Place a toy in the child's hands and observe. If he drops the toy, pick it up, shake it or otherwise call attention to it, and give it to him again.

If the child does not hold the toy for more than a few seconds, try placing your hands over his and helping him manipulate the toy. Release your hands and observe.

DAILY ROUTINES & FUNCTIONAL ACTIVITIES

You should offer the child toys throughout the day (e.g., while he is in the infant carrier or stroller, during diaper changes).

CRITERION   The child plays with a toy that is placed in his hands for a few minutes.

■ ■ ■

8e. Persists in efforts to obtain an object or create an effect (e.g., manipulates a busy box or crib gym to create noises and/or interesting sights)

MATERIALS   A variety of interesting toys or household objects

PROCEDURES

Place an object slightly beyond the child's reach and observe her reactions. If she cries or immediately loses interest, bounce the toy or do something else to make it attractive and place it a little closer to her. Make it possible for the child to get the toy with some persistence. Gradually move the object further and further away to increase the amount of effort necessary or the length of time the effort must take.

Sometimes dangling a toy from a string so that it moves when the child tries to get it will help promote persistence.

DAILY ROUTINES & FUNCTIONAL ACTIVITIES

Observe what the child does when she wants an object that is out of her immediate reach. Such events occur frequently in the course of any child's day. Do not immediately give the objects to the child if it looks like she is trying to get them independently. To avoid frustration, you may want to push the object slightly closer or help in some other minimal way that will let the child get the desired object without your actually giving it to her.

CRITERION   *The child consistently persists in her effort to obtain a desired object. This should occur in several different situations.*

■ ■ ■

8f. Repeats activities that elicit interesting reactions from others

8

MATERIALS   None needed

PROCEDURES

When the child is making a face, clapping hands, or performing any desired action, respond to him immediately by laughing, cheering, or imitating him.

If the child does not repeat his own action, say something such as, "That's wonderful! Let's do it again." If the action lends itself to physical prompts, assist the child in doing it again.

DAILY ROUTINES & FUNCTIONAL ACTIVITIES

Watch for opportunities throughout the day to respond positively to something the child does. Observe to see if he will repeat the action.

Note: Some children are initially startled by adults' responses and become quite subdued and even resistant to repeating the activity. If this occurs, make responses to the child's behaviors more muted, but make it clear you enjoyed what he did.

CRITERION   On several occasions, the child repeats activities that elicit interesting reactions from other people.

■ ■ ■

8g. Looks for or reaches toward objects that make a noise while falling from view

MATERIALS   Spoon, bell, rattle, and other objects that would make a noise when striking the floor or other surface around the child

PROCEDURES

Hold an object at eye level, making sure that the child's attention is focused on it. Drop the object from view, making sure it makes a noise loud enough for the child to hear when it hits the floor (or other surface) and that it does not touch the child as it falls.

Observe whether the child searches visually or reaches toward the object in the appropriate direction. If the child does not look or reach, try one or both of the following:

• Show the object to the child again, bang it on the table (or other surface near her), and drop it. Then, bang it on the floor (or other lower surface), trying to attract the child's attention to it there. Return it to the table, and again bang it, then drop it.

• Hold the object at eye level, make a noise with it to attract the child's attention, move it slowly downward to the floor (or other surface below the child's waist level), and make the noise again. Physically assist the child in reaching for the object, if necessary, and allow her to play with it. After two or three trials, try dropping the object again. If necessary, again physically assist the child to reach toward the object, give it to her, and allow her some play time with the object.

DAILY ROUTINES & FUNCTIONAL ACTIVITIES

This is a good activity to try when the child is seated for other activities (e.g., eating, playing). Most children enjoy looking for objects that drop and will eventually drop them to amuse themselves. Note whether the child looks for or reaches toward an object after dropping it.

CRITERION   The child regularly looks for or reaches toward objects that make a noise while falling from view.

■ ■ ■

8h. Looks for or reaches
toward objects that fall quietly from view

MATERIALS   Stuffed animals or other soft toys that will make minimal noise when dropped on the floor

PROCEDURES

Hold an object at eye level, making sure that the child's attention is fixed on the object. Then, drop it from his view.

Watch carefully to see if the child looks for or reaches toward the dropped object. Vary the objects used and the positions from which they are dropped (e.g., away from midline but easily within view of the child).

If the child does not look for or reach toward the fallen object, hold it at midline eye level, then slowly move it vertically out of the child's sight. Move the object slowly enough so that the child can visually track the object.

DAILY ROUTINES & FUNCTIONAL ACTIVITIES

Do this activity whenever the child is seated and an adult or older child is available to drop objects and observe his reactions (e.g., before or after meals, sitting in an infant chair with toys on the tray). Do not provide more than five or six receptions, however, or the child will lose interest.

CRITERION   The child frequently looks for or reaches toward objects that have fallen quietly from view.

■ ■ ■

8i. Looks or moves in correct direction
for objects that fall and roll or bounce to a new location

8

MATERIALS   A variety of interesting toys that combine visual and auditory stimulation and that, when dropped, will bounce and/or roll from the child (e.g., squeaky toys, balls with bells inside)

PROCEDURES

Hold an object at eye level, and make sure that the child is attending to it. Drop the object within the child's view and in an area that allows it to bounce and/or roll, while remaining within the child's sight.

If the child does not look around to find the object, call her attention to where it is, and say something about it having rolled or bounced. Try again with a different object, perhaps one that is larger and/or makes a noise as it rolls or bounces.

Note: As you do this item, think about the language you are using. Stress location concepts such as "Uh-oh, *where* did it go?" "Is it *next* to the chair?" or "Maybe it went *under* the chair."

DAILY ROUTINES & FUNCTIONAL ACTIVITIES

Note what the child does when objects are dropped accidentally throughout the day. If the child does not look around, use the situation for a brief training session (i.e., show the child where the object went and then try dropping it again).

CRITERION   The child looks or moves in the correct direction for an object that has fallen and rolls or bounces. This should occur consistently if the child is attending to the object before it falls.

■ ■ ■

8j. Overcomes obstacles to get toys (e.g., removes covers, pushes barriers out of the way, reaches under a piece of furniture)

MATERIALS   Any favorite toys, various containers

PROCEDURES

Arrange a situation in which the child can see or hear an interesting toy but must overcome some simple obstacle to get it. For example, place the toy in a plastic container or behind a transparent box so that the child must dump the container, remove a loose-fitting lid, push a barrier aside, or do some other activity to get to the toy.

   If the child does not spontaneously overcome the obstacle, demonstrate for him how it can be done and/or physically guide him through the process. Reduce your help as rapidly as possible. Once a child masters one kind of obstacle, try others. Make it a game!

DAILY ROUTINES & FUNCTIONAL ACTIVITIES

Having obstacles between us and what we want is a typical part of everyday life. Observe how the child copes with such situations. If the child does not try to overcome obstacles and either cries for help or just gives up, provide help by encouraging him, demonstrating the task for him, and/or making the task a little easier for him. Do not solve the problem for the child, but help him solve it with your guidance.

CRITERION   The child overcomes an obstacle to get a toy or other desired object. This should occur several times with different kinds of obstacles.

■ ■ ■

8k. Plays with a variety of toys to produce effects

MATERIALS   Busy box or other responsive toys (i.e., toys that have an effect when pushed, pulled, poked, squeezed, or rocked).

PROCEDURES

Present the child with one toy that creates several different effects in response to different actions (e.g., a busy box) or two to three toys each creating a different sound or sight if acted on. Demonstrate for the child how to produce one of the effects from a toy. Then let the child explore the toy independently.

If the child does not imitate what you did to get the effect, demonstrate again, and physically guide her hand to push the button, pull the lever, and so forth.

After several trials with one effect, show the child how to get another effect from the same toy or from a different toy. Again physically guide her to create the effect if she does not do it spontaneously.

Later, give the child the two toys (or the busy box) and observe what she does. Does she try different actions to get the different effects?

Note: Be sensitive to the motor capabilities of the child. Select toys that require actions she is able to do. Work toward as much variety in movement and activity as the child's limitations and temperament will allow.

DAILY ROUTINES & FUNCTIONAL ACTIVITIES

Observe the child's play with a variety of responsive toys during the course of the day. Does the child manipulate the toys in such a way as to produce sight or sound effects? Does she experiment with novel toys or objects to determine what they can do? When the child tries these different activities with the toys, show interest and excitement about her accomplishments. Imitate what the child did with the toy or object.

CRITERION   The child plays with several different toys (or different parts of a busy box) to produce interesting effects. A child with severe motor impairments may pass the item by reliably operating a switch to create effects in two or more toys.

■ ■ ■

8I. Increases rate of usual activity with toy when it stops working or tries another activity to make toy work

MATERIALS   Toys with moving parts, toys that move when something is pushed or pulled, other interesting toys

PROCEDURES

The goal of this item is to observe what happens when the child is playing with a toy that breaks or stops working in the way he expects. You may want to take the batteries out of a favorite toy, or try taping together two parts on a toy that normally move. In cases when toys are not working as expected, the child may try doing the usual activity with the toy more frequently or with more force, or he may examine the toy, shake it, try another activity with the toy, and so forth. If the child does not attempt to get the toy to work and either cries or puts the toy aside, talk about what has happened, and try to fix the toy. Try to explain and demonstrate to the child that if an object doesn't work, he can try to do other things with it.

Try to set up situations in which you can interfere with the way the child usually plays with an object to see if he will try to remedy the situation. For example, if the child likes to bang a toy on the table to make a noise, place a towel or other sound-absorbing cover on the table so that the toy no longer makes the same noise. See what the child does.

DAILY ROUTINES & FUNCTIONAL ACTIVITIES

This kind of problem solving is best encouraged in natural events that occur throughout the day. Encourage and praise persistence when the child attempts to make something work.

CRITERION   The child increases his rate of usual activity with a toy when the toy stops working, or he tries another activity to make the toy work. This should be observed on a number of occasions with different toys or objects.

■ ■ ■

8m. Retrieves toys from container when they have been dropped through a hole in the top of container

MATERIALS   A variety of small toys, containers with holes to drop objects through (e.g., toy mailbox, shape boxes, a round oatmeal box with one or more holes cut in the top). The holes should be just large enough to accommodate the toys being dropped. It should be somewhat difficult to see the toys in the container after they have been dropped through the hole.

PROCEDURES

Drop one or more toys through the opening at the top of the container, saying, "Oops, where did it go?" Wait to see if the child lifts up the box, removes the lid, or does some other appropriate activity in an effort to retrieve the toy that indicates she understands where the toy is and how to get it back.

If the child does not attempt to retrieve the toy, demonstrate for her how to get it. Physically assist the child, if necessary, as she tries to get the toy.

Note: Although shape boxes are appropriate for teaching this activity, they may be frustrating to some children. If the child is having difficulty getting the toy into the container through the hole, change containers. It may be helpful to make your own containers from boxes, and begin with only one hole so that the child does not have to master shape or size discrimination along with retrieving the objects she has dropped into the container.

DAILY ROUTINES & FUNCTIONAL ACTIVITIES

Identify containers in use around the house or classroom (e.g., trash cans with lids) that would demonstrate the principles being taught in this item (i.e., an object drops when you let it go, the object is present even though you can no longer see it, and the object can be retrieved). For example, let the child drop some easily identifiable, heavy object in a can filled with waste paper. The object should sink to the bottom and out of sight. Ask, "Is the [object] in there?" Then, dump out the contents of the can on some newspaper, and find the object. Use this as an opportunity to expose the child to words such as *down, heavy, light, out, in,* and so forth.

CRITERION   On several occasions, the child retrieves toys from a container after they have been dropped through a hole in the top. Or, if the child is unable to retrieve the toys, she indicates *their location. The child is credited for this item even if she does not retrieve the toys until an adult asks where they are (i.e., the child may have the spatial concept but not the motivation to retrieve those particular toys until asked).*

■ ■ ■

8n. Reaches object from behind a barrier

MATERIALS   A variety of barriers that are common in the child's environment (e.g., partially opened door, upholstered armchair, cardboard box, box lid); various toys, including some of the child's favorites

PROCEDURES

Show the child a preferred toy, and make sure that he is paying attention to it.

While the child is watching, hide the toy behind a barrier, close enough to the child so that he can reach behind it. If the child does not reach behind (or move the barrier) to get the toy, demonstrate how to do so.

Make this a game. Laugh and talk as you play, making comments such as, "Here's Bunny," "Oops, there goes Bunny," "Where's Bunny?" "I found Bunny," and "Can you find Bunny?"

DAILY ROUTINES & FUNCTIONAL ACTIVITIES

Look for opportunities throughout the day to join the child's play, and try this item with a toy that he has nearby. Use furniture, magazines, curtains, or anything else that is handy for a barrier. The greater the variety of materials, the more the child will generalize the idea that he can retrieve objects hidden from him.

CRITERION   The child retrieves several different objects from behind a variety of different barriers. The child should know what to do on the first trial with a toy and a barrier that have not been used for training.

■ ■ ■

8

8o. Pulls string to get object from behind a barrier

MATERIALS   A variety of barriers common in the child's environment (e.g., partially opened door, upholstered armchair, cardboard box, box lid), various toys with strings attached (e.g., stuffed animal with a long tail, pull toys)

PROCEDURES

Show the child a toy, being sure that she is attending to and interested in it. Place the toy slightly out of the child's reach and demonstrate pulling the string to get it. Place the toy out of reach again with the string near the child's hand. Wait to see if the child pulls the string to get the toy. If she does not, physically prompt her to pull the string, then let her play with the toy. Next, while the child is watching, place a toy behind a barrier (e.g., behind the door or a piece of furniture, under or inside an open box) with the string near the child. See if she pulls the string to get the toy. If the child does not pull the string, pull it toward her, and let her play with the toy for a few minutes. During this process, talk to the child about what is happening (e.g., "Where did it go?" "Is it behind the door?" "Can you get it?").

DAILY ROUTINES & FUNCTIONAL ACTIVITIES

When the child is playing with a pull toy or other toy that could be used for this item, stop to play with her for a few minutes, using a magazine, box lid, or nearby piece of furniture for a barrier. Most children love hiding games and will respond well, even if it interrupts an ongoing activity for a few minutes.

CRITERION   The child retrieves an object from behind (inside or under) a barrier by pulling a string. This should occur with several different objects and several different barriers. The child should know what to do on the first trial when a new toy and barrier are introduced.

■ ■ ■

8p. Moves self around a barrier to get object

MATERIALS   A variety of barriers common to the environment (e.g., furniture, doors, curtains, boxes), numerous interesting toys

PROCEDURES

While the child is watching, place a preferred toy behind a barrier that the child must go around to get to the toy (e.g., drop the toy behind a chair, toss a toy behind the door). If the child does not go around the barrier to get the toy, go around the barrier and call to him, and talk about the toy that is there. If necessary, put the toy out into the child's view, shake it to attract his attention, then put it back behind the barrier.

DAILY ROUTINES & FUNCTIONAL ACTIVITIES

Watch throughout the day to see what the child does if a toy goes behind (or under) a barrier.

CRITERION   The child moves himself around a barrier to retrieve an object at least twice, with a different barrier each time. This would include scooting under a piece of furniture or going around it to get a toy or other object.

■ ■ ■

8q. Uses adults to solve problems

MATERIALS   Toys that create an interesting sight and/or sound for a period of time and then stop (e.g., wind-up toys, shape boxes, toy cash register, Jack-in-the-box)

PROCEDURES

Select a toy that requires a new and/or moderately difficult motor response from the child. Show the child how to get the desired effect from the toy. For example, wind up a toy car and let it run down. Observe the child's reaction when the effect stops. If she loses interest, try a new toy, or try the first one again, acting more excited about what happens.

If the child picks up the toy and tries but cannot work it, or if she cries, hold out your hand and say, "Do you want some help?" Be sure that the child watches how you make the toy work. Observe her reaction when the effect stops again.

If the child makes no attempt to imitate what you did to make the toy work, place your hands over her hands and demonstrate what to do. When the effect stops, encourage the child to try it on her own. If the child is unsuccessful, offer your help again and assist her. Provide as much help but no more help than the child requires to be successful.

DAILY ROUTINES & FUNCTIONAL ACTIVITIES

Children frequently ask for help with problems throughout the day. Do not simply do a task for the child. Demonstrate how it can be done and encourage the child to try. If she is unsuccessful, physically assist, but no more than necessary. Help the child feel that she has accomplished the task and that she should be proud of that fact.

CRITERION   On several occasions, the child requests help from an adult to make a toy work (e.g., the request can be in the form of handing the toy to the adult or looking back and forth between the adult and the toy to communicate that the adult should do something).

■ ■ ■

8r. Solves simple problems without adult assistance

MATERIALS   A variety of toys, various containers

PROCEDURES

Collect a box of toys or materials that are new to the child and will create some problems for him. Select materials carefully to fit a child's sensory and motor capabilities. Play with the child a while, showing him how some of the items work, but don't focus too much attention on your actions. Then, let the child play on his own as you observe, responding naturally to his attempts to involve you in play. Encourage the child to figure out his problems on his own, but give as much help as necessary to avoid undue frustration. Watch for the child's efforts to solve simple problems on his own (e.g., opening drawers to remove objects, removing various kinds of lids to get objects out of containers, finding an opening on a simple puzzle box).

DAILY ROUTINES & FUNCTIONAL ACTIVITIES

Observe the child's reactions to typical problems in the environment. At this developmental level, getting into drawers, closets, tool chests, and so forth is enjoyable for the child. While making the environment safe, allow the child to do some of this exploration. It will allow you to observe his problem-solving skills.

CRITERION   The child independently solves several simple problems, such as opening unfamiliar containers to get objects, discovering ways to make a new toy work, finding ways to get a toy he cannot reach, and so forth.

■ ■ ■

8s. Retrieves familiar objects
from usual locations in another room on request
8t. Puts away objects in correct places

MATERIALS   Toys and typical household or school objects that are placed on shelves or in other areas that are accessible to the child

PROCEDURES

Have the child gather some toys from the child's shelves or from her classroom. Play with the child using the toys. Then tell the child that it is time to clean up. Hand the child the toys, one at a time, and tell her to put them away. If she does not put it in the correct place, show her the correct place, and help her put it there.

DAILY ROUTINES & FUNCTIONAL ACTIVITIES

Keep the child's toys and other items in specific locations in the home or classroom whenever they are not in use.

Have the child observe you putting objects away and removing them so that she knows their location. Also, involve the child in picking up objects and putting them away. As you clean up, talk to the child about the location of items (e.g., "The ball goes on the bottom shelf"; "Help me remember, where do we keep this doll?").

When the child is able follow requests to bring you things that she can see (i.e., it is clear she understands the verbal direction, "Bring me the [object]"), begin asking her to bring toys or objects from another room. Do not tell the child where the object is if it is in its expected or usual location.

If the child is unable to get an item, go with her to get it. Point out and label its location. Arrange an opportunity to ask for that same object later in the day to reinforce the child's memory.

CRITERION 8s   On several different days, the child retrieves a familiar object from its usual location on request. The object should not be in sight when the request is made.

CRITERION 8t   The child puts away familiar objects in their correct place. The child should be able to put all familiar toys in their correct places when asked (or, if her motor impairment is too severe, she should be able to indicate the object's correct location).

■ ■ ■

8u. Uses tools to solve problems
(e.g., reaches with a stick, extends height with a stool)

MATERIALS   Small dowels, a broom, strings with loops at the ends, stools, chairs, a variety of toys (Everything necessary for this item should be available in a typical home or group care environment.)

PROCEDURES

Create spatial problems for the child and have various tools available for him to solve the problems. For example, engage the child in playing with a set of blocks that includes one or more dowels. Show the child how you can pull a toy toward you with the dowel. A few minutes later, "accidentally" push a block or other toy out of the child's reach (e.g., under a chair or other stable piece of furniture), and say, "Oops, I can't reach the block. How can we get it?"

Also, after using a stool several times to get something out of reach, place something up out of the child's reach and ask, "How do you think you could get that?"

If the child becomes frustrated with these problems, make suggestions, and provide physical assistance so that he can solve the problem. Make a point of not solving problems for the child, but, instead, encourage him to solve them independently or with only hints or suggestions from you. For example, if the child is trying to reach something that is too far away, put the broom or some other object next to the child and say, "Do you think it would help to use this?"

DAILY ROUTINES & FUNCTIONAL ACTIVITIES

Observe the child's responses when spatial problems naturally occur throughout the course of the day. Give the child hints or make suggestions that might help him solve the problem. Also, model a problem-solving approach to daily events. For example, when you are trying to carry too many items and keep dropping one, put some of the items in a grocery bag. Or, when you can't reach something on the top shelf, pull a chair over and climb up to get it. As you do these activities, describe for the child what you are doing.

CRITERION   The child spontaneously uses a tool to solve one or more spatial problems (i.e., without any physical or verbal prompts). Children with significant physical disabilities may get credit for using a switch to make something move from one place to another.

■ ■ ■

8v. Independently plays
with toys that require pushing buttons,
pulling strings, and/or operating switches to get effects

8

MATERIALS   A variety of toys that have different buttons, strings, and switches that produce different effects when manipulated (e.g., busy boxes, See 'n Say, other pull toys that make noises, music boxes, Jack-in-the-boxes). Just be certain the child is capable of the motor activity required for an effect.

PROCEDURES

When you introduce a new responsive toy to the child, show her how it works. Help her manipulate it by placing your hands over hers if she does not imitate you readily. When the child loses interest in one toy, introduce another toy that can be manipulated in a different way. Model for the child how to make the toy work, and help her use the toy on her own. Observe the child when she is playing independently to see if she spontaneously tries to make the toys work.

DAILY ROUTINES & FUNCTIONAL ACTIVITIES

Place the toys in different parts of the house or in different parts of a room so that they do not compete for the child's attention and so that she will stay with one for a reasonable period of time. Observe what the child does when she first notices a toy that can be manipulated to create an effect.

Observe whether the child is interested in the buttons on the TV or other electronic equipment. An interest in these buttons is a sign of curiosity about how things work, and it is better not to punish a child for this sort of curiosity. You may need to keep the remote control out of reach and temporarily cover reachable buttons with cardboard, however, until you can teach the child which buttons are "her" buttons to push and which are "yours."

CRITERION   The child plays with several toys that require pushing buttons, pulling strings or other devices to get an effect.

■ ■ ■

8w. Experiments with cause and effect when playing

MATERIALS   Empty gift-wrap or paper towel tubes, small toys, a funnel, jar lids

PROCEDURES

Gather together some common household items such as those listed above. Sit with the child, and show him some things you might do with these objects. For example, you could put a toy car in a tube and watch it roll out the other end when you place the tube at an angle, you could pour liquid into a funnel and watch it drain into a glass, or you could spin a jar lid on its side. After performing these tasks in front of the child, let him explore and play with the objects on his own. Observe to see if he imitates activities you have tried or tries variations on them.

DAILY ROUTINES & FUNCTIONAL ACTIVITIES

Make it clear to the child that you are interested in how everything works (e.g., when giving the child a bath, show him how heavy toys sink to the bottom of the tub and how light ones float; show him how cars and trucks stay still on a level surface but roll downward when the surface is tilted). Provide many objects for free play that will lend themselves to experimentation (e.g., blocks, cars, paper tubes, containers of different sizes).

Observe the child when he is playing alone or with other children. Watch for activities that indicate that he is either experimenting with the ideas that you have shared with him or experimenting on his own.

In a group setting, have the children collect rocks, sticks, or leaves when out walking. Put them, one by one, in a tub of water to see what floats and what sinks. Also, have each child bring in something in order to show others how it works—encourage parents to provide some sturdy household items so that the children can experiment with them (e.g., an old-fashioned egg beater that will make bubbles in the water if a little soap is added).

CRITERION   The child experiments with some materials or objects, apparently trying to understand how they work, on several occasions.

■ ■ ■

8x. Independently nests four containers, or stacks rings or blocks of graduated sizes

MATERIALS   Nesting cups (six or more), set of five or six blocks of graduated sizes, stacking rings (the center column should be in the form of a cone rather than a cylinder so that not all of the rings will fit unless placed in the proper order)

PROCEDURES

Show the child a set of nesting cups, separate them, and then show the child how they all fit together. Take them apart again and give them to the child to see if she can put them together properly. Do not provide help unless she begins to show signs of frustration. Take out any cup that has been placed incorrectly, and point to the one that it should go in. Give as much help in this way as necessary to complete the task. Let the child continue to play with the cups if she wishes, but do not insist on it. When doing the task yourself, use size words to emphasize what you are doing, and help the child master these concepts (e.g., "That one is too *big* to fit in there"; "Put the *little* one in last").

In the same manner as the cups, show the child how the rings can all fit on the pole.

Stack the blocks with the largest on the bottom and the smallest on top. Knock them down, and encourage the child to stack them. Do not correct the child unless she requests help or gets frustrated. Unless the blocks fall down, she may not see the point of attending to their sizes. You can encourage her, however, to attend to the sizes by making a tower with one set of blocks and asking her if she can make one just like it, giving verbal hints (e.g., "Find the biggest one, and put it on the bottom").

Keep these materials available for the child to explore on her own when she is interested. Many children find the challenge of these stacking and nesting toys irresistible and are delighted when they finally master them on their own.

DAILY ROUTINES & FUNCTIONAL ACTIVITIES

Look for opportunities in the environment to help the child attend to the relative sizes of objects. For example, when putting groceries away, show that you put the little can on top of the big can. At another time you should ask the child which of two cans you should put down first.

When the child tries to put something into a container that is too small, provide a larger container and, perhaps, show how one container fits into the other.

CRITERION   *The child nests or stacks at least four objects of graduated sizes without help.*

■ ■ ■

8y. Comments that something is not working when expected effects are not produced

MATERIALS   Battery-operated toys or other toys that can be made inoperable but are readily fixed (e.g., a truck with wheels that can be snapped in and out)

PROCEDURES

Present the child with some familiar toys that have been rendered inoperable (e.g., remove the batteries from a battery-operated toy). Observe what the child does when he tries to play with a toy and it does not work in the expected fashion. Does he describe it as broken or not working? Does he ask you to fix it?

DAILY ROUTINES & FUNCTIONAL ACTIVITIES

There are many opportunities in the course of the day for a child to learn that something is not working properly and needs to be fixed. When the battery in a toy runs down, the child may push the buttons harder or do other ineffective things to make it work. Be alert to these situations and talk about them (e.g., "It's not working. I wonder why. Maybe it needs new batteries. Let's see if that helps").

Whenever anything does not work for the caregiver or teacher, he or she should make comment such as, "It's broken" or "It's not working. What can we do to fix it?" If the problem is irreparable or requires help beyond what the caregiver can provide, it is important to communicate that as well (e.g., "Let's wait for Mommy and see if she can fix it"; "I guess we'll have to call the plumber so he can fix it"; "I don't think we can fix it. Let's throw it away and play with something else").

CRITERION   The child comments on several occasions when a toy or something else is not working and seeks to fix it or asks for help.

■ ■ ■

8z. Independently explores objects to determine their functions and/or shows other people how they work

MATERIALS   A few novel toys or other objects

PROCEDURES

Present the child with some novel toys or other objects, and allow her to explore them on her own. If she asks for help, suggest she try different actions with them or ask her what she thinks the objects might be used for. Try to avoid demonstrating what to do with the object so that the child will be challenged to experiment independently. Do not frustrate the child, however. Provide enough help for her to feel successful.

When the child does achieve some effect with an object, comment on it, and get her to show you how she did it.

DAILY ROUTINES & FUNCTIONAL ACTIVITIES

Observe throughout the day what the child does with toys or other objects. Does she immediately take them to someone to ask what to do with them, or does she begin experimenting to see what happens with them? If she immediately asks for help or a demonstration, do not show her; rather, make suggestions to encourage her to explore more effectively on her own.

Occasionally present the child with some common household object that is not dangerous and see what she does with it (e.g., old-fashioned egg beater, turkey baster, pliers, potato masher, flashlight). Also provide opportunities for the child to play with play dough or other art materials that encourage exploration.

Encourage the child to show another person (child or adult) how a toy or other object works.

Note: Typically, curious children will attempt to explore and use objects that may be dangerous for them. It is important to avoid punishing the child for her exploration but also to teach her that certain things in the environment are dangerous and must be left alone.

CRITERION   *On several occasions the child independently explores objects to determine their functions and/or shows other people how they work.*

■ ■ ■

8aa. Answers at least one "why do" question correctly (e.g., "Why do we have umbrellas?")

MATERIALS   None required

PROCEDURES

As you interact with the child, ask him some "why do" questions, such as "Why do we have shoes?" "Why do we have stoves?" "Why do we have eyes?" If he does not answer, tell him the answer and then ask the question again. Move on to another question. After a few days, ask the same questions to see if the child remembers. Also try new ones. It may help if the questions are related in some way to some objects the child is playing with or to an event that is happening (e.g., If it is a rainy day, ask, "Why do we have umbrellas?").

DAILY ROUTINES & FUNCTIONAL ACTIVITIES

Talk about why you do different chores in your daily routine. Provide reasons for many of the requests you make of the child (e.g., "You need to put on your boots to keep your feet dry. It is cold and wet out there"). When the child begins to ask, "Why?" provide an answer. Occasionally ask questions and then answer them yourself in order to model appropriate responses (e.g., "Why do we drink our milk? Because we want to get big and strong"). Then, gradually begin to ask the child "why" and "why do" questions.

A discussion of home or classroom safety rules provides a good opportunity to practice "why" and "why do" questions.

When reading stories to the child or a group of children, stop and ask, "why" and "why do" or "why did" questions.

Note: Do not focus on a child's motives when asking these questions. That is, don't ask the child, "Why do you hit your sister?" or "Why do you color on the walls?" Children of this age have little understanding of their motives. For this item, the issue is encouraging the child's understanding of the world around him.

CRITERION   *The child correctly answers several "why" or "why do" questions.*

REFERENCES

Gopnik, A., Meltzoff, A.N., & Kuhl, P.K. (1999). *The scientist in the crib: Minds, brains and how children learn.* New York: William Morrow & Co.

Hauser-Cram, P., & Shonkoff, J.P. (1995). Mastery motivation: Implications for intervention. In R.H. MacTurk & G.A. Morgan (Eds.), *Advances in applied developmental psychology: Vol. 12. Mastery motivation: Origins, conceptualization, and applications* (pp. 257–272). Norwood, NJ: Ablex Publishing.

9
Number Concepts

A child's ability to understand numbers begins during the toddler years when the child has concrete experiences with objects and hears others use words such as "more," "less," "just one," and so forth. Too often, however, in an effort to prepare children for school, the focus is on counting rather than on understanding quantity. Thus, a child may be able to count to 20 before he or she has any idea that the number names relate to quantities—that "one" is a different quantity from "two." Of course, the child needs to be able to say numbers in sequence before he or she can count objects, but *it is much more important for the child to learn to count objects by moving his or her finger from one object to the next (one-to-one correspondence) than it is to simply say the numbers.* It is also important for the child to be developing other concepts related to quantity (e.g., "more," "less," "lots," "few"). Although an adult takes these concepts for granted, a child must learn them through concrete experiences and through conversations with adults.

This sequence is short because most children do not begin to master concepts of number and quantity until around their second birthday. The groundwork for that mastery, however, begins with children manipulating objects and developing an understanding of some of the size concepts (e.g., "big," "little," "tiny"; see Sequence 10), as well as by hearing people use quantity and number words in their transactions with each other and with the child (e.g., "He has *lots* of toys," "Just *one*, please").

ADAPTATIONS

Children with Motor Impairments

Children whose motor impairments prevent both speech and reaching to touch objects may not be able to do some of the items in this sequence as they are written. Children with motor impairments can learn and demonstrate mastery of number concepts through eye gaze, but their progress may be slower. Active manipulation of materials greatly enhances the mastery of concepts of quantity.

Children with Visual Impairments

Children with visual impairments may need materials modified so that they are larger, have more contrast with the background, or have different colors.

It is much more difficult for children with severe visual impairments to develop a sense of quantity because people's first number concepts are usually very visual in nature. It may be necessary to teach children with severe visual impairments to move an object from one place to another as they say a number when counting rather than to point or touch.

Children with Hearing Impairments

Use signs to teach these items for children who use signs to supplement (or replace) speech.

9. NUMBER CONCEPTS

a. Understands "more" as an addition to some existing amount

b. Selects "just one"

c. Points and recites at least three numbers in correct sequence when asked to count objects

d. Correctly answers "how many" for one and two objects

e. Gives/selects two and three objects

f. Follows instructions including "all," "none," and "not any"

■ ■ ■

9a. Understands "more" as an addition to some existing amount

MATERIALS   Groups of blocks or other small objects

PROCEDURES

Give yourself and the child each a small group of blocks (three or four). Place a box of blocks nearby. Tell the child you are going to try to build a big house. Begin stacking your blocks, and encourage the child to stack his blocks on top of yours. When you both run out of blocks, say, "I think we need some more blocks. Please get us some more." If the child does not get the blocks, point to the box and say, "There they are. Get us some more blocks." If he still does not get them, you should get a handful and say, "Here's some more blocks. Let's build our house bigger." Try a similar activity using some other objects.

DAILY ROUTINES & FUNCTIONAL ACTIVITIES

When the child is eating a meal or having a snack, make a point of asking him if he wants more before giving him an additional amount. Also use the term "more" when you distribute play materials (e.g., "Here are some more blocks" or "Let me get you some more crayons").

Check the child's understanding of this use of "more" by asking him to give you more of something (e.g., "Thank you for giving me a bit of your cookie. May I have some more?" or "I need some more blocks to build this tower. Please get me some more").

Note whether the child says or signs "more" when he wants more.

CRITERION   *The child appropriately says or signs "more" and/or follows directions to give more on several occasions.*

9

■ ■ ■

9b. Selects "just one"

MATERIALS   Five or six toys (e.g., small cars, blocks, animals, other toys), a box or other container

PROCEDURES

Give a group of objects to the child to explore and play with. After a few minutes say, "May I have just one of your [toys]?" Other instructions, for example, might be to put just one in a box or to give just one to Mommy. Hold out your hand when asking for the object, and continue to hold it out for a few seconds after the child has placed one object in it to be sure that she understands "just one" and is not going to continue placing objects in your hand.

DAILY ROUTINES & FUNCTIONAL ACTIVITIES

Focus the child's attention on numbers by counting out loud at every opportunity (e.g., when getting the dinnerware to set the table, when getting mittens or socks for the child to put on). Hold up your fingers as you count. For example, hold up two fingers and say, "I need two socks." Then count the socks, *one* (hold it up), *two* (hold the second one up). Concentrate on the numbers up to 5, as these are the numbers that will first become meaningful. After concentrating on the numbers, begin giving instructions that involve *just one* (e.g., "You can have just one cookie"; "Bring me just one spoon"). Always correct errors by counting (e.g., "Whoops, you took three cookies. See, one, two, three. I said just one. Here is one cookie").

Play finger games or sing songs that involve counting and showing the quantity with fingers.

In a group, pass around the container of scissors, hunks of clay, or markers with the instruction to take *just one*. Always correct errors by counting the objects one by one.

CRITERION   *The child selects "just one" on several occasions without errors.*

■ ■ ■

9c. Points and recites at least three numbers in correct sequence when asked to count objects

MATERIALS   Groups of 5–10 objects

PROCEDURES

Place five objects in a row in front of the child. Be sure to leave at least 1 inch between objects. Say, "Let's count these [objects]. One, two, three, four, five. Now you do it. One . . ." Touch an object each time you say a number. Encourage the child to point to the objects as he imitates your counting. Prompt the child as much as necessary to get him to say the numbers.

After the child has begun to say two or three numbers in sequence without prompting, begin asking the child to count the objects before you model the behavior. If he does not begin counting say "one . . ." to see if that will get him started.

Many children will learn the correct sequence of numbers but always wait for the adult to say "one" before adding "two, three, four." Do not try to correct the child, but continue to model counting appropriately yourself.

Note: It is easier for a child to count if you place the objects in a row rather than in other configurations. Do not expect the child to touch the objects in an orderly sequence as he is learning to count. Show that you are happy he is touching them and continue modeling touching them in sequence.

DAILY ROUTINES & FUNCTIONAL ACTIVITIES

Count various objects (10 or fewer) as opportunities arise throughout the day. Point with your finger as you count. Encourage the child to point as you count and to say the numbers with you.

CRITERION   On three different occasions the child correctly says a sequence of any three numbers when asked to count a group of objects (e.g., two, three, four; four, five, six). It is permissible for the adult to begin the count.

■ ■ ■

9d. Correctly answers "how many" for one and two objects

MATERIALS   Various interesting objects or toys

PROCEDURES

Place one object in front of the child and say, "How many [objects] are there?" If she does not answer say, "There is one [object]. How many?"

When the child is reliably identifying one object, begin placing two and asking "How many?" Correct errors.

DAILY ROUTINES & FUNCTIONAL ACTIVITIES

Frequently ask the child number questions during the course of the day (e.g., "How many cookies do you have?" "Look at this bear, how many eyes does he have?"). If the child does not answer correctly, count aloud for her while pointing to the objects in question (e.g., "One, two. He has two eyes"). Then, move on to another similar question (e.g., "Now, how many eyes does Mommy have?").

Use snack time as well as other activity times to ask questions about numbers. If there is a group of children, make sure that each child has a chance to respond before another child answers the question for him or her. Get the group to count together to check an answer (e.g., "Let's see if John is right. Let's count the cookies. One, two, three . . .").

CRITERION   The child correctly answers three or more questions involving "one" and correctly answers three or more questions involving "two."

■ ■ ■

9e. Gives/selects two and three objects

MATERIALS   A box of blocks

PROCEDURES

Give the child a box of blocks. Tell him you are going to make something. Ask him to give you two blocks. If he gives you some other number, count them as you point to them and say, "That's not two, it is [number of] blocks. Here are two blocks." Begin constructing a tower and then ask for two more blocks. Continue building and asking for two until he is selecting two reliably. Follow the same procedure in asking for three blocks.

DAILY ROUTINES & FUNCTIONAL ACTIVITIES

Build this into daily routines such as setting the table ("Please give me two forks"), serving snacks ("You may take three cookies"), and cleaning up ("You pick up three toys, and I'll pick up three toys").

In a group setting, let the children take turns handing out crayons or other objects (e.g., "Give everyone two pieces of paper"; "Give everyone three cookies").

CRITERION   The child selects two and three objects without error on at least five occasions.

■ ■ ■

9f. Follows instructions
including "all," "none," and "not any"

MATERIALS   Blocks and other small toys

PROCEDURES

Put a group of toys in front of the child and give instructions involving "all," "none," and "not any." For example, "Put all of the blocks in the box," "Pick up the cars until there are not any left on the table," "One of these boxes has some blocks in it, one has none. Show me the box that has none." If the child makes errors, correct her using the words or phrases again.

DAILY ROUTINES & FUNCTIONAL ACTIVITIES

Use the words "all," "none," and "not any" as you talk about what you are doing with the child (e.g., "Let's gather up all of the toys. Oops, we missed one. Let's get all of them. Now we've done a good job. There are not any toys left"). Look for opportunities throughout the day to ask the child to bring you (or pick up or give you) all of a group of objects (e.g., "Put all of the spoons in the dishwasher"). Also, look for opportunities to say things such as, "I don't have any. You see, there are none there." Also, pay attention to these words as you read stories or nursery rhymes (e.g., Old Mother Hubbard: "and then the poor dog had none").

In a classroom, use the terms "all," "none," and "not any" as appropriate to describe daily activities (e.g., "I want all of the girls over here and all of the boys over there," "There are not any blocks on the shelves. Please put all the blocks on the shelves"). Also, look for stories to read that include these words. Put your finger on the picture to show that "all" includes everyone. Make it clear that when objects are all gone, there are "none." Give instructions to individual children that involve giving you all of the crayons and putting all of the toys on the shelf.

CRITERION   The child correctly follows instructions involving "all," "none," and "not any" on several different occasions.

10
Concepts/Vocabulary: Receptive

In the period between birth and 3 years, children progress from making simple discriminations to attaching labels to relatively abstract characteristics of objects (e.g., color, size, shape). This sequence focuses on children's growing ability to relate their perceptions of the world to the words they hear. For example, a young child may initially label all four-legged animals *dogs*, but as the child's experience broadens, he or she will recognize characteristics that distinguish dogs from other animals and will begin to correctly label cats, dogs, cows, and so forth. Later, the child will learn more inclusive categories (e.g., animals) and more exclusive categories (e.g., puppies). Likewise, the child may learn to think of a particular object as soft, gradually include other objects in the soft category, and only then begin to develop the idea that softness is a relative term (i.e., although two things are soft, one is softer than the other). This refining and broadening of concepts continues for a lifetime.

This sequence is concerned with children's understanding of verbal labels. Before labels can be learned, however, a child must be able to make certain discriminations. As a general rule, a child is able to match before he or she can sort, sort before select, and select before naming on the basis of abstract characteristics. For example, a child may be able to match colored discs to pictures of colored discs before he or she can sort a collection of blocks into separate piles based on color. The child may be able to sort the blocks into piles based on color before he or she can select a red block from a pile of mixed blocks. Finally, the child may be able to match, sort, and select but still not be able to name the colors of the blocks. Some children appear to go through these four steps almost simultaneously; others progress from one to the other slowly. Because it is necessary to know whether a child is able to discriminate objects on the basis of abstract characteristics before trying to teach labels for those characteristics, several of the items in this sequence are cross-referenced with matching and sorting tasks in Sequence 6: Visual Perception.

ADAPTATIONS

Children with Motor Impairments

Consult with children's physical and/or occupational therapists to determine the best position and adaptive equipment to allow the children to point to or select pictures/objects. If necessary, use eye gaze or a yes/no response to identify the object a child is choosing. Likewise, it is possible to do sorting activities by having the child indicate through pointing, eye gaze, or a yes/no response where the objects are to be placed. See Appendix D at the end of the book for a description of an object board that may be used for sorting activities and some suggestions for increasing the reliability of eye-gaze responses.

Children with Visual Impairments

Help children with severe visual impairments to feel objects carefully in order to get a sense of size, shape, and other characteristics. Talk about these characteristics as the children explore the objects. Select objects that emphasize the particular characteristics you want the children to notice. Depending on the extent of the impairment, it may be impossible for some children to discriminate colors. If a child is able to match and sort on the basis of size and shape (through tactile cues) but cannot match or sort colors, he or she will not be able to label colors. It is, however, important to continue to use color names. As the child gets older, he or she will know that grass is green and the sky is blue even though she will not have the same mental constructs for those words as people with vision do.

Children with Hearing Impairments

The adaptations required for children with hearing impairments depend largely on the kind of communication program that each child's parents and therapist have determined to be appropriate. Some children will be in an oral program. Natural gestures may be used along with speech, but the use of manual signing will be discouraged. Some children will be using *total communication* in which speech is accompanied by American Sign Language or some other signing system. Some parents who have severe hearing impairments and communicate only by signing may want signing to be the child's primary means of communication. It is important to discuss these issues with the parent's and the child's therapist to determine what kinds of signs and gestures are suitable for the child's educational program.

   If the child is using a communication system that includes signing, all of the items in this sequence can be considered mastered if the child follows signed directions.

   Note: Some therapists recommend supplementing speech with signs for children who do not have hearing impairments but who are having difficulty mastering language. For these children, it is also acceptable to give the directions in a combination of speech and signs.

10. CONCEPTS/VOCABULARY: RECEPTIVE

a. Points to three objects or people on request

b. Shows shoes, other clothing, or object on request

c. Points to most common objects on request

d. Points to three pictures of animals or objects on request

e. Points to three body parts on request

f. Sorts objects/pictures into simple categories (e.g., dogs, cats, houses, chairs) when given an example

g. Follows directions to indicate an understanding of "you," "me," "your," and "my"

h. Points to 15 or more pictures of animals and/or common objects on request

i. Points to five body parts on request

j. Selects "big" and "little" when given a choice between two objects/pictures

k. Selects examples of two or more inclusive categories

l. Points to or shows three or more of the following: tongue, chin, neck, shoulder, knee, elbow, ankle

m. Selects pictures of actions

n. Follows directions including "in," "out," "on," and "off"

o. Selects a similar object/picture when shown a sample and asked to find "another one"

p. Selects objects/pictures that are "the same" or "like this"

q. Selects "biggest" and "littlest" (or "smallest") from a group of three objects/pictures

r. Select objects/pictures to indicate an understanding of at least two relative concepts or comparisons

s. Points to five or more colors on request

t. Selects objects and pictures to indicate which are square and which are round

u. Selects objects by usage

v. Understands part–whole relationships

■ ■ ■

10a. Points to three objects or people on request

10

MATERIALS   A group of familiar objects or toys

PROCEDURES

Place three objects in front of the child. Say, "Show me [object]" or "Touch [object]." If she does not do what you ask, touch the object and name it. Then, place the child's hand on it and name it again. Ask for other objects in the same way.

   If a parent, sibling, or other familiar person is nearby, ask, "Where's [person]?" Point to the person if the child does not point or look directly at that person.

DAILY ROUTINES & FUNCTIONAL ACTIVITIES

Throughout the day, notice what or who is capturing the child's attention. Label whatever the child seems to be interested in (e.g., "Here comes Daddy," "Nice doggie. Pat the nice doggie," "Ball. Roll the ball").

Call the child's attention to items that interest you by handing them to the child or by pointing to them as you call them by name. If you are carrying the child, let her touch the object, and then back up a little so that her arm is still extended toward the object but not touching it as you talk about it and point with your free hand. If the child does not begin to imitate your pointing, hold up her arm in the direction that you pointed as you say, "See the [object]?"

Begin to ask the child, "Where's [person]?" or "Where is the [object]?" beginning with things you have named several times for her. If the child does not point or otherwise indicate the object, you point and say, "There it is, right there. See the [object]?" Physically prompt the child to point if that is reasonable in the situation.

CRITERION   *The child points to three objects or people, each on several occasions. Most children will point with the whole hand or a finger. It is also acceptable for the child to touch or pick up the objects that were named. Eye gaze may be used instead of pointing, if appropriate.*

■ ■ ■

10b. Shows shoes, other clothing, or object on request

MATERIALS   None required

PROCEDURES

Ask the child, "Where are your shoes?" If he does not reply, touch his shoes and say, "There they are. These are your shoes." Touch them (or look at them, or hold them up if the child cannot reach). Then ask for two other articles of clothing following the same procedure. Finally, repeat asking for each of them in turn, prompting as necessary.

DAILY ROUTINES & FUNCTIONAL ACTIVITIES

When you dress the child, talk about his clothing, labeling each piece and noting relationships between them and the part of the body they cover. For example, "Give me your foot. First we put on the sock. Then the shoe goes over the sock." Ask the child to hand you different items of clothing.

When the child gets some new article of clothing, ask him to show it to another person. If he does not, you should point it out for him.

CRITERION   *The child shows his shoes, other clothing, or some object in response to the request to show or touch that object.*

■ ■ ■

10c. Points to most common objects on request

MATERIALS   Objects found in a typical home or group care environment (e.g., cup, spoon, fork, ball, toy truck or car, comb, book)

PROCEDURES

Place three or four objects in front of the child. Hold out your hand and say, "Please give me the [object]." If she does nothing or gives you the wrong object, say, "Here is the [object]. Please give it to me." Physically prompt her to hand it to you if necessary. Repeat with other objects.

Change the instruction to "Show me the [object]," "Touch the [object]," and "Point to the [object]" to teach the child different ways of identifying objects. Prompt as necessary.

DAILY ROUTINES & FUNCTIONAL ACTIVITIES

Proceed as for Item 10a—Regularly name objects in which the child shows an interest; present other objects to her, label them, and talk about them; ask the child where one of her favorite toys is; ask her where other things are.

Note: Most young children do not have systematic scanning skills and may have trouble pointing to an object simply because they do not see it among the other things around it. Focus on asking the child to identify objects within reach or directly in front of her.

CRITERION   *The child points to most common objects (at least 10). Identification may be by any clear response, including touching, pointing, giving, and eye gaze.*

■ ■ ■

10d. Points to three pictures of animals or objects on request

MATERIALS   Books, magazines

PROCEDURES

Place three or four pictures in front of the child. Say, "Show me the [animal/object]," "Touch the [animal/object]," "Where is the [animal/object]?" or "Point to the [animal/object]." If he does nothing or indicates the wrong picture, say, "Here is the [animal/object]. Touch it". Physically prompt the child to point if necessary. Repeat with other pictures. Vary the instructions so that the child learns that "where is," "show me," "touch the," and "point to" are similar instructions.

10

DAILY ROUTINES & FUNCTIONAL ACTIVITIES

Spend at least 5–10 minutes each day reading to the child, using books with colorful pictures of animals and common objects. Tell or read as much of a story as the child will sit still for. Do not restrain an active child, but try to keep him interested by moving quickly from picture to picture and speaking with as much animation as possible. Point to pictures and label them. If necessary, help the child point to or touch the pictures as you label them.

Once the child has begun to point at pictures in books you have read several times, try showing him other books or magazines to see if he will point to less familiar pictures.

When you are with the child in the car, at the grocery store, or in other situations in which pictures are around on signs, food cartons, and so forth, point to and label what you see. Ask the child to find the items that you name.

CRITERION   *The child points to at least three pictures of animals or objects.*

■ ■ ■

10e. Points to three body parts on request

MATERIALS   None required

PROCEDURES

Sit facing the child. Ask her, "Where is my nose?" Help her touch it if she does not do it spontaneously. Then ask, "Where is your nose?" Repeat with eyes, ears, hair, mouth, hands, feet, stomach, and so forth. Introduce a doll or a stuffed animal, and ask the child to find its body parts.

DAILY ROUTINES & FUNCTIONAL ACTIVITIES

When you are dressing or bathing the child, talk about her hair, hands, feet, stomach, nose, eyes, ears, and other body parts as you touch them. Also, give instructions that aid in dressing, and use the body part names (e.g., "Lift up your hands," "Let me wipe your nose").

When the child is playing with a stuffed animal or doll, ask her to find the eyes, ears, feet, and so forth. Talk about the differences between the animals (e.g., the dog's big floppy ears and the mouse's little ears) or between a doll and an animal.

When you look at books with the child, point out the various parts of the animals or people. Ask the child to point to them as well.

If in a group situation, sing songs that include pointing to (or otherwise indicating a knowledge of) body parts (e.g., "When you're happy and you know it, clap your hands [stomp your feet, shake your head, touch your nose, and so forth]").

CRITERION   *The child points to or otherwise indicates three body parts. The child should be able to do this spontaneously (i.e., not just after a period of trying to teach her).*

■ ■ ■

10f. Sorts objects/pictures into simple categories (e.g., dogs, cats, houses, chairs) when given an example

MATERIALS   Several containers, a variety of toys and objects. (Objects in the same category should include different kinds and sizes of members in that category—e.g., dogs should include different breeds; beads should include square, round, oblong, big, and small.)

PROCEDURES

Give the child two or three containers and a mixed group of toys or other objects. Select objects that he can sort easily into the number of containers provided. For example, give the child three containers and a mixed assortment of toy dogs, small blocks, and wooden beads (three to five of each). Show him how to sort the objects, placing one item in each container and naming it. Ask the child to sort the remainder of the objects into the containers.

DAILY ROUTINES & FUNCTIONAL ACTIVITIES

Enlist the child's help in clean-up activities that often involve sorting toys into different containers.

Keep a collection of objects to sort near the telephone. When you are talking on the telephone or are busy in some other capacity, give the collection to the child to sort (changing it frequently so that the child will maintain interest).

CRITERION   The child sorts objects/pictures into simple categories on several occasions when given an example.

■ ■ ■

10g. Follows directions to indicate an understanding of "you," "me," "your," and "my"

MATERIALS   A variety of small toys and a doll or stuffed animal

PROCEDURES

Divide a group of toys, placing some in front of you, some in front of a doll, and some in front of the child. Give instructions such as, "I am going to give you one of my [objects], and I will give one to her (the doll). Please give me one of your [objects]. Now, give one to her," "Take one of my [objects]. Give it to her," "Pick up one of her [objects]. Give it to me." Correct the child if she makes errors. Prompt correct responses with hand-over-hand assistance if necessary.

DAILY ROUTINES & FUNCTIONAL ACTIVITIES

Use pronouns regularly in interactions with the child. She may still be using only names when talking about people but you should use a combination of names and pronouns so that she learns to associate the name and the pronoun. For example, say, "Give it to me" (instead of "Give it to Mommy"), "Please put your shoes in the closet," "Whose hat is this? It is your hat. May I wear it? Okay, you wear it."

Look for opportunities to stress these pronouns as you give instructions to the child so that you can determine if she understands them.

10

CRITERION   The child follows one or more directions that indicate an understanding of "you," "me," "your," and "my" without the adult pointing or saying the name of the person. Note that most children can follow directions involving pronouns before they are able to use them correctly.

■ ■ ■

10h. Points to 15 or more pictures of animals and/or common objects on request

MATERIALS   Books, magazines, picture cards

PROCEDURES/DAILY ROUTINES & FUNCTIONAL ACTIVITIES

See instructions for Item 10d.

CRITERION   On several occasions, the child points to or otherwise indicates knowledge of at least 15 pictures of common animals and/or objects.

■ ■ ■

10i. Points to five body parts on request

MATERIALS   None required

PROCEDURES/DAILY ROUTINES & FUNCTIONAL ACTIVITIES

See instructions for Item 10e.

CRITERION   On several occasions, the child points to or otherwise identifies at least five body parts.

■ ■ ■

10j. Selects "big" and "little" when given a choice between two objects/pictures

MATERIALS   Similar toys that are of distinctly different sizes (e.g., Matchbox cars and cars 6–8 inches long, large and small stuffed animals)

PROCEDURES

Work on this item at the same time you work on sorting big and little (Item 6-IIa). After the child is able to sort items according to whether they are big or little, begin showing him two objects that vary widely in size, and ask him to give you the big one or the little one. Continue with other pairs of objects, gradually reducing the amount of difference in the sizes so that the child learns that "big" and "little" are relative terms.

DAILY ROUTINES & FUNCTIONAL ACTIVITIES

Use the terms "big" and "little" frequently as you talk about or show objects to the child. There should be many opportunities throughout the day to ask the child to bring you something that you can describe as big or little. Or, you can incorporate this into meal times by talking about big bites or little bites, asking the child if he would like a big cracker or a little one, and so forth.

CRITERION   The child correctly identifies big and little objects five or more times.

10k. Selects examples of two or more inclusive categories (e.g., animals, toys, foods)

MATERIALS   Pictures, magazines, books, small toys

PROCEDURES

Look at a book or a magazine with the child and say, "Let's see how many animals we can find in this book. Do you see any animals on this page? How about this page?" Give her an example if necessary (e.g., "Here's a horse. It is an animal. Can you find another animal?"). Point to ones she misses, and correct any errors. Follow the same procedure with another category.

Place a group of toys in front of the child (e.g., four cars, four animals, four trucks, four pieces of dinnerware from a child's tea set). Ask her to find all of the animals and put them in one place. Return the animals to the mix, and ask the child to find all of the trucks. Continue with the other categories.

DAILY ROUTINES & FUNCTIONAL ACTIVITIES

As you talk to the child, you will probably introduce category words without being aware of it. One of the first category words that children learn is *toys* because caregivers usually ask them to pick up the toys or bring them the toys. When looking at a picture book of animals, it is natural to say, "Look at all these animals! Here's a pig, and here's a cow."

Pay attention to the words that you are using with the child. If you have not introduced category words or have introduced only a few, make a conscious effort to interject more new words. Some good ones to begin with are toys, clothes, dishes, animals, vegetables, fruits, drinks, and desserts. Help the child to understand what belongs in a particular category by sorting. For example, when picking up the toys, you may find a sock or some other "nontoy" on the floor with the toys. Ask the child, "Is this a toy?" If the child says "yes," say, "No, it is not a toy. It's a sock and should go in the basket with the dirty clothes." Or, when you are unloading the dishwasher, show the child how to sort the forks, spoons, and knives as they are put in the drawer.

Note: There will always be some confusion about categories because an object may belong to one or another depending on usage or other characteristics. For example, doll clothes may be put in the pile with the toys, rather than in the hamper with the clothes of family members. When a child sorts in a way you would not sort, try to figure out her reasoning. Talk about it with the child.

10

CRITERION   The child understands two or more category words. This may be demonstrated by sorting, by correctly indicating how someone else should sort, by using category words correctly to describe an object or a group of objects, or by any other means, as long as it is clear that the child understands the categories.

■ ■ ■

10l. Points to or shows three or more of the following: tongue, chin, neck, shoulder, knee, elbow, ankle

MATERIALS   Dolls, animals, pictures of people and animals

PROCEDURES

Ask the child to show you each of the above body parts. If he does not, show them to him on yourself. Then ask him to find his. Physically prompt him to touch these parts if necessary.

DAILY ROUTINES & FUNCTIONAL ACTIVITIES

Play games with the child in which you name and touch parts of his body (e.g., "Here comes a little bug, walking up your arm and tickles your chin"). When the child is touching you, name the part that he is touching (e.g., "That's Mommy's neck"). If you hurt yourself or the child hurts himself, name the part that is hurt ("Oh, dear, you skinned your knee").

Sing songs that involve touching body parts. For example, "If You're Happy and You Know It Clap Your Hands (touch your chin, stomp your feet, touch your knee, and so forth)" or "Head, Shoulders, Knees, and Toes" (substituting other parts in different verses, e.g., "tongue, neck, tummy, and ankles").

Occasionally, ask the child to point to the body parts listed above on himself, on you, or on a doll or stuffed animal.

CRITERION   The child points to or shows three or more of the following: tongue, chin, neck, shoulder, knee, elbow, ankle. Each part must be identified in several trials, without errors.

■ ■ ■

10m. Selects pictures of actions (e.g., eating)

MATERIALS   Books, magazines

PROCEDURES

Look at a book with the child and say, "Look at this page. Who is sleeping?" (There should be at least one other person or animal doing something else on the same page.) Or, say, "Let's look through this book and see if you can find someone who is running." Point out pictures the child omits. Repeat this activity often using a variety of books.

DAILY ROUTINES & FUNCTIONAL ACTIVITIES

Read often to the child using colorful picture books. Talk about the pictures as well as read the story. Once the child is familiar with the book, begin asking her to show you who is doing some action, such as eating, sleeping, or jumping.

When you sit to look at a magazine, encourage the child to sit with you. Talk about the ads and what the people are doing in them. Ask the child to point to people or animals doing various activities.

CRITERION   *The child selects (by pointing, touching, naming) action pictures of people or an-imals. The child should be able to identify at least three different actions.*

■ ■ ■

10n. Follows directions
including "in," "out," "on," and "off"

MATERIALS   Typical household objects and containers

PROCEDURES

Place some small toys or blocks and a container in front of the child. Give instructions that include "in," "out," "on," and "off." For example, tell the child, "Put the car in the box," "Take the blocks out of the box," "Put the ball on the chair," "Take the ball off the chair." Correct errors by demonstrating the action you requested. Then repeat the instruction. Use hand-over-hand assistance if necessary to help the child understand instruction. Always praise the child for accomplishing the task even if it is with your assistance.

DAILY ROUTINES & FUNCTIONAL ACTIVITIES

Think about these prepositions as you give children instructions. Give special emphasis to them (e.g., "The blocks go *in* the box, and the books go *on* the shelf," "Please take the book *out* of the box," "Please take your elbows *off* the table"). Use these words to talk about what you are doing, and play games with the child that will involve these words. For example, hide something and say, "Can you find the [object]? Look in the drawer; look on the table."

In a group setting, set up simple obstacle courses that require the children to go into, crawl out of, and climb onto various pieces of furniture or play equipment. As they are doing this ask, "Hey everybody, where is Nell? There she is in the tunnel. Now she's coming out!" Give instructions including these words to individual children as well as to the group to assess whether each child has mastered the concepts.

CRITERION   *The child follows instructions that require an understanding of "in," "out," "on," and "off." The child must demonstrate an understanding of each word in at least two different instructions (e.g., "Put the block in the box," "Take the spoons off the table," "Put the book on the shelf," "Take the shoes out of the box").*

10

■ ■ ■

10o. Selects a similar object/picture
when shown a sample and asked to find "another one"

10p. Selects objects/pictures that are "the same" or "like this"

MATERIALS   Picture books; picture cards from a memory game; common objects found in a home, classroom, outdoors, or elsewhere.

PROCEDURES

Give the child a collection of 8–10 objects/pictures representing three or more classes, such as cars, trucks, airplanes, blocks, spoons, and so forth. Have one representative from each of the classes for yourself. Hold out one of your objects and say, "I have one [object], can you find me another one?" If he does not give you another object of the same class, help him look through his objects to find one. If he gives you some other object, describe how it is similar to or different from the object you have, and help him find the object in the same class as yours (e.g., "That is sort of like a car because it has wheels, but it is a truck. I need another car").

Give the child another collection of objects in which there are exact duplicates of the objects you have. Hold up one of your objects, and tell him to find one that is just like or the same as the one you have. If he gives you one that is in the same class but is not ex- actly the same, tell him that he did a good job of looking but that he needs to find one that is just the same. Help him find it. Put the two next to each other and say, "See, these are just the same. They are alike." Try again with other objects.

Follow similar procedures using pictures instead of objects. An animal memory or lotto game will provide good pictures. Practice until the child understands that "another one" is less specific than "one just the same" or "one just like this."

DAILY ROUTINES & FUNCTIONAL ACTIVITIES

Children learn concepts of similarity and difference from daily exposure to them. When helping the child play with blocks, ask him to find "another one." Or, looking at a book say, "There's a dog. Can you find another one?" If the child selects something different than you have in mind (e.g., a cow instead of a dog), talk to the child about how the two things are the same (both animals) and how they are different (e.g., size, shape, sounds they make).

Proceed to more difficult discriminations in which you ask the child to find "one just like this" or "the same as this one." For example, show the child a picture of four different dogs, and ask him to find the one that is the same as one of the dogs.

CRITERION 10o   On several occasions, the child follows directions to find "another one" when shown a sample. Remember that "another one" is less specific than "same" or "just like" (the other dog may look quite different from the one you first selected).

CRITERION 10p   On several occasions, the child finds "one that is the same" and "one just like this," when shown a sample.

■ ■ ■

10q. Selects "biggest" and "littlest" (or "smallest") from a group of three objects/pictures

MATERIALS   Various objects of different sizes or pictures of objects of different sizes

PROCEDURES

Lay out three objects or find pictures that have three objects of different sizes, and ask the child to point to the biggest and the littlest. Correct the child if she makes an error. Try another set of three objects or pictures.

DAILY ROUTINES & FUNCTIONAL ACTIVITIES

Use the terms "biggest" and "littlest" (or "smallest," depending on your preference) in addition to just "big" and "little" as you describe things in the environment (e.g., "I'm going to give you the biggest cookie. I will save the littlest cookie for me").

As you read books or look at the pictures in books, describe the objects in size terms. An especially good book to use for this item is *The Three Billy Goats Gruff.*

Note: Although this item emphasizes "biggest" and "littlest" because "big" and "little" tend to be the first size terms children use, it is a good idea to introduce a variety of terms such as "large," "tiny," "small," and so forth.

CRITERION   *The child identifies the "biggest" and the "littlest" (or "smallest") among several different sets of three objects or pictures.*

■ ■ ■

10r. Selects objects/pictures to indicate an understanding of at least two relative concepts or comparisons (e.g., "soft/hard," "heavy/light," "rough/smooth," "fat/skinny," "thick/thin," "short/tall," "tiny/large," "short/long," "bumpy/smooth")

MATERIALS   A variety of objects (e.g., stuffed animals, blocks, pillows, chairs, rocks, feathers, pieces of string) that differ in the above characteristics and pictures of objects that differ in these characteristics

PROCEDURES

For each of the relative concepts being taught, present the child with two objects/pictures that are very different. For example, show the child a stuffed animal and a rock for teaching "soft/hard," a rock and a feather for teaching "heavy/light," a ruler and a yardstick for teaching "long/short," cylinders of different widths for teaching "thick/thin," and sandpaper and a scrap of satin for teaching "rough/smooth." Encourage the child to feel, lift, and explore the objects as appropriate as you talk about their characteristics.

After the child appears to understand a comparison with one set of materials, try another set in which the contrast is not quite so great. When the child regularly identifies the characteristics in two objects that he can manipulate, try to find pictures that exemplify these characteristics (e.g., a picture of a brick and a pillow), and ask him to identify which of the objects is soft, hard, heavy, light, and so forth.

10

DAILY ROUTINES & FUNCTIONAL ACTIVITIES

Remember to use words to describe the characteristics of objects throughout the day and to select books that help to reinforce the ideas. For example, the story *Goldilocks and the Three Bears* gives an opportunity to talk about "hard," "soft," "hot," "cold," "big," and "little."

Have children collect materials while they are outside or have them each bring something from home to show to the other children. Pick out objects to compare on varying characteristics (e.g., "rough/smooth"), and encourage the children to identify other objects that could be compared using the same characteristic.

Line up dolls and/or stuffed animals, and have the children pick out some that are tall, short, fat, or skinny or have clothes that are rough or smooth. During snack time, discuss "hot," "cold," "warm," and "cool."

CRITERION   The child selects objects/pictures to indicate an understanding of at least two relative concepts on two or more occasions.

■ ■ ■

10s. Points to five or more colors on request

MATERIALS   Objects of different colors

PROCEDURES

Before trying to get the child to point to colors when you name them, be sure that the child is able to match colors (see Item 6-IIb). If the child is not yet pointing to colors correctly after mastering matching tasks, begin teaching by naming the color of an object you are holding and asking the child to find another one that color. Go on to other colors and then come back to the first and ask the child to find something that color without showing her a matching item.

DAILY ROUTINES & FUNCTIONAL ACTIVITIES

Give instructions frequently in the home or classrooms that involve colors (e.g., "Please bring me the red cup"). When working with a group of children, ask them to point to someone whose shirt is blue, whose ribbon is red, and so forth. Or, have the children look around the classroom and find something that is green, for example, and then let each child tell what he or she has found.

CRITERION   The child points to objects to demonstrate an understanding of five or more colors (each color should be identified several times).

■ ■ ■

10t. Selects objects and pictures
to indicate which are square and which are round

MATERIALS   A variety of square and round objects (e.g., blocks, balls, square and round pieces of construction paper), pictures of square and round objects

PROCEDURES

Before trying to get the child to point to shapes when you name them, be sure that the child is able to match and sort shapes (see Item 6-IIc). If he is not yet pointing to varying shapes correctly after mastering sorting and matching, begin teaching by showing him a round object and asking him to find another round object. Repeat with square objects. Then ask for something round or square without having an example. Once the child is able to give round and square objects on request, show him pictures of round and square objects and circles and squares. Ask him to point to something round and square. Go back to having him find a "round one like mine" if he is unable to make the transition from objects to pictures.

DAILY ROUTINES & FUNCTIONAL ACTIVITIES

Describe objects as square or round (e.g., point out signs when shopping, traveling, or walking outdoors). Ask the child to give you the shapes by name (e.g., "This is a round dish. Can you find me a round lid?" "I need a square block to go on this tower. Can you find me a square one?").

In a classroom, incorporate the learning of shape names into cleanup activities or art work (e.g., say, "Put all of the round blocks in this box and all of the square blocks in this one," have different colored circles and squares and say, "Let's make a picture using just round circles." Then make another out of just squares).

Play a game in which you ask each child to find something square (or round) in the classroom. Work individually with children who have difficulty with the concepts.

CRITERION   *The child selects at least five square and round objects and at least five pictures of such objects from groups containing both shapes.*

■ ■ ■

10u. Selects objects by usage (e.g., "Show me what we drink out of")

MATERIALS   A variety of functional objects

PROCEDURES

Talk about objects as you use them (e.g., "Let's drink out of the blue cup today," "I'm going to cut the paper with these scissors"). Occasionally place three or four objects in front of the child and say, "Show me the one that we . . ." (e.g., drink out of, cut with, use to wash our face, carry money in).

Gather together a collection of interesting objects, and ask the child to tell you their uses. Tell and show the child the uses of the objects that she does not recognize. Let her use or pretend to use the objects. On the next day, bring out the objects again, and ask the child to identify them by use (e.g., "Show me the one we use to pound in the nails," "Show me the one we throw").

Note: It is important to use varying instructions so that the child can accomplish this task when asked to "show me," "point to," "give me," and "find the."

10

DAILY ROUTINES & FUNCTIONAL ACTIVITIES

When shopping with the child or reading to her, ask her to show you objects or pictures when you describe their functions.

CRITERION   The child identifies five or more objects by usage.

■ ■ ■

10v. Understands part–whole relationships (e.g., points to the tail of the dog)

MATERIALS   Toys, pictures, common household objects

PROCEDURES

Give the child two stuffed animals or pictures of two animals. Say, "Show me the tail of the [animal]," "Show me the nose of the [animal]," and so forth.

Give the child a car, a truck, and a train (or pictures of various vehicles). Tell him to show you the wheels of the train, the door of the car, or the window of the truck.

Follow a similar procedure with other pictures and objects. Praise the child for pointing correctly. Correct errors, and ask the child to show you again.

DAILY ROUTINES & FUNCTIONAL ACTIVITIES

When you and the child are engaged in reading a story or some other common activity, comment about the different parts of objects or pictures (e.g., "Look at that squirrel's tail," "That truck has big wheels," "That is the cat's paw. You have hands and feet; the cat has paws"). Occasionally ask the child to show you a part of an object or picture. Help him point to the right place if he makes an incorrect choice.

Increase the difficulty of the task by choosing two or more similar objects, and ask the child to show you a part on one of them. For example, present him with a toy dog and a toy cat (or pictures of a dog and a cat), and ask him to show you the dog's tail. This ensures you that the child is attending to both parts of the question (the object and the part).

CRITERION   The child identifies a part of an object or a picture on five or more occasions. At least two of these must be in situations in which he must choose both the correct object and the correct part.

11
Concepts/Vocabulary: Expressive

A person's ability to communicate depends both on his or her understanding of the words that other people say and the ability to put his or her own thoughts and perceptions into words. This sequence begins with the first word-like sounds that children make and ends with children's emerging understanding of the power of words and their awareness that they should be alert to new words in order to understand and use these new words.

Children form many concepts perceptually before they attach verbal labels to them. For example, children may match colors, clearly recognizing the differences between one color and another, before associating specific names with the colors. Other concepts are discerned through active manipulation of objects and other experiences in the environment. If a child is having difficulty moving through the items in this sequence, it is important to look at his or her progress in other sequences in order to determine whether the child has mastered the foundation of perceptual discriminations (Sequence 6-II: Visual Perception: Matching & Sorting) and has an understanding of the relationships and qualities of objects (Sequence 10: Concepts/Vocabulary: Receptive).

ADAPTATIONS

Children with Motor Impairments

11

When motor impairments interfere with articulation, listen carefully and accept poorer approximations than you might for other children. Consult a speech-language pathologist for help in developing an alternative or augmentative communication system if a child's word production is lagging far behind his or her understanding of language.

Children with Visual Impairments

For children with severe visual impairments, place their hands on your mouth as you make different sounds so that they can feel these sounds as well as hear them. Occasionally, help the children touch their own mouths when making different sounds.

Children with severe visual impairments often imitate speech well but have difficulty establishing the meanings of words. Make a special effort to help these children explore objects by feeling and handling them and experience people by touching their hair and faces as well as by hearing their voices.

Children with Hearing Impairments

Always consult the specialists who are working with children with hearing impairments so that a consistent program is developed. If a child is learning speech through a total communication program, it will be necessary for you to learn the signs the child's therapist is teaching him or her and use them with the child daily. Consistent signs may be credited as words throughout this sequence.

If a child is trying to communicate with signs, accept approximate signs as you would accept approximations of words, but model the correct sign. You may need to physically assist the child to form a sign if he or she is making little progress through imitation.

It may help children with hearing impairments to feel sounds by letting them touch your mouth or larynx and also by having them touch their own mouth or larynx. It may also help to work on sounds and words in front of a mirror and/or amplify the children's vocalizations with a microphone and speakers so that they can hear the sounds.

Note: Consistent manual signs may also be credited as words for children who do not have hearing impairments but are being taught sign language to facilitate communication.

11. CONCEPTS/VOCABULARY: EXPRESSIVE

a. Vocalizes repetitive consonant–vowel combinations

b. Uses two or more gestures associated with verbal concepts

c. Uses one or more exclamations

d. Uses two or more words to label objects or to name people

e. Says "bye-bye" (or equivalent) at appropriate times

f. Uses seven or more words to label objects or people

g. Labels two or more pictures

h. Appropriately uses 15 or more words

i. Meaningfully says "no"

j. Names most common objects

k. Names objects touched or handled but not seen

l. Names six or more pictures of common objects

m. Uses at least 50 different words

n. Names eight or more line drawings of common objects

o. Uses "other" or "another" to refer to additional or similar objects

p. Names most pictures and line drawings of familiar objects

q. Listens carefully to new words (may ask for repetition)

r. Repeats new words to self

■ ■ ■

11a. Vocalizes repetitive consonant–vowel combinations

MATERIALS   None required

PROCEDURES

Carefully listen to the child's vocalizations. Note any consonant–vowel combinations that he makes (e.g., "ba," "duh," "ma," "pa"). Talk back to the child by stringing together repetitions of one of the child's frequent sounds (e.g., "ba, ba, ba, ba," using an interesting inflection pattern). Listen to see if the child repeats a syllable, either the one you modeled or another one. When he repeats a syllable, smile and continue talking to him so that he knows you are pleased.

DAILY ROUTINES & FUNCTIONAL ACTIVITIES

Mealtime is an especially good time to stimulate sound production. As you feed the child, make sounds (e.g., "Mmmmm, mmmmm, yummy"). If the child does not vocalize, you may occasionally apply gently rhythmic pressure at the child's lips with the spoon or your finger as you say, "ma, ma, ma," making it more likely that a sound will be made as pressure is released.

11

Always try to make vocalizing fun for the child. Make it into a turn-taking game and be excited when the child takes his turn.

CRITERION   *The child frequently vocalizes at least two repetitive consonant–vowel combinations.*

■ ■ ■

11b. Uses two or more gestures associated with verbal concepts (e.g., "all gone," "so big," "more," "bye-bye")

MATERIALS   None required

PROCEDURES

Select three or four gestures that you plan to use consistently with the child so that she can associate a particular situation and/or verbal phrase with the gesture. For example, wave as you say "bye-bye" when it is time to go somewhere or when someone is leaving. Physically prompt the child to wave if she does not imitate. Then, begin saying "bye-bye" slightly before you wave to see if the child will wave on the verbal cue alone.

When the child has finished her food at mealtime, show her the empty container and say, "all gone" accompanied by a gesture you choose to use for that concept. Hold her hands and help her make the same gesture as you again say "all gone." Similarly, make a sign for "more," as you ask the child, "Do you want more?" Watch for evidence that she is learning the signs, either imitating you or using them spontaneously.

DAILY ROUTINES & FUNCTIONAL ACTIVITIES

Play games that have gestures that are associated with word concepts, such as, "How big is Keiko? So big!" (as you raise your hands up as high as you can reach). See if the child will imitate and, later, if she will answer the question "How big is Keiko?" by holding up her hands.

Note: A child's first gestures or signs are usually not accurate imitations of the adult. Give the child credit if she approximates the gesture.

CRITERION   *The child uses two or more gestures/signs associated with verbal concepts. The child should use these gestures spontaneously in an appropriate situation or during her turn in a turn-taking game.*

■ ■ ■

11c. Uses one or more exclamations

MATERIALS   None required

PROCEDURES

Think about exclamations that you naturally use (e.g., "uh-oh," "oops," "whew"). Select one or two to teach the child. Frequently, the first exclamation that a child learns is "uh-oh," which is said whenever something goes wrong (e.g., you drop or spill something).

Deliberately drop something and say "uh-oh." Pick it up, handle it briefly, drop it, and say "uh-oh" again. Give the object to the child. If he drops it, say, "uh-oh." Then give it to him again. When he drops it, wait to see if he says "uh-oh." If he does not, you say it. Continue to use the exclamation each time he or you drop something or spill something. Listen for him to begin using it spontaneously.

DAILY ROUTINES & FUNCTIONAL ACTIVITIES

Use exclamations in a natural way throughout the day. Try to be consistent in the expressions you use for particular events, and listen for the child's attempts to imitate and appropriately use them.

Occasionally play with the child using puppets, dolls, or stuffed animals. Say "ouch" when you make the puppet fall down and "uh-oh" or other exclamations when appropriate to the events you create. After you have done this several times, pause to see if the child will insert the exclamation.

CRITERION   *The child uses at least one appropriate exclamation on several different occasions.*

■ ■ ■

11d. Uses two or more words to label objects or to name people

MATERIALS   A variety of toys or objects

PROCEDURES

Ask the child's caregivers if she makes any consistent sounds (or signs, if she is being taught signs) in the presence of particular people or objects. Also, ask the caregivers to tell you the child's preferred toys. Hold one of these toys in front of the child, and listen to the sounds she makes. Name the toy and give it to her. After a few minutes, present another toy. Listen to the child's sounds and then name the toy. Try the first toy again.

Pay attention to the child's vocalizations when a parent, sibling, or other familiar person enters the room. Listen to see if the child makes any attempt to approximate words (e.g., "Daddy," "bottle," "doggie," "Mama"). Reinforce these attempts by smiling and repeating what she has said.

DAILY ROUTINES & FUNCTIONAL ACTIVITIES

Talk to the child throughout the day naming objects, describing what you are doing, and so forth. Be particularly attentive to objects, people, or events to which she is paying attention. It will be easier to teach the child labels that she pays attention to because they already have the child's interest and attention.

When the child reaches to indicate that she wants something, name it, and wait momentarily to see if she will make some effort to imitate the word.

If the child is very slow to attempt to say words, try holding the desired object out of reach until you hear some vocalization; gradually require a closer approximation to the name before giving the object to the child. *Do not,* however, unduly frustrate the child. It is more important that she learns that communication is valuable than that she produce

11

a particular word (and don't forget that reaching or pointing is a form of communication). If you have been making little progress with speech production, you may want to try a total communication approach (e.g., using both signs/gestures and speech) so that the child may learn signs to use until speech becomes easier for her.

Note: Do not be concerned about articulation when the child is trying to learn to speak. A vocalization can be counted as a word for the child if it is used consistently for the same object or event, even if it is quite different from the standard form of the word (e.g., "buh" for "ball"). Continue modeling the correct pronunciation, but do not require the child to repeat the word. Respond to the communication, not to the pronunciation.

CRITERION   *The child spontaneously (not in imitation) uses two or more words to label objects or to name people (or the child can indicate two objects, events, or people using a communication board).*

■ ■ ■

11e. Says "bye-bye" (or equivalent) at appropriate times

MATERIALS   None required

PROCEDURES

Each time you leave the child, wave and say "bye-bye." Physically prompt the child to wave if necessary, and try to get him to imitate your saying "bye-bye." Once the child has learned to wave, he may spontaneously begin to say "bye-bye" as well. If he does not, continue to model the behavior, and occasionally ask him to say "bye-bye."

DAILY ROUTINES & FUNCTIONAL ACTIVITIES

Introduce a toy to the child, join him in playing with the toy, and then drop the toy in a box and say "bye-bye [toy]." Quickly produce another toy and repeat. Again, listen for the child to imitate your saying "bye-bye." Once he begins to imitate, wait to see if he will say "bye-bye" spontaneously (e.g., as he leaves, as he sees someone waving, as he sees some toy disappear).

Note: Many children will wait to say "bye-bye" until after the other person is gone. They should still get credit for saying it because it is clear that they understand the concept (that "bye-bye" means "we are leaving one another").

CRITERION   *The child says or waves "bye-bye" (or equivalent) at an appropriate time (e.g., when he is leaving someone, when someone is leaving him) on several different days.*

■ ■ ■

11f. Uses seven or more words to label objects or people

MATERIALS   A variety of toys or objects

PROCEDURES/DAILY ROUTINES & FUNCTIONAL ACTIVITIES

See instructions for Item 11d.

CRITERION   The child uses seven or more words to label objects or people (or she can indicate seven objects, events, or people using a communication board).

■ ■ ■

11g. Labels two or more pictures

MATERIALS   Sturdy picture books, magazines

PROCEDURES

Spend time every day reading to the child with him seated on your lap so that you can encourage him to touch the pictures. In the beginning, select books with simple pictures that include only one or two objects per page. Name the objects and talk about them (e.g., "See the ball. It is round and red"). Help the child point to the objects that you name. Then, begin turning the pages, waiting for the child to name the objects or ask what they are. Always indicate your pleasure when the child points to the objects or names them.

As the child becomes familiar with a book, do not begin reading immediately. Wait to see if he will point to the pictures and name them on his own. If he does not, ask, "What's that?" Name the object for him if he does not label it.

DAILY ROUTINES & FUNCTIONAL ACTIVITIES

Maintain a selection of simple picture books on a low shelf so that the child can look at them independently. Listen to his vocalizations as he turns the pages. Encourage the child to sit with you as you read a magazine. Point to the pictures and talk about them.

CRITERION   The child labels two or more pictures (not in imitation) at one sitting on several different days.

■ ■ ■

11h. Appropriately uses 15 or more words

MATERIALS   A box of books and small toys

PROCEDURES

Give the child a box containing two books and a variety of small familiar toys. Play with the child. Listen for the child to name objects as she explores them. Name things for her and listen for her to say their names as she picks them up again. Also, listen for words not directly related to the toys. Keep a list of the different words she uses. You should also ask her caregivers to record the words she says.

DAILY ROUTINES & FUNCTIONAL ACTIVITIES

Continue to talk to the child frequently. Respond to all of the child's efforts to communicate. Try to understand what she is trying to say even if the words are pronounced poorly. If a word is unclear, tell the child what you think she said. If she corrects you by repeat-

11

ing what she said before, take another guess at what she means. This process will improve both your understanding of her speech patterns and her ability to pronounce words so that you can understand what she is saying.

CRITERION   *The child spontaneously and appropriately uses 15 or more words (or communicates 15 words through a communication device).*

■ ■ ■

11i. Meaningfully says "no"

MATERIALS   None required

PROCEDURES

Try to get the child to tell you "no" by starting to take a toy from him, by interfering with his play in some other way, or by asking him a question that would likely elicit a refusal.

Ask the child's caregivers if he is saying "no" to their questions or when trying to stop someone from doing something. If he is not, ask the child's caregivers the circumstances under which they use the word *no*. Encourage them to use it when trying to stop him from an unacceptable activity, when refusing to accept something, and so forth.

DAILY ROUTINES & FUNCTIONAL ACTIVITIES

Consistently say "no" when the child engages in inappropriate activities. Use a logical restraining action, if necessary (e.g., remove the child from the area).

Be sure that the child also hears "no" in other contexts (e.g., to indicate refusal or denial). For example, the child may be giving you some of his crackers. After a few, say, "No more, I'm too full," or, if the child indicates that he wants something that you cannot provide, say, "No, you can't have that" and explain why.

When the child begins to say "no," it is important to communicate respect for his feelings. If it is reasonable, stop doing whatever prompted the refusal (e.g., don't give him a particular food). In situations in which it is not reasonable to let the child have his own way, say something to indicate that you understand the child's wishes but have to make a different decision (e.g., "I know you don't want to take a bath, but look at all that dirt. We have to get you clean"). Offer some incentive to the child for complying with your wishes (e.g., "Would you like to take this cup and bowl to play with in the water?").

Note: Many children will say "no" or "no-no" when they are about to do something they know is forbidden. This is an appropriate use of the word. Reinforce it by saying, "You're right, that is a no-no. Let's do this" (and provide an alternative activity).

When children first learn to say "no," they frequently say it to any question, regardless of what they really mean. Respond to such refusals as if they were intended. That is, if the child says "no" to an offer of juice, start to put the juice away. If the child protests, say, "You said no, but you must mean yes. Say, 'yes.' " Whether or not the child says "yes," give him the juice. Gradually, the child will learn not to say "no" automatically to questions.

CRITERION   *The child meaningfully says "no" on several occasions.*

■ ■ ■

11j. Names most common objects

MATERIALS   Objects found in a typical environment

PROCEDURES

Present the child with a box of common toys. As she explores them, ask her what each one is. Walk around the room with the child pausing in front of objects to ask, "What is this?" If she does not respond, name the object for her, and try to get her to imitate the name.

DAILY ROUTINES & FUNCTIONAL ACTIVITIES

Name objects in the child's environment as she plays with them, looks at them, or otherwise indicates an interest in them. Comment on the object's characteristics (e.g., "See this ball. It is round and can roll," "Let's use this sponge to clean up your juice. Feel how soft and squishy it is").

If the child reaches or points to something to indicate that she wants you to get it for her, always try to get her to say the word ("What do you want? Tell me what you want"). If the child does not label the object, label it for her and give it to her.

CRITERION   The child names most of the objects (at least 20) that she sees in her environment.

■ ■ ■

11k. Names objects touched or handled but not seen

MATERIALS   A cloth sack and a variety of toys and typical household or classroom objects that have different textures or consistencies (e.g., sponge, washcloth or towel, block, cookie, stuffed animal)

PROCEDURES

Tell the child you are going to play a guessing game. Put a common object in the sack, and tell the child to reach in, feel it, and then tell you what it is. Begin with something such as a ball or a block. Move on to more difficult items if the child guesses correctly. Always let the child see the object after he has guessed. If the child has difficulty with a ball or a block, show him three objects that are very different from one another. Have him feel and name each one. Then take them away and put one in the sack to see if he can name it.

DAILY ROUTINES & FUNCTIONAL ACTIVITIES

11

Whenever you introduce a new object to the child, name it and let him feel it. Comment on its shape, its softness or hardness, its smoothness or roughness, and so forth. This is the way a child learns to attend carefully to the way things feel and also a way for the child to master a variety of verbal concepts (you may rub the objects over the skin of the children whose physical impairments prevent them from manipulating them on their own).

Putting an object in a sack for children to feel and name is a great activity to keep children occupied during long car trips.

This is also a good activity for children to do in a group, letting each child have a turn putting a toy in the sack and letting the others feel it and guess what is there.

CRITERION   *The child names three or more objects that he cannot see but can feel.*

■ ■ ■

11l. Names six or more pictures of common objects

MATERIALS   Books, magazines, pictures

PROCEDURES/DAILY ROUTINES & FUNCTIONAL ACTIVITIES

See instructions for Item 11g.

CRITERION   *The child names six or more different pictures of objects spontaneously or when asked, "What is that?" This must occur several hours or a day after a session in which the names of the objects were taught.*

■ ■ ■

11m. Uses at least 50 different words

MATERIALS   None required

PROCEDURES

Make a note of each different word the child uses in the time you spend with her. Request that her parents or caregivers try to keep a list of her words as well. It may help for them to have several notebooks in different parts of the house. You should count as a word any sound that the child makes consistently for a particular object, even if it is a poor approximation of your pronunciation of the word (e.g., "bawa" for water). Say the word correctly after the child, both to let the child correct you if you have misinterpreted the word and to give her a better model to imitate. *Do not, however, try to force the child to correct her pronunciation.* She is probably doing the best she can, and her ability to pronounce words should improve gradually.

DAILY ROUTINES & FUNCTIONAL ACTIVITIES

Talk to the child and listen to what she says throughout the day.

CRITERION   *The child spontaneously uses at least 50 different words in her speech (e.g., when asking for objects, telling you about something, looking at books).*

■ ■ ■

11n. Names eight or more line drawings of common objects

MATERIALS   Books with line drawings (i.e., black and white drawings with relatively few details rather than colored pictures—coloring books are good for this purpose)

PROCEDURES

Show the child a book of line drawings, and talk about the pictures. Ask the child, "What is that?" focusing on objects or animals that the child has previously named in colored pictures. If he does not name the pictures, tell him the names, pointing out particular features that characterize the object or animal (e.g., "That is a flower. See, it has a stem and some leaves and some petals," "That is a good guess, but it is not a horse, it is a donkey. See his long ears?"). Check the next day to see if he remembers what the drawings represent.

DAILY ROUTINES & FUNCTIONAL ACTIVITIES

Introduce books with line drawings in them for story time. Tell stories about the pictures, and have the child point to objects in the pictures.

   Note: Some children readily make the transition from colored pictures to line drawings. Others do not. This item is included to help those children who have difficulty making the transition.

CRITERION   The child names eight or more line drawings of common objects at least several hours after a session in which those names were taught.

■ ■ ■

11o. Uses "other" or "another" to refer to additional or similar objects

MATERIALS   A transparent sack or box containing a mixed group of small objects including several members of different categories (e.g., two to four trucks, cars, animals, and blocks)

PROCEDURES

Show the sack or box to the child and say, "I have some toys for us to play with. We will start with this one. (Hand her one of the toys.) When you need more, please ask me for one." When the child begins making requests, listen for her to use "other" or "another." Model the use of these words if she does not use them. For example, if she is playing with a car and says, "I want a car," you say, "Oh, you want another car. Okay, here it is." If she says, "No, not that one," you say, "Do you want the other one?" Listen for her to begin using these words.

DAILY ROUTINES & FUNCTIONAL ACTIVITIES

There are usually many opportunities to use the terms "other" and "another" as you go about daily activities. It is always helpful to young children if you talk about what you are doing. They feel as though you are including them, and they learn how to describe actions and events. Notice whether you use terms such as "other" and "another," as in "I don't like this dress. I think I'll put on the other one," or "It looks like you need another sock. Shall I get you one?" If you are not saying these terms, try to work them into your comments, slightly emphasizing them to call the child's attention to them.

   Listen for the child to begin using these terms when she is interacting with you or with others.

11

CRITERION   The child spontaneously uses "other" or "another" appropriately on several different occasions.

■ ■ ■

11p. Names most pictures and line drawings of familiar objects

MATERIALS   Books, magazines, pictures

PROCEDURES/DAILY ROUTINES & FUNCTIONAL ACTIVITIES

See instructions for Item 11l and Item 11n.

CRITERION   The child names most pictures and line drawings of familiar objects when asked, "What is that?" or names them spontaneously while looking at a book or a magazine.

■ ■ ■

11q. Listens carefully to new words (may ask for repetition)
11r. Repeats new words to self

MATERIALS   Some objects or pictures that the child is unfamiliar with and does not know the names of. (Try to have objects/pictures with unusual sounding names, such as unfamiliar foods or animals.)

PROCEDURES

Select an object/picture that is unfamiliar to the child. Introduce the name of the object before you show him the object. For example, say, "I have a tangerine." Wait and listen to see if he tries to imitate the word or ask a question about it. If not, ask, "Do you know what a tangerine is?" Show him the fruit (what it looks like on the inside as well as the outside), and let him taste it. Say "tangerine" several times as you show it to him. Follow the same procedure with another object.

DAILY ROUTINES & FUNCTIONAL ACTIVITIES

Observe the child as you read stories or talk to him. Deliberately use words that he is unlikely to have heard before, and watch for a reaction. If there is no response, say the word several times, and show or tell the child what it means (e.g., point to the object, do the activity). Make it clear that you think words are fun.

Read books with unusual sounding words in them (e.g., Dr. Seuss books), talk about the words, and identify them with the characters, objects, or events in the stories.

CRITERION 11q   On several occasions the child asks you to repeat a word, asks what a word means, or otherwise indicates an interest in a new word.

CRITERION 11r   On several occasions the child repeats a new word to himself shortly after hearing it and without being prompted to repeat it by an adult.

12
Attention & Memory: Auditory

Many other skills aside from language depend on our ability to hear sounds, identify them, remember them, and associate them with what is seen, smelled, or felt. These skills allow us to be aware of dangers that cannot be seen. They allow us to associate shapes with sounds, a fundamental requirement for learning to read. They also play a major role in the transmission of culture in stories, songs, and music.

This sequence begins with items related to simple attention to sounds. It progresses through items related to remembering the locations from which sounds were heard, and concludes with items important for literacy, including the memory of stories, rhymes, and songs.

ADAPTATIONS

Children with Motor Impairments

Head turning and/or reaching may be disrupted by physical impairments. Children with motor impairments may perform best when positioned on their stomachs over a bolster or placed in other adaptive equipment. Seek the advice of a physical or occupational therapist as to the best positions for these children to be able to reach for objects.

If possible, perform songs and rhymes with movements that are within the children's motor capabilities. If a child has severe impairments that interfere both with speech and with hand movements, include him or her in singing activities, but do not use these items as part of the intervention plan.

12

Children with Visual Impairments

This sequence is especially critical for children with severe visual impairments who may need to use sound to locate objects and make sense of the world they cannot see. It is important to recognize, however, that sound disappears more rapidly than visual stimuli. Thus, children with visual impairments may be slower to learn to localize sounds than children whose vision reinforces their auditory localization skills.

When working with children who have visual impairments, choose objects for making noise that have striking visual characteristics, such as shiny and/or bright colors, unusual shapes, and so forth. Keep the noise going longer than for other children. Touch the children with the objects or place the children's hands on them so that the children can identify the objects by touch as well as sound. If a child is not localizing, guide his or her hands to the object. When working on rhymes or songs with actions, physically guide the child through the actions.

Children with Hearing Impairments

Seek advice from audiologists for the best noisemakers to use to optimize the chance for a response from children with hearing impairments. Children with severe hearing impairments may not be able to master many of the items in this sequence. Upon the advice of their audiologists, those items should be omitted. However, many children with severe to profound hearing impairments respond well to the rhythm of songs and rhymes and should be encouraged to participate in these activities. Be sure to emphasize the rhythm as you sing (a drum helps), and accompany the songs or rhymes with gestures, pictures, or signs (if the speech-language pathologist feels it is appropriate). If the child is using signs, give him or her credit for signing in the items involving singing or saying words.

Sometimes, other developmental problems make a child appear to have a hearing impairment. In such cases, a child's responses to sounds will, as the child develops further, begin to appear more like those of children who can hear. Be sure to share this kind of information with the child's audiologist if you notice that this is happening.

12. ATTENTION & MEMORY: AUDITORY

a. Quiets when presented with noise

b. Visually searches for sound

c. Turns head and searches for or reaches toward sound at ear level while on back

d. Turns head or reaches toward sound at ear level while sitting

e. Turns head toward sound and looks or reaches directly when sound is at shoulder level

f. Responds differently to a new sound

g. Looks or reaches directly toward a noisemaker when sound is to the side at waist level

h. Turns head back and forth or reaches to either side for two sounds

i. Anticipates frequently occurring events in familiar games involving sounds after two or three trials

j. Anticipates frequently occurring events in familiar games involving sounds on first trial

k. Actively searches for source of sound when sound is not visible

l. Shows recognition of a few familiar sounds

m. Makes sounds associated with pictures or objects

n. Attends to stories, repeating words and/or sounds

o. Matches objects to their sounds

p. Identifies objects, people, and events by their sounds

q. Anticipates parts of rhymes or songs

r. Joins in saying nursery rhymes (repeats parts of them)

s. Says or sings at least two nursery rhymes or songs in a group with an adult

t. Independently says or acts out parts of rhymes or songs

u. Notices and reacts to changes in familiar rhymes, songs, or stories

■ ■ ■

12a. Quiets when presented with noise

MATERIALS   A variety of noisemakers that are shiny and/or colorful

PROCEDURES

Make sounds with a noisemaker for 3–5 seconds about 6 inches from the child's ear at ear level. Begin with toys that make relatively soft and pleasant sounds. Observe the child for any indications of decreased activity in response to the sound presented.

Present the same noisemaker to the other ear and observe. Change noisemakers and try again. If the child does not respond, gradually increase the loudness of the sounds that you present to her. When the child quiets, bring the noisemaker in view (and/or touch it to the child). Make the noise again.

Note: This response cannot be taught, although you can experiment with noises to see what is most effective in promoting a response from the child (e.g., take the child to a

12

very quiet room and do not talk prior to presenting the noisemaker, vary the distance of the noisemaker from the ear, try noisemakers with different pitches or different intensities).

Some children habituate (i.e., stop responding) to sounds rather quickly, so it is important to change noisemakers frequently and try this item for only five to six trials at one time.

DAILY ROUTINES & FUNCTIONAL ACTIVITIES

This is an easy item to try throughout the day (e.g., as you change a child's diaper, when you simply pass by the child). Keep noisemakers at the changing table and/or in a box or bag near the child.

CRITERION   The child regularly quiets when a sound is presented. That is, you should see this response almost every time you present a novel sound over a period of several days.

■ ■ ■

12b. Visually searches for sound

MATERIALS   A variety of noisemakers with interesting appearances

PROCEDURES

Make sounds with a noisemaker for 3–5 seconds about 6 inches from the child's ear at ear level. Begin with noisemakers that make relatively soft and pleasant sounds.

Observe the child's eyes. If he does not look back and forth for the noise, attract his attention to the object by bringing it to the midline and making the noise, and then move it back and forth again, in an attempt to obtain the child's attention. Then, remove the object, wait for a few seconds, and present it at his side again.

Present the same noisemaker to the other ear and proceed as above.

Change noisemakers and repeat the trial. If a child does not respond, gradually increase the loudness of the sounds that you present. Keep a record of the kinds of sounds to which the child responds.

Wiggle the toy again to create a visual effect, as well as a sound, when the child does not search for it.

Note: For some children, it will be necessary to work on this skill in a quiet room with no distracting noises.

DAILY ROUTINES & FUNCTIONAL ACTIVITIES

Take the opportunity throughout the day to watch the child's responses to environmental sounds (e.g., the telephone, closing doors, toys being used by other children).

Note: Many children with visual impairments will respond with searching eye movements, even if they cannot see the object. Look for this response as an indication of attention, and reinforce the response by touching the child with the object on the hand or cheek of the same side in which the sound was presented. If a child with a visual impairment does not visually search, look for other indications of attention (e.g., moving head from side to side, increased motor activity).

CRITERION   The child visually searches for a variety of sounds. This should be observed throughout the course of daily activities, not just in training sessions.

■ ■ ■

12c. Turns head and searches for or reaches toward sound at ear level while on back

MATERIALS   A variety of noisemakers that have gotten the best response in previous items

PROCEDURES

Make sounds with a noisemaker about 6 inches from the child's ear at ear level, and observe her response.

Randomly test each ear with the noisemaker, changing toys frequently for six to eight trials at a time.

If the child does not turn her head to find the toy, gain the child's visual attention to the toy at her midline, then move the toy to one side slowly while making noise. Remove the toy, wait for a few seconds, and again present it at the child's side. If this procedure does not work after five trials, present the sound at the side, and gently turn the child's head in the direction of the sound. As the child's head is turned, make the sound again, and move the object in such a way as to produce an interesting visual effect.

Note: It may be unclear whether a child has a visual impairment. Always work for the visual response first, even if the child has been described as cortically blind. If you cannot get any indication that the child is looking at the noisemaker, guide the child's hand to the toy.

DAILY ROUTINES & FUNCTIONAL ACTIVITIES

Look for opportunities throughout the day to try this item for a few minutes (e.g., when changing a diaper, when placing the child on the floor to play). Many exposures throughout the day will work better than concentrated training sessions. Also, watch for the response to occur naturally to environmental sounds.

CRITERION   The child turns her head in the direction of a sound and visually searches or reaches when lying down. This should be observed during several trials on different days and in the everyday care of the child.

■ ■ ■

12d. Turns head or reaches toward sound at ear level while sitting

12e. Turns head toward sound and looks or reaches directly when sound is at shoulder level

12

MATERIALS   A variety of noisemakers

PROCEDURES

Make sounds with a noisemaker about 6 inches from the child's ear at ear level and observe his response.

Randomly test each ear with the noisemaker, changing toys frequently for only six to eight trials at a time.

If the child does not turn his head to find the toy, gain the child's visual attention to the toy at midline, then move the toy to one side slowly while making noise. Remove the toy, wait for a few seconds, then present the toy again at the side. If this procedure does not work after five trials, present the sound at the child's side, and gently turn his head in the direction of the sound. As the child's head is turned, make the sound again, and move the object in such a way as to produce an interesting visual effect.

Follow these same procedures again while presenting the noise at shoulder level instead of at the child's midline.

DAILY ROUTINES & FUNCTIONAL ACTIVITIES

Try these activities for a few minutes several times a day when the child has been seated for some other activity (e.g., just after a meal).

CRITERION   *The child turns his head or reaches toward the source of a sound while sitting. This response should occur spontaneously throughout the course of daily events, not only in training sessions.*

■ ■ ■

12f. Responds differently to a new sound

MATERIALS   A variety of noisemakers

PROCEDURES

After playing with the child using one noisemaker for several minutes, introduce another sound out of the child's sight. Observe to see if she quiets, looks for the other sound, or gives other indications of noticing the sound. If she does not seem to notice the new sound, show her the object that caused the sound and activate it while she is looking at it. Activate it six or seven times within sight. Then, introduce a different noisemaker out of view. Observe responses to indicate that she hears and attends to the new sound.

DAILY ROUTINES & FUNCTIONAL ACTIVITIES

Observe the child throughout the day to note any changes in response to new sounds. It may not be in response to toys but in response to footsteps, a different person's voice, the telephone ringing, and so forth.

CRITERION   *The child's behavior indicates attention to a novel sound on at least five occasions.*

■ ■ ■

12g. Looks or reaches directly toward a noisemaker when sound is to the side at waist level

MATERIALS   A variety of noisemakers

PROCEDURES

Make sounds with a noisemaker on one side of the child about 8 inches from his body at waist level.

Repeat this procedure on the child's other side. Then, randomly present the sound to one or the other side on successive trials. Many children will turn their heads to the correct side but will not look down to find the noisemaker. If this occurs, make the noise again while the child's head is turned. If the child still does not look down, bring the toy up to his eye level, and make a noise with it as you move it down to waist level, trying to get the child to visually track it. Then, attract the child's attention to you back at midline and again make the noise at waist level.

Whenever the child does look at the toy, be sure to move it, give it to the child, or otherwise let him know it was good that he found the noisemaker.

DAILY ROUTINES & FUNCTIONAL ACTIVITIES

Keep noisemakers available throughout the child's living area. Try this item each time you prepare to give one of these toys to the child to play with or just happen to pass the child and can make use of a toy near him.

CRITERION   *The child turns his head toward a sound and looks at or reaches for the noisemaker when sound is presented at waist level. This should occur in several trials on different days throughout training, or frequently in the course of typical daily activities.*

■ ■ ■

12h. Turns head back and forth or reaches to either side for two sounds

MATERIALS   A variety of noisemakers with interesting visual characteristics

PROCEDURES

Hold a different toy in each hand, approximately 10–11 inches from the child's midline at ear level but 6–8 inches in front of her face. Make a noise with one of the toys for 2–3 seconds. Pause for 1–2 seconds, then make a noise with the other toy. Continue alternating noisemakers three times.

Repeat this same procedure with two different toys. If the child does not look at the toy that is making the noise, move it to midline to her visual attention, and then take it slowly back to the side. Then, make noise with the second toy. Bring it to midline and back if necessary to get the child's attention. Wait and be quiet for 5 seconds or more, then do it again. If the child looks back and forth at the two toys, place them in the child's hands and let her manipulate or touch them.

DAILY ROUTINES & FUNCTIONAL ACTIVITIES

12

Keep noisemakers at the diaper changing area and in other areas in which you frequently interact with the child. Perform the above procedure each time you change the child and, periodically, when you take time to play with the child.

Observe what the child does in situations in which sounds are alternating. For example, when two people are having a conversation, does she look back and forth between them as each takes a turn speaking?

CRITERION   *The child turns her head back and forth or reaches to either side for two sounds on several trials on different days.*

■ ■ ■

12i. Anticipates frequently occurring events in familiar games involving sounds after two or three trials

12j. Anticipates frequently occurring events in familiar games involving sounds on first trial

MATERIALS   None required

PROCEDURES

Play a game you have previously played with the child, hesitating slightly at some important point. For example, in This Little Piggy you might stop just before you say "and this little piggy went wee, wee, wee all the way home" to see if the child makes the "wee, wee" sound. If not, repeat the game several times, alternating feet.

DAILY ROUTINES & FUNCTIONAL ACTIVITIES

Play games with the child throughout daily care activities. For example, when bathing or dressing the child, play This Little Piggy with his toes, or walk your fingers slowly up his arm saying, "Here comes a little bug," suddenly increasing the speed and tickling the child under his arm or chin. When the child is accustomed to the game and enjoying it, wait a few seconds before a critical line and observe the child. Does he pull up the shoulders expecting the tickle when you get to his arm or chin?

Note: Children generally enjoy games that include touching or tickling, and it is easy to observe their anticipation as they prepare for the tickle or the touch to come. Some children, however, do not enjoy either touch or tickle. Play other games that rely on interesting sounds for their effects.

. Most bookstores have a collection of books with rhyming games for children. One of the more recent is *The Complete Book of Rhymes, Songs, Poems, Fingerplays, and Chants* (Silberg & Schiller, 2002). Smaller collections include *Fabulous Fingerplays* (Kitson, 2000; accompanied by an audio tape) and *Wee Sing and Play: Musical Games and Rhymes for Children* (Beall & Nipp, 1981). You should familiarize yourself with many rhyming games so you can continue to try new ones.

CRITERION 12i   *The child shows anticipation of an event in one or more familiar games after they are played two or three times in sequence. This should be observed on a number of occasions over a period of several days.*

CRITERION 12j   *On several different days, the child shows anticipation of an event in one or more familiar games the first time it is played on a given day.*

■ ■ ■

12k. Actively searches for source of sound when sound is not visible

MATERIALS   A variety of objects that make noise, typical environmental sounds

PROCEDURES

When the child is engaged in some activity or has her back turned to you, introduce a new and interesting sound. Observe whether she becomes alert, looks around to find the sound, and moves toward the object that made the noise.

Hold a noisemaker under a cloth, behind your back, or behind some kind of curtain or barrier and activate it. See if the child tries to find it.

DAILY ROUTINES & FUNCTIONAL ACTIVITIES

Watch for the child's reaction to naturally occurring new sounds throughout the day.

CRITERION   The child actively searches for the source of a new sound (e.g., a dropped object, another child's manipulation of a toy) on several different occasions.

■ ■ ■

12l. Shows recognition of a few familiar sounds

MATERIALS   Possibly a tape recorder

PROCEDURES

Call the child's attention to frequently occurring sounds such as a caregiver's voice, the doorbell, the theme song of some television program the child enjoys—any sound that is being produced by something outside of the child's range of vision. Tell the child to listen and ask, "What's that?" or "Who's that?" If he does not respond, tell him what or who it is. Take him to see it if it is not someone coming in to see him.

If it is feasible, make a recording of environmental sounds the child may recognize (e.g., the doorbell, caregivers and siblings' voices, music). Play one sound and then pause to see if the child shows signs of recognition.

DAILY ROUTINES & FUNCTIONAL ACTIVITIES

Observe the child during the course of the day for signs of recognition of familiar sounds (or ask the caregiver/teacher to observe and record).

CRITERION   The child demonstrates recognition of three or more familiar sounds by naming them or reacting in a joyous way (or even a frightened way) that you can readily interpret.

12

■ ■ ■

12m. Makes sounds associated with pictures or objects

MATERIALS   A variety of toys or other objects whose sounds can be imitated (e.g., cars, animals, trains) or pictures of those objects

PROCEDURES

Use toy cars to play with the child. Run the car around making a motor noise. Listen for the child to imitate you. Then, become quiet and see if the child will spontaneously make the sound of a motor when she is playing with a car.

Show a book to the child with pictures of animals. Make different noises for the animals—a roar for a lion, a quack for a duck, a heehaw for a donkey, and so forth. When you look at the book again, wait for the child to make the sound. If she does not, you should make the appropriate sound. React with pleasure when she imitates the sounds or makes them spontaneously.

DAILY ROUTINES & FUNCTIONAL ACTIVITIES

Make appropriate sounds throughout the day for the toys the child plays with. Make different sounds for different stuffed animals. Encourage the child to imitate you, and then watch for her to make the sounds spontaneously when playing.

Make sounds you associate with different appliances when you get ready to use them (e.g., "Here comes the vacuum cleaner. Varoom!").

When on walks or drives, point to animals or objects, and make sounds associated with them. Encourage imitation. Watch to see if the child makes the sounds spontaneously when she sees the same or similar animals or objects.

CRITERION   The child makes sounds associated with three or more objects either spontaneously or when asked.

■ ■ ■

12n. Attends to stories, repeating words and/or sounds

MATERIALS   Picture books

PROCEDURES

Each day read one or two simple picture books to the child—be sure that he can see the pictures as you read. Books with flaps that children can lift to see a picture underneath are particularly engaging to young children. You can enhance the stories by changing the pitch or loudness of your voice for different characters or for different events (e.g., read Goldilocks and the Three Bears with a deep voice for Papa Bear, a typical voice for Mama Bear, and a high-pitched voice for Baby Bear; read The Little Engine That Could making different varieties of choo choo noises for the different trains). The next time you read the book to the child (or the next time he picks it up and looks at it independently), observe to see if he makes the sounds or says a word or two associated with the pictures.

DAILY ROUTINES & FUNCTIONAL ACTIVITIES

Maintain a shelf or box of sturdy books that the child can explore independently at any time. Listen to him as he turns the pages. Talk with him about what he see if he is looking but not saying anything.

Note: Reading with animation and including different sounds will engage young children with books even if they do not understand the story. If a child's attention is too short for you to read the whole story, tell it to him in a more simplified form, making your narrative fit the pictures. Do not interfere with his turning the pages too fast, but adjust your story to fit the pictures he is observing. As his attention increases, include more of the story as written.

CRITERION   The child listens to stories (or looks at books on her own) for five or more minutes and imitates sounds or produces them spontaneously.

■ ■ ■

12o. Matches objects to their sounds

MATERIALS   Toys or objects that make different noises, a piece of cardboard or other material for a screen

PROCEDURES

Give the child two different objects that make distinctive noises (e.g., a bell and a squeaky toy). Let her play with the toys for a short while. Then, place the toys quickly behind a screen and say, "Watch me. We're going to play a game." Cause one toy to make a noise. Quickly remove the screen and ask, "What was that? Which one made that noise?" (Point to each in turn.) If the child chooses incorrectly, cause each object to make its noise, cover them again, and give a second trial using the second object. Continue until the child makes the correct choice for each object. When the child is answering correctly, try another pair of objects. (These are all practice trials.)

Once the child clearly understands the process, begin with different but familiar objects behind the screen. Make a noise with one and raise the screen. Say, "What was that?" Help the child explore the objects to correct errors. Once the child has mastered two objects, increase the number of choices to three.

DAILY ROUTINES & FUNCTIONAL ACTIVITIES

During the course of the day, make a point to identify objects by their sounds, and ask the child (or another child in the room) to tell you what made that noise.

CRITERION   The child matches sounds to at least five familiar objects without a practice trial.

■ ■ ■

12

12p. Identifies objects, people, and events by their sounds

MATERIALS   A variety of objects that make different sounds

PROCEDURES

Play a game with the child in which you make a sound with a toy behind your back and say, "Listen, what's that?" If the child doesn't tell you, bring it out, show it to him, name it, and then try it again. Repeat with another toy. After you have tried several, try each of them again. When another member of the family or another familiar person is approaching, ask them to speak to the child before they can be seen. When you hear the voice say, "Listen, who is that?" or "Who is here?" Name the voice for the child if he does not name it.

DAILY ROUTINES & FUNCTIONAL ACTIVITIES

As you hear environmental sounds (e.g., a car in the driveway, the telephone ringing, the vacuum running in the next room), stop what you are doing, look interested, and say, "Listen, what's that?" Take the child to see the source of the sound and talk about it.

Make a point of reading stories to children with different voices for the different characters. At the end, ask, "Who talks like this?" and imitate one of the characters from the story.

Note: If the child is in a noisy classroom, it is more difficult to isolate sounds. Be sure to use the activities described in the Procedures section during circle time when it is relatively quiet.

CRITERION   The child identifies a variety of sounds (at least 10) either by naming them, making a sign for them, or otherwise making a clear indication.

■ ■ ■

12q. Anticipates parts of rhymes or songs

12r. Joins in saying nursery rhymes (repeats parts of them)

12s. Says or sings at least two nursery rhymes or songs in a group with an adult

12t. Independently says or acts out parts of rhymes or songs

MATERIALS   None required

PROCEDURES

Frequently say rhymes or sing songs to the child. Try to include some rhymes or songs that emphasize different sounds (e.g., Old MacDonald) and some that have actions to them (e.g., The Itsy, Bitsy Spider; The Wheels on the Bus; Little Jack Horner). After the child is imitating your actions well, begin to wait slightly before you do the actions to see if she will do them without your model. Or, after the child has learned to sing along with you, start a song, and see if the child can sing part of it without you. Again, help as needed.

DAILY ROUTINES & FUNCTIONAL ACTIVITIES

Singing songs or saying rhymes is a good way to keep a child entertained when you are riding in the car, waiting in a doctor's office, or waiting for other events. A singing period is also an important part of a group care schedule. The children learn from one another as well as from the adult.

At home or in the classroom, encourage the child to perform, showing others the songs or rhymes she knows. Praise the child. Do not be critical of mistakes.

CRITERION 12q   On two or more occasions, the child anticipates some part of the rhyme or song by doing an action or saying/singing a phrase when the adult pauses.

CRITERION 12r   The child joins with an adult or a group of children in singing or saying two different rhymes or songs, saying one or two phrases, and/or doing one or two actions.

CRITERION 12s   The child sings/says at least two complete songs/rhymes with an adult or with a group of children, getting nearly all of the words and actions correct.

CRITERION 12t   The child says or acts out parts of two or more rhymes or songs independently. The child may start independently or the adult may start the song, but the child must say or sing one phrase without the adult singing, or the child must do a good approximation of at least one of the movements associated with the song at the appropriate time without an adult concurrently modeling the movements.

■ ■ ■

12u. Notices and reacts to changes in familiar rhymes, songs, or stories

MATERIALS   Books

PROCEDURES

After a child is familiar with a rhyme, a song, or a story, deliberately make mistakes or change it in some way. If the child does not react by looking puzzled, laughing, or correcting you, laugh and say, "Oops, I made a mistake. How does it go?" Try to make this into a joke. Wait for a day and try it again with another rhyme, song, or story the child has learned.

DAILY ROUTINES & FUNCTIONAL ACTIVITIES

Use this as a game to entertain throughout the day (e.g., when riding in the car, waiting in line, doing household chores).

CRITERION   The child reacts to changes in at least two different rhymes, songs, or stories by looking puzzled, laughing, or correcting the adult.

REFERENCES

Beall, P., & Nipp, S. (1981). *Wee sing and play: Musical games and rhymes for children.* Los Angeles: Price Stern Sloan.
Kitson, J. (2000). *Fabulous fingerplays.* Albany, NY: Delmar.
Silberg, J., & Schiller, P. (2002). *The complete book of rhymes, songs, poems, fingerplays, and chants.* Beltsville, MD: Gryphon House.

12

13
Verbal Comprehension

This sequence is concerned with how well children understand the instructions others give to them. This understanding is not a passive event for children; rather, it is a part of ongoing interactions between the children and their caregiver(s) in which each teaches the other. By their responses to instructions, children show caregivers how much they understand. Caregivers, in turn, increase children's understanding through demonstration, prompts, and indications of pleasure when the children succeed.

Many children with disabilities rely on some alternate form of communication at various times throughout their development. In this sequence, it is suggested that gestures and manual signs accompany speech for many children. You could also use communication boards. Be sure to consult with your communication disorders specialist for advice on the extent to which manual signing and other forms of augmented communication are appropriate for any given child.

ADAPTATIONS

Children with Motor Impairments

If a child has severe motor impairments, it may challenge your creativity to find activities that you can ask the child to do that will give you an opportunity to assess his or her understanding of verbal directions. In some cases, you may need to use eye gaze as the primary signal by which you can discern the child's understanding of words (e.g., "Look at Mama," "Look at the cow," "Look at the thing we use to fix our hair"). If the child is able to use eye gaze or any other consistent voluntary response to communicate understanding, you should arrange a consultation with an augmentative communication specialist to determine what form of communication system may be effective for the child.

If the child has few means of communication, make sure that he or she has many opportunities to observe other children listening to and following instruc-

13

tions. Make this observation more meaningful by talking to the child about what the other children are doing.

Children with Visual Impairments

Children with visual impairments may be especially sensitive to sounds and may use their caregivers' tone of voice to infer feelings more than other children. Be particularly aware of what you may be communicating through the tone of your voice.

Experiment with visual materials to find out whether the child attends better if objects or pictures are made larger, are given more contrast, are given brighter colors, and so forth.

Provide hand-over-hand assistance if necessary when teaching the child to follow directions that are usually accompanied by a gestural cue.

Children with Hearing Impairments

Make sure that children with hearing impairments look at you as you speak. It may be necessary to touch these children in order to get their attention. For some children with hearing impairments, a loud hand clap will be sufficient to get attention. Once you learn how to attract a child's attention, use the signal consistently so that the child will learn it means, "Look at me. I have something to tell you."

Facial expressions and gestures will be particularly important for children with hearing impairments to comprehend what people are trying to say to them. Use more and somewhat exaggerated facial expressions and gestures than you would with children who have normal hearing.

Consult with a speech-language pathologist about the possibility of using signing or some other form of augmentative communication if a child is not progressing in his or her understanding of language.

13. VERBAL COMPREHENSION

a. Appropriately reacts to tone of voice and/or some facial expressions

b. Turns to the direction from which name is being called

c. Stops activity when name is called

d. Does previously learned task on verbal or gestural cue

e. Responds with correct gestures to "up" and "bye-bye"

f. Responds to "no" (briefly stops activity)

g. Responds to "give me" (spoken or signed)

h. Follows two or more simple commands (one object, one action), spoken or signed

i. Appropriately indicates "yes" or "no" in response to questions

j. Retrieves objects within view on verbal or signed request

k. Understands "look"

l. Understands words used to inhibit actions

m. Follows commands in familiar contexts

n. Follows two-part related commands in novel contexts

o. Follows three-part commands (three objects and one action, three actions and one object, or three objects related by activity)

■ ■ ■

13a. Appropriately reacts to tone of voice and/or some facial expressions

MATERIALS None required

PROCEDURES

Lean over the child, smile, and talk in a gentle, loving voice. Watch the child's reactions. Then, frown and speak in a firm "I don't want you to do that" kind of voice. Observe to see if the child responds differently. Also, try a look of surprise with some appropriate statement (e.g., "My goodness, what are you doing?").

DAILY ROUTINES & FUNCTIONAL ACTIVITIES

Talk to the child often. Naturally express your feelings, and try to reflect back to the child what you believe he is feeling. Smile when he smiles, and make happy sounds. When he cries, look distressed and make comforting sounds. If the child is chronologically and physically old enough to be biting or producing other unacceptable behavior, respond with a serious face and a firm "no, no" message.

Note: Without being aware of it, many adults exaggerate their facial expressions when talking to an infant or young child. This probably helps the child associate facial expressions with other events in the environment and is, no doubt, useful. Listen to yourself and watch yourself in the mirror. If you are not exaggerating your facial expressions, you should make a conscious effort to do so.

13

CRITERION   The child appropriately reacts to tone of voice and/or facial expressions that communicate at least two different emotional states. For example, the child might look solemn if the caregiver sounds angry or hurt, fearful if the caregiver is afraid, excited when the caregiver is excited, or happy when the caregiver is happy or laughing. At least one other person besides the primary caregiver should be able to confirm that the child is responding differently to the different vocal and facial expressions.

■ ■ ■

13b. Turns to the direction from which name is being called
13c. Stops activity when name is called

MATERIALS   None required

PROCEDURES

When the child is playing independently, stand out of her view and call her name. See if she stops what she is doing and/or looks for you. If she does not, call her name again. Repeat several times. If she does not respond, approach her, touch her on the shoulder, and say her name again.

DAILY ROUTINES & FUNCTIONAL ACTIVITIES

Regardless of how young a child is, call her by her name as you talk to her. Call the child's name in order to get her attention. Initially, the child will primarily attend to you because your voice alerts her. Soon, however, she should associate the name with the call to attention.

Note: Many families have two or more pet names for a child in addition to the child's given name (e.g., sugar, sweet pea, little man). Children often enjoy these pet names. There is nothing wrong with using them, but it is important to use one name (either the given name or a consistent nickname) most of the time so that the child will respond to it.

CRITERION 13b   The child frequently turns toward a beckoning voice when her name is called (or, if the child has a hearing impairment, she turns to some other signal and looks at the adult to see her name sign).

CRITERION 13c   The child frequently stops her activity when her name is called (or, if the child has a hearing impairment, she stops her activity to the same signal that is used in Item 13b).

■ ■ ■

13d. Does previously learned task on verbal or gestural cue

MATERIALS   None required

PROCEDURES

Select any behavior that a child has learned to do when playing with you (e.g., kissing, hugging, clapping, playing Pat-a-cake). Try to initiate that activity with just a verbal cue. For example, say, "Pat-a-cake, Pat-a-cake" without doing any actions yourself. Wait momentarily to see if the child claps. If he does, go on and play the game. If the child does not clap, again say, "Pat-a-cake," and start clapping or physically guide the child to start clapping. Then play the game. The next time, start again with just the verbal cue.

If the child is not yet participating in any activities that lend themselves to being initiated by a verbal cue, begin creating games that can be used in this way. For example, kiss the child, and then say, "Give me a kiss," placing your face close to the child. Or, lean toward the child so that his mouth touches your face and then hug him.

Other cues to try include "How big is Johnny? So big" (raising the child's hands above his head) or "Knock, knock" (as you rap on the table and then wait for the child to imitate).

DAILY ROUTINES & FUNCTIONAL ACTIVITIES

Use such games to fill in moments throughout the day when the child needs attention. Teaching the child to play games on verbal cues will allow you to keep him entertained for short periods while you are doing other activities.

CRITERION   *On several occasions, the child does a previously learned task on spoken or signed cue.*

■ ■ ■

13e. Responds with correct gestures to "up" and "bye-bye"

MATERIALS   None required

PROCEDURES

With the child on the floor or on a bed, say, "Do you want to get up?" Hold your hands out, but do not touch the child. Wait to see if she will reach for your hands. If not, reach down, take the child's hands, and hold them a second or so before you pick her up. Gradually reduce the help you provide. Instead of reaching down and taking the child's hands, just touch her gently on one arm and take your hands back, beckoning the child to reach.

When someone is leaving, say, "bye-bye," wave yourself, and then physically prompt the child to wave. Gradually reduce the amount of help you give the child, until she is waving in response to the situation and the verbal cue.

DAILY ROUTINES & FUNCTIONAL ACTIVITIES

Consistently match your verbalization of "up" and "bye-bye" with the appropriate gestures (i.e., reaching for the child, waving) throughout the day.

CRITERION   *The child regularly responds with correct gestures to "up" and "bye-bye."*

13

■ ■ ■

13f. Responds to "no" (briefly stops activity)

MATERIALS   None required

PROCEDURES

When the child engages in inappropriate activity that should be stopped, say, "no" firmly, and distract the child with a new activity, move him to a different location, or do something else that stops the activity and communicates to him, "Do this, instead of that."

After you have said, "no," always respond to even momentary cessation of activity with praise, and give the child special attention as he begins to do the substitute activity. It is important that the child learn *what to do* as well as *what not to do*.

DAILY ROUTINES & FUNCTIONAL ACTIVITIES

Most children present numerous opportunities for their caregivers to say "no." It is important that homes be "child proofed" so that there are not too many forbidden activities. The child will learn "no" more effectively if it is applied consistently but not continuously.

Note: Children with severe disabilities may not be able to do any activity that would require you to respond with a "no." This item is inappropriate for those children, but caregivers should use the word with each other and with other children so that the child will come to understand its meaning.

CRITERION   The child usually briefly stops activity when told "no."

■ ■ ■

13g. Responds to "give me" (spoken or signed)

MATERIALS   None required

PROCEDURES

When the child is involved in playing with a small toy, say or sign, "Give me the [toy]," while you hold out your hand. If the child does not give you the toy, gently take it from her, say (or sign), "Thank you," and immediately give the toy back to the child. Make a game of taking and returning a variety of toys. Avoid asking for favorite toys until the child clearly understands that you will give the toys back. Do not take a toy if the child vigorously protests.

DAILY ROUTINES & FUNCTIONAL ACTIVITIES

Model giving throughout the day. That is, when the child reaches for something, ask, "Do you want me to give you the [object]? Here it is." Hand items to the child and others in the environment, saying, "Let me give you some [objects]," and so forth. Look for opportunities to ask the child to give you some object.

CRITERION   The child regularly responds to "give me" (spoken or signed) by giving whatever is requested.

■ ■ ■

13h. Follows two or more simple
commands (one object, one action), spoken or signed

MATERIALS   A group of toys

PROCEDURES

Put three or four toys in front of the child. Give a series of directions to him such as, "Pick up the truck," "Make the car go," "Put the doll over here," or "Bounce the ball." If he does not follow the command, repeat it as you do the action with the object. Then say, "Now, you do it" while you repeat the command. Praise the child when he does follow the command.

DAILY ROUTINES & FUNCTIONAL ACTIVITIES

There will be many opportunities and reasons throughout the day for making requests of the child. Be sure to keep the requests simple (e.g., "Put the [object] down," "Bring the [object] to me," "Take this to Mary"). Always say "thank you" or otherwise indicate your appreciation when the child complies. If the child does not do as requested, try to help him by demonstrating what you expected or physically guiding the child through the actions that are involved. If you guide the child through the actions, conclude with a "thank you," a hug, or some other indication of approval.

CRITERION   The child follows at least three different simple commands (signed or spoken).

■ ■ ■

13i. Appropriately indicates
"yes" or "no" in response to questions

MATERIALS   None required

PROCEDURES

Put one of your shoes and one of the child's shoes in front of the child. Hold the child's shoe up and ask, "Is this my shoe?" If she doesn't respond, shake your head and say, "No, that isn't my shoe. That is your shoe." Then, pick up your shoe and ask, "Is this my shoe?" If she does not reply or replies incorrectly, nod your head and say, "Yes, that is my shoe. Watch me put it on." Ask several other questions such as "Is this your mommy?" or "Do you want a cracker?"

DAILY ROUTINES & FUNCTIONAL ACTIVITIES

Throughout the day, ask the child simple questions that require a yes/no answer (e.g., "Do you want some ice cream?"). Begin with questions to which you are quite sure the child knows the answers.

Recognize, however, that children frequently learn to indicate no before they indicate yes and may respond to every question by saying "no." Be sure to be consistent in acting on what the child says, rather than on what you think she means. If the child appears dis-

13

tressed by your actions after she has responded to a question, ask the question again to see if she will change her response.

CRITERION   The child regularly and appropriately indicates "yes" or "no" in response to questions. The answers can be in the form of gestures or words. The appropriateness of the response is determined by the way in which the child behaves when the caregiver acts on what the child says.

■ ■ ■

13j. Retrieves objects within view on verbal or signed request

MATERIALS   None required

PROCEDURES

Look around the room. Tell the child to bring you some object that is familiar to him (e.g., "Please bring me the ball"). If the child looks puzzled when you ask for something, turn toward the object and point to it. If the child picks up the wrong item, say, "No, I need the [other object]." If necessary, go over to the object and say, "This is the [name of object]. Please take it over there." Give as much help as necessary to ensure that the child is successful. Always thank the child, give him a hug, tell him he is a good helper, and so forth.

DAILY ROUTINES & FUNCTIONAL ACTIVITIES

Include the child in your activities during the course of the day by asking him to hand items to you, get something for you that is across the room, and so forth.

CRITERION   The child retrieves at least three different objects from the same room on verbal or signed request (without prompts from the caregiver).

■ ■ ■

13k. Understands "look"

MATERIALS   None required

PROCEDURES

Look around the room and identify several objects the child is likely to recognize. Say, "Look at that [object]. It is [description] (e.g., beautiful, big, funny)." Observe what the child does. If she does not look at the object, point to it yourself, and see if she looks in that general direction. Repeat with other objects.

DAILY ROUTINES & FUNCTIONAL ACTIVITIES

Call the child's attention to objects and occurrences in the environment by saying, "look," and pointing. Gradually stop pointing and say, "Look at the [object]." If the child does not look with that instruction, prompt her to look by pointing. When you are showing the child how to do something, say, "Look at me. See how I [action]." When you are looking at books together, say, "Look at the [picture]."

CRITERION   The child looks when told to look at something. For this item it is less critical that she look at the correct object (that is more vocabulary) than that she does something to indicate that she is looking (e.g., turns her head, moves her eyes as if to search).

■ ■ ■

13l. Understands words used to inihibit actions (e.g., "wait," "stop," "get down," "my turn")

MATERIALS   A variety of small toys

PROCEDURES

Present a variety of toys to the child, and let him play freely with them for a while. Then, look for (or create) opportunities to inhibit his actions. For example, say, "Wait, don't feed the doll yet," "Stop kicking the table," "It's my turn to use the blue car," or "Stay right there. I am going to get some paper." Observe his reactions. If he does not appropriately inhibit his actions, repeat the instruction, and physically stop him from the activity or show him what he should do. If he does inhibit appropriately, thank him and show your pleasure.

DAILY ROUTINES & FUNCTIONAL ACTIVITIES

Most typically active children provide ample opportunities for their caregivers to use words intended to inhibit behavior. The important element is for the caregiver to follow the word(s) with some kind of action so that the child knows it is important to inhibit the behavior. For example, when the caregiver removes the child from the car seat and stands him by the car, the instruction "wait" or "stand right there" should be accompanied by a hand on the shoulder or some other physical restraint until the child demonstrates an understanding of the command.

Note: There may be few behaviors that need to be inhibited for children who are relatively inactive; however, these children still need to learn to understand these words. They will probably learn best if they have many opportunities to be with other children who are active and need to be inhibited by adults.

CRITERION   The child inhibits behavior following a command used to inhibit actions. This should occur in several different situations and with at least two different commands.

■ ■ ■

13m. Follows commands in familiar contexts

13n. Follows two-part related commands in novel contexts

MATERIALS   A variety of small toys

PROCEDURES

Place a variety of toys in front of the child, and let her play with them for a few minutes. Then, begin giving instructions that are similar to activities that she would typically do

13

and involve performing two tasks with one object (e.g., "Pick up the doll, and put it on the chair") or one task with two objects (e.g., "Put the doll and the truck in the box"). Praise the child if she follows the instructions correctly. If she does not, show her what you asked her to do, then repeat the instruction to see if she will do it.

When the child is following these relatively familiar kinds of instructions, introduce instructions of similar complexity (two objects and one action, one object and two actions) but involve unexpected activities ("Pick up the doll, and stand it on its head," "Make the horse ride the dog").

DAILY ROUTINES & FUNCTIONAL ACTIVITIES

Throughout the day, include the child in your activities by asking her to do tasks with you and for you. Pay attention to the complexity of the instructions that you give the child. Focus on requests that involve doing two tasks with one object ("Pick up your socks, and bring them to me") or one task with two objects ("Put the doll and the truck on the shelf").

The earliest commands the child learns to follow will be in familiar contexts in which she has already practiced the actions that you will request of her (e.g., picking up toys, getting undressed, taking a bath). When the child has begun to follow directions in these familiar situations, give her two-part commands in less familiar contexts. For example, go for a walk and suggest that the child pick up a leaf and give it to you or that she put a rock in a container.

Always give the child enough help to be successful, and demonstrate your pleasure and appreciation of her success. Help may consist of pointing and other gestures or physically assisting the child.

CRITERION 13m   *The child correctly follows three different two-part commands in familiar contexts. This should be done without additional prompts from the caregiver (i.e., no pointing, repeating, or physically assisting).*

CRITERION 13n   *The child follows several different two-part commands in less familiar or novel contexts. For example, she does a new action with a familiar object or does a familiar action with a new object without prompts from the caregiver.*

■ ■ ■

13o. Follows three-part commands (three objects and one action, three actions and one object, or three objects related by activity)

MATERIALS   A collection of small toys

PROCEDURES

Place the toys in front of the child, and let him play with them for a few minutes. Then begin giving instructions that include the following:

- One action and three objects (e.g., "Give me the doll, the brush, and the comb")
- Three actions and one object (e.g., "Take this spoon, go in the dining room, and put it on the table")

- Three objects that are related by an activity (e.g., "Put your baby in the bed, and give her a bottle")

Always give the child enough help to be successful, and demonstrate your pleasure and appreciation of his success. Help may consist of pointing and other gestures, physically assisting the child, and so forth.

DAILY ROUTINES & FUNCTIONAL ACTIVITIES

During the course of the day, pay attention to the requests you make of the child while you interact with him. Make sure that you are giving a variety of simple three-part requests or demands

CRITERION   The child correctly follows three or more different three-part commands. This should be done without additional prompts from the caregiver.

13

14
Conversation Skills

This sequence is at the heart of all of the communication sequences. Children's abilities to communicate are highly dependent on interactions with adults who are sensitive to children's needs and behaviors. Early conversations are not made up of words but of reciprocal interactions. These interactions are the foundation for developing a desire to communicate, generating the meaning of communicative acts, and establishing the "rules" of communication exchanges.

These interactions also lay the foundation for children's social and emotional development. A child who can maintain interactions with others, make requests, and communicate basic expectations regarding the behavior of others has the building blocks for healthy social-emotional development. The development of these capabilities, however, is highly dependent on the sensitivity and responsiveness of the adults who provide the child care.

Early in children's lives, adults probably attribute more intentional communication to them than is actually there. Yet, this attribution is critical to communication development. When an adult acts on a child's "message," the child begins to learn which of his or her behaviors influence the adult's actions. For example, when a child first begins to say "da da," he or she is simply experimenting with sounds. But, when a father pays attention and repeats "Daddy," the stage is set for the child to use the sound intentionally to identify the father.

The same is true of nonverbal communications. A child learns to hold his or her hands up to mean *I want to be picked up* only after many experiences of raising arms in anticipation of being picked up and having a parent or caregiver interpret arms up as a wish to be picked up.

Some disabilities may interfere with the vocal and motor behaviors that typically form the basis for early communicative acts, such as smiling, babbling, reaching, and so forth. Because these conditions limit children's behavioral repertoire, adults may cease to attribute intentional communication and may interact with the children less frequently, slowing the development of the children's intentional communication. It is especially important, therefore, that caregivers for young children with disabilities remain alert to behaviors that can be interpreted and used in communication exchanges.

ADAPTATIONS

Children with Motor Impairments

It may be more difficult for children with significant motor impairments to request by reaching or pointing. You may need to be especially sensitive to directed eye gaze as a communicative signal until you can discern differences in vocalizations that indicate requests, refusals, and so forth.

Be creative in developing activities for children with motor impairments. Consult their therapists and make use of any voluntary acts (e.g., movement, vocalization, eye gaze) that you can incorporate into activities and games.

If a child's motor impairments interfere with speech, seek the help of a speech-language pathologist to work toward an alternative system of communication.

Children with Visual Impairments

Children with little usable vision may seem inattentive when you talk to them because eye contact is not established. Smiling may also be absent or delayed. In such cases, look for other signs that indicate a child is paying attention to your conversations. In very young children with severe visual impairments, changes in movement, particularly in the hands, may be cues of attention.

Choose activities and toys that include tactile stimulation, movement, and sound. Help children explore the objects as you talk about them. It may help you to close your eyes as you describe the objects so that you focus on tactile and auditory characteristics rather than on visual characteristics.

Children with severe visual impairments often imitate the speech of others without having a sense of its meaning. It is especially important to help these children explore the world by feeling it and smelling it so that these senses can help give meaning to the words they hear.

When you read to children with severe visual impairments, choose books with textured pictures, and help the child feel them. When the child becomes familiar with a book, ask the child the name of the picture that he or she is exploring with his or her hands.

Children with Hearing Impairments

Always respond to the vocalizations that children with hearing impairments make, regardless of whether you believe the children can hear you. Speak slowly and clearly but with animation to make the most of the child's residual hearing. Make clear gestures to increase the meaningfulness of what you say. Use signs if a child's language therapist recommends total communication. Be especially attentive to the gestures the children use. Many children with severe hearing impairments develop their own "sign language" through natural gestures. It is important to watch for consistencies in these gestures and respond to them, thereby maintaining the children's interest in communication. Choose activities and toys that provide movement and visual displays.

14. CONVERSATION SKILLS

a. Smiles to person who is talking and/or gesturing

b. Provides consistent signals for states of hunger, distress, and pleasure

c. Protests by vocalizing disapproval of actions and/or events

d. Vocalizes five or more consonant and vowel sounds

e. Laughs

f. Repeats vocalizations and/or gestures that elicit reactions

g. Indicates interest in toy or object through eye gaze, reaching, or vocalization

h. Requests continued action of familiar toy, song, or activity by body movements, eye contact, and/or vocalizations

i. Waits for adult to take a turn

j. Begins to coordinate looking with listening

k. Makes requests by directing caregiver's attention

l. Indicates "no more" and "I don't like this" by vocalization, turning, or pushing away

m. Notices and vocalizes when primary caregiver prepares to leave

n. Uses eye gaze to select another person as partner for a communication exchange

o. Changes pitch/volume to signify intensity of desires

p. Raises arms to be picked up

q. Indicates desire to "get down" or "get out" in some consistent fashion other than fussing or crying

r. Plays reciprocal games

s. Uses words or signs to express wants

t. Seeks adult's assistance in exploring the environment by vocalizing, pointing, or using other communicative signals

u. Uses inflection patterns when vocalizing (or uses gestures as if signing)

v. Greets familiar people with an appropriate vocalization or sign

w. Directs caregiver to provide information through pointing, a questioning look, vocal inflection, and/or words

x. Says (or signs) "no" to protest when something is taken away

y. Experiments with two-word utterances or two-sign gestures to achieve specific goals

z. Spontaneously says (or signs) familiar greetings and farewells at appropriate times

aa. Says (or signs) "yes" and "no" to indicate desires or preferences

bb. Spontaneously uses words (or signs) in pretend play

cc. Uses words or signs to request actions

dd. Answers simple questions with a verbal response, gesture, or sign

ee. Asks simple questions with a vocalization or gesture

ff. Asks yes/no questions with appropriate inflection

gg.   Requests assistance

hh.   Uses word or sign combinations to describe remote events

ii.   Comments on appearance or disappearance of objects or people

jj.   Sustains conversation for several turns

kk.   Reads books to others by making multiple-word utterances

ll.   Responds appropriately to "where" and "why" questions

■ ■ ■

14a. Smiles to person who is talking and/or gesturing

MATERIALS   None required

PROCEDURES

Try to establish eye contact with the child as you talk to her. Vary the pitch of your voice and add gestures, especially if the child has a hearing impairment. If the child does not smile back, try to elicit a smile by being especially animated as you talk and by touching or patting her. At first, the child may just watch you, but gradually, she may begin to smile. Repeat this procedure daily until talking will elicit the smile without additional stimuli (e.g., touching, patting).

DAILY ROUTINES & FUNCTIONAL ACTIVITIES

Talk to the child frequently throughout the day (e.g., when feeding, diapering, or bathing; when you walk by as the child is lying awake; when you can just take a few minutes to sit and hold the child for a conversation).

   Note: Most of a child's earliest smiles (at age 2–4 weeks in a child without impairments) are in response to inner states such as feeling full or comfortable. The child then begins to smile at certain tactile stimuli (e.g., being kissed, patted, tickled, rubbed) and at sounds. It is important to respond to all of these early smiles by talking, gesturing, and otherwise interacting with the child. In this way the smiles become truly interpersonal and a part of the child's communication system.

CRITERION   The child frequently smiles to the person who is talking and/or gesturing to her on a daily basis.

■ ■ ■

14b. Provides consistent signals
for states of hunger, distress, and pleasure

MATERIALS   None required

PROCEDURES

Children's abilities to produce consistent signals for different states depends, in large part, on caregivers' attending to different behaviors, guessing from context what they mean, responding on the basis of that guess, and altering the response if it does not appear to satisfy the child. Thus, the only procedure for this item is for the child's caregivers to be attentive and responsive to the child. For example, if a child is "just fussing a little," the caregiver may try moving him to a new area of the room, talking to him, or otherwise trying to provide a change in stimulation. If the fussiness increases in intensity, the caregiver may intervene more (e.g., change a diaper, pick up and rock the child, offer milk). In this exchange, the child learns the kind of cry that produces particular results, and the adult learns to discriminate various cries from one another.

DAILY ROUTINES & FUNCTIONAL ACTIVITIES

If the child has several caregivers, it is important that they share information with one another about the child's signals so that the caregivers' responses can be as consistent as possible.

Note: It is very important to respond to a child's cries rather than ignore them out of concern for spoiling the child. Cries are especially important when other forms of communication have not yet developed. Responding to cries teaches the child that he has some control over the environment and that communication is important. As other forms of communication develop, the child will substitute them for crying. It is more likely that a child will become a chronic crier if caregivers respond inconsistently to crying. A child may also become a chronic crier, however, if caregivers respond to crying but are not sensitive to other communicative cues or signals from the child (e.g., changes in activity level, different vocalizations).

CRITERION   The child provides consistent signals for states of hunger, distress, and pleasure that can be discriminated by the primary caregiver(s). That is, the caregiver should be able to label the state and appropriately respond. This should occur daily, although there may be periods in which a child will again become difficult to read, usually during periods of illness or when new behaviors are emerging.

■ ■ ■

14c. Protests by vocalizing disapproval of actions and/or events

MATERIALS   None required

PROCEDURES

When the child is playing with (or attending to) some object, remove it and notice her reactions. Return the object whether or not she protests. Try other actions you and/or her caregiver believe might be slightly distressing, such as dropping something to make a loud sound, trying to feed her a food she has previously rejected by turning her face away, and so forth. Do not, however, try more than one or two potentially negative events within a 30-minute period.

DAILY ROUTINES & FUNCTIONAL ACTIVITIES

When, in the natural course of events, you give the child something she does not like (e.g., a new food), there is a loud noise or other startling event, or the child is hurt, respond appropriately to the crying or other protest. Take the rejected food away, and perhaps try again another time, pick up the child to comfort her, and so forth. Cries and other vocalizations of protest may begin as simple reactions to the situation but rapidly become an intentional communication if adults respond to them as communication.

CRITERION   *The child regularly protests by vocalizing disapproval of actions and/or events.*

■ ■ ■

14d. Vocalizes five or more consonant and vowel sounds

MATERIALS   None required

PROCEDURES

Listen to the child while you are interacting with him. Keep a record of the sounds he makes. If he is not making very many in typical play interactions, work with him during his snack or lunch time. Eating tends to stimulate vocal production. As you feed him, smile, and make babbling sounds. After he swallows a mouthful of food, wait before giving another to see if his vocalizations will increase.

DAILY ROUTINES & FUNCTIONAL ACTIVITIES

Throughout the day, take time to look directly at the child, try to establish mutual gaze, and then talk to the child. This should occur as part of all routine care activities.

Listen to the child. As he begins to vocalize, imitate those vocalizations or talk back as if having a conversation. Smile and laugh as you talk to the child. Making sounds should be fun for you both.

Attach an unbreakable mirror to the child's crib or to the wall by the crib or mat where the child spends time so that the child can see his face as he makes different sounds.

CRITERION   *The child vocalizes five or more consonants and vowel sounds.*

■ ■ ■

14e. Laughs

MATERIALS   None required

PROCEDURES

Notice the activities that frequently cause the child to smile (or ask the caregiver what they are). Do these activities with the child in a playful fashion. Such activities may include making various noises, making faces, tickling, and so forth. If the child smiles, smile back at her, and continue to stimulate her for a few minutes. If she does not laugh, go on to other activities and try again later.

DAILY ROUTINES & FUNCTIONAL ACTIVITIES

Take time during daily care activities and at times set aside for playing to interact with the child—make various noises, tickle her gently, and/or say nursery rhymes or songs that include tactile stimulation (e.g., Pat-a-cake, This Little Piggy). Always laugh, repeat the activity, or otherwise respond with enthusiasm when the child smiles or laughs.

CRITERION   *The child laughs at least three times each day.*

■ ■ ■

14f. Repeats vocalizations and/or gestures that elicit reactions

MATERIALS   None required

PROCEDURES

When the child vocalizes, imitate the sound(s) that he has just made. Wait to see if he will make the sound again. Likewise, if the child makes a gesture (e.g., slaps the table), imitate it and wait to see if he will repeat it. Also notice what the child does if you laugh at something he does.

DAILY ROUTINES & FUNCTIONAL ACTIVITIES

Attend to the child's vocalizations throughout the day. Imitate the sounds that he makes, or smile and say something to the child as if he had just made a statement to you. At times, you will spontaneously laugh because the child will make a funny sound. Watch to see if the child vocalizes again. If so, respond again. These exchanges are the basis for later conversations.

CRITERION   *The child repeats vocalizations and/or gestures that elicit reactions at least two times a day for three to four days. The child may repeat the same sound or experiment with a new one, as long as the vocalization and/or gesture appears to be in response to the reaction of the adult.*

■ ■ ■

14g. Indicates interest in toy or object through eye gaze, reaching, or vocalization

MATERIALS   A mixed group of interesting toys

PROCEDURES

Place four or five toys within the child's visual field but not too close to each other (you want to be sure you can tell when the child is looking at a particular one). Observe to see if she will reach toward one, vocalize while looking at one, or simply just look at one for an extended period (e.g., 30 seconds). If you see any of these indications of interest, give her the toy, or put it close to her and assist her with play. Vary toys and the distance at which you place them to determine what is most effective for getting the child's interest.

DAILY ROUTINES & FUNCTIONAL ACTIVITIES

Observe what the child attends to throughout the day. When she is looking at a particular object, reaching toward an object, or vocalizing as the object appears, talk about it, take the child to it to look at it more closely, point to it, or pick it up and give it to the child. Such actions let the child know that you are interested in the object in which she is interested. The more you respond to the child's interests in this way, the more she will try to communicate with you.

Note: At this stage, the child is probably not intentionally trying to get you to attend to an object. As the child discovers that you attend to what she is attending to, however, she will learn to use eye gaze, reaching, and vocalizations to communicate in a more intentional manner.

CRITERION   The child's interest in objects is usually apparent through behaviors such as eye gaze, reaching, or vocalization.

■ ■ ■

14h. Requests continued action of familiar toy, song, or activity by body movements, eye contact, and/or vocalizations

MATERIALS   None required

PROCEDURES

Play games with the child such as riding a horse (bouncing him on your knee) or Pat-a-cake (clapping hands). Stop while the game is still pleasing to the child, and wait to see if he will signal you to continue. Signaling may be in the form of beginning to bounce in the riding-a-horse game, taking your hands and trying to make them clap in the Pat-a-cake game, and so forth. As soon as you believe the child is signaling you to continue, begin the game again. If the child makes no such signal, try to prompt one. For example, you may jiggle the child a bit rather than bouncing him and this may help the child to start moving. When he moves, begin the bouncing game again.

Start a moving toy (e.g., wind it up, rock it, push it) and place it in front of the child. While he is enjoying this activity, stop the toy and wait to see what the child does. The child may signal you to continue the activity by looking back and forth between you and the toy, by looking at the toy and vocalizing, by pushing the toy toward you, or by some other behavior appropriate to the situation. As soon as you believe the child is signaling you to continue, immediately make the toy move again.

DAILY ROUTINES & FUNCTIONAL ACTIVITIES

Watch for what may be signals from the child throughout the day. For example, when feeding him, provide one or two bites and then stop for a minute or two to see if he will look at the food and back at you, open his mouth, or give some other sign that he wants you to continue feeding him. Also, play games with him several times a day as in the Procedures section.

Note: A child's signals to continue may be somewhat unclear at first. It is better to assume you are getting a signal from the child when you are not than to fail to respond to an intended signal. Your responses to the child's signals will make it more likely that he will try to signal again the next time the game stops. After a while, you may want to delay your continuation of the activity to see if the child will give a more vigorous or clear signal. In this way, you can shape clear communicative signals.

CRITERION   *The child frequently requests continued action of familiar toys, songs, or activities by starting body movements, directed eye gaze, vocalization, or other consistent communicative signals at least twice a day for 3 days.*

■ ■ ■

14i. Waits for adult to take a turn

MATERIALS   None required

PROCEDURES

Model turn taking for the child. That is, imitate something the child does, and wait for her to act again. As soon as she does, imitate that action and wait again. Or, put a piece of paper between you and the child, and play Peek-a-boo several times. Then, hide behind the paper and wait. If the child does not try to look around the paper to find you, show your face again.

DAILY ROUTINES & FUNCTIONAL ACTIVITIES

As you interact with the child throughout the day, make up games to play. These can be as simple as imitating something that the child does (e.g., making a particular sound, banging on the table) and waiting for the child to do it again or as complex as Peek-a-boo or other games with words. The point is to set up a turn-taking routine. Observe to see if the child waits after her action so that you can take your turn.

Note: This activity should continue long after the child has met the criterion for passing this item because it promotes a good social interaction and lays the foundation for the child to develop increasingly complex imitation skills. Once a turn-taking routine is established, challenge the child's imitative skills. For example, begin a game by imitating the child. Once you have each had two or three turns, do a new behavior and see if the child will imitate the new action (See Sequence 17: Imitation: Motor).

CRITERION   *The child waits for an adult to take his or her turn in an exchange. The child should pick up on the turn-taking routine and wait for the adult after only three to five turns in any newly initiated game.*

■ ■ ■

14j. Begins to coordinate looking with listening

MATERIALS   A group of interesting toys or objects

PROCEDURES

Place four or five toys/objects within the child's visual field but not close together. When the child looks at one of the objects (or something else in the environment), bring the object close to him and talk to him about it. Notice whether he looks back and forth between you and the object. If he only looks at you, do something with the object to get him to attend to it again (e.g., point to its parts as you speak, make it produce a noise or spectacle of some sort).

DAILY ROUTINES & FUNCTIONAL ACTIVITIES

As you care for and interact with the child during the day, pay attention to what interests him. Talk about that object or person, take the child to it, or bring it to the child. Observe to see if the child maintains interest as you talk, occasionally looking back and forth between you and the object.

Begin to try to expand the child's interests. Point at or take the child up to something in which you are interested and talk about it. Watch for the child to begin listening and focusing his attention on that object.

CRITERION   *The child occasionally (two to three times per week) coordinates looking with listening as an adult calls attention to and talks about an object, person, or event of interest.*

■ ■ ■

14k. Makes requests by directing caregiver's attention

MATERIALS   None required

PROCEDURES

This is an extension of Item 14g. After routines of joint attention have been established, the child will begin to deliberately direct the adult's attention by reaching out toward objects to indicate a desire for them, by looking at the adult and crying to indicate a need for comfort, by looking back and forth between the object and the adult to indicate a desire for the adult to do something with the object, and so forth. It is critical for the adult to be sensitive to these early communicative signals—giving or showing the child those items that she appears to be desiring, comforting the child when she seems to need comfort, and so forth.

DAILY ROUTINES & FUNCTIONAL ACTIVITIES

Throughout the day, respond to the child's attempts to direct your attention toward objects in the environment.

Note: If the child wants something that she cannot have or touch, do not ignore the communicative signal. Talk about the object to communicate your desire to share her interests, and then distract the child with some other interesting object or interaction.

CRITERION   *The child makes requests three to four times per day by directing caregivers' attention through reaching, vocalizing, alternating gaze between the adult and the object, and so forth.*

■ ■ ■

14l. Indicates "no more" and "I don't like this" by vocalization, turning, or pushing away

MATERIALS   None required

PROCEDURES

The first situation in which a child indicates rejection of something is usually during feedings. It is important to respond to the child's turning away as a valid communication attempt. Put words to the child's behavior (e.g., "Oh, you don't want any spinach," "No more?"). It is all right to offer the child the same item again (e.g., "Please try some spinach"), but if the child continues to indicate rejection, do not insist that he take the item. It is important that the child learns that you understand and respect his communication.

DAILY ROUTINES & FUNCTIONAL ACTIVITIES

Throughout the day, pay attention to what the child does. If he pushes a toy away, remove it, and say something such as, "You don't want that any more? Okay, let's try this." Even if the child did not intend to communicate rejection, your removing the toy will help teach him that pushing things away is an effective way to get you to remove them.

CRITERION   On three to five occasions the child indicates "no more" and "I don't like this" by turning his head or body away or by pushing away what he does not want.

■ ■ ■

14m. Notices and vocalizes when primary caregiver prepares to leave

MATERIALS   None required

PROCEDURES

Engage the child in play. Then ask her parent or other primary caregiver to say goodbye to the child and leave the room but to come back in 5 minutes. Observe the child's reactions both when the caregiver leaves and when he or she returns. If the child is distressed when the caregiver leaves, try to comfort her, indicating that the caregiver will soon return.

DAILY ROUTINES & FUNCTIONAL ACTIVITIES

To facilitate the emergence of the skill of noticing and vocalizing when the primary caregiver prepares to leave, make sure the child has an opportunity to observe the routines that lead up to the person's departure. It is important for the caregiver to announce his or her intent to leave (e.g., by saying "bye-bye," by waving) and, if the child appears distressed, to respond to the child with words and gestures of reassurance.

Note: Sometimes parents or caregivers will try to sneak away to avoid the child's protest. This is apt to make the child more insecure because she can't predict whether a parent will be there. It is much better to say goodbye with reassurances as necessary (keeping this to a very brief exchange) and then make a point of seeking out the child and demonstrating affection on return.

CRITERION   The child usually notices and vocalizes when the primary caregiver is preparing to leave. The child's responses should occur during preparations for leaving, not just when the caregiver opens the door and steps out. Vocalization may be in the form of crying or other protests.

14n. Uses eye gaze to select another person as partner for a communication exchange

MATERIALS   None required

PROCEDURES

Make a point of saying something to the child each time he establishes eye contact with you. If this occurs infrequently, make a point of leaning over the child and waiting until he looks at you to begin talking. It is not necessary to talk for more than a few seconds, but try to engage the child. If the child's caregiver is not available, ask another person to join you and the child. Talk to the other person while observing the child. As soon as he establishes eye contact with you, turn your attention to him and talk to him. Instruct the other person to do likewise. Once again, begin the conversation with the other adult and observe the child.

DAILY ROUTINES & FUNCTIONAL ACTIVITIES

Observe the child when several other people are nearby. Does he use eye gaze to try to engage you or one of the other people?

CRITERION   *Frequently and in a variety of settings, the child uses eye gaze to select another person as a partner in a communication exchange.*

14o. Changes pitch/volume to signify intensity of desires

MATERIALS   None required

PROCEDURES

Attend to the sounds that the child makes. Early in life, an infant tends to fuss and then work into a louder, more intense cry if attention does not come. Gradually, the child learns that more intense vocalizations get quicker results, so she begins to use the more intense vocalizations (e.g., crying, yelling) to signal an intense need or desire. In order to facilitate the child's intentional use of pitch and/or volume to indicate intensity of desire, respond differently to different kinds of vocalizations—respond especially quickly to more intense (e.g., louder, higher pitched) vocalizations.

DAILY ROUTINES & FUNCTIONAL ACTIVITIES

Encourage all of the people who interact with the child to be sensitive to changes in her vocalizations and respond as previously noted.

CRITERION   *The child changes pitch and/or volume to signify the intensity of her desires at least once per day.*

■ ■ ■

14p. Raises arms to be picked up

MATERIALS   None required

PROCEDURES

When you begin to pick up the child, put your arms out and say something such as, "Do you want to get up?" or "Up we go." Wait for a few seconds to see if the child will raise his arms toward you. If the child does not raise his arms, touch your hands to the child's hands and again wait a few seconds. Observe to see if the child raises his arms when you come near or when you ask, "Do you want to get up?" but before you put out your arms.

DAILY ROUTINES & FUNCTIONAL ACTIVITIES

Always respond to the child's outstretched arms. If you cannot pick him up at that moment, say something to indicate that you understand that he wants to be picked up but that he will have to wait.

CRITERION   *The child raises his arms to be picked up two or more times a day for 3 days. This must occur before the adult has put out his or her arms, but may be in response to a question such as, "Do you want up?"*

■ ■ ■

14q. Indicates desire to "get down" or "get out" in some consistent fashion other than fussing or crying

MATERIALS   None required

PROCEDURES

When you are holding the child or she is sitting in a high chair, watch for signals that the child wants to get down or get out of whatever is confining her (e.g., increased restlessness, reaching for the floor, fussiness). Ask something such as, "Do you want to get down?" or "Want out?" and remove the child to some other situation. Check out your interpretation of the child's behavior by her response to being moved (e.g., Does the child seem happy or does the behavior that prompted you to move the child persist?). If getting down or getting out doesn't seem to satisfy the child, try again to determine what she really wants.

DAILY ROUTINES & FUNCTIONAL ACTIVITIES

If the child has several people providing her care, tell them (and show them, if possible) the way the child acts when she wants "down" or "out." Encourage them to respond consistently to such cues *and* use words to describe their interpretation of the child's signals (as previously noted).

Note: When young children are bored or uncomfortable, they usually work through a series of behaviors that culminate in fussing or crying when the other behaviors do not work. Try to notice cues that indicate that the child may want to get down or get out before the fussing and crying begin so that you can teach the child that behaviors other than crying are an effective means of communication.

CRITERION   The child regularly indicates desire to "get down" or "get out" in some consistent fashion other than fussing or crying.

■ ■ ■

14r. Plays reciprocal games (e.g., Peek-a-boo, clapping, taking turns making sounds)

MATERIALS   None required

PROCEDURES

One of the best ways to start games with a young child is to pay attention to what he is doing, identify some simple behavior, imitate that behavior, and wait for the child to do the behavior again (see Item 14f.). Introduce turn-taking games that are not just simple imitation such as Peek-a-boo (e.g., your turn is saying, "Where's [child's name]?" and the child's turn is peeking around the corner of a barrier) or Pat-a-cake (e.g., you say all of the words, but stop the hand movements at particular intervals and wait for the child to do them).

DAILY ROUTINES & FUNCTIONAL ACTIVITIES

Take a few minutes during routine care activities (e.g., eating, bathing, dressing) to play a game with the child that involves reciprocal interactions. If he does not take his turn, physically prompt him to do so.

Note: Children vary as to how long it takes them to organize themselves to take a turn. This is especially true of many children with Down syndrome. The adult must learn to wait (e.g., count to 10 or 15) after doing his or her turn to allow the child time to prepare to take a turn. Timing is critical for helping a child learn to play reciprocal games.

CRITERION   The child plays two to three reciprocal games. That is, the child will take his turn as soon as the adult starts the familiar game.

■ ■ ■

14s. Uses words or signs to express wants

MATERIALS   None required

PROCEDURES

Attend carefully to the child, and try to determine what she is interested in or what she wants. When she looks back and forth between you and an object, say, "Do you want the [object]? Say [object's name]." You may wish to add a sign for the object as you say the word and use a hand-over-hand prompt to help the child make the sign.

At mealtimes, notice when the child acts as if she is full. Say, "Are you finished?" or "All done?" You may wish to also make a sign for "finished" and physically prompt the child to make the sign.

Watch and listen to the child to see when she begins to spontaneously make approximations of the signs or words.

DAILY ROUTINES & FUNCTIONAL ACTIVITIES

Attend to the child's attempts to communicate both vocally and through gestures or signs throughout the day. Try to guess from context cues what the child wants if the vocalizations are unintelligible or the gestures or signs are unclear. Check your guesses with the child (e.g., "Do you want some juice? Crackers?"), and continue guessing until you get it right. Let the child know that you respect and will respond to her requests. Repeating what you think the child is saying will help the child refine her gestures or articulation of the word.

CRITERION   *The child uses words or signs to express wants three or more times a day for several days (or, if the child has a severe motor impairment, she is able to make choices through eye gaze or other indicator response).*

■ ■ ■

14t. Seeks adult's assistance in exploring the environment by vocalizing, pointing, or using other communicative signals

MATERIALS   None required

PROCEDURES

Spend time with the child when you are not actively directing his activities. Be sure to have some interesting objects out of his reach. Watch what he does. How does he try to get your attention? Does he hand things to you to indicate an interest he wishes to share? Does he combine pointing and/or eye gaze with vocalization to indicate a wish for you to get something? Does he pull your hand toward something? Respond to the child's overtures, putting into words what you think he is trying to communicate. If the child makes no effort to initiate communication of this sort, talk about objects he looks at, hand objects to him, and help him explore for several minutes. Then, become more passive to see if he will begin to seek your attention/assistance.

DAILY ROUTINES & FUNCTIONAL ACTIVITIES

As you go about your daily activities, respond to the child's efforts to engage you in helping him explore the environment. The child's interest and exploration will often be guided by the activities in which you are engaged.

Take the child to less familiar environments (e.g., other people's homes, the mall, the grocery store), and observe if or how he tries to engage you in exploring the environment.

Note: This item is one example of the child's learning to coordinate attention to objects and people. Look for other indications of this as well (e.g., the child's bringing objects to another adult, the child's sharing her food with an adult).

CRITERION   *The child engages the caregiver's assistance in exploring the environment through vocalizations, pointing, or other clear communicative signals on a daily basis.*

■ ■ ■

14u. Uses inflection patterns when vocalizing (or uses gestures as if signing)

MATERIALS   None required

PROCEDURES

When you are interacting with the child, listen for the beginnings of vocalizations that sound like sentences even though no individual words can be understood. Respond to these vocalizations as if they were sentences. You can do this by repeating back to the child what you heard, by saying in clearly articulated words what you thought the child might have said under these circumstances, by answering as if the child said a particular comment, and so forth. Often, the child is not particularly interested in the content of what you say but is very interested in the fact that you respond as if having a conversation. Your talking to the child gives more examples of the inflection patterns she is learning.

DAILY ROUTINES & FUNCTIONAL ACTIVITIES

Talk to the child throughout the day and pay attention to her vocalizations, repeating back what you think she may be trying to say.

CRITERION   *The child uses inflection patterns on a daily basis when vocalizing.*

■ ■ ■

14v. Greets familiar people with an appropriate vocalization or sign

MATERIALS   None required

PROCEDURES

Always greet the child and others in an appropriate fashion (e.g., "Good morning, Bobby," "Hi, Bobby"). Encourage the child to greet others as well (e.g., "Say hi to Hakim"), but do not repeat instructions to greet others more than once or twice. The child will learn best by having those whom he greets respond appropriately (e.g., greet the child, give him a hug).

For some children, it is helpful to focus on a nonverbal greeting before focusing on a verbal greeting. For example, smile and raise one hand as you say "hi." Physically prompt the child to raise her hand.

DAILY ROUTINES & FUNCTIONAL ACTIVITIES

Model greeting people appropriately whenever you encounter them. Encourage the child to greet as well.

CRITERION   *The child frequently greets familiar people with appropriate vocalizations or signs. Several individuals in addition to the immediate family should observe these actions.*

■ ■ ■

14w. Directs caregiver to provide information through pointing, a questioning look, vocal inflection, and/or words

MATERIALS   A toy or other object unfamiliar to the child (perhaps a wind-up toy)

PROCEDURES

Place an interesting but unfamiliar object in front of the child. Allow her to explore it, and watch for signs that she wants you to tell her about it or show you how it works. If you have given her a wind-up toy, gently take it from her after she has explored it and wind it up. When it stops, just sit and wait. Respond to any efforts she makes to communicate that she wants you to wind it up again.

DAILY ROUTINES & FUNCTIONAL ACTIVITIES

Respond to the child's attempts to communicate throughout the day. Try to determine what she is trying to tell you both through her vocalizations and gestures as well as through her awareness of objects and events in the environment. Be particularly sensitive to the child's attempts to elicit more information. Listen for the inflection pattern of a question and/or a word (e.g., "That?" + a pointing finger = "What's that?"). Also, look for a puzzled look on the child's face as she looks to you. Answer the question you think the child is asking, or repeat the question that you think the child is asking and then answer it. Let the child know that you are interested in her questions.

CRITERION   *The child directs her caregiver to provide information through pointing, a questioning look, vocal inflection, or words on a daily basis.*

■ ■ ■

14x. Says (or signs) "no" to protest when something is taken away

MATERIALS   None required

PROCEDURES

Do not set up an artificial situation to teach or assess this skill. Simply observe what the child does in situations in which something must be taken from him or in which other children are present and the typical competition for toys is taking place. Demonstrate saying, "No, no, I have it now" when the child tries to take something from you. Prompt the child to say "no" when someone takes something from him. If it is a situation in which the child must be parted from the object, say something to indicate you understand what he is trying to communicate, then explain why he cannot have the object (e.g., "I know you want the ball, but we must put it away now and have dinner").

DAILY ROUTINES & FUNCTIONAL ACTIVITIES

Watch for the child to say "no" as a protest throughout the day. Let the child know that you have heard and are sympathetic to his protest, but note that there will be times when you will have to insist that he give up the object (e.g., "Greg, give the ball back to Mary. She was playing with it").

CRITERION   The child says or signs "no" on a daily basis to protest when something is taken away.

■ ■ ■

14y. Experiments with two-word utterances or two-sign gestures to achieve specific goals (e.g., "Me go," "Daddy sit")

MATERIALS   None required

PROCEDURES

When the child is making one-word utterances to communicate, expand her statement with a two- or three-word sentence. For example, if the child looks at you and says, "Sit," sit down, and as you do so say, "[Name] sit down." As the child begins to put two words together, expand with three- and four-word sentences. Listen for the child to imitate you and then begin using such utterances spontaneously.

DAILY ROUTINES & FUNCTIONAL ACTIVITIES

Caregivers will probably expand the child's sentences automatically if they spend much time alone with the child. However, in a child care or preschool setting, it becomes particularly important to think about this item. Adults have a tendency to talk over children to other children or to an adult rather than paying careful attention to what kind of sentences a child is forming.

CRITERION   The child experiments with two-word utterances (signed or spoken) three or more times on a daily basis to achieve specific goals such as "Me go," or "Daddy sit" (or communicates similar ideas through a communication device).

■ ■ ■

14z. Spontaneously says (or signs) familiar greetings and farewells at appropriate times

MATERIALS   None required

PROCEDURES

Model appropriate greetings and farewells whenever another person comes into the room, when meeting someone outside the home, when someone leaves, and so forth. Encourage the child to imitate, but do not pressure him to do so. The best encouragement will be others' responses when the child does say (or sign or gesture) "hi," "bye-bye," and so forth.

DAILY ROUTINES & FUNCTIONAL ACTIVITIES

Encourage others in the child's environments to use appropriate greetings and farewells with each other and with the child. If the child is signing, it is particularly important to teach others the signs the child is using.

In group care environments, it is appropriate to occasionally encourage the group to imitate the caregiver in greetings and farewells when a visitor comes to visit (e.g., "Let's say it all together, 'Good morning, Mr. Edwards' "). There are also songs that children can sing that include such greetings (e.g.. "Where is Thumbkin? . . . Here I am. . . . How are you today, sir? Very well, I thank you").

CRITERION   The child spontaneously says (or signs) appropriate familiar greetings and farewells most of the time.

■ ■ ■

14aa. Says (or signs) "yes" and "no" to indicate desires or preferences

MATERIALS   A few of the child's favorite foods or toys

PROCEDURES

Hold up the child's favorite food or a favorite toy. If the child reaches for it, say, "Do you want [object]?" You may need to prompt the child to say "yes" by trying to get her to imitate saying it (e.g., as you are handing a cookie to the child ask, "Do you want a cookie? You do? Okay. Say, 'Yes please.' " If the child does not imitate the yes, repeat it and give the object/food to the child. Continue modeling and prompting the yes until the child uses it spontaneously.

DAILY ROUTINES & FUNCTIONAL ACTIVITIES

Rather than simply providing the child with what you think she needs or wants throughout the day, make a point of asking, "Do you want some ice cream?" "Would you rather have juice?" "Do you want to go outside?" Try to focus on questions that you believe will be answered in the affirmative. If the child says "no," act as if that genuinely reflects her desires. If the child complains, repeat the question and say, "Yes, you do want some [object]." Emphasize the "yes."

Model saying "yes" for the child. For example, if she offers you a block as a cookie in pretend play say, "Oh, yes. Thank you. I will have one of your good cookies."

Note: Most young children learn to say "no" when asked a question several months earlier than they genuinely understand the meanings of "yes" and "no," perhaps because they hear "no" more frequently. They often say "no" to any question, even when they really mean "yes." The goal of this item is to help the child understand the meaning of the two words.

CRITERION   The child answers questions with either "yes" or "no" (or their equivalent signs) three or more times a day, and it is clear that she answered appropriately to her desires.

■ ■ ■

14bb. Spontaneously uses words (or signs) in pretend play

MATERIALS   None required

PROCEDURES

Engage in pretend play with the child. For example,

- Talk for dolls, stuffed animals, or puppets; have them engage in activities that are familiar to the child (e.g., eating, going to bed, taking a bath); and have them ask the child questions or otherwise involve him in the play.
- Have pretend tea parties in which you and the child share cookies and juice from empty containers.
- Build houses and roads with blocks and talk about them.
- Take animals or other toys for rides in trucks or cars and talk about where they are going, whom they will visit, what they will do, and so forth.

Listen for the child to begin using words spontaneously in his pretend play.

DAILY ROUTINES & FUNCTIONAL ACTIVITIES

Pretend play is an effective way to entertain a child while waiting in lines, riding in a car, or while doing routine activities around the house. It is an excellent way for the child to hear new words and to think about their meanings.

CRITERION   *The child spontaneously uses words (or signs) in pretend play. These should not just be immediate imitations of what a partner has said, but an integral part of the child's play. This should be observed on a daily basis.*

■ ■ ■

14cc. Uses words or signs to request actions

MATERIALS   An interesting object in a transparent container that is difficult to open, wind-up toys, jar of bubble liquid, other objects that require adult actions to be most entertaining

PROCEDURES

Present the child with an interesting toy in a transparent container. When the child is unsuccessful in removing the lid, wait to see what she does. If she hands it to you say, "Do you want me to open it? Say, 'open.'" Reward any vocalization other than a fuss with opening the box.

Proceed similarly with a jar of bubble liquid—blow some bubbles, close the container, and wait for the child to request you to blow more bubbles. Try to get the child to say "bubbles."

DAILY ROUTINES & FUNCTIONAL ACTIVITIES

Carefully observe the child's attempts to communicate her wishes throughout the day. If her words are difficult to understand, tell her what you think she has said (e.g., "Open? Do you want me to open it?" "Come? Do you want me to come?"). Respond to these requests, if possible. If you cannot respond because you are doing something else, tell the child she must wait but then do what she asked as soon as you can. It is important that the child has success with her early requests so that she knows she is communicating them.

CRITERION   The child uses words or signs to request at least three different actions on three different days.

■ ■ ■

14dd. Answers simple questions with a verbal response, gesture, or sign

14ee. Asks simple questions with a vocalization or gesture (e.g., "What doing?" "Where going?")

14ff. Asks yes/no questions with appropriate inflection

MATERIALS   Several toys or other functional objects

PROCEDURES

Place a few objects in front of the child, and ask him questions that he can answer by saying either "yes" or "no" (e.g., "Is this a spoon?" "Do I use this cup for drinking?").

After the child is answering yes/no questions, hide a toy behind or under another object and ask, "Where is the [object]?" Also, hold up the object and ask, "What is this?" If the child does not respond or responds incorrectly, model the correct response and try another question.

Place an interesting, novel object in front of the child without saying anything. As he explores the object, listen for him to ask a question about it. If he does not, ask him one (e.g., "Do you know what that is?" "Do you know what we can do with that?"). You can also make something out of paper (e.g., make a paper airplane) to see if the child will ask what you are doing, what the object is, and so forth.

DAILY ROUTINES & FUNCTIONAL ACTIVITIES

Ask the child questions frequently in the course of daily activities. If he does not answer, model appropriate answers for him. For example, if you ask the child, "What are you doing?" and he does not reply, you might say, "It looks like you're taking your dog for a ride in the truck. Is that what you're doing?"

Respond quickly when the child asks questions of you. If he rarely asks questions, set up situations throughout the day where you attract his attention and do some interesting activity, but do not talk about it as you do it. If this does not prompt the child to ask questions, begin asking him some to model the behavior.

CRITERION 14dd   The child regularly answers simple questions with a verbal response or gesture. The answers must be other than just "yes" or "no."

CRITERION 14ee   The child asks at least three different questions a day on three different days. (It is not necessary for the child to have the correct word order as long as the inflection indicates a question—"Mommy's going to the store?" is all right if the inflection is correct).

CRITERION 14ff   The child asks three different yes/no questions per day on 3 days

■ ■ ■

14gg. Requests assistance (e.g., "Help," "You do it")

MATERIALS   Toys or other objects that will challenge the child (e.g., puzzles, wind-up toys)

PROCEDURES

Give the child a challenging toy to work with. If she becomes frustrated but does not ask for help, ask, "Would you like some help?" or "May I help you?" If she nods or gives other nonverbal evidence that she wants help, tell her, "Say, 'Help me.'" Provide assistance. Try other tasks and continue to prompt her to ask for help if she becomes frustrated. Whenever possible, give the child a choice as to whether you help her—don't just do activities for her. Some children have a strong need to do activities on their own.

Respond positively to requests for help. Indicate an appreciation for how hard the task is, do only as much as necessary to help the child, and praise the child for trying hard.

DAILY ROUTINES & FUNCTIONAL ACTIVITIES

Model asking for help within the family or classroom (e.g., "Please help me pick up the toys," "Please hold this box so I can open the door"). Prompt the child (and other children) to ask for help when a task is difficult.

CRITERION   The child requests help from an adult or another child when a task is difficult on three different occasions.

■ ■ ■

14hh. Uses word or sign combinations to describe remote events

MATERIALS   None required

PROCEDURES

When you first see the child after he has been on an outing or after you have been away, ask him about his experiences (e.g., "Where did you go with Grandma?" "What did you do at school today?"). If the child does not respond, ask more specific questions (e.g., "Did you go to the store?" Did you play outside?"). The child may simply answer "yes" or "no," but these questions give him some cues as to how to answer the more open-ended questions.

DAILY ROUTINES & FUNCTIONAL ACTIVITIES

Frequently engage in conversations with the child. Talk about what the child is doing or what he did earlier in the day. Listen carefully to what the child tries to say. Repeat back what you think you understand to check it out with the child. Ask the child questions about what he wants, what he is doing, and so forth. Listen for the child to describe events or make requests.

CRITERION   The child uses word or sign combinations to describe remote events two or more times in a week.

■ ■ ■

14ii. Comments on appearance or disappearance of objects or people

MATERIALS   None required

PROCEDURES

Put away something that has been a standard part of the home or classroom for some period of time. Notice whether the child comments on the disappearance or asks questions about it. Add something to the room or classroom and observe to see if the child comments on it.

Enlist the child's parent or caregiver to be in the room with you and the child and to interact with the child in a typical way. Then, when the child is engaged in some activity alone or with you, have the caregiver step out of the room quietly. Observe to see if the child comments as the person leaves or afterward.

DAILY ROUTINES & FUNCTIONAL ACTIVITIES

Help the child become aware of her world by commenting on what you see and do not see. As the child empties her cup, look in it and say, "All gone," or "No more milk." If the child asks for a parent or caregiver who has gone to work, say, "Mama's gone to work." Ask the child "where" questions (e.g., "Where's Daddy?" "Where are your potatoes?") Listen for the child to ask you "where" questions or to comment on objects or people who are coming or leaving, appearing or disappearing.

If you are in a group setting and one child is absent, ask the child if she knows who is missing.

CRITERION   On at least three occasions, the child comments on the appearance or disappearance of objects or people without being prompted or asked questions.

■ ■ ■

14jj. Sustains conversation for several turns

MATERIALS   None required

PROCEDURES

Talk to the child about activities that he is doing, activities that you are doing, or plans for such activities. Take time to listen to the child's responses, and let him direct the conversation. Pay attention to how many turns each of you takes during the conversation.

DAILY ROUTINES & FUNCTIONAL ACTIVITIES

Pay attention to the child when he is playing with other children. Does he have conversations that last for several turns?

CRITERION   *The child sustains a conversation for three or four turns on several occasions.*

■ ■ ■

14kk. Reads books to others
by making multiple-word utterances

MATERIALS   A variety of interesting books appropriate for infants and toddlers

PROCEDURES

Read a familiar book to the child and then ask her to read it to you or to tell you all about it. Do not correct her if she is telling a familiar story in an abbreviated or incorrect manner. Listen for her to make a two- to three-word utterance as she looks at a page. If she does not, ask questions about the pictures (e.g., "What is happening there?" "Who is that?").

DAILY ROUTINES & FUNCTIONAL ACTIVITIES

Read to the child daily. Observe her as she looks at a book on her own. Does she tell part of the story or describe the pictures? Suggest that the child show the book to someone else and tell that person about it.

CRITERION   *On three or more occasions, the child reads books to others by making multiple-word utterances.*

■ ■ ■

14ll. Responds appropriately to "where" and "why" questions

MATERIALS   None required

PROCEDURES

Ask the child several "where" questions that can be answered by pointing or by stating a location (e.g., "Where are your shoes?" "Where is your nose?" "Where is the lamp?").

Read a story to the child and then ask him "why" questions (e.g., "Why did the third little pig build his house out of bricks"?). If the child does not respond, give him some choices for a response (e.g., "Was it because she wanted a strong house to keep out the wolf?"). Ask the child to bring you something that you know will be difficult for him to carry. Then ask her, "Why is that so hard to carry?" If he does not reply, say, "Is it because it is too big to carry?"

DAILY ROUTINES & FUNCTIONAL ACTIVITIES

As you do activities with the child throughout the day, talk about the places you can find different objects or people, introducing the topic with a "where" question (e.g., "Where's Daddy? He's in the kitchen," "Where did we leave your ball? It must be outside," "Where are the crayons? Oh, they are here in this box").

Sing Where Is Thumbkin? ("Where is Thumbkin? Where is Thumbkin? Here I am [hold up one thumb]. Here I am [hold up second thumb]. How are you today, sir [one thumb bows several times to the other]? Very well, I thank you [the other bows]. Run away [one hand behind the back]. Run away [the other hand behind the back]"—continue with Pointer, Tall Man, Ring Man, and Pinkie.)

Use the term "why" as you discuss how various objects work in the environment (e.g., "Why is this chair so hard to move? I guess it is because it is so heavy," "Why are you crying? Is it because you fell down?"). Give reasons for decisions or instructions (e.g., "You can't do that because . . .," "I can't lift it because it is too heavy," "I can't look now because I am driving"). Ask the child "why" questions in a variety of contexts supplying answers if he cannot.

Note: Avoid asking "why" questions to assess a young child's motives (e.g., "Why did you hit Johnny?" "Why did you write on the wall?" "Why did you wet your pants?"). Children at this stage usually do not understand their own motives. If you are unhappy with something a child has done, it is much better to tell him you do not like for him to do that act than to ask him why he did it.

CRITERION   The child points to indicate where, retrieves an object, or tells a location in response to three or more different "where" questions and responds appropriately (gives reasons) to three or more "why" questions. In neither case is it necessary that the child's answer be correct. Rather, the issue is that he understands a "where" question requires a location response and a "why" question requires some kind of a reason, usually prefaced by because.

15

Grammatical Structure

Human beings appear to be "wired" to learn language with its complex grammatical structures. Although it is unclear how much caregivers can influence the rate at which their children learn these structures, it is obvious that children must hear the structures (or see them, in the case of signed speech) and have the opportunity to practice them. Most caregivers naturally adapt their speech so that they are always just one step ahead of the child in the complexity of the speech they use, thereby giving the child models for the next structures to be learned. For typically developing children, this is enough. For children with special needs, however, more repetition and greater emphasis may be needed to encourage development. Caregivers should be sure not to nag children about grammar, as this may interfere with the communication.

This sequence includes grammatical forms roughly in the order they are mastered by the majority of typically developing children and suggestions for encouraging the mastery of those forms. Some children may need time to work individually in speech-language therapy, concentrating on sentence construction. The rest of the time, however, you should encourage learning by listening to the children, reinforcing correct structures by responding to the structures in a typical communicative fashion, and simply repeating incorrect structures in a correct form to provide a model for the children. Avoid paying too much attention to errors.

ADAPTATIONS

Children with Motor Impairments

It is important to provide opportunities for children to learn these grammatical forms, even if the children cannot talk. This can be done by reading and talking to the children so that they hear the forms repeatedly.

If a child's motor impairments make it impossible for him or her to produce a variety of sounds, seek the help of an augmentative communication system specialist in developing an alternate form of communication. Also, be sure to keep talking to the child, and try to focus on the language structures he or she would typically be developing. It is important that the child hear the structures even though he or she cannot say them. It is also helpful for children with motor impairments to be with other children of a similar age who are developing speech. Your interactions with the other children not only provide model sentences but also help you speak at an appropriate level for the children's understanding. When a child does not talk, adults tend to talk over him or her to another adult or maintain baby talk long after it has become inappropriate.

Children with Visual Impairments

Children with visual impairments usually learn these structures at a rate consistent with their general learning ability. In fact, those children with severe visual impairments may speak long, grammatically correct sentences even though the sentences have little relevance to what is going on in the environment. These children's major problem in learning language is learning the referents for the words and sentences they hear. Caregivers must be alert to helping such children understand the meaning of the words and sentences they hear and say.

Children with Hearing Impairments

With children with hearing impairments, pay particular attention to their words in isolation as well as to their attempts to communicate through gestures and signs. Respond appropriately. Credit signs mixed in with other gestures if the children are being exposed to signs.

Note: The focus of this sequence is on English, not American Sign Language.

15. GRAMMATICAL STRUCTURE

a. Uses inflection patterns in a sentence with one or two understandable words (or mixes recognizable signs with gestures)

b. Uses two-word utterances to indicate possession and action

c. Uses two-word utterances to indicate nonexistence and recurrence

d. Uses two-word utterances to indicate specificity and characteristics

e. Uses "-s" on the ends of some words to form plurals

f. Uses auxiliary verbs, usually shortened

g. Uses "-ing" on verbs

h. Uses negative terms

i. Uses personal pronouns

j. Uses prepositional phrases

k. Uses three-word phrases to specify, to indicate rejection, and/or to describe

■ ■ ■

15a. Uses inflection patterns in a sentence with one or two understandable words (or mixes recognizable signs with gestures)

MATERIALS   None required

PROCEDURES

After a child has begun to vocalize inflection patterns (something that sounds like a sentence), it will usually not be long until you are able to distinguish one or more words in such a vocalization. Try to determine what the child might mean, and repeat back a simple two- or three-word phrase summarizing the child's vocalization and using the words you think he has said. Respond to the child's jargon as if he were communicating clearly (i.e., look at him, listen, and take turns speaking).

DAILY ROUTINES & FUNCTIONAL ACTIVITIES

Listen carefully throughout the day to the child's vocalizations, and try to extract the child's meaning from the sounds and the context. Speak back to him, expressing what you think you understood. Letting the child know that you value his vocalizations will increase his desire to talk and his ability to communicate.

CRITERION   The child often uses inflection patterns in a sentence with one or two understandable words.

■ ■ ■

15b. Uses two-word utterances to indicate possession and action (e.g., "Mommy's sock," "my doll," "eat cookie")

15c. Uses two-word utterances to indicate nonexistence (e.g., "no juice," "Daddy gone") and recurrence (e.g., "more juice," "Daddy here")

15d. Uses two-word utterances to indicate specificity (e.g., "this toy," "that box") and characteristics (e.g., "hot stove," "pretty bunny")

MATERIALS   None required

PROCEDURES

When the child is using one-word utterances, respond to her by repeating her word and expanding on it. For example, when the child says "hot," you say, "Yes, hot. Hot stove." When the child holds out her glass and says "juice," you say, "You have no juice. Do you want more juice? Here is some more juice" (give a special emphasis to the word you are using to expand the child's statement). When she says "sock," say, "Yes, sock. Daddy's sock." Listen for the child to imitate you and then use two-word utterances spontaneously. At this stage, it is acceptable if the child uses an incorrect form of a verb (e.g., "Daddy goed," "Mommy wented").

DAILY ROUTINES & FUNCTIONAL ACTIVITIES

Talk to the child frequently during the course of the day. Do not use "baby talk" but do place extra emphasis on short phrases that the child will be more likely to imitate.

CRITERION 15b   The child uses several two-word utterances indicating possession or action.

CRITERION 15c   The child uses several two-word utterances indicating nonexistence or recurrence.

CRITERION 15d   The child uses several two-word utterances indicating specificity or particular characteristics.

■ ■ ■

15e. Uses "-s" on the ends of some words to form plurals

MATERIALS   Groups of similar toys (e.g., several cars, several dolls, several blocks, several stuffed bears), pictures or picture books

PROCEDURES

Place one car in front of yourself and two cars in front of the child. Say, "I have one car. You have two . . ." (waiting for him to fill in the word). If he does not fill in the correct word, say, "You have two cars" (emphasizing the "s"). Now, add another car to your pile. Say, "Look, now you have two cars and I have two . . ." Try a similar procedure with several other sets of toys.

Look at pictures or a book with the child. Point to the pictures and ask questions to elicit the use of plurals (e.g., "What does that boy have? He has some [objects]").

DAILY ROUTINES & FUNCTIONAL ACTIVITIES

Throughout the day, make a special effort to pronounce the "s" on the end of words indicating a plural. Use numbers and other quantity words when talking about objects that you are seeing or playing with (e.g., "I have just one block. You have a lot of blocks," "Here, you can have two cookies," "Look at this picture. There is only one puppy. In this picture, there are three puppies—one, two, three"). Listen for the child to begin using "s" on the ends of words to indicate plurals.

Sing songs, read nursery rhymes, and do fingerplays that involve both singular and plural nouns. Emphasize the "s" on the plurals so that the child will hear it.

CRITERION   The child uses plurals for several different words. At this stage, it is counted as correct if the child incorrectly forms plurals for irregular words (e.g., says "mans" instead of "men").

■ ■ ■

15f. Uses auxiliary verbs, usually shortened (e.g., "gonna," "wanna," "hafta")

MATERIALS   A variety of interesting toys

PROCEDURES

Sit with the child and talk as you manipulate the toys together. Create sentences using auxiliary verbs, and ask the child questions that are likely to elicit such verbs. For example, say, "I'm going to put this ball right here. What are you going to do with your ball?" "I want to see what is in this box. What do you want to do?" "We made a mess. I have to get a towel" (don't get one for the child and see if she will say, "I have to get one, too"). If the child does not imitate you or use the auxiliary verbs spontaneously as you play, try to prompt her to do so. For example, ask, "What are you going to do?" If she does not answer but shows you, say, "Oh, you are going to zoom that car. Say, 'I'm going to zoom the car.' "

DAILY ROUTINES & FUNCTIONAL ACTIVITIES

Make sure that you are using auxiliary verbs in your conversations with the child throughout the day. They will come very naturally if you describe your activities to the child as you do them (e.g., "Now I'm going to wash the dishes," "I have to change your diaper before we go out," "I want to go outside").

CRITERION   The child uses at least two auxiliary verb forms several times.

■ ■ ■

15g. Uses "-ing" on verbs

MATERIALS   Picture books

PROCEDURES

Look at a book with the child and ask questions such as "What is that boy doing?" or create a fill-in-the-blank sentence such as "Look at that dog. He is . . ." If the child does not respond with an "ing" verb, answer your own question ("The boy is running"), or complete your sentence ("That dog is eating").

DAILY ROUTINES & FUNCTIONAL ACTIVITIES

Throughout the day, talk to the child frequently about what you are doing and about what he is doing. It will be natural to include verbs with the "-ing" ending (e.g., "We are going . . .," "I am doing . . .," "Grandma is coming"). Listen for the child to begin using "-ing" on the end of verbs. Repeat the "-ing" verbs to the child when he does use them (e.g., "Yes, we are going home").

CRITERION   The child using "-ing" on the end of several different verbs.

■ ■ ■

15h. Uses negative terms (e.g., "can't," "won't," "do not")

MATERIALS   A variety of interesting toys

PROCEDURES

Use the toys to play with the child. Create opportunities to insert negative terms (e.g., "I can't make this piece fit. Will you hold it for me?" "That car won't go. It lost a wheel"). Listen for the child to use these terms. If she does, repeat what she says and expand it in some natural way (e.g., if the child says "can't go," you say, "The car can't go. The car must be broken. Let's see if I can fix it").

DAILY ROUTINES & FUNCTIONAL ACTIVITIES

You will use these terms naturally with the child as you talk to her about your daily activities. Listen to the child so that you will hear when she begins to use such negative terms. Let the child know you have heard her and understand her by repeating her sentence and expanding it in some natural way.

CRITERION   The child uses at least two different negative terms (e.g., "can't," "won't," "do not") on several different days.

15

15i. Uses personal pronouns
(e.g., "me," "you," "mine," "your")

MATERIALS   A group of interesting toys

PROCEDURES

Play with the child in a natural way, letting him take the lead. Try to maintain a conversation, and make a point of using personal pronouns (e.g., "That's your truck. This one is mine," "I want the ball. Will you please hand it to me?"). Listen for the child to use these pronouns. If he does not, ask questions to try to elicit them.

DAILY ROUTINES & FUNCTIONAL ACTIVITIES

As soon as it is clear that the child understands the name of familiar people, begin to use personal pronouns. For example, caregivers should begin to say, "I love you," rather than "Mommy loves you." Likewise, the caregiver should begin to use *you* and *your* with the child (e.g., "You are my big boy," rather than "Johnny is my big boy"). Listen to the child so that you will hear when he begins to use these pronouns. Do not correct the child if he gets them wrong (e.g., "Me going to the store"), but continue to model the correct usage.

Read stories to the child with many conversations in them. These will include the usage of numerous personal pronouns.

CRITERION   *The child uses at least three personal pronouns, each on several occasions.*

15j. Uses prepositional phrases
(e.g., "in house," "on table")

MATERIALS   A variety of interesting toys

PROCEDURES

Use the toys to play with the child. Place them in various relationships to one another (e.g., on top of, next to, behind, between, under) and talk about what you are doing. If the child does not take the cue from you and begin talking about what she is doing, ask questions that are likely to elicit prepositions (e.g., "Where is the [toy]?" "Where did you put the [toy]?"). If the child does not answer, answer for her, and try to get her to repeat your answer (e.g., "There it is, it is *on* the chair. Where is it?").

DAILY ROUTINES & FUNCTIONAL ACTIVITIES

Throughout the day, emphasize prepositions as you talk to the child about activities that you are doing or about what is happening (e.g., "Your ball is *under* the table," "Let's put the sheets *on* the bed," "Put your toys *in* the toy box"). Listen for the child's first attempts to use these words. Encourage the child to use prepositions by asking her where objects are (e.g., "Where is your book?"). If the child does not reply or just points, say, "I see it.

It is on the table." You can also make a game of hiding objects in, on, or under containers and have the child (or children) guess where they are.

CRITERION   The child uses at least two different prepositions in phrases, each several times.

■ ■ ■

15k. Uses three-word phrases to specify (e.g., "that big one," "this finger hurt"), to indicate rejection (e.g., "no scary book," "no want that"), and/or to describe (e.g., "the big dog")

MATERIALS   None required

PROCEDURES

Play with the child, allowing him to take the lead. Try to maintain a conversation about what you are doing. Ask open-ended questions (i.e., questions that are not easily answered with "yes" or "no"), such as "What would you like to play with?" or "What do you want?" Listen for three-word phrases that include adjectives or other specifying words.

DAILY ROUTINES & FUNCTIONAL ACTIVITIES

As the child uses two-word phrases, expand on them to encourage the child to produce longer phrases. For example, if the child says "that one," say, "Oh, you want that big one?" Read simple picture books to the child, and talk about the pictures. Encourage the child to talk about them, too. Listen for three-word phrases.

CRITERION   The child uses several three-word phrases on several different days.

16
Imitation: Vocal

A child's ability to speak depends on hearing a language spoken and on the ability to imitate the sounds within that language (or languages in a setting where more than one language is spoken). For most children, vocal imitation appears to happen automatically, beginning with watching a speaker, making a variety of sounds, and then learning to match mouth movements and sounds to those of the caregivers. Various impairments, however, may interfere with this form of imitation. Some children do not pay sufficient attention to imitate what caregivers do. Others have problems with motor coordination or motor planning, which interfere with the production of sounds. Still others do not hear the sounds well enough to imitate them.

This sequence is designed to help caregivers promote vocal imitation through paying attention to children's attempts to imitate, reinforcing those attempts, and trying to shape more accurate and complex imitation as the children develop. At the beginning, the focus is on speech sounds, but at the end, the focus is on imitation of complete sentences with accuracy.

ADAPTATIONS

Children with Motor Impairments

Some children with motor impairments will find it very difficult (or impossible) to control the lips, jaw, and tongue well enough to imitate sounds. It is important to keep trying to elicit the imitation and to reinforce the child's attempts.

Children with Visual Impairments

When children with significant visual impairments are first beginning to attend to sounds and experiment with vocal play, make a point of touching the children to draw their attention to you. Also, encourage these children to touch your face and mouth as you talk or make noises.

Children with Hearing Impairments

Make extra efforts to be sure children with hearing impairments are attending to you when you make sounds or speak words. You may need to work in a very quiet environment. Be sure to consult a child's audiologist and/or speech-language pathologist regarding the pitch and loudness that will be likely to get the most reliable reactions from the child.

Encourage children with hearing impairments not only to touch your mouth but also to hold their hands on your throat to feel the vibrations of your speech. Take a child's hands to his or her own throat to help the child compare the way it feels.

Children with profound hearing losses may never imitate sounds very effectively. Consult with a child's audiologist or speech-language pathologist to determine if it is appropriate to emphasize motor imitation (see Sequence 17: Imitation: Motor) so that gestures can take the place of early words for communication purposes.

16. IMITATION: VOCAL

a. Quiets to voice

b. Looks at person who is talking

c. Repeats sounds just made when imitated by caregiver

d. Shifts sounds (imitates sounds in repertoire when made by caregiver)

e. Imitates inflection

f. Experiments with making own mouth move like that of an adult

g. Attempts to match new sounds

h. Imitates familiar two-syllable words without syllable changes

i. Imitates familiar two-syllable words with syllable changes

j. Imitates most novel one-syllable words

k. Imitates a variety of novel two-syllable words

l. Imitates familiar words overheard in conversation or from books

m. Imitates the vocalizations others use for environmental sounds

n. Imitates two-word phrases or sentences

o. Imitates three-syllable words (or two-word phrases containing three syllables)

p. Repeats novel two-word or two-number sequence

q. Repeats three-word sentences

■ ■ ■

16a. Quiets to voice

MATERIALS   None required

PROCEDURES

When the child is lying down and alert, or when the child is just beginning to fuss, move over to her and talk in an animated but comforting fashion. Observe to see if the child's motor activity decreases, if she stops fussing, or if there is some other behavioral change to suggest that she is listening and interested. If the child does not stop fussing, pick her up and comfort her. It is through associating the voice with comfort that she will learn to quiet to just a voice alone.

Begin to talk to the child before you are within her field of vision. Observe to see if her behavior changes to just your voice or to both the sight and sound of you.

DAILY ROUTINES & FUNCTIONAL ACTIVITIES

Always speak to the child when you pick her up in response to her fussing. Then, try speaking to the child when she begins to fuss rather than immediately picking her up to see if she will quiet to your voice alone. Then, pick up the child, and attend to her needs.

Note: Be sure to give the child time to respond to your voice. Some children seem to either process information very slowly or have difficulty organizing a response to incoming information.

CRITERION   *The child quiets to a voice on four or more different occasions. That is, the child's motor activity decreases or fussing diminishes on hearing a voice. This should occur prior to seeing the person who is talking.*

■ ■ ■

16b. Looks at person who is talking

MATERIALS   None required

PROCEDURES

Talk to the child in an animated fashion, using hand gestures that are appropriate to what you are saying. If the child looks at you, continue to speak to him, touch him, smile, and/or pick him up. Try to maintain eye contact with him for as long as you can.

DAILY ROUTINES & FUNCTIONAL ACTIVITIES

Make a point of looking directly at the child and talking to him while you are changing his diaper, feeding him, bathing him, or engaging in other routine activities. Try to maintain eye contact with him for as long as you can.

CRITERION   *On four or more different occasions, the child looks at the person who is talking and gesturing. The child should orient to the person as the person begins to talk, and the child should continue looking at the person who is talking for at least 1 minute (although there may be momentary looking away and then back again).*

■ ■ ■

16c. Repeats sounds
just made when imitated by caregiver

16d. Shifts sounds (imitates sounds
in repertoire when made by caregiver)

MATERIALS   None required

PROCEDURES

Attend to sounds that the child spontaneously makes. Imitate the sound a child makes, and pause to see if she makes the sound again. If the child makes another sound, imitate that one, and wait again.

When the child has learned to continue an exchange in which you imitate a sound she is making and she repeats it, change the rules of the "game." Instead of continuing to imitate the child, answer the child's vocalization with a different sound, one that you have heard the child make on other occasions. Wait to see what the child does. If she repeats the original sound, say the different sound again. Watch for the child to make an effort to change her sounds to match yours.

DAILY ROUTINES & FUNCTIONAL ACTIVITIES

As you interact with the child throughout the day, make a point of imitating the sounds she makes, waiting to see if she will repeat them or will make some other sound. Once the child is repeating a sound in this fashion, begin introducing another sound you have heard her make instead of just imitating her. See if she attempts to change her vocalization to match yours. This imitation and turn taking is the beginning of conversation.

16

Note: There is a period in many children's development when they will become very quiet if a person talks when they are talking. If the child does stop vocalizing when you attempt to start this turn-taking game, just wait until the next vocalization and try again. Eventually, the child will learn the turn-taking pattern.

CRITERION 16c   The child repeats sounds just made when imitated by the caregiver several times a day on a daily basis.

CRITERION 16d   On four or more different occasions, the child shifts sounds when the caregiver responds to the child's vocalization with another sound from the child's repertoire.

■ ■ ■

16e. Imitates inflection

MATERIALS   None required

PROCEDURES

When engaging in vocal turn taking with the child, introduce some exaggerated inflection pattern(s). For example, if you are saying "ba ba ba ba ba" in a normal tone of voice, begin to say it with a high-pitched, squeaky voice. Watch the child's reactions, and wait to see if he attempts to imitate you. If the child does not attempt to imitate, go back to your normal voice for a few turns and then again try the squeaky voice or, perhaps, a big, deep voice.

DAILY ROUTINES & FUNCTIONAL ACTIVITIES

Play vocal games with the child as you go through your daily child care routines. Vary the pitch, speed, and volume in your voice, and listen for the child's attempts to imitate you.

Note: Some children will find exaggerated shifts in pitch amusing and will smile or laugh instead of trying to imitate. Laugh along with them, but try again.

CRITERION   On three or more occasions, the child changes his pitch in an attempt to imitate a caregiver's pitch changes.

■ ■ ■

16f. Experiments with making own mouth move like that of an adult

MATERIALS   None required

PROCEDURES

Hold the child so that she is facing you and near enough to reach out and touch your mouth. Talk to the child, exaggerating your lip and tongue movements. Also, try making faces (e.g., stick out your tongue, pucker your lips as if to whistle, move your tongue back and forth quickly between your lips). Watch the child's mouth and lip movements. When she imitates you, make that same movement again. If the child makes no attempt to imitate you, try to prompt imitation by doing movements with your lips slowly and using your fingers to encourage her lips to move like yours.

DAILY ROUTINES & FUNCTIONAL ACTIVITIES

Spend time several times a day holding the child on your lap or in another position that allows her to see and reach for your face as you talk. Allow the child to touch your face and mouth.

Watch the child's mouth as you talk. Notice whether the child moves her mouth as you talk, as if trying to do what you are doing. Exaggerate your mouth movements (e.g., make a big "o" shape, whistle, tighten your lips and say "mm-mm-mm-mm").

Note: This item is different from earlier efforts in which the child attempts to move her mouth when seeing the adult talking in that now the child is both more deliberate and more precise in her imitations and is actively interested in the mouth of the speaker and the sounds it produces.

CRITERION   The child experiments on four or more occasions with making her own mouth move in a manner similar to that of the adult.

■ ■ ■

16g. Attempts to match new sounds

MATERIALS   None required

PROCEDURES

Get a vocal turn-taking game going by imitating the sounds the child makes and introducing other sounds you have heard him make (see Items 16d and 16e). Then, introduce a sound you have not heard the child make. For example, the child may be saying, "dadada," "bababa," "gagaga," and other sounds incorporating a consonant and an "ah" sound and may readily change from one to the other in imitation of you. If so, you might introduce one of the same consonants with an "oo" sound (e.g., "doo, doo, doo," "boo, boo, boo," "goo, goo, goo"). Pause a while to allow the child time to imitate the sound. React with enthusiasm when he does imitate these new sounds.

DAILY ROUTINES & FUNCTIONAL ACTIVITIES

Include the above procedure in your interactions with the child throughout the day. Mealtimes are especially good for eliciting different sounds from a child. Try to have relaxed mealtimes with a lot of conversation with the child.

CRITERION   The child attempts to match new sounds on a daily basis. The imitation does not have to be exact, but it should be evident that the child is trying to change the way he shapes his mouth, moves his lips or tongue, and so forth.

■ ■ ■

16h. Imitates familiar two-syllable words without syllable changes (e.g., "baba," "Dada," "Mama")

16i. Imitates familiar two-syllable words with syllable changes (e.g., "baby," "uh-oh," "all gone")

MATERIALS   None required

PROCEDURES

Establish a vocal turn-taking game with the child and begin to introduce familiar two-syllable words that do not require a change in syllables (e.g., "Dada," "Mama," "Nana"). Pause to see if the child will imitate the words you say.

You may be most successful if you introduce a word when the child is making sounds similar to that word. For example, children frequently babble "dadadada" long before they actually say "Dada" (stopping after two syllables). When the child babbles "dada-dada," you should say "Dada" with uneven emphasis on the two syllables, making it sound more like a single word than part of a stream of babble. Again, wait for the child to imitate. If she continues to babble, continue to take your turn with similar sounds, but in word form.

Once the child has begun to imitate two-syllable words with repetitive syllables, start trying to get her to imitate words with syllable changes (e.g., "baby," "uh-oh," "all gone," "Daddy"). Always smile and talk to the child to reward her efforts.

DAILY ROUTINES & FUNCTIONAL ACTIVITIES

Initiate a vocal imitation game, following the above procedure, several times a day during play or regular caregiving activities.

CRITERION   The child imitates at least two familiar two-syllable words on four or more occasions.

■ ■ ■

16j. Imitates most novel one-syllable words

16k. Imitates a variety of novel two-syllable words

MATERIALS   A variety of toys or interesting objects, picture books

PROCEDURES

Select objects or pictures to show the child what can be labeled with simple one-syllable words (e.g., "ball," "car," "boat," "star," "shoe," "dog"). Hold an object up for the child to see, and say the word clearly. Wait to see if the child will imitate what you say.

When the child is reliably imitating one-syllable words, introduce two-syllable words (e.g., "monkey," "puppy," "berry," "flower"). Give credit for approximations (e.g., "bah" for ball, "bo" for boat, "muh-key" for monkey) The issue is not whether the child has good articulation but whether he changes his sounds consistently when imitating words that are new to his expressive vocabulary.

DAILY ROUTINES & FUNCTIONAL ACTIVITIES

Make a point of noticing what the child seems to be interested in, and label these items for him. Look at picture books with the child and point to and label the pictures. Always wait after you have said a label to see if the child will try to imitate you. If he does not, say the word again and ask, "Can you say [word]?"

CRITERION 16j   The child imitates four or more novel one-syllable words.

CRITERION 16k   The child imitates a variety of novel two-syllable words (six or more).

■ ■ ■

16l. Imitates familiar words overheard in conversation or from books

MATERIALS   Picture books

PROCEDURES

This is a difficult skill to elicit in an artificial fashion. One possible way to do it is to read one or two books to the child. The books should be relatively new to her and should contain pictures of objects or animals that are familiar to her. Give the child the books to look at while you talk to another adult or do some other activity. Listen for the child to repeat words that she heard when you read the books to her.

DAILY ROUTINES & FUNCTIONAL ACTIVITIES

Periodically observe the child when you are talking to another adult or to another child to see if she is listening and repeating one or more of the words that she hears. Also, pay attention to the sounds that the child makes after the conversation is over. She may practice some of the words she heard. Likewise, the child may practice words she hears on television, or she may use the words while looking at books. Listen for them.

CRITERION   On three or more occasions, the child imitates familiar words overheard some time beforehand.

■ ■ ■

16m. Imitates the vocalizations others use for environmental sounds

16

MATERIALS   A variety of toys and picture books

PROCEDURES

Read to the child or play with him, and make appropriate nonspeech noises that are associated with different animals or objects. For example, "moo" at the picture of a cow after you say "cow," bark for a dog, meow for a cat, make "rhmm, rhmm, rhmm" noises for a car, and make "choo choo" noises for a train. After you have made each sound, listen to see if the child imitates the sound. Also listen to see if the child makes this sound spontaneously when he looks at the pictures or plays with his toys.

DAILY ROUTINES & FUNCTIONAL ACTIVITIES

Read books to the child daily, introducing nonspeech sounds that may not be a part of the book's text. For example, the child may not be able to sit still for you to read *The Little Engine That Could* but may greatly enjoy when you read one sentence for each page that includes different engine sounds for the different engines. You can also make up sounds to go with the child's toys. He will likely to try to imitate these sounds.

CRITERION   The child imitates two or more different environmental sounds.

■ ■ ■

16n. Imitates two-word phrases or sentences

MATERIALS   A variety of toys and picture books

PROCEDURES

Play with the child (or read to her), and try to get her to name objects and/or imitate your labels for them. When she says one word, expand it with an adjective or a verb. For example, if the child says "ball," you can say "big ball" or "Throw the ball." Listen for the child to imitate these two-word phrases. If she does not, try to elicit the imitation by saying "big ball. You say it: 'big ball' " or by saying, "Say 'big.' Now say 'ball.' Now say 'big ball.' " Do not focus on this artificial practice, however, for more than a few trials at a time.

DAILY ROUTINES & FUNCTIONAL ACTIVITIES

As the child begins to use more single words to communicate, begin stressing two- and three-word sentences as you talk. Be sure to pause after you speak, giving the child an opportunity to try to imitate you. If she does not imitate you, repeat what you said and wait again. Try two or three times but no more at one time. Always let the child know you like it when she imitates you. Also, continue to provide experiences that reinforce the meaning of the words that you introduce.

CRITERION   The child imitates three or more two-word sentences or phrases.

■ ■ ■

16o. Imitates three-syllable words
(or two-word phrases containing three syllables)

MATERIALS   A variety of toys and picture books

PROCEDURES

Begin focusing on three-syllable words as you play with the child or read to him (e.g., "butterfly," "elephant"). Also, focus on two-word sentences that contain three different syllables (e.g., "Daddy gone," "Baby eat"). If he does not imitate spontaneously, try to elicit imitation by repeating the words slowly and asking him to say them.

DAILY ROUTINES & FUNCTIONAL ACTIVITIES

The child will hear many three-syllable words throughout the course of the day. Pay attention to his efforts to begin to imitate more complex sound sequences—either three-syllable words (e.g., "Granddaddy") or two-word phrases containing three syllables (e.g., "Doggie gone"). Speak some of these words or phrases more slowly and distinctly to facilitate imitation. Show your pleasure at the child's attempts to imitate.

CRITERION   *The child imitates four or more three-syllable words (or two-word phrases containing three different syllables) on several different occasions.*

■ ■ ■

16p. Repeats novel two-word or two-number sequence

MATERIALS   None required

PROCEDURES

Play a game with the child that involves each of you repeating what the other says. Most children who have been imitating two-word sentences will find such a game fun. Always start easy, that is, with only one number or a short word. Then move on to a two-word or number sequence (e.g., "Say 'apple.' Say 'Daddy.' Now say 'apple, Daddy' "). If the child gets a two-word sequence correct after having repeated each word alone first, try a new two-word sequence, or try two numbers.

DAILY ROUTINES & FUNCTIONAL ACTIVITIES

If there are several children around, include them in playing this game. They can take turns or all repeat it together. Begin with single words or numbers and move on to two-word or two-number sequences. Children like it if you put words together that do not typically go together (e.g., "Yummy dirt," "Pickle ice cream").

   Note: Young children may have trouble waiting their turn, and several may call the phrases out. Do not be critical of this; just say, "You all remembered it. Now let's see if Mary can do the next one all by herself."

CRITERION   *The child repeats four or more two-word or two-number sequences.*

■ ■ ■

16q. Repeats three-word sentences

MATERIALS   None required

16

PROCEDURES

Tell the child you want to see if she can say what you say. Begin with one word, then two, and then a three-word sentence (e.g., "Say 'Johnny.' Now say 'Johnny likes.' Now say 'Johnny likes candy.' ") If the child repeats the three-word sentence, try another without presenting it in parts.

DAILY ROUTINES & FUNCTIONAL ACTIVITIES

Listen to the child. Many children repeat things they hear without being asked to do so. If she does not, see if you can get her to repeat phrases you say by starting with a two-word phrase she is already saying. Once the child readily says the phrase, try a three-word sentence.

Repeating sentences also works well when you are reading simple books. Read a short sentence and then say, "Now you read it." Prompt as necessary by providing the first word or the first two words.

CRITERION   *The child repeats four or more different three-word sentences without prompts.*

17
Imitation: Motor

I mitation is as natural to typically developing children as breathing. It is the means by which they learn to manipulate materials, solve problems, and relate to other people. Most children, with or without disabilities, do not have to be taught to imitate, although there may be significant limitations in the kinds of actions children with disabilities can imitate. For these children, this sequence will primarily serve as a means of noting their progress in developing more complex imitative skills. Some children, however, will require coaching both to begin to imitate and to develop the more complex forms of imitation.

ADAPTATIONS

Children with Motor Impairments

All of the items included in this sequence may need to be modified to accommodate children with significant motor impairments. You should seek help from an occupational or physical therapist to determine what movements are possible for a particular child and then design imitation activities that use these movements. For example, if a child can only move his or her hand a few inches to the right or left, a sequence of two motor acts may be moving that hand from a block to a toy dog or from touching a red circle to touching a blue square. In this case, the child is imitating a sequence (as in Item 17n) but is making minimal motor movements.

Children with Visual Impairments

It is obviously difficult to teach children to imitate motor actions if they are unable to see those actions. Children with moderate visual impairments may benefit if you select motor acts that create noises for teaching imitation. When children attempt to imitate, the sounds they create give them feedback about their success.

It may be necessary to help children with severe visual impairments experience another person's movements by exploring the other person's face or body with their hands. It is also helpful for these children to explore their own movements. You should not, however, devote an inordinate amount of time to teaching motor imitation to these children. It is more adaptive for children with visual impairments to simply learn to do motor acts that allow them to move through the environment and manipulate objects appropriately.

Children with Hearing Impairments

No adaptations are necessary for children with hearing impairments beyond touching the children or otherwise ensuring that the children are looking at you when you do the motor acts.

17. IMITATION: MOTOR

a. Looks at caregiver and makes facial movements when caregiver is talking or making noises

b. Continues movement if it is imitated by caregiver

c. Imitates an activity in repertoire after observing caregiver doing that activity

d. Imitates unfamiliar movements

e. Imitates simple gestures, such as signaling "bye-bye" or "no"

f. Imitates frequently observed actions with objects

g. Imitates actions related to the function of objects

h. Imitates gestures or signs caregiver commonly uses

i. Imitates activities involving a combination of objects or two actions with one object

j. Imitates activities involving a combination of objects several hours after observing actions

k. Incorporates sequence of imitated adult activities into solitary play

l. Attempts to solve problems (including activating toys) by imitating adult actions

m. Imitates postures or actions that do not involve props

n. Imitates sequence of two unrelated motor acts

17

■ ■ ■

17a. Looks at caregiver and makes facial movements when caregiver is talking or making noises

MATERIALS   None required

PROCEDURES

Hold the child so that your faces are 12–14 inches apart, and try to establish eye contact. Make noises or talk to the child, exaggerating your facial expressions and mouth movements. Watch for the child to begin moving his mouth as he looks at you.

DAILY ROUTINES & FUNCTIONAL ACTIVITIES

Spend time several times a day holding the child and making sounds, exaggerating your facial expressions and your mouth movements. Watch for the child's efforts to move his mouth as if trying to imitate.

   Note: Because some children with special needs are slow to respond to their caregivers' attempts to engage them with animated facial expressions and unusual sounds, the caregivers gradually stop providing this kind of stimulation. It is important, however, to continue in order to help the child begin to imitate.

CRITERION   On four or more occasions the child begins to make movements with his lips, jaw, and/or tongue as he watches a caregiver who is talking to him.

■ ■ ■

17b. Continues movement if it is imitated by caregiver

MATERIALS   None required

PROCEDURES

As you interact with the child, watch for her to make some discrete movement you can readily imitate. For example, she may slap or finger the table. Imitate this action and wait to see if she will do it again. If she does not, look for another behavior and imitate that. Continue until she repeats a behavior you have imitated. When she does, smile and immediately imitate her again. Try to establish a turn-taking pattern for several turns.

DAILY ROUTINES & FUNCTIONAL ACTIVITIES

Try this activity several times a day when you are sitting with the child during routine activities (e.g., mealtimes).

CRITERION   On four or more occasions, the child continues a movement if it is imitated by a caregiver. Unless the child has a severe motor impairment, at least two different behaviors should be continued for several turns.

■ ■ ■

17c. Imitates an activity in repertoire after observing caregiver doing that activity

MATERIALS   None required

PROCEDURES

As you talk or play with the child, model some simple motor activity that you have seen the child engage in at other times. For example, you might clap your hands or stick out your tongue. Watch to see if the child will imitate you.

If the child does not imitate you, repeat the action. If feasible, physically prompt the child to do the action and then repeat it again.

DAILY ROUTINES & FUNCTIONAL ACTIVITIES

During routine care activities, take a little time to do some simple motor act you have seen the child do spontaneously, and see if he will imitate you.

CRITERION   On four or more occasions, the child imitates an activity that is already in his repertoire after observing a caregiver do the activity. Unless the child has a very limited repertoire of movements, he should imitate at least two different activities.

■ ■ ■

17d. Imitates unfamiliar movements

MATERIALS   None required

PROCEDURES

Try to establish a turn-taking game with the child in which you alternately make the same or similar motor actions (e.g., clapping hands, banging hands on table) that are already in the child's repertoire. Then, introduce a new action (e.g., putting the hands over the eyes, raising the hands high above the head), and see if the child will imitate you.

If the child does not change her behavior in an attempt to imitate the new action, model the behavior again, and physically assist the child to do it. If she does imitate you, respond by laughing, praising, or doing whatever pleases the child.

DAILY ROUTINES & FUNCTIONAL ACTIVITIES

Use turn-taking games to occupy the child in situations that are likely to produce boredom and fussiness (e.g., waiting in grocery lines, waiting for lunch).

Note: It is often helpful (and fun!) to do this activity in front of a mirror.

CRITERION   The child imitates three or more unfamiliar actions on two different days.

■ ■ ■

17e. Imitates simple gestures, such as signaling "bye-bye" or "no"

MATERIALS   None required

PROCEDURES

Select two or three meaningful gestures to teach the child. For example, shaking the head for "no" is one of the first gestures that children imitate. Many parents also emphasize waving "bye-bye." It is also helpful to have a consistent gesture for "more" and "finished."

Use the gestures you select consistently with the words that go with them. For example, when someone says "bye-bye" to the child, watch for him to lift his hand as if beginning to wave. If he does not, gently move his arm back and forth and say "bye-bye." Likewise, when you say "no," be sure to shake your head, and watch for the child to imitate you (head shaking is hard to prompt physically because the child may resist). If you are using other gestures (e.g., *more, finished*), always make the gestures when you say the words. If the child does not imitate you, hold his hands and guide him through the movements. The child's first efforts at imitation may be gross approximations but should be credited. They should gradually become more precise.

DAILY ROUTINES & FUNCTIONAL ACTIVITIES

All of the child's caregivers should be informed of the gestures you are trying to get the child to imitate so that they can be used in different contexts. Develop other gestures that are appropriate to particular events, and prompt the child to imitate them until he begins to imitate you without prompts.

CRITERION   The child imitates at least one simple action, such as waving "bye-bye" or shaking his head, on a daily basis.

■ ■ ■

17f. Imitates frequently observed actions with objects (e.g., stirs with spoon)

17g. Imitates actions related to the function of objects

MATERIALS   Spoon, bowl, small broom, cleaning cloth, other objects appropriate to the setting

PROCEDURES

Place a spoon and a cup in front of the child. Pick up the spoon and pretend to stir something in the cup. Place the spoon down and observe what the child does. If she does not imitate stirring, demonstrate again and say, "Your turn. You stir." If she does not, physically guide her hand to pick up the spoon and stir. Smile and say "good stirring." Use a similar procedure to try to get her to imitate using a cloth to wipe the table, using a broom to sweep, or using other familiar objects in an appropriate manner.

Introduce a less familiar object or new toy to the child (e.g., a wind-up toy, tongs). Demonstrate using it, put it down, and observe the child. If she does not imitate your actions, do them again and ask the child to try. Physically assist her if necessary.

DAILY ROUTINES & FUNCTIONAL ACTIVITIES

When you are preparing the child's meal, doing laundry, dusting, or performing other daily activities, give the child materials that will encourage her to imitate you. For example, if you are mixing some food in a bowl, give her a small bowl and spoon; if you are doing laundry, let her pull clothes from the hamper; if you are dusting, give her a cloth to dust as well.

If the child does not imitate spontaneously, physically guide her hands to do the activity, and hug or praise her for being a good helper.

When you play with the child, demonstrate the function of objects (e.g., push a truck and make a motor noise, use a hair brush to brush a doll's hair). Give the child the materials. Observe to see if she immediately imitates the action. If not, place your hand over hers and help her.

When you introduce an unfamiliar toy, demonstrate its function, and observe to see if the child imitates your actions with the toy.

Note: Children vary in their ability to imitate motor acts accurately. The goal of these items is to get the child to make a reasonable approximation of the adult's actions, regardless of whether the child is fully accurate or successful. For example, the child may put her fingers on the key to a wind-up toy and move her fingers in a back-and-forth motion but not turn the key or make the toy work.

CRITERION 17f   The child imitates two or more frequently observed actions with objects without prompts.

CRITERION 17g   The child imitates actions with at least two unfamiliar objects without prompts.

■ ■ ■

17h. Imitates gestures or signs caregiver commonly uses

17

MATERIALS   None required

PROCEDURES

In addition to continuing to use the gestures or signs selected for Item 17e, develop some playful routines that involve gestures. For example, say to the child, "You are so big," as you raise your hand up over your head; say, "Do you want to eat?" as you put your fingers to your mouth; or say, "Listen to Mommy," as you put your hand by your ear. If the child makes no attempt to imitate you, guide his hands to do the appropriate action.

The next time you do that action, wait to see if the child will imitate without a prompt. If not, prompt again. Continue until he imitates spontaneously.

DAILY ROUTINES & FUNCTIONAL ACTIVITIES

Pay attention to the gestures you naturally use (e.g., putting a finger in front of the lips when you ask someone to be quiet). Watch for the child to begin imitating these gestures.

Note: Most children can produce good approximations of gestures before they can articulate words. Caregivers can promote communication as well as imitative skills by developing consistent gestures to accompany common words such as *more, finished, eat, drink,* and *come.* Using consistent gestures has also been found to help children to learn basic sign language. (See Appendix B at the end of the book for books on early signs.)

CRITERION   The child imitates at least two gestures or signs without prompts.

■ ■ ■

17i. Imitates activities involving
a combination of objects or two actions with one object
17j. Imitates activities involving
a combination of objects several hours after observing actions

MATERIALS   Broom (or brush) and dustpan, small sponge and pan, a container of bubble liquid and a bubble wand, or other materials of your choice

PROCEDURES

Show the child how to brush crumbs or dirt into a dustpan with a broom (or brush). Put the broom and dustpan down, and observe what the child does. If she does not imitate your actions, show her again, and ask her to clean up. Physically assist her if necessary. Follow the same steps to try to get her to imitate putting a sponge in a pan of water and then using it to wipe the table. Or, show her how to put a bubble wand in the bottle and then blow bubbles. Try other actions with other materials.

Put away these materials and bring them out several hours or a day later. Observe what the child does with them. Does she spontaneously use them to imitate the actions you did with them earlier?

DAILY ROUTINES & FUNCTIONAL ACTIVITIES

Give the child access to materials that you use daily in the house (e.g., broom, dustpan, sponges or cloths for cleaning, wooden or plastic spoons, small pans). It may be helpful to reserve one drawer or cabinet in the kitchen for such objects that the child is free to use.

Observe to see if the child tries to imitate daily activities that involve combining objects. Does she, for example, try to sweep dirt into the dustpan with a brush or a broom after watching you do this, or does she imitate your pouring something from a bowl into a pan?

When you use toys to play with the child, try different activities using different combinations of materials (e.g., use a cardboard box for a garage and push a toy car inside to park it, prop one end of a book on blocks and use it as an incline for cars to run down, place a stuffed animal in a box, and push it around as if the box were a car). When you have finished, give the materials to the child and say, "Now, you do it." Help her imitate if necessary. Observe the child when she is playing by herself to see if she remembers your actions and imitates them.

CRITERION 17i   *The child imitates activities involving a combination of objects or two actions with one object on a daily basis.*

CRITERION 17j   *The child imitates adult actions with objects several hours or more after observing the adult's behavior on three or more occasions.*

■ ■ ■

17k. Incorporates sequence of imitated adult activities into solitary play

MATERIALS   Toys that lend themselves to imitation activities (e.g., cooking utensils, a toy tool chest, a toy doctor's kit, a play telephone)

PROCEDURES

Sit with the child and watch him play, participating if he draws you into the play. Observe to see if you can identify sequences of actions that are clearly in imitation of behaviors he has observed from you or other caregivers. It may be giving a baby doll a bottle and putting it to bed, punching buttons on a play telephone and then talking into the receiver, putting play utensils out as if setting the table, using tools to try to fix a truck tire, and so forth. If you do not see any sequential actions of this sort, suggest an activity to the child such as "I think that truck has a bad tire. Can you fix it?" or "I think that bear is hungry. Maybe you should fix him something to eat."

DAILY ROUTINES & FUNCTIONAL ACTIVITIES

Observe the child when he is playing alone or with other children, and try to identify actions that look like an imitation of a sequence of adult activities.

CRITERION   The child incorporates a sequence of imitated adult activities into play on a daily basis. At least two different sequences of activities should be observed.

■ ■ ■

17l. Attempts to solve problems (including activating toys) by imitating adult actions

MATERIALS   An unfamiliar toy or object that must be activated in order to work (e.g., a tape recorder that requires the child to choose between several buttons to push, a top that must be wound up and then released), yardstick or broom, a couple of small cars

PROCEDURES

Show the child a toy or object and demonstrate for her how it works. Then, give the toy to the child and observe what she does. Does she imitate your actions to make it work?

Push two cars or other small toys out of the child's reach (e.g., under a couch or other low surface). Ask, "Uh-oh, how are we going to get them?" Let the child try to reach the cars and then say, "I have an idea. Let's try this." Use a yardstick or broom to retrieve one of the toys. Then say, "How will we get the other one?" Observe what the child does. Does she try to extend her reach with the broom or yardstick?

DAILY ROUTINES & FUNCTIONAL ACTIVITIES

Observe what the child does when she encounters a problem or tries to activate a toy. Before asking for help, does she try some action she has observed? For example, if something is too high to be reached, does she pull over a chair or stool to reach it? If a toy has a winding mechanism, does she try to wind it as you do?

If the child does not imitate actions seen before or has a problem that she has not observed being solved, do not solve the problem for her; rather, show her how to solve the problem for herself. For example, if a toy is under the couch, use the broom to retrieve it, put it back under the couch, and ask the child to try to get it. Then, see what happens the next time a toy rolls out of reach.

CRITERION   The child attempts to solve two or more problems by imitating adult actions.

■ ■ ■

17m. Imitates postures or actions that do not involve props

MATERIALS   None required

PROCEDURES

Play a game with the child in which you take turns modeling and imitating different actions. For example, say, "We're going to play a game. When I put my hands over my head, you put your hands over your head. Ready?" Put your hands over your head and wait for the child to imitate. If he does not, help him put his hands up and then say, "That's right. Now we'll try another one." Then say, "Now it is your turn. You do something, and then I'll do what you do." Imitate what the child does. Then you take a turn modeling the action. Begin with easy actions (i.e., both hands doing the same thing) and work up to more complicated ones (e.g., one hand on the head, the other on the stomach). Try this with both you and the child facing a mirror.

DAILY ROUTINES & FUNCTIONAL ACTIVITIES

Play the above game with a group of children. Let them take turns modeling different postures for the others to imitate.

There are also songs that encourage this sort of imitation such as The Hokey Pokey or Head, Shoulders, Knees, and Toes.

Note: Getting right and left correct is not an important part of imitation at this level.

CRITERION   *The child imitates four or more postures that do not involve props. The imitation of a complex act need not be exact but should be a good approximation.*

■ ■ ■

17n. Imitates sequence of two unrelated motor acts

MATERIALS   None required

PROCEDURES

As soon as the child is able to imitate a variety of different postures, play an imitation game such as the one in Item 17m, but perform two actions (be sure to ask the child to wait until you finish if she starts to imitate the first action before you have completed the second). Begin with simple combinations such as touching your head and then clapping your hands. Work up to more complex combinations such as stomping your foot and then rubbing your stomach.

DAILY ROUTINES & FUNCTIONAL ACTIVITIES

Play a variation of Simon Says with the child and one or more of her peers. Explain that when you say, "Simon says do this," their job is to try to do what you are doing. Begin with one action at a time, and then proceed to two.

When you provide a new toy for the child, try to get one that requires at least two different motor acts in order for the toy to work (e.g., tops that must be wound before pushing a button to release them, wind-up toys that must be wound and then started by releasing a catch). Demonstrate the actions required in sequence, and observe whether the child imitates approximately, if not exactly.

CRITERION   *The child imitates at least two sequences of two unrelated motor acts. The imitation of a complex act need not be exact but should be a good approximation.*

18
Grasp & Manipulation

T he fine motor skills represented in this sequence are those that are involved in the development of accurate reach, grasp, release, and manipulation of objects. As children learn to use their hands, they learn that they can manipulate their environment. The development of fine motor skills establishes a framework for a child's growing independence in self-help and play skills and ultimately contributes to the child's future success in school.

ADAPTATIONS

Children with Motor Impairments

Children with motor impairments may need extra trunk and head support in order to successfully use their hands. For children who are very involved, sidelying may be a good starting position. An occupational or physical therapist can assist you in developing optimal positioning for hand development.

Some children with motor impairments learn to do manipulative tasks without looking. It is important to encourage the coordinated use of hands and vision together so that the child will not have difficulty moving to a higher level of skills that require the integration of vision and motor abilities (e.g., visual-motor skills).

Although it is important to facilitate the development of good reaching and grasping patterns in both hands, it may be advisable to work though the sequence at a different rate for each hand when clearly asymmetric development is evident. Always record which hand is being used for a particular activity, and devise a means of getting the child to use the nonpreferred hand for some activities.

Children with Visual Impairments

The early items in this sequence tend to be highly dependent on vision. It is important to encourage children with any degree of vision to use that ability in coor-

dination with their hand skills. In particular, reaching skills are facilitated and mo-
tivated by the presentation of visual stimuli. These skills can adequately develop,
although very slowly, even with the absence of vision. In order for children with visual impairments to avoid a major delay in acquiring these skills, be creative both
in selecting and presenting toys. Some points to remember include the following:

- Noisy toys that cease to make noise before a child has a chance to reach them
  may cognitively cease to exist for the child unless he or she has achieved "object permanence," a concept that generally develops later in children with visual
  impairments.

- Although most objects are presented at the midline for children without visual
  impairments in order to maximize their use of vision in reaching, the midline
  is the most difficult place to localize a sound. Thus, it is extremely important
  to be aware of a child's auditory localization skills in order to know the opti-
  mum placement for an object so that the child can find it easily.

The later items in this sequence are not as strongly dependent on vision. Children with severe visual impairments can learn to do these tasks through the use of
tactile cues. As soon as children with visual impairments are able to pick up and
release items efficiently, you should make an effort to involve the children with
these later items (beginning with Item 18k). Of course, you will constantly have to
make decisions as to which activities are most appropriate by considering each
child's tactile skills and motor sophistication.

Children with Hearing Impairments

Children with hearing impairments will require few adaptations to these items.
For young infants, use brightly colored materials rather than noisemaking toys
to capture their attention. Be sure to accompany any verbal instructions with
demonstrations.

18. GRASP & MANIPULATION

a. Actively moves arm after seeing or hearing an object

b. Looks to one side at hand or toy

c. Brings toy and hand into visual field and looks at them when toy is placed in hand

d. Watches hands at midline (actively moves and watches results)

e. Bats at object at chest level

f. Grasps object that is placed in hand (i.e., not reflexive grasp)

g. Reaches out and grasps objects near body

h. Displays extended reach and grasp

i. Rakes and scoops small objects (i.e., fingers against palm)

j. Reaches out for toys and picks them up when toys are in visual field

k. Manipulates objects with hands and fingers

l. Releases one object to take another

m. Grasps an object, using thumb against index and middle fingers

n. Uses inferior pincer grasp (i.e., thumb against side of index finger)

o. Uses index finger to poke

p. Uses neat pincer grasp (i.e., thumb against tip of index finger)

q. Removes objects from holders

r. Releases objects into container

s. Imitates building two-block tower

t. Grasps two small objects with one hand

u. Places round pegs in holes

v. Imitates building three- to four-block tower

w. Pokes or plays with play dough

x. Turns pages one at a time

y. Imitates building six- to eight-block tower

z. Turns doorknob with forearm rotation

aa. Puts small object through small hole in container

bb. Builds tower of 8–10 blocks

■ ■ ■

18a. Actively moves arm after seeing or hearing an object

MATERIALS   Any attractive toys or objects (e.g., bright, shiny, colorful), including some that make noise

PROCEDURES

Place the child on her back or in an infant seat so that her arms are free to move. Hold up a toy near the child, shaking it slightly, if needed, to catch her attention. As the child moves her arms, move the object closer so that the child can touch it.

If the child looks at the object but does not initiate any arm or hand movement, provide occasional physical prompts. Try different objects to find those that might be more interesting to the child. Select toys that also make an interesting sound to help attract the child's attention.

DAILY ROUTINES & FUNCTIONAL ACTIVITIES

Place a mobile in the child's crib. Make sure that the items on the mobile are hung so that they are interesting to the child who is viewing them from below. Change the items on the mobile periodically. Mobiles should be removed when the child begins to sit independently.

Use toys or mobiles that move or make noise independent of the child's action (e.g., wind-up or electronic toys) in order to attract her attention. Do not leave the toys on constantly; rather, use them for brief periods when the child is awake and alert.

CRITERION   On several occasions the child moves either or both hands when presented with an object.

■ ■ ■

18b. Looks to one side at hand or toy

MATERIALS   Brightly colored ribbon; small bells on elastic bands or on loops of yarn or string

PROCEDURES

Tie brightly colored ribbons to the child's wrists and encourage him to look at them. Add a few bells to the ribbons, and give the child's hands a little shake so that the bells jingle. Sometimes just stroking or tapping the child's hands will help to draw his attention to them.

You may want to do this activity several times in succession, making sure that there is a definite break between presentations (e.g., 5 or 6 seconds). Be sure to look at the child for signs of recognition or excitement when you return the ribbon, bell, or yarn to his hand or when you gently shake the toy.

Look for the child to make eye contact with the object. Any affective change (e.g., a smile) when the object is placed in his hand or shaken may indicate that the child is looking at his hand or the toy.

DAILY ROUTINES & FUNCTIONAL ACTIVITIES

Change the toys you are using, sometimes selecting a toy for visual qualities and sometimes for auditory qualities. Do not leave toys attached to the child's wrists for long periods of time, as he will habituate to the toy and lose interest.

CRITERION   The child turns his head to look at his hand or a toy on several different occasions.

18c. Brings toy and hand into visual field and looks at them when toy is placed in hand

MATERIALS   Toys or materials that are brightly colored and/or that make a noise when manipulated

PROCEDURES

Hold the toy in the child's visual field. Manipulate it to gain the child's attention, and then place the toy in the child's hand, allowing her to bring it back into her visual field by herself.

18

    If the child does not bring the toy into her visual field, move her hand with the toy to midline, or gently turn the child's head toward the hand with the toy. Then, manipulate the toy to gain the child's attention.

DAILY ROUTINES & FUNCTIONAL ACTIVITIES

Incorporate this activity during feeding and diaper changing.

CRITERION   The child brings a toy into her visual field or turns toward it when it is placed in her hand.

18d. Watches hands at midline (actively moves and watches results)

MATERIALS   Brightly colored ribbons or mittens with bells, if necessary

PROCEDURES

Observe the child at various times throughout the day. Help the child to bring his hands into midline, and shake the child's hands to draw attention to them (repeat this action several times).

DAILY ROUTINES & FUNCTIONAL ACTIVITIES

If the child does not play with his hands, place a mitten or bright ribbon or elastic with bells attached on the child's hands or wrists. Vary the toys you are using, sometimes selecting a toy for visual qualities and sometimes for auditory qualities. Do not leave toys attached to the child's wrists for long periods of time, as he will habituate to the toy and lose interest.

    Note: Be sure to allow the child to work with both hands.

CRITERION   The child watches his hands at midline on several different occasions.

■ ■ ■

18e. Bats at object at chest level

MATERIALS   Any attractive toys or objects (e.g., bright, shiny, colorful), including some that make noise

PROCEDURES

Hold objects in front of the child at chest level and within her arm's reach. If necessary, shake or move the object to attract her attention. If the child does not bat at the object, move it closer so that it touches one or both of the child's hands and any movement will make the object move. Gradually move the object farther away to promote more active movement on the part of the child.

DAILY ROUTINES & FUNCTIONAL ACTIVITIES

Place a mobile in the child's crib. Make sure that the items on the mobile are hung so that they are interesting to the child who is viewing it from below. Change the items on the mobile periodically. Mobiles should be removed when the child begins to sit independently. Set a free-standing frame in front of the child while she is sitting in an infant seat, and suspend a variety of interesting objects from it.

CRITERION   The child bats her arms at toys on several different occasions.

■ ■ ■

18f. Grasps object that is placed in hand (i.e., not reflexive grasp)

MATERIALS   A variety of small, interesting toys (e.g., rattles, rings, cubes)

PROCEDURES

Place an object in the child's hand and observe his reactions. If the child immediately drops the object, give it back to him or try another object of a different size, shape, and/or weight. Look for the child's fingers to curve around the object so that he is holding it for 10 seconds or more.

If the child does not respond, try placing your hand over his hand, assisting him in holding the object. Gradually reduce your assistance, and watch for the child to continue independently holding the object. Varying the properties of the objects given and the way in which the object is placed in the child's hand may also be useful in promoting independent grasping.

Note: Objects should not be smaller than 1½ inches to avoid accidental swallowing. Do not credit a purely reflexive grasp (i.e., the automatic closing of the hand around any object that touches the palm of the hand). If you get this response, try giving the child toys that are larger in diameter or are of a different shape. Make sure that the child is as relaxed as possible.

DAILY ROUTINES & FUNCTIONAL ACTIVITIES

Hand the child various objects to hold during routine care activities (e.g., diapering, eating, bathing, dressing).

CRITERION   The child grasps an object that is placed in his hand for 10 seconds or more on several different occasions.

■ ■ ■

18g. Reaches out and grasps objects near body

MATERIALS   A variety of interesting toys or objects

PROCEDURES

Place an interesting object within the child's easy reach, and observe her attempts to pick it up. If the child does not pick up the object, place it in her hand for a few seconds to attract her attention to it and then take it and place it within reach again.

　　If there is still no attempt to pick up the toy, physically assist the child to reach toward and touch the toy. The grasp at this point is usually "palmar" (i.e., fingers against the palm of the hand). Be sure to vary the toys so that the child will remain interested in the task.

DAILY ROUTINES & FUNCTIONAL ACTIVITIES

Place various objects near the child at different times of the day. You can set a free-standing frame with a variety of suspended objects in front of the child while she is sitting in an infant seat.

CRITERION   The child reaches out and grasps objects in a coordinated fashion on several different occasions.

■ ■ ■

18h. Displays extended reach and grasp

MATERIALS   A variety of interesting toys or objects

PROCEDURES

Place a toy at a distance, requiring the child to straighten his arm and/or lean forward to reach it. If the child does not reach for and pick up the toy, move it a little closer until he does reach for it. Gradually present the item further and further back until extended reach is obtained.

DAILY ROUTINES & FUNCTIONAL ACTIVITIES

Have different objects or toys available for the child throughout the day. Present the items at varying distances from the child's body and while the child is in different positions (e.g., prone, supine, supported sitting).

CRITERION   The child reaches for and picks up an object at arm's length on several different occasions.

■ ■ ■

18i. Rakes and scoops
small objects (i.e., fingers against palm)

MATERIALS   A variety of small objects (when you begin to work with very small objects, it is a good idea to use edible items because there will be less of a danger when the child puts the items in her mouth)

PROCEDURES

Place small pieces of cereal on a table or tray in front of the child. Encourage her to pick up the food and eat it. If the child does not spontaneously pick up the cereal,

- Place a piece in the child's hand, guide it to her mouth (or simply feed the child a piece), and try again.
- Vary the size and shape of the items (e.g., larger items will be easier to pick up). Reduce the size of items when the child masters picking up the larger size.

DAILY ROUTINES & FUNCTIONAL ACTIVITIES

This activity is readily incorporated into meal and snack time. As the child demonstrates success, begin offering her a wider variety of finger foods that are easy to eat and swallow.

CRITERION   *The child picks up several small objects.*

■ ■ ■

18j. Reaches out for toys
and picks them up when toys are in visual field

MATERIALS   Any preferred toys that are easy to pick up

PROCEDURES

Place a toy within the child's easy reach, but not near the child's hand. The toy should be placed where child can readily see it. The child's hands may or may not be in view. If the child does not pick up the toy, gently move his hand closer to the toy. On subsequent trials, try to increase the distance that the child must move on his own.

DAILY ROUTINES & FUNCTIONAL ACTIVITIES

Place favorite toys near the child throughout the day. This can be done while the child is sitting or lying down.

CRITERION   *The child picks up a toy when it is placed in visual range on several different occasions.*

■ ■ ■

18k. Manipulates objects with hands and fingers

MATERIALS   Paper, cellophane, squeaky toy, busy box

PROCEDURES

Place a piece of paper in front of the child. Tell the child to "get the paper." If she does not respond, crumple the paper and, if needed, guide the child's hands to the paper. Try the same activity with cellophane, which makes an interesting crackling sound when manipulated.

DAILY ROUTINES & FUNCTIONAL ACTIVITIES

Hand the child a piece of paper while changing her diaper. Show the child how to squeeze a soft squeaky toy. Demonstrate the functions on a busy box, and help the child manipulate the various activities.

CRITERION   *The child uses her fingers and hands to manipulate an object on several different occasions.*

■ ■ ■

18l. Releases one object to take another

MATERIALS   A variety of interesting toys and objects

PROCEDURES

Give the child a toy. Allow the child a moment to explore and play with that toy. Then, offer a second toy, and encourage the child to take the second toy as well. If the child does not take the second toy, place it in his hand. It may be helpful to reserve a favorite toy to offer as the second choice.

Note: In the typical developmental sequence, when a child first learns to reach for a second object, he usually drops the first. It is a more mature response for the child to continue holding both objects.

DAILY ROUTINES & FUNCTIONAL ACTIVITIES

Carry a bag of small, interesting toys on outings. When the child has one toy, offer him a different toy, and watch for him to drop the toy he is holding so that he can take the new one that you are offering.

CRITERION   *The child releases one object to take or pick up another on several different occasions.*

18

■ ■ ■

18m. Grasps an object, using thumb against index and middle fingers

MATERIALS   Several 1-inch blocks, objects of gradually decreasing size (edible items are good for this activity)

PROCEDURES

Present small objects near the thumb side of the child's hand. Encourage the child to use her thumb and fingers to pick up the objects. If the child continues to pick up the objects using her fingers against the palm, try holding an object between your thumb and index finger so that the child cannot take it from you without using a thumb-against-fingers grasp.

If the child is not successful, do not frustrate her. Let the child continue to pick up the items with her fingers against the palm for several more weeks and then try this activity again.

Note: This grasp may also be referred to as the radial-digital grasp or the three-jaw chuck.

DAILY ROUTINES & FUNCTIONAL ACTIVITIES

Offer the child frequent opportunities to finger feed herself various sizes and shapes of food—this should encourage development of more mature grasp patterns.

CRITERION   The child spontaneously picks up small objects using her thumb against index and middle fingers on several different occasions.

■ ■ ■

18n. Uses inferior pincer grasp (i.e., thumb against side of index finger)

MATERIALS   A variety of small objects or finger foods

PROCEDURES

Provide the child with small objects and observe how he picks them up. Using very small edible items is often the best way to encourage the development of this grasp pattern.

Note: As a child develops better skills with his hands, he will use a variety of different grasps. Within the course of one meal or playtime, it is typical to see a child pick up objects by raking his fingers against the palm, by using thumb and first two fingers, and by using thumb against index finger.

DAILY ROUTINES & FUNCTIONAL ACTIVITIES

Routinely include small foods that the child can pick up during meals and snacks. These small finger foods are particularly good for "on the go" snacks. Continue to encourage pointing activities or poking objects with the index finger to increase the separation of that finger from the others.

CRITERION   On several occasions, the child picks up small objects with his thumb against the side of the index finger.

18o. Uses index finger to poke

MATERIALS   An empty pegboard with small holes, busy box toy

PROCEDURES

Present an empty pegboard to the child, and demonstrate how to poke your finger into the holes and pull it out. Guide the child to try this activity with her own index finger.

Cut a hole in a piece of wood or cardboard that is big enough for you to stick your finger through. Stick your finger through it and wave it at the child, making a game of it. The child will probably reach for your finger. If so, withdraw it gradually, enticing the child to come after it with her finger. If the child puts her finger through the hole, turn the board slightly so that child can see her finger wiggle.

Note: The point of this item is to obtain good separation of the index finger from the rest of the fingers. Watch for other activities in which the child spontaneously does this (e.g., pushing food or toys around with her index finger).

DAILY ROUTINES & FUNCTIONAL ACTIVITIES

Provide a busy box-type toy for the child to play with at various times throughout the day. Demonstrate for the child how to push a button to produce a sound or pop-up reaction with the toy.

CRITERION   *The child spontaneously pokes or places her index finger into openings in an empty pegboard or similar item on several different occasions.*

18p. Uses neat pincer grasp (i.e., thumb against tip of index finger)

MATERIALS   A variety of small objects or finger foods

PROCEDURES

Give the child a lot of practice picking up small objects, particularly small pieces of food at mealtime. Observe the grasp patterns that the child uses. If the child persists in using a raking motion (i.e., fingers against palm) when other patterns would be more efficient, try handing the items to the child. Hold them between your thumb and index finger in such a way that the child cannot get them with a raking movement.

DAILY ROUTINES & FUNCTIONAL ACTIVITIES

Routinely include small foods that the child can pick up during meals and snacks. These small finger foods are particularly good for "on the go" snacks. Continue to encourage pointing activities or poking objects with the index finger to increase the separation of that finger from the others.

CRITERION   *The child spontaneously picks up a small object between his thumb and the tip of the index finger on several different occasions.*

■ ■ ■

18q. Removes objects from holders
(e.g., rings from post, pegs from holes)

MATERIALS   A post with several rings, a pegboard with small round pegs (approximately ⅜ inch)

PROCEDURES

Place a toy post with several rings on it in front of the child. Demonstrate how to remove the rings one at a time. Then, replace the rings and ask the child to take one ring off.

Present the child with a pegboard that contains several small pegs. Space them far enough apart so that they are easy to grasp. Tell the child to take out the pegs. If the child removes a peg, praise her and encourage her to remove others.

Provide physical prompts and verbal cues as needed for the child to be successful. Gradually fade your assistance.

DAILY ROUTINES & FUNCTIONAL ACTIVITIES

Keep a post with rings and pegboard and pegs on a low shelf so that the child can play with them frequently. If the child has difficulty removing the rings from a commercial stacking toy, try temporarily replacing them with hard plastic bracelets that are easier to remove and replace.

CRITERION   The child removes items from two different toys on several different occasions (e.g., rings from post, pegs from pegboard).

■ ■ ■

18r. Releases objects into container

MATERIALS   A variety of small objects (e.g., 1-inch blocks, clothespins, bells), a container with a wide opening (e.g., kettle, cookie jar, oatmeal box)

PROCEDURES

Place a container in front of the child. Demonstrate how to drop objects into the container. Then dump the objects back out and encourage the child to drop them into the container again. If the child does not attempt the activity, place one object into the child's hand, and tell him to "put it in." If the child loses interest quickly, try handing him another object as soon as he drops one in.

If the child does not respond, help him by holding his hand over the container. Tell the child to put the object in the container. If he still does not, tap the top of the child's hand until he lets go of the object. If that does not work, gently press on the back of the child's hand, bending it forward until he releases the object. Praise his release.

Using a metal container that makes a loud sound when an object is dropped in may be motivating for some children. Also, experiment with various objects to find some that the child may be interested in dropping in.

DAILY ROUTINES & FUNCTIONAL ACTIVITIES

Encourage the child to clean up his toys at the end of a play session by picking them up and dropping them into a container.

Make "dumping out and putting in" a game. Vary the task with different sizes of objects and containers. Challenge the child's motor skills (e.g., if the child easily puts clothespins into a big container, try a container with a smaller opening, such as a milk jug). During bath time, the child can retrieve floating objects and drop them into a basket.

CRITERION   The child will drop four or more objects into a container on several different occasions.

■ ■ ■

18s. Imitates building two-block tower

MATERIALS   Several blocks of identical size (1 inch to 1½ inches)

PROCEDURES

Let the child play with the blocks for several minutes. Tell the child that you are going to build a tower. Build a three- to four-block tower. Knock it down, start to build another, and tell the child to build a tower like yours. Begin with two or three blocks. If the child does not respond, you may need to physically assist her in putting one block on top of another. Express a lot of praise for the child's attempts.

DAILY ROUTINES & FUNCTIONAL ACTIVITIES

Children often enjoy stacking household items such as small cans or boxes. Let her have fun doing so through the day.

CRITERION   The child imitates building or spontaneously builds a two-block tower on several different occasions.

■ ■ ■

18t. Grasps two small objects with one hand

MATERIALS   Several 1-inch blocks or other small objects

PROCEDURES

Place two blocks or other small toys on a table next to each other, and tell the child to get the blocks. If needed, demonstrate how to pick up both of the blocks with one hand. Provide physical prompts, placing the child's hand on top of both blocks. It may be helpful to give the child something to hold in his other hand so that he will need to pick up both blocks with only one hand.

DAILY ROUTINES & FUNCTIONAL ACTIVITIES

The child may spontaneously pick up two pieces of cookie or other finger food in one hand.

CRITERION   The child picks up two small objects with one hand on several different occasions.

■ ■ ■

18u. Places round pegs in holes

MATERIALS   Pegs (½-inch or smaller or knob-type pegs), a pegboard

PROCEDURES

Present a pegboard with the pegs in place to the child. Remove the pegs (or ask the child to remove them). Then, tell the child to put all of the pegs back into the pegboard. If the child has difficulty with this activity, demonstrate how to do it, and then repeat the command. If the child fails to put all of the pegs into the pegboard, encourage her to finish. If necessary, physically assist the child in putting all of the pegs in the holes.

If the child rapidly loses interest, it may be helpful to give her the pegboard with some of the pegs already in it, and encourage her to finish the activity or to take turns with you until the pegs are in place. Gradually decrease the amount of help that you provide.

DAILY ROUTINES & FUNCTIONAL ACTIVITIES

Encourage the child to play with small, plastic figures that fit into toy vehicles or furniture. Placement of these figures requires much the same skill as putting pegs in a pegboard and can be expanded into a language or pretend play activity.

CRITERION   The child puts five to six round pegs into the holes.

■ ■ ■

18v. Imitates building three- to four-block tower

MATERIALS   Eight blocks of identical size (1 inch to 1½ inches)

PROCEDURES

Let the child play with the blocks for several minutes. Tell him that you are going to build a tower. Build a tower with four blocks. Knock it down, start to build another, and tell the child to build a tower like yours. If the child does not respond, you may need to physically assist him in putting one block on top of another. Express a lot of praise for the child's attempts.

DAILY ROUTINES & FUNCTIONAL ACTIVITIES

Children often enjoy stacking household items, such as small cans or boxes. Encourage the child to practice building with household materials.

CRITERION   The child imitates building a three- to four-block tower on several different occasions.

■ ■ ■

18w. Pokes or plays with play dough

MATERIALS   Play dough (homemade or commercial)

PROCEDURES

Hand the child a piece of play dough. Take a piece yourself and show the child that you can roll it, pat it flat, stretch it, and so forth. Give the child positive descriptions of the material (e.g., "This feels good," "It's fun to squeeze this").

If the child merely holds the play dough, physically assist her to poke, pat, and stretch it. Reinforce all attempts to do something purposeful with the play dough.

Note: Be sure that the play dough is soft enough for small hands to manipulate.

DAILY ROUTINES & FUNCTIONAL ACTIVITIES

Make play dough with the child. Have her assist you in mixing together the ingredients with her hands. Vary the colors of the play dough by mixing in tempera paints or food coloring. Vary the textures of the play dough, as well, by adding sand, flour, water, oil, soap, and so forth.

Have the child make imprints in the dough with her fingers, hand, foot, or small objects. (Footprints/handprints can be saved and later painted.)

For a child who imitates well, try modeling several activities with the clay, such as patting it flat, rolling it into a ball, or making a dough snake.

CRITERION   The child independently pokes at or plays with play dough.

■ ■ ■

18x. Turns pages one at a time

MATERIALS   Children's book with thick pages

PROCEDURES

Look at a book with the child, turning the pages and pointing out the pictures on each page. Then tell the child to turn the page for you. If needed, lift up one page part of the way and then tell the child to turn the page. If he does not respond, give physical assistance to turn the page.

DAILY ROUTINES & FUNCTIONAL ACTIVITIES

Plan a daily reading time with the child. At this time, encourage him to turn the pages of the book for you. Also, have sturdy books readily available for the child should he be interested in looking at them alone.

CRITERION   The child turns the pages of a book, one at a time, on several different occasions.

■ ■ ■

18y. Imitates building six- to eight-block tower

MATERIALS   Twelve to sixteen blocks of identical size (1 inch to 1½ inches)

PROCEDURES

Let the child play with the blocks for several minutes. Tell her that you are going to build a tower. Build a tower with eight blocks. Knock it down, start to build another, and tell the child to build a tower like yours. If the child does not respond, you may need to physically assist her in putting one block on top of another. Express a lot of praise for the child's attempts.

DAILY ROUTINES & FUNCTIONAL ACTIVITIES

A good set of wooden blocks will provide a wealth of play and learning opportunities for a number of years. Encourage the child to make buildings using blocks of various sizes.

CRITERION   *The child imitates building a six- to eight-block tower on several different occasions.*

■ ■ ■

18z. Turns doorknob with forearm rotation

MATERIALS   A door with an easy-to-turn doorknob

PROCEDURES

When entering or leaving a room, tell the child to open the door for you. If the child has difficulty with this task, give him verbal cues such as "turn" (physically prompting in the correct direction), then "push" (or "pull"). It is usually easier to open a door that needs to be pushed.

If the child is unsuccessful, practice with other activities that involve turning (e.g., nested barrels, plastic nuts and bolts, unscrewing loosely fastened lids from various jars). Incorporating supination (i.e., palm up) patterns into activities also may be helpful (e.g., using one hand to drop small objects into the other hand [palm up] to see how many objects the child can hold before dropping any).

Note: Once a child has mastered door opening, doors should be kept locked to prevent the child from leaving the building.

DAILY ROUTINES & FUNCTIONAL ACTIVITIES

Allow the child opportunities to open doors without assistance

CRITERION   *The child opens a doorknob using a forearm rotation.*

■ ■ ■

18aa. Puts small object
through small hole in container

MATERIALS   Containers with holes in them and objects to put into them (e.g., a box with a slot and poker chips, coins and a bank, blocks and a shape box with a single opening, bottle and clothespins, small pellets [or edible items such as raisins], and a bottle with a 1-inch neck opening)

PROCEDURES

Demonstrate for the child how to put a small object through a hole or slot in a container (e.g., poker chips through a slot in a box). If needed, physically guide the child through the motions. If she lacks the accurate control, start with a slightly larger opening, then reduce the size as the child gains skills.

Note: This is often a favorite play activity for young children; however, they should be supervised carefully if small objects are being used.

DAILY ROUTINES & FUNCTIONAL ACTIVITIES

Holes or slots can be easily cut into the plastic lids of margarine containers or coffee can lids. Vary the demands by offering slots for pennies or checkers and small, round openings for pegs or short dowels.

18

CRITERION   *The child places a small object in or through a small hole on several different occasions with at least two different objects and containers.*

■ ■ ■

18bb. Builds tower of 8–10 blocks

MATERIALS   Ten 1-inch blocks

PROCEDURES

Place 10 blocks on the table in front of the child. Tell the child to build a tower (or tall building). If needed, demonstrate building a tower and then knock it down (or let the child knock it down). Tell the child to make a tower (or tall building) like you did. Start with larger blocks and a smaller tower if the child has difficulty. For a child experiencing difficulty in motor control, try magnetic blocks or blocks with small Velcro spots attached. Beginning stacking games also can be done with beanbags.

DAILY ROUTINES & FUNCTIONAL ACTIVITIES

Encourage the child to build roads and buildings with a large selection of blocks. Build towers of blocks (or small boxes) to knock down with beanbags.

CRITERION   *The child builds a tower of 8–10 blocks.*

19
Bilateral Skills

The items in this sequence involve the development of bilateral hand use. The items begin with activities in which both hands perform essentially the same movements and progress to activities in which each hand performs a different function to accomplish a single task (e.g., one hand holds a bead while the other pushes a string through it), including the emergence of hand dominance. The activities also progress from unrefined movements to those requiring considerable coordination.

During the first 2 years of life, children generally do not demonstrate a clear hand preference. If a child demonstrates a strong preference for one hand before the age of 1 year, evaluation by an occupational or physical therapist is indicated to rule out any possible difficulties that the child may have in using the nonpreferred hand.

ADAPTATIONS

Children with Motor Impairments

If children with motor impairments have difficulty bringing their hands to midline, try early activities in a sidelying position, which naturally facilitates a midline orientation. For later activities, if a child does not sit well independently, try sitting the child in a corner chair that provides support and helps to bring his or her arms forward and toward midline. If a child has one side that is more affected by his or her motor impairments than the other, encourage the child to use the more involved hand to assist the other hand (e.g., hold the stick with the less skilled hand, and place rings on the stick with the more skilled hand).

Note: It is important for curriculum users to recognize that not all activities in this sequence are appropriate for all children. For example, a child with athetoid cerebral palsy might be able, with a great deal of effort, to put beads on a string, but such an activity would never be functional. The activity would teach this child more about frustration tolerance than a useful fine motor skill, even though the latter is the item's intent. The more severe a child's disability, the more important it is to seek the advice of a physical and/or occupational therapist in choosing those activities that will be functional and enjoyable for the child.

Children with Visual Impairments

Use toys that offer interesting textures and make sounds when working with children with visual impairments. Many rhythm instruments are useful for encouraging bilateral hand skills in young children with visual impairments. Provide hand-over-hand assistance, give verbal feedback, and describe what you are doing.

Children with Hearing Impairments

Children with hearing impairments will require no adaptations to these items as they are based on visual and motor skills. For young infants, use brightly colored materials to capture their attention. Be sure to accompany any verbal instructions with demonstrations.

19. BILATERAL SKILLS

a. Raises both hands when object is presented (hands partially open)

b. Looks at or manipulates toy placed in hands at midline

c. Brings hands together at midline

d. Places both hands on toy at midline

e. Transfers objects from hand to hand

f. Glances from one toy to another when a toy is placed in each hand, or alternately plays with the toys

g. Plays with own feet or toes

h. Claps hands

i. Uses both hands to perform the same action

j. Plays with toys at midline (one hand holds the toy and the other manipulates it)

k. Pulls apart pop beads

l. Holds dowel in one hand and places ring over it

m. Puts dowel through hole in piece of cardboard

n. Unwraps edible item or other small object

o. Unscrews small lids

p. Puts loose pop beads together

q. Strings three large beads

r. Demonstrates hand preference (typically in eating)

s. Unbuttons large buttons

t. Strings small beads

u. Screws on lids

■ ■ ■

19a. Raises both hands
when object is presented (hands partially open)

MATERIALS   Any attractive toys or objects that the child favors

PROCEDURES

While the child is lying on his back, hold or dangle an object at the child's chest level and observe his reactions. If the child does not reach up with his hands, try lowering the toy until it briefly touches one of his hands, then raise it slightly, finally returning it to midline.

DAILY ROUTINES & FUNCTIONAL ACTIVITIES

At various times throughout the day, suspend toys in front of or over the child using a freestanding frame. This would be a good activity to do when a parent or caregiver is busy, as it offers the child an early opportunity to begin developing independent play skills. Observe to see if the child raises both hands toward the objects.

CRITERION   The child spontaneously raises or reaches with both hands toward an object with his hands partially open on several different occasions.

■ ■ ■

19b. Looks at or manipulates toy placed in hands at midline

MATERIALS   Bright, shiny objects that will gain the child's attention or toys that emit a noise if shaken or squeezed

PROCEDURES

Hold a toy within the child's reach, and try to gain her attention by shaking, rattling, or squeezing the toy. With your free hand, bring the child's hand to the toy at midline. Once the child's hand is on the toy, shake or rattle it for her.

See if the child will hold the toy independently. Rather than holding the toy for the child, merely try supporting it lightly with one or two fingers to facilitate the child's holding it.

DAILY ROUTINES & FUNCTIONAL ACTIVITIES

Take regular opportunities throughout the day to present different toys to the child. You can also attach brightly colored ribbons and bells to her hands or wrists to encourage her to bring her hands to midline to look at them.

CRITERION   The child looks at or manipulates a toy that is placed in her hands at midline for 5 or more seconds on several different occasions.

■ ■ ■

19c. Brings hands together at midline

MATERIALS   Stick-on bows, if needed

PROCEDURES

If this behavior is not observed in general free play, put something colorful and easy to remove on one of the child's hands or wrists (e.g., a stick-on bow). Observe to see if the child brings the other hand over to touch it. If he does not, physically guide his two hands to midline by gently pushing his shoulders and upper arms.

DAILY ROUTINES & FUNCTIONAL ACTIVITIES

When holding the child on your lap, encourage him to find his own hands by gently guiding his hands together. Play Pat-a-cake with the child, taking him through the motions.

CRITERION   The child brings his hands together at midline on several different occasions.

■ ■ ■

19d. Places both hands on toy at midline

MATERIALS   Any attractive toys (e.g., rattles and other toys that make noise)

PROCEDURES

Hold a toy at midline within the child's reach. Shake or move the toy in order to gain the child's attention. If she does not reach for the toy, place her hands on the toy. Repeat this activity with various toys at different times.

DAILY ROUTINES & FUNCTIONAL ACTIVITIES

Have toys available to offer the child when you are giving her a bath or changing her diaper.

CRITERION   *The child spontaneously places both hands on a toy at midline.*

19

■ ■ ■

19e. Transfers objects from hand to hand

MATERIALS   Easy-to-grasp toys that are likely to promote transfer (e.g., plastic bracelet, large yarn pom-pom, lightweight toys with several handles)

PROCEDURES

Place a toy in one of the child's hands. As the child plays with it, see if he will take hold of both sides of the toy, let go with one hand, and then transfer it back to the original hand. If the child does not transfer objects from hand to hand, try placing a sticky bow or tape with sticky side out on one hand. Encourage the child to pull it off with his other hand. Provide physical prompts as needed.

DAILY ROUTINES & FUNCTIONAL ACTIVITIES

Look for opportunities throughout the day (e.g., while changing the child's diaper, while the child is in his car seat or the grocery cart) to hand the child a toy. Observe to see if he transfers objects from one hand to the other. Take turns offering toys first to one hand and then to the other.

CRITERION   *The child transfers an object from one hand to the other on several different occasions.*

■ ■ ■

19f. Glances from one toy to another when a toy is placed in each hand, or alternately plays with the toys

MATERIALS   1-inch blocks, squeaky toys, rattles

PROCEDURES

Place a toy in one of the child's hands. Attract the child's attention to look at it and then place another toy in the child's other hand. Encourage her to look at the other toy. You can tap or squeak the toy or do whatever to attract the child's attention to it. Be sure to allow the child time to look at the first toy before adding the second toy.

Sometimes the child will drop the first toy as soon as a second one is placed in the other hand. Try placing objects in both hands several times and, perhaps, gently holding the child's hands with the toys in them for a few seconds to encourage looking back and forth. Do not frustrate the child, however, if she clearly wants to attend to one toy and to ignore the other. If this happens, go on to the next item in the sequence.

DAILY ROUTINES & FUNCTIONAL ACTIVITIES

Offer small toys to the child when you are giving her a bath, feeding her, or changing her diaper.

CRITERION   The child glances from one hand to the other when an object is placed in each hand (or alternately plays with toys) on several different occasions.

■ ■ ■

19g. Plays with own feet or toes

MATERIALS   Ribbons, bells, or booties with bright colors or patterns

PROCEDURES

Place ribbons, bells, or brightly colored booties on the child's feet or shoes. If the child does not play with his feet, gently shake them to gain his attention. Call attention to the bells, ribbons, or "pretty shoes." Shake the child's foot gently, saying, "Look at the ribbons, hear the bells!" If the child does not reach for his feet, try lifting the child's buttocks slightly, with legs in flexion, bringing the feet nearer to the child's hands. If needed, prop the child's buttocks up on a small pillow, while you physically prompt bringing both hands to his feet. Try to prompt response from the child's shoulders, gently pushing forward.

DAILY ROUTINES & FUNCTIONAL ACTIVITIES

Play This Little Piggy while dressing the child. Wait to see if the child then plays with his feet.

CRITERION   The child spontaneously plays with his feet or toes on several different occasions.

■ ■ ■

19h. Claps hands

MATERIALS   None required

PROCEDURES

Play clapping games (e.g., Pat-a-cake) with the child. Sing clapping songs in which the child can observe you clapping and in which you can physically guide her hands to clap. Gradually reduce the amount of physical assistance you provide the child.

DAILY ROUTINES & FUNCTIONAL ACTIVITIES

Incorporate singing and clapping games on a daily basis. This is a great way to keep the child entertained when needing to wait somewhere. Create your own songs or use one of the many resource books available (e.g., *Pat-A-Cake and Other Play Rhymes* by Joanna Cole, *Games Babies Play: Birth to Twelve Months* by Vicki Lansky).

CRITERION   *The child claps her hands without assistance.*

■ ■ ■

19

19i. Uses both hands to perform the same action

MATERIALS   Large ball, xylophone or drum and two sticks

PROCEDURES

The object of this activity is for the child to use both of his hands at the same time. If you are unable to elicit a behavior with one activity, try a different one. Various activities include

- Sit across from the child (approximately 6 feet away). Push a ball to the child. Tell the child to roll it back to you. If the child does not respond, provide physical assistance. (This activity is easiest to do with two adults, one helping the child and the other receiving and returning the ball.)
- Show the child how to hit a xylophone or drum using two sticks at the same time.
- Play Pat-a-cake with the child.

DAILY ROUTINES & FUNCTIONAL ACTIVITIES

This is an easy activity to incorporate whenever you play with the child, particularly with musical or clapping activities. You many want to participate with the child in an infant music class. Messy play provides another opportunity to encourage bilateral hand use (e.g., patting bubbles in the bath or pudding on the highchair tray).

CRITERION   *The child uses both of his hands to perform the same action.*

■ ■ ■

19j. Plays with toys at midline
(one hand holds the toy and the other manipulates it)

MATERIALS   Interesting toys, particularly those with moving parts

PROCEDURES

Observe the child as she holds a toy at midline. Watch to see if the child holds the toy with one hand and pats, feels, pulls, and so forth, with the other. The point is that both hands are being used, but each hand is doing something different.

You may stimulate the child's play by demonstrating what she can do with the toy, but it is more likely that the characteristics of the toys themselves will stimulate the activity.

DAILY ROUTINES & FUNCTIONAL ACTIVITIES

Have a tub of appropriate toys to give to the child when you are talking on the telephone or when you are busy with some other activity. Periodically observe the child to see if she is holding a toy with one hand and manipulating it with the other hand.

CRITERION   *The child plays with toys at midline, with one hand holding a toy and the other hand manipulating it.*

■ ■ ■

19k. Pulls apart pop beads

MATERIALS   Large pop beads (e.g., approximately 1½ to 2 inches) that are easy to pull apart

PROCEDURES

Show the child a string of four or five pop beads. Pull them apart and put them back together. Give them to the child and ask him to pull them apart. If needed, give physical assistance.

Note: Different brands of pop beads require differing degrees of strength to pull apart. Select beads that are appropriate for the child. Gradually increase their difficulty as the child's skill and strength increase.

DAILY ROUTINES & FUNCTIONAL ACTIVITIES

Have other toys that involve pulling sections apart and putting pieces together (e.g., Duplos, bristle blocks) available to the child during playtime.

CRITERION   *The child pulls apart pop beads in at least one place.*

■ ■ ■

19l. Holds dowel in one hand and places ring over it

MATERIALS   Several ½-inch dowels (5–10 inches long), wooden or plastic rings

PROCEDURES

Sit down with the child; bring a container of dowels and rings. Let the child explore the materials on her own for several minutes, and comment on what she does. If the child makes no attempt to put a ring on a dowel, show her how to do it. If the child has difficulty, try hard plastic bracelets, which will be easier to place over the dowel. Provide phys-ical assistance as needed. As the child becomes more adept, reduce your assistance, and introduce the rings with smaller holes again.

DAILY ROUTINES & FUNCTIONAL ACTIVITIES

Encourage the child to play with rings and bracelets, putting them on her arms and fin-gers. Add a pretend element to the activity (e.g., tell the child to decorate the "tree" [dowel]).

CRITERION   The child places a close-fitting ring over a dowel while holding the dowel in one hand and using the other hand to place the ring.

■ ■ ■

19

19m. Puts dowel through hole in piece of cardboard

MATERIALS   Dowel that is ¼ inch by 10 inches (unsharpened pencils or Tinker Toys will also work), squares of cardboard (4 inches by 4 inches) with various size holes in them (can also use spools or beads that fit easily over dowel)

PROCEDURES

Give the materials to the child and let him explore them. Show the child how to put the dowel through the hole in the cardboard. Have some of the holes in the cardboard squares large enough so that you could put the child's finger through them, and have others that are small enough so that there is just room for the dowel. Play with the child, and show him how you can stick your finger through the hole, put the dowel through the hole, and so forth. If the child makes no effort to imitate the task or to perform the task spontaneously, physically assist him.

DAILY ROUTINES & FUNCTIONAL ACTIVITIES

Provide a basket with beads and dowels for the child to play with. This is a good activity to do while the child is sitting in his highchair and waiting for a snack or meal. Be sure the child does not walk around carrying the dowel so that he is not injured if he should fall.

CRITERION   The child puts a ¼-inch dowel through a bead, a spool, or a small hole in a piece of cardboard.

■ ■ ■

19n. Unwraps edible item or other small object

MATERIALS   A small piece of fruit or candy or a small toy wrapped in wax paper or sim-ilar wrapping

PROCEDURES

Give the child a small edible item or other object that is wrapped up, and ask her to open it. If the child does not respond, demonstrate how to unwrap the item, and then rewrap it in front of her. Return it to the child and tell her to open the candy. Use of a favorite edible item will increase the likelihood of success.

DAILY ROUTINES & FUNCTIONAL ACTIVITIES

Give the child a snack that is wrapped in wax paper.

CRITERION   The child unwraps an edible item or other small object on several different occasions.

■ ■ ■

19o. Unscrews small lids

MATERIALS   Various small jars with lids that are easy to unscrew (i.e., select jars to fit the size of the child's hands—baby food jars are appropriate for many children but may be too large in diameter for very small hands), small toys or edibles

PROCEDURES

Present the child with several jars, each of which has an interesting item inside. Ask the child to open the jars or to get the object inside. If the child makes no attempt to unscrew the lids, show him how to do it. Remove the object from the jar, return it, and replace the lid very loosely (i.e., so that a one-quarter to one-half turn will get it off). Give the jar to the child to try the task again. You may use physical assistance, if necessary, but it will probably be less effective than making the task easier and letting the child master unscrewing the lids on his own.

In general, children may have more success starting with a larger jar and lid (e.g., 2 inches in diameter) that is loosely fastened. Give verbal cues for the child to turn the lid the other way, if needed. Make sure that the child's fingers are touching only the lid when he is attempting to unscrew it. Some children tend to hold on to the lid and the jar with one hand, making turning impossible.

DAILY ROUTINES & FUNCTIONAL ACTIVITIES

Try offering snacks in one or two small jars for the child to open. You can also give the child toy radios, music boxes, or busy boxes with a turn knob/dial so that the child can practice the coordination of finger movements that are needed to unscrew a jar lid.

Look for other toys that involve unscrewing, such as large nuts and bolts or nested barrels. Items that are more challenging to unscrew may be better suited to older children. You might also want to have a basket of various-size jars and bottles with lids available to help the child generalize skills.

CRITERION   The child unscrews lids from several small jars.

■ ■ ■

19p. Puts loose pop beads together

MATERIALS   Loose-fitting pop beads (i.e., adjust size and looseness to motor capabilities of the child)

PROCEDURES

Give the child a box of pop beads that are not connected to one another. Allow the child to explore them. If the child makes no effort to put them together, show her how to do it. Begin making a necklace with the pop beads and encourage the child to make one. Physically assist her, if necessary. Be sure to praise her efforts as well as successes.

DAILY ROUTINES & FUNCTIONAL ACTIVITIES

Provide a basket with pop beads on a low shelf so that the child can play with them whenever she wants. Encourage her to make necklaces for herself or a stuffed animal.

CRITERION   *The child puts loose pop beads together.*

19

■ ■ ■

19q. Strings three large beads

MATERIALS   Large beads of various shapes and colors, lace with stiff tip at one end and knot at the other end

PROCEDURES

Present the child with a container of beads and the string of lace. With a second string of lace, show the child how to make a necklace, stringing slowly so that he can observe the process of putting the tip of the lace through the bead and then pulling it from the other side. Provide physical assistance or verbal instruction, as necessary, to help the child accomplish the task. If the child has difficulty, try using a stiff object, such as aquarium tubing or a swizzle stick, for the child to place beads onto at first.

DAILY ROUTINES & FUNCTIONAL ACTIVITIES

Have the child make a necklace to wear for the day.

CRITERION   *The child is able to string three large beads.*

■ ■ ■

19r. Demonstrates hand preference (typically in eating)

MATERIALS   Spoon, plate, food

PROCEDURES

Present the child with a plate of food, placing a spoon at midline above her plate. Observe the child eating on several occasions, and note if she has a preference for either hand (which may also be evident during other activities, such as waving, coloring, or hammering). If the child demonstrates a preference, continue to support that hand as dominant, and encourage the child to use it consistently. If a preference is not clear, continue to present materials to the child at midline so that she has free choice over which hand to use.

Note: There is a large variation in age regarding achievement of hand dominance, with complete dominance establishment generally not expected until 5–6 years of age. Exclusive use of one hand at a very early age (e.g., before 1 year) is suspect and may be indicative of motor difficulties with the child's other hand. Children do not necessarily need to have established a dominant hand until approaching school age (5–6 years). If a hand preference has not emerged at this age, you should consult an occupational therapist.

DAILY ROUTINES & FUNCTIONAL ACTIVITIES

Observe which hand the child uses for various activities throughout the day and over a period of several weeks to see if you can determine a preference. Until the child begins to clearly demonstrate a preference, continue to present items (e.g., spoon, crayon, toy hammer) at midline.

CRITERION   *The child regularly uses the same hand for a skilled task (e.g., eating with a spoon at lunch).*

■ ■ ■

19s. Unbuttons large buttons (e.g., ¾–1 inch)

MATERIALS   Cloth strip (or dressing vest or doll) with large buttons, buttonholes that are slightly loose

PROCEDURES

Present the item with buttons buttoned, and ask the child to unbutton it. If he does not know how to approach this task, slowly demonstrate for him two or three times. Then, try to physically assist the child. He should hold and lightly pull the cloth next to the hole with one hand and grasp the button and push it through the hole with the other hand. If this task is too difficult for the child, a good preliminary activity is pushing coins or checkers through a slit cut into a plastic jar. The slit should provide a tight fit so that the child has to exert some effort to push the coin through.

DAILY ROUTINES & FUNCTIONAL ACTIVITIES

Play dress-up with very simple clothing that has large buttons. At this age, the goal would be for the children to undo fasteners and remove clothing independently. In another year, the focus will be on independently putting on and fastening the clothing.

Buttoning boards that have a surprise picture hidden under the material can be fun to use with a group of children who can then share what they found under the material.

Playing bank or store during which children place pennies in a piggy bank or through a slotted lid is a good preparatory activity.

CRITERION   *The child unbuttons three large buttons (e.g., ¾–1 inch).*

■ ■ ■

19t. Strings small beads (e.g., ½ inch)

MATERIALS   Bowl with a number of small beads, lace with one stiff end and a knot on the other end

PROCEDURES

Place the bowl of beads and the string of lace in front of the child, and ask her to make a necklace or a snake. Demonstrate the procedure for the child with a second lace. In general, square beads with straight sides may be easier for the child to hold and string than round or oval beads. If the child has difficulty, check first to be sure she can string large beads. If the child can successfully string the larger beads but still cannot do this task, she may need more practice handling small objects (e.g., putting pennies in a bank, placing ½-inch pegs in a pegboard, finger feeding small pieces of cereal or raisins).

DAILY ROUTINES & FUNCTIONAL ACTIVITIES

When you and the child have some down time, you could string wheel-shaped macaroni to make room decorations, or string spools together to make snakes.

CRITERION   *The child strings several small beads (e.g., ½ inch).*

■ ■ ■

19u. Screws on lids

MATERIALS   Small bottles or jars of various sizes with matching lids

PROCEDURES

Give the child a bottle with small objects inside. Tell him to open the bottle and dump out the contents. Then, tell the child to put the lid back on, perhaps as part of cleanup. If the child has difficulty with this task, demonstrate screwing on the lid and then physically assist him. Show him how to hold the lid in an overhand fashion with his fingers around the edge of the rim. Give verbal cues as to which direction the child should turn the lid.

DAILY ROUTINES & FUNCTIONAL ACTIVITIES

Have children hide tiny surprises for each other in opaque jars. If you cannot find any opaque jars, you can make some by taping paper around and over the bottoms of the jars. Close the lids and then exchange the jars. After opening a snack jar, have the child replace the lid.

CRITERION   *The child can screw lids onto various types of jars or bottles.*

REFERENCES

Cole, J. (1992). *Pat-a-cake and other play rhymes*. New York: HarperTrophy.
Lansky, V. (1993). *Games babies play: From birth to twelve months*. Minnetonka, MN: Book Peddlers.

20
Tool Use

C hildren usually first discover their hands and their ability to have an impact on their environment with their hands when they play with a toy, obtain something they want, or feed themselves. After children establish a good awareness of their own bodies, they begin to learn that they can use a tool as an extension of their body to impact their environment. Tool use allows us to manipulate our world in a more sophisticated way than we are able to achieve with just our hands. The ability to use tools is one of the characteristics that identifies humans as an advanced animal species. In addition to the tool use listed in this section, two essential areas of tool development are addressed in other sequences. Sequence 4-I (Self-Help: Eating) includes the use of eating utensils, and Sequence 21 (Visual-Motor Skills) includes the use of writing implements and scissors.

20

ADAPTATIONS

Children with Motor Impairments

If children with motor impairments have difficulties holding a tool, ask an occupational therapist for assistance in exploring adaptive gloves, splints, or Velcro devices that may help these children hold the tools. Stabilizing the toy or object being acted on with the tool also may be helpful. Dycem mats are sticky mats that can be placed under toys to stabilize them.

Children with Visual Impairments

Use toys that offer interesting textures and make interesting sounds with children with visual impairments. Many rhythm instruments are useful for encouraging young children with visual impairments to use tools. Be sure to provide hand-over-hand assistance, give verbal feedback, and describe what you are doing.

Children with Hearing Impairments

Children with hearing impairments will require no adaptations, as these items are based on visual and motor skills. You can eliminate Item 20e for children with a severe to profound hearing loss.

20. TOOL USE

a. Pulls string to obtain object or make effect

b. Hits drum with stick

c. Uses stick to obtain object

d. Uses hammer to pound in balls

e. Uses mallet to play xylophone keys

f. Holds bowl and stirs

g. Uses hammer to pound pegs in pounding bench

h. Transfers material with spoon

i. Spreads with knife

j. Cuts with edge of fork

■ ■ ■

20a. Pulls string to obtain object or make effect

MATERIALS   Crib gym, string, a variety of toys including pull toys

PROCEDURES

Dangle a toy by a string in front of the child, and then place it out of her reach but with the string toward the child and within easy grasp. If the child does not pull the string to get the toy, demonstrate for her how to do it.

Repeat and observe to see if the child pulls the string without further demonstration. If she does not, place the string in her hand and wait. If there is no effort to pull the string, physically prompt the child, providing only as much help as necessary. Be sure to let the child play with the toy when she gets it.

DAILY ROUTINES & FUNCTIONAL ACTIVITIES

Place one or two pull toys available for the child throughout the day. Periodically place one toy near the child with the string toward her. Observe to see if the child pulls the string to bring the toy closer.

Have a crib gym in the child's crib (or attached to a frame that fits over an infant seat) that has rings or other handles to pull and create effects. Periodically observe the child to see if she is learning how to pull the string, ring, or other device to create an effect. It is important to note that while such a toy may keep the child entertained while you are doing other activities, it can become boring to the child if she is left alone with it for long periods at a time.

CRITERION   The child spontaneously (i.e., without an immediately preceding demonstration) pulls a string to get a toy. Except for children with severe motor impairments, the child should pull a string to get a toy in several different situations (e.g., in free play, in training sessions) with several different toys.

■ ■ ■

20b. Hits drum with stick

MATERIALS   Toy drum, stick

PROCEDURES

Place the drum and stick in front of the child. Use a second stick to demonstrate hitting the drum. If the child does not spontaneously imitate you, place the other stick in the child's hand, and provide him physical assistance to hit the drum. You can also begin drumming with just the child's hand before adding the drumming stick. Some children enjoy having a stick in each hand to drum with.

DAILY ROUTINES & FUNCTIONAL ACTIVITIES

Play music and hit the drum while playing music. Show the child how to drum on different materials with different tools (e.g., use a spoon on a can or the bottom of a cup). Give the child drumming materials to play with when he is in his highchair waiting for food.

CRITERION   *The child spontaneously uses a stick or similar tool to hit a drum on several occasions.*

■ ■ ■

20c. Uses stick to obtain object

MATERIALS   Dowel or similar stick (approximately ⅜ inch by 10 inches), interesting small toys

PROCEDURES

Seat the child at small table or in her highchair. Place one of her favorite or another interesting toy in front of child but out of reach. Demonstrate using the dowel to obtain the toy. Return the toy to its original position, and hand the child the dowel. Tell her to "get the toy." It may be helpful to have a second dowel in case you need to repeat your demonstration. If the child does not respond, provide hand-over-hand assistance.

DAILY ROUTINES & FUNCTIONAL ACTIVITIES

Make a game of this activity, using your own dowel to move the toy about and, perhaps, bring it closer to you. You could also place a snack food just out of reach on the child's highchair tray. Give the child a dowel and tell her to "get the food."

CRITERION   *On several different occasions, the child uses a stick to obtain a toy that is out of her reach.*

■ ■ ■

20d. Uses hammer to pound in balls

MATERIALS   Pounding toy with balls and hammer

PROCEDURES

Present the pounding toy and hammer to the child, and demonstrate for him how to hammer in the balls. Reset the balls, and give the hammer to the child. Tell him to hit the balls. Provide physical assistance and repeated demonstrations as needed. Encourage the child to replace the balls on top and repeat the activity. Typically, the ball-hammering toys are highly motivating because the ball usually travels through the toy and comes out through a hole at the bottom, reinforcing cause and effect concepts.

DAILY ROUTINES & FUNCTIONAL ACTIVITIES

Have a pounding toy readily available for free play. In group settings, children should not be encouraged to play close to each other when hammering so that they do not accidentally hit someone.

CRITERION   The child uses a hammer to pound in balls on several different occasions.

■ ■ ■

20

20e. Uses mallet to play xylophone keys

MATERIALS   Xylophone, two mallets

PROCEDURES

Place the xylophone and one mallet in front of the child. Use the second mallet to demonstrate how to play different keys on the xylophone. The goal of this item is for the child to use more precise control in order to hit individual keys, rather than using the random hitting motion highlighted in Item 20b. If the child does not spontaneously imitate you, place the mallet in her hand, and provide her with physical assistance to hit the xylophone. Encourage the child to use one mallet in each hand in order to develop bilateral coordination.

DAILY ROUTINES & FUNCTIONAL ACTIVITIES

Play the drum and xylophone together with the child—have the child play one instrument while you play the other. Try playing slower or faster to see if the child will imitate you.

CRITERION   The child spontaneously uses a mallet to play individual keys on a xylophone.

■ ■ ■

20f. Holds bowl and stirs

MATERIALS   Bowl or cup with spoon

PROCEDURES

Hold the bowl with one hand, and demonstrate a stirring motion with your other hand. Give the child a bowl and spoon, and tell him to stir. Repeat your demonstration and give physical assistance as needed. A bowl or a cup with a handle may be easier for the child to hold and stabilize while stirring.

DAILY ROUTINES & FUNCTIONAL ACTIVITIES

When possible, involve the child in simple cooking activities. Put a small amount of mixture/batter into a cup or a small bowl for the child to stir. Encourage him to stir in additions to cereal (e.g., pieces of fruit).

CRITERION   *The child holds a bowl and stirs with spoon.*

■ ■ ■

20g. Uses hammer to pound pegs in pounding bench

MATERIALS   Pounding bench with pegs and hammer

PROCEDURES

Present the pounding bench and hammer to the child. Demonstrate for her how to hammer in the pegs. Give the hammer to the child, and tell her to hit the pegs. Provide physical assistance and repeated demonstrations as needed. Encourage the child to turn the bench over or replace the pegs, and repeat the activity. Pounding benches are typically made of wood and require greater strength and more repeated hammerings than the pounding toys with balls (see Item 20d).

DAILY ROUTINES & FUNCTIONAL ACTIVITIES

Have a pounding toy readily available for the child during free play. In group settings, children should not be encouraged to play close to each other when hammering due to the risk of accidentally hitting someone.

CRITERION   *The child uses a hammer to pound in pegs on several different occasions.*

■ ■ ■

20h. Transfers material with spoon

MATERIALS   Two bowls, teaspoon, loose materials (e.g., small stones, lentils, rice, sand; if mouthing is a problem, use edibles)

PROCEDURES

Fill one bowl with lentils, for example, and set it in front of the child next to an empty bowl. With a spoon, demonstrate scooping the lentils from one bowl and dumping them into the second bowl. Then, give the spoon to the child, and ask him to fill up the second bowl. Give physical assistance as needed. Using heavy bowls that will not tip over easily may offer the child greater success. If the child tends to lose most of the material before reaching the second bowl, let him use a measuring cup at first.

DAILY ROUTINES & FUNCTIONAL ACTIVITIES

If you have access to a sandbox or table, be sure to provide scoops, shovels, spoons, and a variety of containers for the child to play with. The children can also use shovels to fill up pails and then use that sand to build a sand castle.

At snack time, have children serve themselves a snack (e.g., dry cereal, raisins) from a large bowl using a spoon or a scoop.

CRITERION   *The child uses a spoon to scoop and transfer material from one container to a second container.*

■ ■ ■

20i. Spreads with knife

MATERIALS   Toast or firm bread, soft butter, knife, plate

PROCEDURES

Place a piece of toast on a plate and set it on the table in front of the child with a knife and butter. With a second piece of toast, show the child how to spread on the butter, covering its entire surface. Encourage the child to spread the butter on her piece of toast. Teach the child to stabilize the toast with one hand and spread the butter with the other. Give the child physical assistance as needed.

20

DAILY ROUTINES & FUNCTIONAL ACTIVITIES

Encourage the child to fix simple foods independently. She can spread peanut butter or jelly on top of crackers, or she can decorate cookies by spreading soft frosting on top of them.

CRITERION   *The child uses a knife for spreading on several occasions.*

■ ■ ■

20j. Cuts with edge of fork

MATERIALS   Easy-to-cut food (e.g., pancakes), fork, plate

PROCEDURES

Place a pancake on a plate and set it on the table in front of the child with a fork. Show the child how to cut the pancake with the edge of his fork. Position the fork sideways in the child's hand, and help him cut the pancake by pushing down with the edge of the fork and then pulling away the fork. Then, ask the child to do the activity independently. Encourage him to keep his index finger on the top edge of the fork to apply pressure.

DAILY ROUTINES & FUNCTIONAL ACTIVITIES

Roll play dough into snakes or flatten with a rolling pin. Encourage the child to use the edge of a fork to cut the play dough into smaller pieces.

CRITERION   *The child cuts with the edge of his fork on several occasions.*

21
Visual-Motor Skills

V isual-motor refers to skills involving the use of tools with paper (e.g., drawing, coloring, painting, writing, cutting) and generally involves the coordinated use of vision and hands together. The emergence of visual-motor skills requires integration of visual-perceptual and fine motor skills. Young children benefit from early exposure to art materials that allow them to explore and develop the motor control needed to do more skilled work in the preschool period. For toddlers, easel work provides a great opportunity to explore different mediums (e.g., paint, chalk, crayons) in a position that contributes to the development of a mature grip and hand posture. As the child draws or paints against a vertical surface, he or she develops not only greater shoulder stability but also better wrist extension, bringing the thumb and fingers into a natural readiness to hold a pencil. Often, a mature pencil grip does not emerge before the age of 3 years. Typically, there is considerable variability in visual-motor development, with girls often demonstrating the developmental advantage.

ADAPTATIONS

Children with Motor Impairments

Children with severe motor impairments may never be able to do these activities independently, but there are some things you can do to help. For example, if a child is unable to hold a crayon or marker, focus initially on doing writing/drawing activities with his or her hand or finger in fingerpaint. Children with motor impairments may need some type of adaptive device in order to hold a crayon. Consult an occupational therapist regarding various possibilities.

Children with Visual Impairments

Children with severe visual impairments will have considerable difficulties with these items. It is important to consult an occupational therapist or vision specialist to determine whether it is appropriate to include these items in a child's program and, if so, what adaptations will be necessary.

Some adaptations include using contrasting colors, such as bright yellow paper and black markers, or making marks in thick fingerpaint, play dough, or shaving cream so that the child can trace them with his or her finger.

Children with Hearing Impairments

Children with hearing impairments will require no adaptations to these items as they are based on visual and motor skills. Be sure to accompany any verbal instruction with demonstrations.

21. VISUAL-MOTOR SKILLS

a. Marks paper with writing implement
b. Scribbles spontaneously
c. Fingerpaints with whole hand
d. Imitates vertical stroke
e. Imitates shifting from scribble to stroke and back
f. Imitates horizontal stroke
g. Pretends to write
h. Copies a circle with a circular scribble
i. Snips with scissors
j. Makes continuous cuts across paper

■ ■ ■

21a. Marks paper with writing implement

MATERIALS   Large crayon, pencil, or marker; several pieces of paper

PROCEDURES

Place a piece of paper in front of the child. Pick up a crayon and make several slow strokes on the paper, drawing the child's attention to what you are doing. Tell the child to write or draw on the paper like you are doing. If needed, place the crayon in the child's hand. If he does not mark on the paper, physically assist him to do so. Watch for the child to continue after you stop providing assistance.

DAILY ROUTINES & FUNCTIONAL ACTIVITIES

Let the child practice making strokes in fingerpaint using his hands or fingers. A good time to introduce and practice drawing activities is while you are preparing a meal. Seat the child in his highchair and provide him with paper and crayons. This way, you are there to talk to him and supervise him, but you still have your hands free to prepare the meal. It is often helpful to use sturdy paper and tape it to the tray top.

CRITERION   *The child makes several marks on a piece of paper with a writing implement.*

■ ■ ■

21b. Scribbles spontaneously

MATERIALS   Two crayons, pencils, or markers; several pieces of paper

PROCEDURES

Give the child a crayon (or other writing implement) and a piece of paper. Show the child how to scribble on the paper, and physically assist her if necessary.

Then, give the child the crayon and paper (without a demonstration), and observe what she does. If the child does not spontaneously scribble, ask her to draw or write on the paper you gave her. Continue demonstrations until the child scribbles spontaneously.

DAILY ROUTINES & FUNCTIONAL ACTIVITIES

Set up an easel with paper for the child. Vary the drawing materials you provide for the child (e.g., crayons, markers, paint, chalk). Use soap crayons or foaming soap on the edge of the tub during bath time.

CRITERION   *The child spontaneously scribbles.*

■ ■ ■

21c. **Fingerpaints with whole hand**

PROCEDURES

Place a small amount of fingerpaint on a piece of paper in front of the child. Demonstrate for him how to move the paint around the paper using your entire hand. Ask the child to paint, and observe what he does. Provide physical assistance as needed.

If the child is resistant to touching the paint, encourage him to sit and watch you paint. Repeated exposure may reduce his resistance. For children who will not touch the paint, try putting some in a large resealable bag and letting them squish the paint around, while keeping hands clean. If the child does not become comfortable with finger-painting, consult with an occupational therapist, as the child may be demonstrating sensory defensiveness.

DAILY ROUTINES & FUNCTIONAL ACTIVITIES

Similar exploratory play can be done with foaming soap or shaving cream. For children who are still mouthing, try pudding or whipped cream instead. You may want to laminate the child's fingerpainting to create a placemat.

CRITERION   *The child uses his whole hand to spread fingerpaint on paper on several different occasions.*

■ ■ ■

21d. **Imitates vertical stroke**

MATERIALS   Large pieces of paper, crayons or markers

PROCEDURES

Place a piece of paper in front of the child, and demonstrate how to make a vertical stroke. While drawing, say to the child, "Watch me. I am making lines that go up and down." Try adding a sound as you make each line (e.g., "zip").

After you demonstrate these movements for the child, ask her to do what you did. If she does not, take her hand and help her make the vertical stroke several times. Then, ask the child to make one by herself. If the child is having a lot of difficulty with vertical lines, you can use a cardboard guide with a slot to help her. Assist the child in making the lines using the slot. Then, see if the child can do the activity independently.

Note: To make a cardboard guide, cut a slot ½ inch wide by 8 inches long.

DAILY ROUTINES & FUNCTIONAL ACTIVITIES

Encourage the child to make lines and circular scribbles with her index finger in finger-paint, foaming soap, a sandbox, or in a small amount of sand or salt on a cookie sheet. Tape a piece of sturdy paper to the child's highchair tray, and provide her with one or two crayons for drawing.

CRITERION   The child imitates a vertical stroke with a writing utensil.

■ ■ ■

21e. Imitates shifting from scribble to stroke and back

MATERIALS   Large crayon, pencil, or marker; several pieces of paper

PROCEDURES

When the child is marking on a piece of paper, say, "Watch me," and make a quick vertical stroke on your paper. Then say, "Can you do it?" If the child imitates the stroke, say, "Good, now do this," and scribble for the child. If he then imitates the scribble, shift back again to the stroke. Make a game of it. If the child does not shift from scribble to stroke, physically assist him, keeping the activity fun.

DAILY ROUTINES & FUNCTIONAL ACTIVITIES

Encourage the child to make lines and circular scribbles with his index finger in finger-paint, foaming soap, a sandbox, or in a small amount of sand or salt on a cookie sheet. Tape a piece of sturdy paper to the child's highchair tray, and provide him with one or two crayons for drawing.

CRITERION   The child imitates shifting from scribble to stroke and back again.

■ ■ ■

21f. Imitates horizontal stroke

MATERIALS   Large pieces of paper, crayons or markers, cardboard

PROCEDURES

Place a piece of paper in front of the child, and demonstrate how to make a horizontal stroke. While drawing, say to the child, "Watch me. I am making lines that go back and forth." Try adding a sound as you make each line (e.g., "vroom").

After you demonstrate these movements for the child, ask her to do what you did. If she does not, take her hand, and help her make the horizontal stroke several times. Then, ask the child to make one by herself. If the child is having a lot of difficulty with horizontal lines, you can use a cardboard guide with a slot to help her. Assist the child in making the lines using the slot. Then, see if the child can do the activity independently.

Note: To make a cardboard guide, cut a slot ½ inch wide by 8 inches long.

DAILY ROUTINES & FUNCTIONAL ACTIVITIES

Encourage the child to make lines and circular scribbles with her index finger in finger-paint, foaming soap, a sandbox, or in a small amount of sand or salt on a cookie sheet. Tape a piece of sturdy paper to the child's highchair tray, and provide her with one or two crayons for drawing.

CRITERION   The child imitates a horizontal stroke with a writing utensil on several occasions.

■ ■ ■

21g. Pretends to write

MATERIALS   Paper, pencil

PROCEDURES

Sit at a table with the child and begin to write something (e.g., a letter to Grandpa, a grocery list). Give the child a pencil and piece of paper, and ask him to write whatever you are writing. Most children will pick up the pencil and begin to make marks on the paper. If the child does not, place the pencil in his hand and provide hand-over-hand assistance to mark the paper. Gradually fade your assistance.

DAILY ROUTINES & FUNCTIONAL ACTIVITIES

During down times (e.g., when waiting for lunch, when waiting for an appointment), give the child a small notepad and pencil so that he can write.

In a classroom, provide pencils and notepads in the housekeeping and other centers so that the children can pretend to make lists or do office work.

CRITERION   The child pretends to write with a writing utensil.

■ ■ ■

21h. Copies a circle with a circular scribble

MATERIALS   Large pieces of paper, crayons or markers

PROCEDURES

Place a piece of paper in front of the child, and demonstrate how to make a circular stroke. While drawing, say to the child, "Watch me. I am going around and around." Try making discrete circles, but if the child does not respond, use a circular scribble.

After you demonstrate these movements for the child, ask her to do what you did. If she does not, take her hand and help her make the circular stroke several times. Then, ask the child to make one by herself.

DAILY ROUTINES & FUNCTIONAL ACTIVITIES

Encourage the child to make lines and circular scribbles with her index finger in finger-paint, foaming soap, a sandbox, or in a small amount of sand or salt on a cookie sheet. Tape a piece of sturdy paper to the child's highchair tray, and provide her with one or two crayons for drawing.

CRITERION   The child produces a circular scribble when attempting to copy a circle.

■ ■ ■

21i. Snips with scissors

MATERIALS   Paper, safety scissors

PROCEDURES

Place a piece of paper and the safety scissors in front of the child. Ask him to cut the paper. If he does not know how to do this, place the scissors in his preferred hand and guide him through the motion.

For best control, place his thumb and middle fingers in the handle holes, with his index finger on the bottom handle next to the hole. Hold the paper taut between your hands and ask the child to cut. Verbal cues such as "open" or "squeeze" may be useful. If the child is having a lot of difficulty, use small squeeze scissors or training scissors that have extra handle holes for your hand. When the child is successful in making cuts, encourage him to hold the paper on his own. Using stiff paper or index cards may make this activity easier.

Note: If the child's hand preference is not clear, teach cutting with the right hand, as most scissors are righthanded, and a number of lefthanded people cut with their right hand. Quality scissors can make a big difference in a child's level of success in cutting. Children who are lefthanded should be provided with lefthanded scissors. The blades need to be sharp (not pointed) and fit closely together.

DAILY ROUTINES & FUNCTIONAL ACTIVITIES

Make placemats by cutting fringe around the edge of the paper.

CRITERION   The child snips paper with scissors several times.

■ ■ ■

21j. Makes continuous cuts across paper

MATERIALS   6-inch square pieces of paper, safety scissors

PROCEDURES

Place a piece of paper and the safety scissors in front of the child. Ask her to cut the paper in half or to cut all of the way across the paper. Give her verbal cues (e.g., "open, squeeze, open, squeeze") as well as physical assistance, if needed, to maintain continuous cutting. It may be helpful if you hold the paper for the child initially. Then, when she is having some success cutting, have her hold the paper herself. Try stiff paper or index cards initially to make the activity easier.

DAILY ROUTINES & FUNCTIONAL ACTIVITIES

Make simple puzzles by cutting a picture glued on cardboard into several pieces

CRITERION   *The child makes several continuous cuts across a piece of paper.*

22-1
Upright: Posture
& Locomotion

The ultimate goal of motor programming is for children to function efficiently in upright positions—sitting, standing, and walking. These abilities are based on the strength gained in the prone (on stomach) and supine (on back) positions. For overall program planning, however, it is important to distinguish between the use of upright positioning for motor development and the usefulness of this position to promote cognitive and social development (although these purposes often overlap).

Sitting, for example, is a motor skill that involves strength and balance. The motor activities performed in prone and supine positions strengthen the muscles, while those performed in the sitting position are used to increase balance and control. Sitting is also, however, an important position for promoting cognitive and social development. Sitting provides children with a wider view of the world around them, different experiences with object manipulation, and greater opportunity for social interaction. Sitting will only serve these functions, though, if the head can move freely and the hands are free for play and not used for support. A child who must use his or her hands for support should be placed in the appropriate supportive seating devices for cognitive and social activities.

Standing is another important motor skill. Standing promotes musculo-skeletal development and circulation. Proper position in standing helps prevent tightening of the hips, knees, and ankles and promotes strength in the back. Same-age peers will also perceive a standing child as more mature; thus, standing can also promote social interaction.

Some children will not function well in prone or supine and should be routinely placed in sitting or standing. Therapists will provide guidance on appropriate positions.

ADAPTATIONS

Children with Motor Impairments

Children with motor impairments will often prefer to cuddle into an adult's shoulder rather than lift their heads. For such children, it is particularly important to emphasize independent head control and utilize special positioning for activities requiring visual attention or arm use.

Extra time and physical assistance may be necessary to promote sitting. A child with severe motor impairments may never achieve independence in assuming a sitting position; however, the child should still be given the opportunity to control whatever parts of the transitional movement he or she can. A child who cannot change position independently should be repositioned by caregivers at least once an hour. This will help prevent joint contracture and skin breakdown and will help to ensure changes in the child's visual environment. Back-lying, stomach-lying, and supported sitting and standing also should be used.

A child with motor impairments who wants to sit but lacks adequate postural control will usually use various strategies to remain stable. Some children will sit with their heels next to their hips (i.e., W-sit). If a child has stiff muscles, you should discourage this position by praising the child for sitting with his or her feet to the front and by providing a supported seating alternative. If W-sitting is used frequently by a child with stiff muscles, make sure that the child is being checked regularly by an orthopedist because that position can promote hip dislocation as well as knee and ankle problems. For children with weak, floppy muscles, W-sitting is not a great orthopedic concern but usually indicates a need for specific strengthening.

A child who sits with his or her back rounded, head tipped back, and legs stiffly extended should have his or her posture corrected. Some children will need specially manufactured seating devices that should be selected by a therapist. Other children can achieve good sitting posture by using straight-back chairs with nonslip shelf liner on the seat.

Be sure to assist children with motor impairments to stand as straight as possible, with both feet flat on the floor and their ankles in a normal position. Children with severe motor impairments may never achieve independent standing, so you should provide them with alternatives (e.g., a prone stander). Consult a physical therapist for advice.

The nature of a child's motor impairment will determine whether independent walking is possible. Consult a physical therapist about each child's potential and the adaptive aids that may assist the child to walk. Many children who use wheelchairs for general transportation can function without them in the classroom if they are given physical assistance to move about. This ability is important for general health and has an impact on the way these children view themselves and are viewed by others. Make sure that children with motor impairments have a safe means of falling before working on balance activities. The most important consideration is to be sure that a child will not hit his or her head on the floor in the event of a fall. Children who are at high risk for injuring their face or head by falling should wear protective helmets.

Stair climbing is an important motor skill both for functional reasons and for strengthening of leg muscles. Whenever possible, assist a child with motor impairments in climbing stairs rather than carrying him or her.

Children with Visual Impairments

When working with children with visual impairments, it is important to pay particular attention to the position of the upper trunk. Try to prevent a child with visual impairments from letting his or her head and shoulders slope forward. Most children with visual impairments have some degree of usable vision that you can use to encourage head lifting. You can pair auditory stimuli with brightly colored, shiny, or high-contrast visual stimuli, or you can use toys that make a continuous sound, and physically guide the child through the movement.

For children with visual impairments who are mobile, keep the arrangement of the room and toys in their same predictable location. Walking alone is often delayed in children with visual impairments, so working on this activity will probably require more perseverance on your part. Practice repeatedly in a familiar, predictable play space. Consider using a playpen or corner of a room. Try standing a child with visual impairments on your feet and walking together to convey the idea. As soon as the child is able, start teaching the child to feel walls and furniture to find his or her way around. For children with sufficient functional vision, use bright or fluorescent floor markings. For children who have little or no vision, work on pushing a cart along a clear quiet hallway toward a meaningful auditory goal.

22-1

Children with Hearing Impairments

Children with hearing impairments sometimes have problems standing and walking. This is because the structures that control hearing and balance are located in the same part of the brain. Children with hearing impairments may require more practice but will eventually attain standing and walking.

22-I. UPRIGHT: POSTURE & LOCOMOTION

a. Holds head steady when held

b. Holds trunk steady when held at hips

c. Moves to sitting position from stomach or all-fours position

d. Sits alone

e. Pulls self to standing position

f. Steps sideways holding a support

g. Stoops to pick up toy while holding a support

h. Removes hands from support and stands independently

i. Takes independent steps

j. Moves from hands and knees to hands and feet to standing

k. Squats down to retrieve object

l. Walks sideways

m. Walks backward at least 5 feet

n. Walks up three stairs, same-step foot placement, with rail

o. Walks down three stairs, same-step foot placement, with rail

p. Maintains a squatting position in play

q. Runs stiffly

r. Jumps on floor

s. Walks up three stairs, same-step foot placement, without rail

t. Jumps off stair

u. Walks backward 10 feet

v. Walks on all types of surfaces without falling

w. Uses heel–toe pattern (arms free to carry objects)

x. Takes three to four steps on tiptoes

y. Runs at least 10 feet without falling

z. Jumps down from 8-inch height (one foot leading)

aa. Walks up three stairs, alternate pattern, with rail

bb. Walks at least 20 feet on tiptoes

cc. Avoids obstacles when running

dd. Walks up three stairs, alternate pattern, without rail

ee. Walks down three stairs, same-step foot placement, without rail

ff. Jumps over 2-inch hurdle

gg. Jumps down from 16-inch to 18-inch height (one foot leading)

hh. Broad jumps 4 inches to 14 inches

■ ■ ■

22-Ia. Holds head steady when held

MATERIALS   Any visual stimuli that hold the child's attention

PROCEDURES

Hold the child without supporting her head. If necessary, keep your hand near the base of the child's skull, ready to hold her head in position.

DAILY ROUTINES & FUNCTIONAL ACTIVITIES

Present interesting visual stimuli (e.g., bright pictures, toys, masks) to the child. Strive for a symmetrical midline position for the child as well as for the child to have the ability to turn to the right and left. Use this procedure as much as possible throughout the day whenever you are holding or carrying the child. Carrying the child face out is a good way to promote head control.

CRITERION   The child holds her head erect and steady while in an upright position for at least 2 minutes and can turn to the right and left. The child is able to do this consistently on 3 consecutive days.

■ ■ ■

22-1

22-Ib. Holds trunk steady when held at hips

MATERIALS   None required

PROCEDURES

Carry the child with support at the hips. Provide support to the trunk with your hand, and withdraw assistance whenever you can. At first, your hand will be higher on the child's trunk, but as he gains strength, you can move your control down until it is at his hips.

DAILY ROUTINES & FUNCTIONAL ACTIVITIES

Carrying the child face out is a good way of promoting trunk control; you should use this position whenever practical throughout the day. When you are carrying the child, encourage him to turn to his right and left. Once the child can hold his trunk erect and steady, riding on an adult's shoulders can be fun and beneficial.

CRITERION   The child holds his trunk erect and steady for at least 2 minutes and can turn to the right and left. The child consistently demonstrates this ability on 3 consecutive days.

■ ■ ■

22-Ic. Moves to sitting position
from stomach or all-fours position

MATERIALS   None required

PROCEDURES

If starting from a stomach-lying position, lift the child's hips, wait for her to bend her knees under her chest, then rotate the child over one hip into a sitting position. If starting from a hands-and-knees position, rotate the child back and over one hip into a sitting position.

DAILY ROUTINES & FUNCTIONAL ACTIVITIES

Give the child plenty of time to participate in the movement. Incorporate this activity into position changes when they occur naturally throughout play or caregiving activities.

CRITERION   The child independently moves to a sitting position from her stomach or an all-fours position, and she demonstrates this ability on 3 consecutive days.

■ ■ ■

22-Id. Sits alone

MATERIALS   A variety of large and small toys, low bench

PROCEDURES

Move the child into a sitting position as in Item 22-Ic. Give support either at the hips or slightly above. Provide toys for the child that are small enough to be picked up or that have a mobile at eye level so it can be activated by reaching out. You can also place a large toy, such as a busy box, on a low bench and position the child in front of it. This will encourage him to lift his arms while keeping a straight back. Once the child is fairly stable in a sitting position, start placing toys to elicit reaching to the side and rotating to the right and left. If the child's back is rounded, rock the pelvis forward to create a small arch in his lower back.

DAILY ROUTINES & FUNCTIONAL ACTIVITIES

Use sitting as a play position throughout the day. If necessary, place pillows around the child for light support. Look at other daily activities, such as feeding time, to see if sitting can be used as a functional position. As much as possible, ensure that the child assumes a variety of sitting positions (e.g., cross-legged, both legs to one side, both legs in front, sitting on a low chair).

CRITERION   The child can sit with his trunk erect and with his hands free for play, and he can rotate from side to side without losing balance. The child can play in this manner for at least 3 minutes at a time on 3 consecutive days.

■ ■ ■

22-Ie. Pulls self to standing position

MATERIALS   Favorite toys, low table or couch

PROCEDURES

Place toys on a low table or couch. Use a variety of starting positions for the child (e.g., sitting, prone, hands-and-knees, kneeling). Show the child where the toys are, and assist her, if necessary, in moving up to a standing position. Most children will start by simultaneously straightening both legs. The more mature pattern consists of first kneeling, then placing one foot flat on the floor, and finally, pulling into a standing position. If necessary, assist the child in keeping a flat foot and turned-out knee.

DAILY ROUTINES & FUNCTIONAL ACTIVITIES

Make a point of placing toys on elevated surfaces. If there is a heavy chest of drawers, place the toys in a partially pulled-out drawer. Always make sure that the items being used to pull up on are very stable.

CRITERION   *The child can independently pull to a standing position by first placing one foot on the floor. The child is able to do this several times a day on 3 consecutive days.*

■ ■ ■

22-If. Steps sideways holding a support

MATERIALS   Favorite toys, low table or couch

PROCEDURES

With the child standing at a support, place toys several inches out of his reach so that he will take sideways steps to get to them. Do this to both sides, gradually increasing the distance at which you place the toys. At first, the child will lean against the support, then he will stand upright using only hand contact. Once the child is able to easily step sideways, position the toys to elicit stepping around the corner of the support.

DAILY ROUTINES & FUNCTIONAL ACTIVITIES

Set up play areas at couches, tables, or drawers so that favorite toys are displayed in a long row. Removing cushions from a couch and placing toys on the couch often helps when children are starting to take sideways steps.

CRITERION   *The child can step freely along a support and around corners using light hand support. The child is able to do this several minutes at a time on 3 consecutive days.*

■ ■ ■

22-Ig. Stoops to pick up toy while holding a support

MATERIALS   Favorite toys, low table or couch

PROCEDURES

While the child is playing in a standing position at a support, take a toy and place it on the floor. Give light assistance, if necessary, to help the child retrieve the toy and return

22-1

to an upright position. If the child cannot reach down all the way to the floor, place the toy on a low stool at first. Make sure that the child bends at the knees, not at the waist, and that she keeps her feet flat on the floor while holding onto the support with one hand. Place the toys to the right and left.

DAILY ROUTINES & FUNCTIONAL ACTIVITIES

This activity can be incorporated into many fine motor, cognitive, and language activities, such as stacking blocks, sorting, matching, and naming objects.

CRITERION   The child can independently pick up a toy from the floor and return to a standing position while maintaining support with one hand. The child can do this several times in a row on 3 consecutive days.

■ ■ ■

22-Ih. Removes hands from support and stands independently

MATERIALS   Small toys, low table or couch

PROCEDURES

While the child is standing at a support, offer him a toy that he must grasp with both hands, or play two-handed games with the child. Offer light hand support, if necessary, and then gradually withdraw it. It is usually best to speak quietly and not call attention to the fact that the child is standing. You can also kneel in front of the child, away from any furniture, and use these procedures.

DAILY ROUTINES & FUNCTIONAL ACTIVITIES

Place the child in a standing position for dressing and eating snacks. Keep the child's attention on the functional activity rather than on the act of standing.

CRITERION   The child can stand alone for at least 30 seconds, and he demonstrates this ability several times a day on 3 consecutive days.

■ ■ ■

22-Ii. Takes independent steps

MATERIALS   None required

PROCEDURES

Place the child in a standing position, either between two adults or against a wall. Encourage the child to take steps by holding your arms out—at first, just a few feet away. Gradually increase the distance between you and the child. Children often want light support to maintain confidence when they are learning to walk. You can do this in several ways. For example, you can hold one of the child's hands while walking, and then gradually loosen your grip. You can have the child hold an object such as a wooden spoon while you hold her other end. Or, you can also have the child hold one hand of a baby doll while you hold the other. Gradually lessen the amount of support you give.

DAILY ROUTINES & FUNCTIONAL ACTIVITIES

Offer opportunities throughout the day for the child to take independent steps. Let the child walk with support rather then being carried when practical.

CRITERION   The child can walk alone 5–10 feet several times a day on 3 consecutive days.

■ ■ ■

22-Ij. Moves from hands and knees to hands and feet to standing

MATERIALS   None required, but favorite toys may be helpful

PROCEDURES

Move to a clear space on the floor, and entice the child to stand by offering him your hands or a toy. Give physical assistance, if necessary, by standing behind the child and helping him with limb movements. First, place the child's hands on the floor, then place his feet under his hips. Show the child how to rock back and stand up. When feasible, take time to use this procedure rather than picking the child up into a standing position.

22-1

DAILY ROUTINES & FUNCTIONAL ACTIVITIES

Assist the child in standing up at various times during the day.

CRITERION   The child independently moves from his hands and knees to a standing position and remains steadily standing for at least several seconds. The child should routinely uses this as a method of attaining a standing position, rather than creeping over to a support and pulling himself up.

■ ■ ■

22-Ik. Squats down to retrieve object

MATERIALS   Small objects or toys that the child likes

PROCEDURES

While the child is walking, entice her to squat down and pick up small objects and then stand up again. Make sure she is bending her knees.

DAILY ROUTINES & FUNCTIONAL ACTIVITIES

Encourage the child to pick up toys to put in a bucket, pick flowers, or help in cleaning up the room. At home she can take laundry from a small pile and put it in the dryer or take small grocery items from a bag and hand them up to an adult to put in the cupboard.

CRITERION   *The child can easily and smoothly squat down and stand up several times in a row while keeping her feet flat on the floor. The child is able to do this on 3 consecutive days.*

■ ■ ■

22-Il. Walks sideways

MATERIALS   Tables, ball, toys

PROCEDURES

Start by having the child push a small toy along a table. Then, have him carry a larger toy with two hands while walking sideways alongside the table. You can also have the child pull a string toy sideways.

DAILY ROUTINES & FUNCTIONAL ACTIVITIES

Play games in which sideways steps are required. For example, place the child on a step facing you. Then, move sideways and encourage him to come to you.

CRITERION   *The child spontaneously takes several steps sideways during play on 3 consecutive days.*

■ ■ ■

22-Im. Walks backward at least 5 feet

MATERIALS   Pull toys

PROCEDURES

Present the child with a pull toy, and place both of her hands on the string. Guide her through the action of walking backward, then withdraw.

DAILY ROUTINES & FUNCTIONAL ACTIVITIES

You can play a game of "I'm going to get you" to elicit backward walking.

CRITERION   *The child takes several backward steps during play on 3 consecutive days.*

■ ■ ■

22-In. Walks up three stairs, same-step foot placement, with rail

22-Io. Walks down three stairs, same-step foot placement, with rail

MATERIALS   A set of at least three steps (approximately 6 inches high and 6 inches deep) that has a railing

PROCEDURES

To teach going up stairs, position yourself close to the child at first. Start the climb by having the child face the railing, holding on with both hands. As the child gains confidence, he will let go of the railing with one hand and face forward, up the steps. If the child has one leg that is stronger than the other, the stronger leg should be placed on the first step when going up the stairs. From time to time, assist the child in reversing this pattern. If the child's motor impairment prevents him from walking up stairs, consult a physical therapist for an alternate strategy. If the child is fearful, start by stepping up only one step, then gradually add steps. Use the same strategy when teaching going down stairs. The stronger leg will remain on the upper step, so attempt to reverse this pattern from time to time.

To teach going down stairs, position yourself close to the child at first, giving physical assistance as necessary. Start by having the child face the railing, holding on with both hands. As the child gains confidence, he will let go of the railing with one hand and face forward. If the child has one leg that is stronger than the other, the stronger leg should stay on the top stair when going down the stairs. From time to time, assist the child in reversing this pattern. If the child is fearful, start by using the bottom stair only, then add stairs. If the child's motor impairment prevents him from walking down stairs, consult a physical therapist for an alternate strategy.

DAILY ROUTINES & FUNCTIONAL ACTIVITIES

Whenever practical during the day, take the time to assist the child on the stairs rather than carry him.

22-1

CRITERION 22-In   *The child uses one hand on the railing while walking up at least three stairs using same-step foot placement. The child does this spontaneously on 3 consecutive days.*

CRITERION 22-Io   *The child uses one hand on the railing while walking down at least three stairs using same-step foot placement. The child does this spontaneously on 3 consecutive days.*

■ ■ ■

22-Ip. Maintains a squatting position in play

MATERIALS   Large toys placed on the floor

PROCEDURES

Assist the child in maintaining a squatting position while playing with large toys on the floor. Make sure the child's thighs are horizontal and that the child is not resting her bottom on her heels.

DAILY ROUTINES & FUNCTIONAL ACTIVITIES

Playing a toy xylophone, reading a book, or playing in the sandbox are all good opportunities to practice this skill. If necessary, kneel behind the child, and let her start by sitting on your knees while you guide her into the position.

CRITERION   *The child plays in a squatting position for about 10 seconds at a time on 3 consecutive days.*

■ ■ ■

22-Iq. Runs stiffly

MATERIALS   Open space

PROCEDURES

Early running should take place indoors on a smooth surface. Use verbal commands to "go fast" accompanied by hand clapping and demonstrations of running. Most children enjoy kicking a ball and chasing it. At this stage, children should not be competing with others, following rules, or using equipment.

DAILY ROUTINES & FUNCTIONAL ACTIVITIES

Running skills should progress with practice. Offer opportunities to run freely in spaces with few obstacles or uneven surfaces. Chasing, controlled racing, and musical play can be used to prompt running.

CRITERION   *The child can run 5–10 feet without falling, lands on flat feet, and shows little arm movement on 3 consecutive days.*

■ ■ ■

22-Ir. Jumps on floor

MATERIALS   Open space, trampoline

PROCEDURES

For children who are having difficulty learning to jump, you can have them start by standing in front of you while you are sitting and placing their hands on your knees as they practice the leg movements of jumping. Small trampolines are also useful to help the child jump.

For all jumping items, the child must only land on his feet without touching his hands to the floor.

DAILY ROUTINES & FUNCTIONAL ACTIVITIES

Jumping activities are easily incorporated into imaginative play or active music games. You can have the children jump on carpet squares or pretend to be animals that jump.

CRITERION   *The child is able to jump one or two times with both feet off the floor at the same time. The child can demonstrate this ability on 3 consecutive days.*

■ ■ ■

22-Is. Walks up three stairs, same-step foot placement, without rail

MATERIALS   A set of at least three steps (approximately 6 inches high and 6 inches deep)

PROCEDURES

To teach going up stairs without using a rail, stand behind the child (away from the rail if the stairs have one) and offer light support at the hips. Gradually withdraw support as the child gains confidence. If the child tends to lean back, try standing in front of her. Look for stairs of varying heights on which the child can practice. If she is having difficulty with balance, use lower and fewer stairs at first. You can also place books on the floor onto which the child can step up.

DAILY ROUTINES & FUNCTIONAL ACTIVITIES

Practice this activity in both indoor and outdoor naturally occurring situations. Let the child step up onto curbs and other low surfaces.

CRITERION   The child walks up at least three stairs (same-step foot placement) without using a rail. She spontaneously does this activity on 3 consecutive days.

■ ■ ■

22-It. Jumps off stair

MATERIALS   Step that is 6 inches high, boards or books of varying thickness

PROCEDURES/DAILY ROUTINES & FUNCTIONAL ACTIVITIES

22-1

Teach jumping down by starting with low objects. Determine the highest object from which the child can jump. Place a mat on the floor. Hold the child's hand at first, then gradually move off to the side. First attempts will be little more than stepping down, with no real flight. As skill and confidence increase, the child will start jumping with one foot leading, frequently touching the floor with hands at landing. With practice, a two-foot take-off and landing will emerge, and the child will be able to jump from greater heights.

CRITERION   The child independently jumps down from a 6-inch step with both feet together. The child demonstrates this ability on 3 consecutive days.

■ ■ ■

22-Iu. Walks backward 10 feet

MATERIALS   Pull toys, large empty boxes, small carts or wagons with wide handles, a smooth surface to walk on

PROCEDURES

Encourage the child to take backward steps by pulling a wheeled toy backward, giving a ride to a friend in a small wagon or cart, or pulling a cardboard box backward. You can also play, "I'm going to get you," while facing the child, or you can simply move the child backward gently with your hands.

DAILY ROUTINES & FUNCTIONAL ACTIVITIES

All of these activities can be done easily in small groups, either indoors or out. They can be structured into simple routines that help the children learn to move to music, listen to instruction, and stay in a group.

CRITERION   *Child walks backward 10 feet without pausing or falling. She can do this several times a day on 3 consecutive days.*

■ ■ ■

22-Iv. Walks on all types of surfaces without falling

MATERIALS   A variety of surfaces to walk on (e.g., sidewalk, grass, slopes, gravel)

PROCEDURES

Gradually introduce the child to the outdoor surfaces in his environment.

DAILY ROUTINES & FUNCTIONAL ACTIVITIES

Start by offering hand support and moving slowly, then gradually withdraw support and encourage faster movement.

CRITERION   *The child routinely navigates all surfaces in his environment without falling.*

■ ■ ■

22-Iw. Uses heel–toe pattern (arms free to carry objects)

MATERIALS   Balls or other toys large enough to require two hands to hold

PROCEDURES

As the child practices various mobility skills, a heel–toe walking pattern should emerge. At this point, the child will have sufficient stability to carry objects when walking.

DAILY ROUTINES & FUNCTIONAL ACTIVITIES

Encourage the child to help with cleanup and carry objects from place to place.

CRITERION   *The child routinely walks with a heel–toe pattern while carrying objects, without losing balance.*

■ ■ ■

22-Ix. Takes three to four steps on tiptoes

MATERIALS   Any toys or materials that will encourage reaching high, open space

PROCEDURES

Encourage the child to rise onto her tiptoes while holding onto a support to reach objects on shelves. This can be made a part of a routine by selectively placing favorite toys just out of reach. Then, encourage tiptoe stepping away from a solid support. At first, offer one of your hands for support.

DAILY ROUTINES & FUNCTIONAL ACTIVITIES

You can also ask the child to imitate you as you walk on tiptoes, or you can suspend the child lightly so that only her toes touch the floor.

CRITERION   *The child takes three to four consecutive steps on tiptoes, and she can do this several times a day on 3 consecutive days.*

■ ■ ■

22-Iy. Runs at least 10 feet without falling

MATERIALS   Open space

PROCEDURES/DAILY ROUTINES & FUNCTIONAL ACTIVITIES

See instructions for Item 22-Iq.

CRITERION   *The child routinely runs 10–20 feet on a smooth surface without falling.*

22-1

■ ■ ■

22-Iz. Jumps down from 8-inch height (one foot leading)

MATERIALS   Large stable objects of varying heights up to 8 inches (e.g., boxes, stairs)

PROCEDURES/DAILY ROUTINES & FUNCTIONAL ACTIVITIES

See instructions for Item 22-It.

CRITERION   *The child jumps (one foot leading) from an 8-inch height and stays on his feet when landing. The child can do this several times a day on 3 consecutive days.*

■ ■ ■

22-Iaa. Walks up three stairs, alternate pattern, with rail

MATERIALS   A set of at least three stairs (approximately 6 inches high and 6 inches deep) with rail

PROCEDURES/DAILY ROUTINES & FUNCTIONAL ACTIVITIES

To teach the alternating pattern, start with going up stairs because this is easier than going down. At first use only 2–3 steps. You can use demonstration, physical assistance, or verbal instruction. If the child is not using a rail, avoid holding her hand; a snug grip on her shirt will give her a sense of security, and you can loosen your hold as appropriate. It is often helpful to use a nonsense refrain such as "pizza, mac and cheese" to remind the child to take a big step up. You can also place different colored ribbons or socks on the child and place paper footprints in those colors on alternate stairs. Experiment with different heights and depths of stairs. To teach going down stairs using alternate pattern, use similar techniques, again starting with only 2–3 steps.

Note: Leg length is a factor in learning alternating stair patterns; children who are short for their age may have to use a same-step pattern on most stairs but can learn alternate pattern in lower stairs.

CRITERION   The child walks up at least three stairs while using an alternate pattern and holding the rail. The child demonstrates this ability several times a day on 3 consecutive days.

■ ■ ■

22-Ibb. Walks at least 20 feet on tiptoes

MATERIALS   Open space

PROCEDURES

Once the child can take several steps on tiptoes, engage him in games that encourage tiptoeing for longer distances.

DAILY ROUTINES & FUNCTIONAL ACTIVITIES

Tiptoe walking can be integrated into group music time or pretend play.

CRITERION   The child takes consecutive steps on his tiptoes for 20 feet or more. The child demonstrates this activity several times a day on 3 consecutive days.

■ ■ ■

22-Icc. Avoids obstacles when running

MATERIALS   Open space with obstacles

PROCEDURES/DAILY ROUTINES & FUNCTIONAL ACTIVITIES

See instructions for Item 22-Iq but provide space where obstacles (e.g., play equipment) are present.

CRITERION   The child routinely runs in an open space with play equipment without running into the equipment.

■ ■ ■

22-Idd. Walks up three stairs, alternate pattern, without rail

MATERIALS   A set of at least three stairs (approximately 6 inches high and 6 inches deep) with rail

PROCEDURES/DAILY ROUTINES & FUNCTIONAL ACTIVITIES

See instructions for Item 22-In.

CRITERION   *The child independently walks up three stairs using an alternate pattern, without rail on 3 consecutive days.*

■ ■ ■

22-Iee. Walks down three stairs, same-step foot placement, without rail

MATERIALS   A set of at least three steps (approximately 6 inches high and 6 inches deep)

PROCEDURES

To teach going down stairs without a rail, use a similar strategy as in Item 22-Is. Position the child on the stairs, and give her light support by holding her hand or the back of her shirt. Gradually, withdraw support as the child gains confidence. If the child is fearful, start with just the bottom stair, then gradually add stairs.

22-1

DAILY ROUTINES & FUNCTIONAL ACTIVITIES

Practice this activity in both indoor and outdoor naturally occurring situations. Let the child step down from curbs and other low surfaces.

CRITERION   *The child walks down at least three stairs (same-step foot placement) without using rail. She spontaneously does this activity on 3 consecutive days.*

■ ■ ■

22-Iff. Jumps over 2-inch hurdle

MATERIALS   Planks, ropes, or other low obstacles

PROCEDURES

Jumping over hurdles can be initiated by jumping over a line on the floor, progressing to jumping over a rope, then over gradually higher obstacles.

DAILY ROUTINES & FUNCTIONAL ACTIVITIES

Create an obstacle course for the child that includes items to jump over. Play Follow the Leader through the course.

CRITERION   *The child jumps over a 2-inch hurdle, taking off and landing on two feet, without falling, on 3 consecutive days.*

■ ■ ■

22-Igg. Jumps down from 16-inch
to 18-inch height (one foot leading)

MATERIALS   Low benches or other stable surfaces that are 16 inches to 18 inches high

PROCEDURES/DAILY ROUTINES & FUNCTIONAL ACTIVITIES

See instructions for Item 22-It.

CRITERION   The child jumps down from a height of 16 inches to 18 inches, leading the jump with one foot, on 3 consecutive days.

■ ■ ■

22-Ihh. Broad jumps 4 inches to 14 inches

MATERIALS   Patterns or lines on the floor

PROCEDURES

To teach broad jumping, observe the child's attempts, and determine how far he can jump. Initial attempts will be short jumps with a one-foot take-off. The trunk will be upright, and there will be slight upward arm movement. Later, the arms will be held in front of the body and will be used to initiate the jump. A preparatory crouch will be evident but will not be deep, and the legs will be flexed during flight. Early instruction should focus on getting the child to take off with both feet together. The child may be better able to get this idea if you have him jump down a short distance with feet together then repeat the broad jump.

To measure the jump, place your finger at the child's heel before he jumps, then measure the distance to his heel after the jump.

DAILY ROUTINES & FUNCTIONAL ACTIVITIES

Create games that involve a variety of motor activities as well as a broad jump (e.g., Follow the Leader, Simon Says).

CRITERION   The child broad jumps 4–14 inches on 3 consecutive days.

22-II
Upright: Balance

Balance consists of the ability to stabilize the body over a base of support, whether remaining still or moving. Many factors contribute to balance, and impairments in strength, coordination, vision, vestibular function, or skeletal alignment can result in poor balance. Occupational and physical therapists are trained to analyze balance problems. They can provide consultation if a child's balance is not improving, and they can give you guidance on improving or compensating for poor balance.

ADAPTATIONS

Children with Motor Impairments

Children with motor impairments typically take a long time to develop balance skills because of weak musculature in the trunk and legs. You can help them develop the capabilities of unilateral stance and walking on a narrow base by holding them in position, then asking them to tell you when to let go. This gives them the opportunity to focus on what they need to do and prepare themselves. A physical therapist can give you specific suggestions for a particular child. Before teaching somersaults to a child with Down syndrome, have the parents obtain an X-ray of the neck because some of these children have a bony abnormality in the neck that could cause damage with extreme neck movements.

Children with Visual Impairments

Children with usable vision should be trained to use it to help with balance. Coach them to focus on a brightly lit spot in the environment as they practice standing on one leg or walking on a balance beam. Train them also to feel the support surface with their feet. Use bright colors to guide them on a balance beam. To practice kicking, use brightly colored balls and/or balls that emit sound.

Children with Hearing Impairments

Children with hearing impairments often have balance problems because the structures that control hearing and balance are located in the same part of the brain. Teach children with hearing impairments to focus on visual targets and feel their feet on the supporting surface.

22-II. UPRIGHT: BALANCE

a.   Stands on one foot while hands are held

b.   Lifts one leg momentarily

c.   Rises onto tiptoes momentarily

d.   Stands on one leg with stable posture (1–2 seconds)

e.   Stands sideways with both feet on balance beam with stable posture

f.   Walks 5 feet on balance beam with one foot on the balance beam and the other on the floor

g.   Walks along 10-foot line, following the general direction of the line

h.   Stands with stable posture on one leg with hands on hips and opposite knee bent (1–2 seconds)

i.   Walks three steps on balance beam and maintains balance

j.   Walks along 10-foot line, keeping feet on the line and maintaining balance

■ ■ ■

22-IIa. Stands on one foot while hands are held

MATERIALS   Music, shoes, socks, pants, stairs

PROCEDURES

Sit in front of the child and hold his hands. Help him pick up one foot, and ask him to hold it up while you provide support.

DAILY ROUTINES & FUNCTIONAL ACTIVITIES

Hold the child's hands while playing music, and show him how to lift one foot at a time. Assist him in going up stairs while holding his hands. When getting him dressed or un-dressed, have him stand and hold your shoulders as he lifts each leg.

CRITERION   With hands held, the child is able to raise one foot off of the floor and hold it up for 2–3 seconds, demonstrating this ability for 3 consecutive days. (Record right and left feet separately.)

■ ■ ■

22-IIb. Lifts one leg momentarily

MATERIALS   Music, shoes, socks, pants

PROCEDURES/DAILY ROUTINES & FUNCTIONAL ACTIVITIES

See instructions for Item 22-IIa, gradually decreasing the amount of assistance you give the child until she can lift either leg momentarily without support.

CRITERION   The child is able to lift either leg momentarily without support.

22-II

■ ■ ■

22-IIc. Rises onto tiptoes momentarily

MATERIALS   Attractive toys or food

PROCEDURES

While the child is standing away from supports, offer an attractive toy or favorite food several inches above his head, and tell him to reach for it. As he makes efforts to obtain the object, reward him with the toy or food.

DAILY ROUTINES & FUNCTIONAL ACTIVITIES

Present objects to the child that are just beyond his reach to see if he will rise onto his tiptoes. Magnetized toys on the refrigerator or food on a table work well.

CRITERION   *The child rises onto tiptoes momentarily with arms free.*

■ ■ ■

22-IId. Stands on one leg with stable posture (1–2 seconds)

MATERIALS   Low obstacles, lower body clothing

PROCEDURES

Because static balance activities are not intrinsically fun, children will not generally practice them spontaneously as they will with many other gross motor activities. Balance activities are best practiced by taking advantage of naturally occurring activities or by embedding them in games. Gradually increase the amount of time the child can stay on one leg while using her arms for balance. Later, ask the child to keep her arms across her chest as she stands on one foot.

DAILY ROUTINES & FUNCTIONAL ACTIVITIES

Stepping over obstacles, marching, or incorporating leg-lifting into musical games, such as The Hokey Pokey, are all good ways to promote a one-leg stance.

During dressing and undressing, have the child lift a foot to put on pants, pajamas, shoes, and socks. Singing or counting while standing on one foot will help the child to concentrate. Expect to find a difference between right and left legs, especially at first.

CRITERION   *The child stands on each leg with stable posture for 1 or 2 seconds and does this for 3 days in a row.*

■ ■ ■

22-IIe. Stands sideways with both feet on balance beam with stable posture

MATERIALS   A balance beam that is 4 inches wide, 8 feet long, and 4 inches high

PROCEDURES

Help the child step up to a balance beam, standing sideways and facing you. Hold his hands at first, and then gradually withdraw your support.

DAILY ROUTINES & FUNCTIONAL ACTIVITIES

Offer various opportunities to stand on small surfaces. Play areas at home and school generally have ledges, stepping stones, or similar objects.

CRITERION   *The child stands with both feet sideways on a balance beam for at least 5 seconds for 3 days in a row.*

■ ■ ■

22-IIf. Walks 5 feet on balance beam with one foot on the balance beam and the other on the floor

MATERIALS   A balance beam that is 4 inches wide, 8 inches long, and 4 inches high; books

PROCEDURES

Introduce balance beam activities by having the child walk with one foot on the balance beam and one foot on the floor. Let the child try the activity and, if necessary, give her physical assistance. If the child is having difficulty balancing, start by removing the supporting blocks that are under the beam, and place the beam on the floor.

DAILY ROUTINES & FUNCTIONAL ACTIVITIES

You can also place books of various thickness on the floor to practice this skill. The child should practice this activity with her right leg on the beam, as well as her left leg. Use environmental structures such as curbs or other low surfaces to practice this skill throughout the day.

CRITERION   *The child walks 5 feet on the balance beam with one foot on the balance beam and the other on the floor, 3 days in a row.*

22-II

■ ■ ■

22-IIg. Walks along 10-foot line, following the general direction of the line

MATERIALS   Boards, a line on the floor that is 10 feet long and 1 inch wide, footprints or designs on the floor

PROCEDURES

When teaching a child to use a narrow base of support, start by demonstrating walking along a straight path, either on floor markings (e.g., designs on the floor) or between two boards that are placed on the floor. If the child is having problems balancing, start with boards that are placed 12–14 inches apart, and move them closer together as he gains control.

DAILY ROUTINES & FUNCTIONAL ACTIVITIES

You can incorporate narrow base activities into games of walking on footprints or using imagery to go over a bridge, walk on a tightrope, or similar activities.

CRITERION   The child walks along a 10-foot line, following the general direction of the line. The child demonstrates this ability 3 days in a row.

■ ■ ■

22-IIh. Stands with stable posture on one leg with hands on hips and opposite knee bent (1–2 seconds)

MATERIALS   None required

PROCEDURES/DAILY ROUTINES & FUNCTIONAL ACTIVITIES

See instructions for Item 22-IId.

CRITERION   The child stands with stable posture on one leg for 1–2 seconds with hands on hips and opposite knee bent. The child does this 3 days in a row.

■ ■ ■

22-IIi. Walks three steps on balance beam and maintains balance

MATERIALS   A balance beam that is 4 inches wide, 8 feet long, and 4 inches high

PROCEDURES

Begin by holding the child at the shoulders. Gradually decrease your support until you are holding the back of her shirt. Finally, release support. Offer encouragement, but don't give too many verbal instructions; instead, let the child practice walking on the balance beam until she discovers the correct strategy. You can begin with wider balance beams and gradually decrease the width.

DAILY ROUTINES & FUNCTIONAL ACTIVITIES

Explore the child's home, school, and playground environments for opportunities to practice this skill. Walking on elevated surfaces can easily be incorporated into games.

CRITERION   The child walks three steps on a balance beam and maintains his balance, 3 days in a row.

22-IIj. Walks along 10-foot line, keeping feet on the line and maintaining balance

MATERIALS   Boards, lines on the floor, footprints or designs on the floor

PROCEDURES/DAILY ROUTINES & FUNCTIONAL ACTIVITIES

See instructions for Item 22-IIg.

CRITERION   The child walks on a 10-foot line, keeping feet on the line and maintaining balance. The child demonstrates this ability 3 days in a row.

22-II

22-III
Upright: Ball Play

Throwing and catching balls is one of the basic play skills of early childhood. This activity involves motor skills such as strength, dynamic balance, and eye–hand and eye–foot coordination. In addition, early ball play promotes social interaction, which can help children with disabilities feel included and can help typically developing children learn how to play with their peers with disabilities.

The skills in the following sequence are intended to lay the foundation for more advanced games (e.g., baseball, basketball, volleyball) that use equipment. Children in the 2- to 3-year age range should be getting comfortable with kicking, throwing, and catching.

ADAPTATIONS

Children with Motor Impairments

Children with motor impairment should try using different types of balls to find the one that works best (e.g., soft balls that can be grasped in a fist, large balls that are easier to hold, balloons, Koosh balls, suspended balls). Some children can use "ball scoopers" made from cut-open bleach bottles. Games involving rolling balls, such as bowling with empty plastic bottles, are also fun. When initially teaching throwing, coach children with motor impairments to raise the ball high overhead before throwing; this will help increase strength in the arms and back. Children with severe motor impairments should be given physical assistance in moving their arms. This will give them a sense of participation and will teach other children to view them as playmates.

Children with Visual Impairments

Children with visual impairments can use very brightly colored balls or balls that make noise. They will need more physical guidance to learn basic throwing and catching skills. Teach them to attend closely to sounds. Give physical assistance and verbal descriptions to children who are totally blind to help them learn about throwing, catching, and kicking.

Children with Hearing Impairments

Children with hearing impairments should be able to do well with ball activities unless other impairments are present.

22-III. UPRIGHT: BALL PLAY

a. Rolls ball back and forth with an adult

b. Tries to kick ball

c. Hurls ball 3 feet

d. Kicks ball 3 feet

e. Throws 8-inch ball to an adult who is 5 feet away

f. Throws 3-inch ball to an adult who is 7 feet away

g. Throws 3-inch ball to an adult who is 9 feet away

h. Catches 8-inch ball with arms in front of body from an adult who is 5 feet away

i. Kicks ball 4–6 feet

■ ■ ■

22-IIIa. Rolls ball back and forth with an adult

MATERIALS   8-inch ball

PROCEDURES

Sit on the floor facing the child, and show her how to roll the ball back and forth. It may help to keep your legs straight as a barrier so the ball won't roll away when the child pushes it.

DAILY ROUTINES & FUNCTIONAL ACTIVITIES

Practice this activity each day, experimenting with different sizes and weights of balls. Assist the child with hand placement, as necessary.

CRITERION   The child rolls a ball back and forth with an adult for several turns on 3 consecutive days.

22-III

■ ■ ■

22-IIIb. Tries to kick ball

MATERIALS   8-inch ball

PROCEDURES

Place an 8-inch ball on the ground and demonstrate kicking it. Hold one of the child's hands as he attempts to kick it. This will prevent him from picking up the ball. Show him how to kick and chase the ball. Beginning kickers usually put their foot on top of the ball. It helps to move their foot through the kicking motion.

DAILY ROUTINES & FUNCTIONAL ACTIVITIES

Set up situations in which there are several balls on the floor. Engage a small group of children in a game of kick and chase.

CRITERION   The child makes attempts to kick a ball several times a day on 3 consecutive days.

■ ■ ■

22-IIIc. Hurls ball 3 feet

MATERIALS   8-inch ball

PROCEDURES

Demonstrate throwing a ball overhand, then give it to the child and ask her to throw it. If she is having difficulty, assist her in raising her arms above her head in preparation for throwing.

DAILY ROUTINES & FUNCTIONAL ACTIVITIES

Practice this activity daily. At this stage, the child is simply learning the arm movement, not learning to aim.

CRITERION   The child hurls a ball 3 feet several times a day on 3 consecutive days.

■ ■ ■

22-IIId. Kicks ball 3 feet

MATERIALS   8-inch ball

PROCEDURES

Once the child has the idea of kicking without having his hands held, present him with balls to kick.

DAILY ROUTINES & FUNCTIONAL ACTIVITIES

Doing this as a group activity will increase participation by all of the children. You can place several balls on the ground at once. This is also a good indoor rainy day activity.

CRITERION   The child kicks a ball 3 feet.

■ ■ ■

22-IIIe. Throws 8-inch ball to an adult who is 5 feet away

MATERIALS   8-inch ball

PROCEDURES

Observe the child to see what type of throwing pattern she uses. Early throwers will fling the ball forward and down. Later they learn to throw underhand, and then they learn to raise their arms overhead, which allows them to throw farther.

DAILY ROUTINES & FUNCTIONAL ACTIVITIES

Coach the child to look at the target while throwing (i.e., at your hands rather than at your face). She can also start throwing at other targets, such as a poster on the wall. To increase throwing distance, increase the distance between the child and the target.

CRITERION   *The child throws an 8-inch ball to an adult who is 5 feet away several times a day on 3 consecutive days.*

■ ■ ■

22-IIIf. Throws 3-inch ball to an adult who is 7 feet away

MATERIALS   3-inch ball

PROCEDURES/DAILY ROUTINES & FUNCTIONAL ACTIVITIES

See instructions for Item 22-IIIe.

CRITERION   *The child throws a 3-inch ball to an adult who is 7 feet away several times a day on 3 consecutive days.*

■ ■ ■

22-IIIg. Throws 3-inch ball to an adult who is 9 feet away

22-III

MATERIALS   3-inch ball

PROCEDURES/DAILY ROUTINES & FUNCTIONAL ACTIVITIES

See instructions for Item 22-IIIe.

CRITERION   *The child throws a 3-inch ball to an adult who is 9 feet away several times a day on 3 consecutive days.*

■ ■ ■

22-IIIh. Catches 8-inch ball with arms in front of body from an adult who is 5 feet away

MATERIALS   8-inch ball

PROCEDURES

Catching requires a combination of visual, motor, and attention skills. Children learn how to catch in different stages. Early catchers will extend their arms in front with palms up; they scoop the ball with their arms and trap it against the chest. At this stage, the child may avoid the ball by turning his face away. Later, the arms are held at the side, with elbows bent at right angles and palms facing each other; the ball is trapped by the bent arms. Mature catchers will adjust to the flight of the oncoming ball and catch it only with their hands. Use verbal preparation such as "ready, catch" before each throw to the child. Coach him to look at the ball, not at the person throwing. Begin by standing very close to the child and throwing gently and accurately to ensure the child successfully catches the ball. Then, gradually increase the distance between yourself and the child as long as catching remains successful.

DAILY ROUTINES & FUNCTIONAL ACTIVITIES

Start with larger balls and move gradually to smaller ones in order to promote more mature catching patterns. The processes of visual tracking, catching, and aiming can be slowed down by using a balloon; first suspend a balloon on a string and let the child practice catching and hitting, then let the child move a floating balloon around the room.

CRITERION   The child catches an 8-inch ball with his arms in front of himself from someone who is 5 feet away. The child demonstrates this several times a day on 3 consecutive days.

■ ■ ■

22-IIIi. Kicks ball 4–6 feet

MATERIALS   Balls of various sizes and weights

PROCEDURES

Initially, hold the child's hand as you guide her in kicking the ball. This will prevent her from picking up the ball. Demonstrate the activity by taking turns with her. Start with medium-size, lightweight balls.

DAILY ROUTINES & FUNCTIONAL ACTIVITIES

For beginning kickers, play a game of kick and chase. Then encourage the child to kick harder to make the ball travel farther.

CRITERION   The child kicks a ball 4–6 feet, 3 days in a row.

22-IV
Upright: Outdoor Play

Outdoor play activities should be encouraged for all children, including those with serious impairments. Climbing, moving fast, and engaging in ball play all are important activities for developing muscle strength and promoting cardiovascular health. In addition, the playground is one of the most important places to form social relationships. All play areas should be arranged to be safe, with separate areas for nonwalkers, toddlers, and more active older children. Shaded areas should be provided in the summer. Adequate numbers of toys will minimize, though not eliminate, conflict among the children. Children benefit from caregivers who participate in play and use outdoor time to promote creativity, language building, turn taking, and social negotiation as well as active play. Consider using theme-based centers outdoors so that more mobile children will be attracted to play with less mobile peers. Water tables, painting easels, and hanging musical toys would work well at these centers.

Note: Climbing equipment for toddlers should be no more than 3 feet high, and the surrounding ground should be cushioned with wood chips, pea gravel, or rubberod playground covering, for example.

22-IV

ADAPTATIONS

Children with Motor Impairments

Children with mild or moderate motor impairments may shy away from climbing activities. You should give them physical guidance in mastering these skills. Children whose motor impairments preclude them from using equipment should still experience participation in games that caregivers will need to structure (e.g., being pulled in a wagon, holding a ball for others). Most children who cannot move quickly enjoy being pushed fast in a wheelchair or given other experiences in moving fast. Encourage more active children to think of ways of including less active children in games.

Children with Visual Impairments

When children with visual impairments are ready to be active outside, help them explore the playground so that they can memorize where equipment is located. For children with some vision, bright tape or textured material can be placed on bars or steps to help in orientation.

Children with Hearing Impairments

Children with hearing impairments can play well outdoors. Problems sometimes arise, however, because of their lack of attention to environmental sounds. Show these children how to watch other children to avoid collisions on equipment.

22-IV. UPRIGHT: OUTDOOR PLAY

a.   Explores play area with supervision

b.   Enjoys swinging and sliding

c.   Climbs on low equipment

d.   Climbs slanted ladder

e.   Uses slide independently

f.   Runs on playground, pausing at surface changes

g.   Climbs on low jungle gym bars and will drop several inches to the ground

h.   Climbs vertical ladders

i.   Walks on movable surfaces using some hand support

■ ■ ■

22-IVa. Explores play area with supervision

MATERIALS   Play area with low climbing equipment, balls, push toys

PROCEDURES

Observe the child in the play area. He should move about, inspect the play equipment, and play actively with smaller toys.

DAILY ROUTINES & FUNCTIONAL ACTIVITIES

During outdoor play, watch the child's activity. If he is not exploring the playground and equipment, guide him physically through these activities.

CRITERION   The child explores a play area with supervision.

■ ■ ■

22-IVb. Enjoys swinging and sliding

MATERIALS   Bucket-type swing, low slide

PROCEDURES

Observe the child's reactions as you place her in the swing and on the slide. Swinging and sliding should be enjoyable activities for the child. If she shows excessive anxiety or resistance to these activities, consult a physical or occupational therapist, as the child may be showing early signs of sensory dysfunction.

DAILY ROUTINES & FUNCTIONAL ACTIVITIES

Expose the child to these activities daily. Keep close physical contact, if necessary, until she is accustomed to the movement.

CRITERION   The child enjoys being placed on a swing and slide.

■ ■ ■

22-IVc. Climbs on low equipment

MATERIALS   Low climbing equipment that is no more than 3 feet high

PROCEDURES

Observe the child as he approaches toddler climbing equipment that offers opportunities to crawl through spaces, climb up and over edges, and maneuver in small spaces.

DAILY ROUTINES & FUNCTIONAL ACTIVITIES

Offer daily opportunities for climbing on equipment. If the child has more difficulty than his same-age peers, assist him physically to master the skills. It may help to practice without other children in the area.

CRITERION   *The child climbs independently and safely on low equipment, several days in a row.*

■ ■ ■

22-IVd. Climbs slanted ladder

MATERIALS   3- to 6-foot-high ladder attached to a piece of playground equipment

PROCEDURES

Initially, assist the child physically in climbing the ladder. Make sure she is holding on with both hands and can find the rungs with her feet. Gradually withdraw your support. If a child has leg weakness, this is a good opportunity to work on strengthening in both bending and pushing with the legs.

DAILY ROUTINES & FUNCTIONAL ACTIVITIES

Once the child has mastered the basic movements of climbing, include her in a small group of children in which each child takes a turn with this activity.

CRITERION   *The child climbs a slanted ladder, 3 days in a row.*

■ ■ ■

22-IVe. Uses slide independently

MATERIALS   Slide of appropriate height for child's age

PROCEDURES

Initially, stand behind the child as he climbs the ladder and provide support, if necessary, as he slides down the slide. If necessary, show him how to bring his feet in front of him and initiate the sliding movement.

DAILY ROUTINES & FUNCTIONAL ACTIVITIES

Provide daily opportunities for this activity. You may want to place the child halfway down the slide at first so he gets used to the speed.

CRITERION   *The child uses the slide independently, 3 days in a row.*

■ ■ ■

22-IVf. Runs on playground, pausing at surface changes

MATERIALS   Play area with changes in surface (e.g. grass, sand, pavement)

PROCEDURES

Early playground runners usually exhibit caution to avoid falling at surface changes. As the child is running on the playground, observe her behavior at surface changes. If necessary, teach her to look for surface changes and slow down in anticipation.

Note: As the child increases her skill and confidence, she will move actively on the playground without pausing at surface changes and finally will run vigorously on the playground, adapting automatically to surface changes and barriers.

DAILY ROUTINES & FUNCTIONAL ACTIVITIES

Routinely encourage the child to play games that involve running and chasing. At first, use only two surface changes, adding more as the child improves and becomes more comfortable.

CRITERION   *The child runs on the playground, pausing at surface changes*

■ ■ ■

22-IVg. Climbs on low jungle gym bars and will drop several inches to the ground

22-IV

MATERIALS   Low jungle gym bars

PROCEDURES

Guide the child through the activity of climbing and letting go of jungle gym bars. If the child has arm weakness or is fearful of the activity, hold him at the hips during the activity until he gains confidence.

DAILY ROUTINES & FUNCTIONAL ACTIVITIES

Use this as a group activity in which children take turns climbing and dropping down.

CRITERION   *The child climbs on low jungle gym bars and will drop several inches to the ground, 3 days in a row.*

■ ■ ■

22-IVh. Climbs vertical ladders

MATERIALS   Vertical ladder, 4–6 feet high

PROCEDURES/DAILY ROUTINES & FUNCTIONAL ACTIVITIES

See instructions for Item 22-IVd.

CRITERION   The child climbs a vertical ladder independently and safely, 3 days in a row.

■ ■ ■

22-IVi. Walks on movable surfaces using some hand support

MATERIALS   Movable surfaces (e.g., a wiggly bridge)

PROCEDURES

Introduce movable surfaces slowly, allowing the child to explore the surface at her own pace. Initially, show her how to hold on to upright supports with two hands, then with one hand. As the child gains confidence, show her how to release her hold and walk on the surface as it is moving.

DAILY ROUTINES & FUNCTIONAL ACTIVITIES

Include the child in fantasy games (e.g., "walking over the river") with other children, having the children take turns on the moveable surface.

CRITERION   The child walks on movable surfaces using some hand support, 3 days in a row.

23
Prone (On Stomach)

I n the process of physical development, the abilities that children develop as they lie on their stomachs and extend their bodies against gravity are important for adequate motor function in the upright positions of sitting, standing, and walking. Generally speaking, children begin by lifting their head, then trunk, arms, and legs. The arms, and then the legs, are used to bear weight and move forward. It is important to recognize the difference between typical motor patterns and incomplete or atypical ones. Watch infants without motor impairments as they play in a prone position, demonstrating the patterns found on the Motor Milestones in Infant Development chart (Appendix E). Infants are now routinely being placed on their backs for sleep. While this has reduced the incidence of Sudden Infant Death syndrome, it has also increased the incidence of misshapen heads. It is, therefore, very important to routinely place infants on their stomachs for play.

ADAPTATIONS

Children with Motor Impairments

If children with motor impairments do not show adequate extension in prone, ask a physical therapist to show you how to adapt the position and devise other methods to strengthen the back. Every effort should be made to develop symmetrical trunk extension. If a child with motor impairments has tight muscles, use relaxation techniques before and during prone activities. Gently move the child's shoulder blades and rotate the hips. If the child's arms are extremely tight, place a bolster or towel roll under the shoulders to bring the arms forward. If necessary to prevent the child's arms from pulling underneath the body, bring the elbows forward on the floor. If the child's legs are thrusting out straight, relax and bend them. A child with weak, floppy muscles (hypotonia) may hold his or her legs in a "frog" position; correct this by holding the legs together. Positioning a child over a wedge

23

can make head lifting easier. You can also place a child in a prone position over your chest as you recline, and assist with lifting against gravity.

When teaching children to pull forward on the floor, look at the surface on which you place the children. It will be easier for children to move on a hard, smooth surface, and more difficult for children to move on a carpet. It is also easier to move with clothing on than it is with bare skin. For a child with spina bifida, well-padded clothing is necessary to prevent skin damage.

When working on reaching in prone, provide physical assistance if necessary. When working in an all-fours position, use physical assistance to keep children's legs well positioned under their bodies. You can sit on the floor and place a child over one of your extended legs, using your other leg to keep the child's legs bent.

Consult a physical therapist for guidance when working with children with severe motor impairments. For many children with severe motor impairments, prone will never be a functional position. They will work much better in upright positions, and you can devise alternative means of strengthening back muscles.

Children with Visual Impairments

Introduce the prone position as quickly as possible. This is not a preferred position for children with visual impairments, so you will have to use interesting sounds or movement games to maintain a child's position (e.g., try placing bright toys or illuminated toys on the floor). It may be helpful to carry children with visual impairments face-out in front of light sources that they respond to, or you can place them on your stomach and talk to them as you help them lift up. For children who are totally blind, place interesting textures under their hands and faces. For children with low vision, use colored lights, brightly colored toys, or objects with black-and-white patterns with sound added.

To elicit reaching, allow a child to grasp and mouth a toy briefly, then take the toy and hold it a few inches from the child's hand. Sound the toy and intermittently touch it to the child's hand. As the child reaches, allow a brief touch, and then reposition it further away. This task may be delayed in children who are blind until the concept of auditory object permanence is well established.

To elicit movement on the floor, establish a routine of placing a child in a prone position surrounded by a circle of favorite toys within easy reach. Leave each toy in the same position. As the child learns to obtain the toys, very gradually move them farther away. Let the child hold and mouth each object after obtaining it.

Children with Hearing Impairments

Children with hearing impairments should not have difficulties with prone activities unless motor problems are also present.

23. PRONE (ON STOMACH)

a.   Lifts head, freeing nose (arms and legs flexed)

b.   Lifts head to 45-degree angle (arms and legs partially flexed)

c.   Extends head, arms, trunk, and legs in prone position

d.   Bears weight on elbows in prone position

e.   Rolls from stomach to back

f.   Reaches while supported on one elbow

g.   Supports self on hands with arms extended and head at 90 degrees

h.   Pivots in prone position

i.   Pulls forward in prone position

j.   Pulls self to hands and knees

k.   Rocks forward and backward while on hands and knees

l.   Plays with toys in asymmetrical half-sitting position

m.   Moves forward (creeps) while on hands and knees

n.   Raises one hand high while on hands and knees

o.   Creeps up stairs

p.   Creeps down stairs, backwards

■ ■ ■

23a. Lifts head, freeing nose (arms and legs flexed)

MATERIALS   Brightly colored or shiny toys; noisemaking toys

PROCEDURES

Place the child on her stomach, and encourage her to lift her head by placing toys on the floor in front of her face. Shake or otherwise activate the toy when the child's head is lifted, to provide motivation. The muscles at the base of the skull and in between the shoulder blades can be stimulated with your fingers, using firm, not light, strokes. Giving pressure over the buttocks can also help with head lifting.

23

DAILY ROUTINES & FUNCTIONAL ACTIVITIES

During the day, place the child on your chest as you are lying on your back with your head raised, and talk or sing to her. Raising the elevation of your shoulders (i.e., making the child more upright) will make head raising easier. As the child gets stronger, lie flatter so that the effect is the same as being on a flat surface.

CRITERION   *The child lifts her head and holds it up, with arms and legs flexed, for several seconds at a time. The child does this consistently over a period of several days.*

■ ■ ■

23b. Lifts head to 45-degree angle (arms and legs partially flexed)

MATERIALS   Dangling toys

PROCEDURES

When the child is able to lift his head independently in a prone position, place toys in front of his face, and lift the toys so that the child lifts his head at a 45-degree angle. Place the child's elbows in the correct position if necessary. The muscles in the back of the neck and between the shoulder blades can be stimulated with your fingers, using firm, not light, strokes.

DAILY ROUTINES & FUNCTIONAL ACTIVITIES

Be sure to place the child on his stomach on the floor for several play sessions throughout the day. Use a variety of toys for visual interest. A quilt with Velcro or strings to attach different toys is helpful.

CRITERION   *The child lifts his head at a 45-degree angle, keeping his arms and legs partially flexed, for 20–30 seconds at a time. The child should do this consistently over a period of several days.*

■ ■ ■

23c. Extends head, arms, trunk, and legs in prone position

MATERIALS   Favorite toys, therapy ball, towel roll

PROCEDURES

With the child lying on her stomach on the floor, your lap, or a therapy ball, gently pull her shoulders up, and wait for lifting of the head, arms, trunk, and legs. Release your hold when she stays up alone, and resume your hold when she loses control. Use visually interesting toys or toys that make noise to provide motivation.

DAILY ROUTINES & FUNCTIONAL ACTIVITIES

Practice this item and Item 23d together, alternating between them. This is an extremely important item for building postural stability and should be practiced often throughout the day. Carrying children over your hip and facing away from you is a good way to exercise their neck, back, and hip muscles.

Note: Children with developmental problems often need work on this item even after they have achieved functional skills at a higher level. Children with tight or stiff muscles will tend to pull their shoulders up and forward, tip their heads back too far, not flatten their upper spine, and thrust their legs stiffly. Children with weak or floppy muscles (hypotonia) will have similar tendencies in the upper body but will keep their legs spread out. If you cannot easily correct these tendencies, consult a physical therapist.

CRITERION   *The child lifts her head, arms, trunk, and legs off of the supporting surface for at least 5 seconds at a time. The child should do this consistently over a period of several days.*

■ ■ ■

23d. Bears weight on elbows in prone position

MATERIALS   Favorite toys, music

PROCEDURES

Place the child on the floor in a position in which he is taking weight on his elbows. Use toys that encourage the child to lift his head. At first, the child's hands may be closed, but work toward open hands, with palms in contact with the floor. Do this by lightly rubbing the back of the child's hands from the wrist toward the fingers, and then gently opening the hand.

DAILY ROUTINES & FUNCTIONAL ACTIVITIES

Practice this item and Item 23c together, alternating between them. Be sure to place the child on the floor for several play periods throughout the day. Because children at this stage are not yet mobile, be prepared to change toys or stimuli often enough to prevent boredom.

CRITERION   *The child lifts his head and upper trunk into a position in which he is taking weight on his forearms, with hands open on the floor, and can stay there for at least 30 seconds. The child should repeat this activity several times a day for several days.*

■ ■ ■

23e. Rolls from stomach to back

MATERIALS   Favorite toys, blanket

PROCEDURES

Encourage the child to roll from her stomach to her back by dangling a toy in front of her face then moving it to the side and behind the child's line of sight. If this does not promote rolling, physically assist the child at the shoulders or hips, start her in a sidelying position, or place her on a blanket and lift one edge. Try for a pattern in which the head and shoulders lead the movement and the hips follow.

DAILY ROUTINES & FUNCTIONAL ACTIVITIES

Use this procedure whenever lifting or turning the child out of a stomach-lying position. Give the child enough time to participate in the movement.

CRITERION   *The child is able to roll independently from stomach to back and spontaneously does this several times a day for a number of days in a row.*

23

■ ■ ■

23f. Reaches while supported on one elbow

MATERIALS   Toys that elicit sustained reaching (e.g., mobiles, suspended balloons, busy box)

PROCEDURES

Start this activity by requiring the child to reach straight out to activate a toy. Then, gradually reposition the toy so that it is above the child's shoulder level and a little out to the side. Do this activity with each arm, and note any asymmetries. Initially, you may need to shift the child's weight to the nonreaching side by placing your hand on his buttocks.

DAILY ROUTINES & FUNCTIONAL ACTIVITIES

Provide opportunities for the child to reach out with one arm when he is either on the floor or being carried face out.

CRITERION   *The child independently and spontaneously reaches up and out to bat at a toy, without collapse of the supporting arm. The child should do this several times a day on a number of days in a row.*

■ ■ ■

23g. Supports self on hands with arms extended and head at 90 degrees

MATERIALS   Favorite toys, large ball, bolster

PROCEDURES

Place an interesting toy in front of the child's face and then raise it, encouraging her to push up with straight arms. Initially, the child's hands may be closed, but work toward open hands with the child's palms in contact with the floor.

DAILY ROUTINES & FUNCTIONAL ACTIVITIES

Make use of play time on the floor to practice this item. When the child is on the floor, place toys at a higher level in order to attract her attention.

CRITERION   *While lying in a prone position, the child independently and spontaneously pushes up to a fully extended arm position with open hands and head upright. The child should be able to stay in this position for at least 5 seconds several times a day on a number of days in a row.*

■ ■ ■

23h. Pivots in prone position

MATERIALS   Favorite toys, bottle

PROCEDURES

Imagine a circle drawn around the child, and place a toy on the circle to the right or left of his head (sometimes a bottle works best as a lure). After the child obtains the toy (or bottle), move it farther around the circle. Have the child pivot both clockwise and counterclockwise. It is best to not have other toys in sight. Provide assistance if necessary by rubbing the child's back and moving his arm toward the toy.

DAILY ROUTINES & FUNCTIONAL ACTIVITIES

When the child is playing on the floor or in a crib, periodically move his toys to different locations to encourage pivoting.

CRITERION   *The child independently pivots 360 degrees in each direction several days in a row.*

■ ■ ■

23i. Pulls forward in prone position

MATERIALS   Favorite toys

PROCEDURES

Place a favorite toy just out of the child's reach, and encourage her to pull forward to obtain the toy. Initially, you can provide physical assistance in weight shifting, reaching, and pulling.

DAILY ROUTINES & FUNCTIONAL ACTIVITIES

Make a point of placing toys just outside of the child's reach throughout the day. Do not immediately respond if the child fusses for the toy. If she does not go after the toy, give her physical assistance in pulling forward.

   Note: It is common for children to push themselves backward at first, when they really want to move forward. They will soon learn to change the pattern.

CRITERION   *The child pulls forward in prone position on the floor, using her arms and legs, establishing this as a means of locomotion.*

23

■ ■ ■

23j. Pulls self to hands and knees

MATERIALS   Favorite toys to elicit movement, low obstacles (e.g., pillows, bolsters)

PROCEDURES

While the child is pushing up onto extended arms, place your hands under his pelvis and lift up and back, waiting for him to participate by pulling his knees under his hips. Practice this several times a day while the child is playing on the floor. Incorporate the movement into the process of bringing the child from prone to sitting or standing. Give the child plenty of time to participate.

Note: The child who is beginning to do "bottom lifting" in prone position is ready to start this activity. The child who is not yet ready will protest vigorously if you impose this pattern.

DAILY ROUTINES & FUNCTIONAL ACTIVITIES

Presenting low obstacles over which to crawl will promote the necessary leg movements. For example, you can encourage the child to crawl over your legs or over a pillow.

CRITERION   *The child independently and spontaneously pulls to hands and knees and can stay there for several seconds. The child does this several days in a row.*

■ ■ ■

23k. Rocks forward and backward while on hands and knees

MATERIALS   Music

PROCEDURES

While the child is on her hands and knees, place your hand on her abdomen and gently start a forward and backward rocking movement. Pause and wait for the child to start the movement on her own. Children will often rock to a favorite kind of music.

DAILY ROUTINES & FUNCTIONAL ACTIVITIES

Once the child has begun to position herself on her hands and knees, carry out the rocking activity several times a day during floor play. This is a very important activity because it involves the middle ranges of leg movement. Immediately after rocking, the child will usually be ready to either creep or move into a sitting position by rotating the buttocks to the floor.

CRITERION   *The child independently and spontaneously rocks back and forth several times in a row for a number of days in a row.*

■ ■ ■

23l. Plays with toys in asymmetrical half-sitting position

MATERIALS   Favorite toys, pillows

PROCEDURES

Place toys on the floor next to the child at the level of the lower part of his rib cage. Physically guide the child into the asymmetrical half-sitting position shown in the Motor Milestones in Infant Development chart (Appendix D). Gradually release your hold as the child stays in this position. Do this activity to both sides. Using pillows for positioning helps some children stay up longer. This is a very good position for building head, trunk, and shoulder control, as well as rotational patterns. The weight-bearing side develops stability, and the non–weight-bearing side develops more skilled movement. It is also a good transition position for teaching a child how to move to a sitting or standing position.

DAILY ROUTINES & FUNCTIONAL ACTIVITIES

For children who are not yet safe in a sitting position, use this as one play position several times throughout the day.

CRITERION   The child maintains an asymmetrical half-sitting position without support for about 30 seconds on each side. The child should be able to do this several days in a row.

■ ■ ■

23m. Moves forward (creeps) while on hands and knees

MATERIALS   Favorite toys

PROCEDURES

With the child on her hands and knees, place a favorite toy in front of her but beyond her reach. If necessary, place your hand on the child's abdomen to encourage creeping rather than returning to a prone position. The child who is actively rocking on her hands and knees is ready to have creeping encouraged several times a day during floor play. Some children creep more readily on a carpet or on grass than on a smooth floor.

DAILY ROUTINES & FUNCTIONAL ACTIVITIES

Practice this activity periodically throughout the day. It sometimes helps to say, "hand, hand, knee, knee."

CRITERION   The child creeps briskly and uses this as a form of mobility.

■ ■ ■

23n. Raises one hand high while on hands and knees

MATERIALS   Favorite toys, mirror

PROCEDURES

While the child is on his hands and knees, position a desired toy so that the child has to reach out to obtain it. You can also place the child in front of a mirror with toys on suction cups. Start by requiring the child to reach straight in front of his shoulder, and gradually move the toy so that it is above the child's shoulder level and a little out to the side. Perform this activity with each arm, and note any asymmetric movements.

DAILY ROUTINES & FUNCTIONAL ACTIVITIES

At home, children enjoy reaching for refrigerator magnets or batting at suspended toys.

CRITERION   The child independently reaches up high for an object with his supporting arm not collapsing and the upper trunk rotating against the hips. The child demonstrates this ability several days in a row.

23

■ ■ ■

23o. Creeps up stairs

MATERIALS   Set of 6–10 stairs (approximately 6 inches high and 6–8 inches deep), favorite toys

PROCEDURES

Place a desired object on a stair just one or two stairs above the child. If necessary, give physical assistance with arm and leg placement. Assist the child in fully flexing the advancing leg with the knee turned out and placing the foot flat on the next step. Gradually withdraw assistance and increase the number of stairs that you wish the child to climb.

DAILY ROUTINES & FUNCTIONAL ACTIVITIES

Encourage the child to creep up stairs when time allows. Provide other low obstacles (e.g., sofa cushions on the floor) for her to practice climbing on.

Note: Once a child is interested in stairs, you will need safety gates to prevent falls.

CRITERION   *The child safely and independently creeps up 6–10 stairs. The child should be able to do this several days in a row.*

■ ■ ■

23p. Creeps down stairs, backwards

MATERIALS   Set of 6–10 stairs (approximately 6 inches high and 6–8 inches deep), favorite toys

PROCEDURES

Place the child on the stairs just one or two stairs from the bottom. Entice the child to creep down to obtain a toy. Give physical assistance with arm and leg placement, as necessary. Gradually withdraw assistance and increase the number of stairs that you wish the child to descend.

Note: Once a child is interested in stairs, you will need safety gates to prevent falls. Some children prefer to go down stairs by sitting, facing forward, and lowering themselves to the next stair. The most important considerations are safety and independence.

DAILY ROUTINES & FUNCTIONAL ACTIVITIES

Encourage the child to creep down stairs when time allows. Provide other low surfaces, such as small chairs or sofa cushions, on the floor for the child to practice on.

CRITERION   *The child safely and independently creeps down 6–10 stairs. The child should be able to do this several days in a row.*

24
Supine (On Back)

The items in this sequence will help children develop stabilizing functions using the front of the neck, trunk, shoulders, and hips. This stability allows children to lift their arms and legs, bringing them into their visual field and using them for play. Items 24a through 24e help children develop the basic capabilities for self-feeding. The muscle control developed in this position is very important for developing the balanced posture needed for feeding, efficient respiration, sitting, and standing.

ADAPTATIONS

Children with Motor Impairments

For children with motor impairments, a completely supine position is frequently inappropriate for either exercise or general positioning. Children with weak, floppy muscles (hypotonia) cannot act against gravity and usually can lie only on their backs with arms and legs passively on the floor. Naturally, such children prefer a supine position to being on their stomachs because it allows them to observe the environment more readily.

Children with stiff muscles (hypertonia) will often become stiffer when lying on their backs, and this will interfere with the development of more functional patterns.

In order to establish the stabilizing functions that should be acquired with the help of this sequence, the use of sidelying and semireclined positions are frequently more appropriate. A child may progress to performing the functions on her back, or he or she may never achieve this function. A good rule is to always position the child for maximum function while still providing some neuromuscular challenges. A physical or occupational therapist can provide guidance regarding the best position for a particular child.

24

Children with Visual Impairments

Pair auditory stimuli with brightly colored, shiny, or high-contrast visual stimuli for children with visual impairments. Experiment to find a child's preferred stimuli. Be sure to help children touch and mouth the objects (touch them to the child's face to help orient the child to turning movement). Reaching out with the arms may be significantly delayed in children who are blind.

Children with Hearing Impairments

Experiment with different types and intensities of sounds to find preferred stimuli for children with hearing impairments.

24. SUPINE (ON BACK)

a. Turns head from side to side in response to auditory or visual stimuli

b. Bends and straightens arms and legs

c. Brings hands to mouth

d. Maintains head in midline position while supine

e. Reaches out with arm while supine

f. Holds feet in air for play

g. Rolls from back to stomach

■ ■ ■

24a. Turns head from side to side in response to auditory or visual stimuli

MATERIALS   Any visual and/or auditory stimuli that hold the child's attention

PROCEDURES

Position the child comfortably on his back with his head in midline. Move your face to one side so that the child will turn his head to see you. You can also talk to the child from the side to encourage him to turn to the right and left. It may help to touch the child's cheek on the side toward which you wish him to turn.

DAILY ROUTINES & FUNCTIONAL ACTIVITIES

Do this activity throughout the day while holding the child. You can set up the changing table with a visually attractive object on the wall. Also, be sure to alternate the way the child is positioned on the table so that turning to the right and left will be encouraged.

CRITERION   The child independently turns his head completely from side to side in response to auditory or visual stimuli. The child should be able to do this several days in a row.

■ ■ ■

24b. Bends and straightens arms and legs

MATERIALS   Noisemakers on wrist/ankle bands

PROCEDURES

Move the child's arms and legs rhythmically, then pause and wait for her to do the movements on her own. Try different starting positions if the child does not move her arms and legs without assistance. Stroking the skin on the limbs or stomach may also help stimulate movement. Attach wrist/ankle bands with noisemakers that will be activated with movement.

24

DAILY ROUTINES & FUNCTIONAL ACTIVITIES

Work on this activity several times a day while holding the child. While the child is in her crib, use the noisemakers or attach the wrist/ankle bands with ribbons to an overhead mobile.

CRITERION   The child spontaneously bends and straightens her arms and legs several days in a row.

■ ■ ■

24c. Brings hands to mouth

MATERIALS   Soft foods, bracelets or mittens, bottle

PROCEDURES

Put a small amount of food on the child's thumb and hold it close to his mouth. Let the child see and smell the food, and help him lick the food off of his thumb. A few light finger strokes to the child's mouth may help elicit the movements.

DAILY ROUTINES & FUNCTIONAL ACTIVITIES

Place colorful mittens or bracelets on the child's hands to encourage him to look at his hands. During bottle feeding, place the child's hands on the bottle. From time to time, withdraw the bottle and wait for the child to pull it back.

CRITERION   The child spontaneously brings each hand to his mouth several days in a row.

■ ■ ■

24d. Maintains head in midline position while supine

MATERIALS   Any visual and/or auditory stimuli that hold the child's attention, small pillow

PROCEDURES

Engage the child's attention with her head in a midline position while supine, and maintain that position. Whether you are using a toy, your face, or a sound, keep the stimulus in the midline. If the child is having difficulty maintaining her head in a midline position, provide assistance, and then withdraw as the child takes over. You can also start by placing a small pillow around the child's neck.

DAILY ROUTINES & FUNCTIONAL ACTIVITIES

Observe the child's head position throughout the day, and use supportive pillows to maintain midline position. Feed the child with her head in midline.

CRITERION   The child maintains her head in a midline position while lying on her back for at least 30 seconds. The child should be able to do this several days in a row.

■ ■ ■

24e. Reaches out with arm while supine

MATERIALS   Any visual and/or auditory stimuli that hold the child's attention

PROCEDURES

Hold an interesting toy above the child's face and attract his attention to it. If the child does not reach out, briefly touch the toy to his hand and then raise it again. Suspend a mobile above the child's head, and be sure to check the mobile from the child's perspective (some of the commercial ones look interesting only from above). Placing rolled-up towels under the child's shoulders may help with reaching up.

DAILY ROUTINES & FUNCTIONAL ACTIVITIES

During other play and caregiving routines, look for opportunities to ask for reaching. Help the child reach up to get his bottle, to touch your face, or to ask to be picked up. As soon as the child is ready to make choices, reaching can be used to indicate desired objects.

CRITERION   *The child independently reaches up for an object that is held at arm's length above his face. The child should be able to do this several times a day over several days.*

■ ■ ■

24f. Holds feet in air for play

MATERIALS   Brightly colored booties, bells, or bracelets

PROCEDURES

Place objects on the child's feet that both make noise and are visually interesting. Lift the child's feet to her hands, and help her hold on to her feet, if necessary. Place your hand under the child's buttocks to help lift the legs.

DAILY ROUTINES & FUNCTIONAL ACTIVITIES

Invent a game or song using this action and play it several times a day. Have a variety of interesting items to place on the child's feet (e.g., decorated socks, bracelets).

CRITERION   *The child independently and spontaneously lifts her buttocks off of the floor and places her feet in her hands for play. The child should be able to do this several times a day over several days.*

24

■ ■ ■

24g. Rolls from back to stomach

MATERIALS   Blanket, interesting toys

PROCEDURES

Entice the child to roll from his back to his stomach by placing a favorite toy at his side, out of his reach. Assist, if necessary, by pulling gently on the leading hip, then waiting for the child to complete the roll. Try starting the child from a sidelying position, then moving the starting position farther back. You can also place the child on a blanket and lift one edge to assist him in rolling.

DAILY ROUTINES & FUNCTIONAL ACTIVITIES

When the child needs to be lying on his stomach, use the rolling procedures rather than just placing him on his stomach. Give plenty of time for the child to organize a response.

CRITERION   The child independently rolls onto his stomach by first turning his head, then bringing one or both legs across the body using a rotation of the trunk. The child should be able to do this several times a day over a number of days.

Appendices

Appendix A
Selected Impairments and Their Effects on Development

There are many different kinds of conditions that may result in a child having special needs. The most common conditions that may influence a child's development include

- Communication problems (speech and language)
- Dyspraxia
- Sensory defensiveness
- Gravitational insecurity
- Sensory modulation dysfunction
- Mental retardation
- Down syndrome
- Attention-deficit/hyperactivity disorder (ADHD)
- Autism
- Cerebral palsy
- Spina bifida
- Visual impairments
- Hearing impairments

Because developmental expectations vary as infants mature, different impairments become obvious at different stages of development. Children who are referred for intervention in their first year of life tend to be those identified with genetic problems; those considered to be at risk for impairments because of medical or social factors; and those who have obvious and significant impairments in vision, hearing, or motor development. Moderate delays in meeting motor milestones tend to be the primary causes for referral early in the second year, to be replaced by concerns about speech and language between 2 and 3 years. It is also between 2 and 3 years that referrals for poorly developed social skills and difficult behavior increase.

For further information on these conditions, the effects of these conditions on development, tips for intervention, information on specialists who can provide assistance, and resources to help you find the most up-to-date information about current treatments, support groups, and so forth, please visit http://www.brookespublishing.com/ccupdates.

Appendix B
Resources and Recommended Readings

RESOURCES

Here is a selection of materials that may be useful resources for working with young children with special needs and their families.

General

Batshaw, M.L. (Ed.). (2002). *Children with disabilities* (5th ed.). Baltimore: Paul H. Brookes Publishing Co.

Gopnik, A., Meltzoff, A.N., & Kuhl, P.K. (1999). *The scientist in the crib: Minds, brains and how children learn.* New York: William Morrow & Co.

Gowen, J.W., & Nebrig, J.B. (2002). *Enhancing early emotional development: Guiding parents of young children.* Baltimore: Paul H. Brookes Publishing Co.

Communication

Acredolo, L., & Goodwyn, S. (2002). *Baby signs: How to talk with your baby before your baby can talk.* New York: McGraw Hill/Contemporary Books.

Baker, P. (1986). *My first book of sign.* Washington, DC: Kendall Green Publications.

Casey-Harvey, D. (1995). *Early communication games.* Oceanside, CA: Academic Communication Associates.

Hart, B., & Risley, T.R. (1999). *The social world of children learning to talk.* Baltimore: Paul H. Brookes Publishing Co.

Schober-Peterson, D., & Cohen, M. (1999). *Toddler talk.* Oceanside, CA: Academic Communication Associates.

Aids for Teachers and Parents

Henry, D. (1998). *Tool chest for teachers, parents & students.* Youngtown, AZ: Henry OT Services.

Henry, D. (2001). *Tools for parents.* Youngtown, AZ: Henry OT Services.

Masi, W.S. (Ed.). (2001). *Toddler play.* San Francisco: Weldon Owen Publishing.

Morris, L.R., & Schulz, L. (1989). *Creative play activities for children with disabilities* (2nd ed.). Champaign, IL: Human Kinetics Books.

Reitzes, F., & Teitelman, B. (1995). *Wonderplay.* Philadelphia: Running Press.
Silberg, J. (1996). *More games to play with toddlers.* Beltsville, MD: Gryphon House.
Silberg, J. (2002). *Games to play with 2 year olds* (Rev. ed.). Beltsville, MD: Gryphon House.
Silberg, J. (2002). *Games to play with toddlers* (Rev. ed.). Beltsville, MD: Gryphon House.
Silberg, J., & Schiller, P. (2002). *The complete book of rhymes, songs, poems, finger plays and chants.* Beltsville, MD: Gryphon House.
Stern, D.N. (1990). *Diary of a baby.* New York: Basic Books.
Williams, M.S., & Shellenberger, S. (1996). *How does your engine run? A leader's guide to the alert program for self-regulation.* Albuquerque, NM: TherapyWorks.

Emergent Literacy

Dannehl, L., & Rodhouse, A. (1999, October/November). *Literacy software for children with disabilities.* Retrieved from http://www.closingthegap.com
Justice, L., & Kadevarak, J. (2002, March/April). Using shared storybook time to promote emergent literacy. *Teaching Exceptional Children, 11,* 8–13.
Musselwhite, C.R. (1998). *Adaptive play for special needs children.* London: College-Hill Press.
Notari-Syverson, A., O'Connor, R.E., & Vadasy, P. (1998). *Ladders to literacy: A preschool activity book.* Baltimore: Paul H. Brookes Publishing Co.
Pierce, P. (Ed.). (1994). *Baby power: A guide for families using assistive technology with their infants and toddlers.* Raleigh, NC: Department of Human Services, Division of Mental Health. Retrieved from http://www2.edc.org/NCIP/library/ec/power.htm
Ritchie, S., James-Szanton, J., & Howes, C. (2003). Emergent literacy practices in early childhood classrooms. In C. Howes (Ed.), *Teaching 4- to 8-year-olds: Literacy, math, multiculturalism, and classroom community* (pp. 71–92). Baltimore: Paul H. Brookes Publishing Co.

RECOMMENDED READINGS

Many helpful books about children with special needs can be found in your local bookstore. Here are a few examples.

Armstrong, T. (1995). *The myth of the A.D.H.D. child.* New York: PLUME/Penguin Books.
Geralis, E. (Ed.). (1998). *Children with cerebral palsy* (2nd ed.). Bethesda, MD: Woodbine House.
Hart, C.A. (1993). *A parent's guide to autism.* New York: Simon & Schuster.
Kranowitz, C. (1998). *The out-of-sync child.* New York: Perigee/Penguin Putnam.
Kranowitz, C. (2002). *The out-of-sync child has fun.* New York: Perigee/Penguin Putnam.
Lutkenhoff, M. (Ed.). (1999). *Children with spina bifida: A parents' guide.* Bethesda, MD: Woodbine House.
Ozonoff, S., Dawson, G., & McPartland, J. (2002). *Parent's guide to Asperger syndrome and high functioning autism.* New York: Guilford.
Pueschel, S.M. (2001). *A parent's guide to Down syndrome: Toward a brighter future* (Rev. ed.). Baltimore: Paul H. Brookes Publishing Co.
Stray-Gunderson, K. (1995). *Babies with Down syndrome: A new parents' guide.* Bethesda, MD: Woodbine House.
Yack, E., Sutton, S., & Aquilla, P. (1998). *Building bridges through sensory integration.* Weston, Canada: Pocket Full of Therapy.

Appendix C
Play and Children
with Motor Impairments

Play is the natural activity of children. It is through play that children learn and practice their cognitive, language, social, and motor skills. Although instrumental in learning, play is very different from *work* because it is directed by the child and has no other immediate goal than the pleasure of the activity. Much of the play of typically developing children involves motor activity. Children whose motor impairments limit play often depend on others for entertainment and can easily become fussy or passive if not continuously attended to. They also lose out on opportunities to discover on their own how the world works, and they may lose their urge to master the environment—a critical factor in mental development. Children with significant motor impairments may need help in learning to play, explore, and persist. You can help the child by assessing his or her stage of play and then carefully selecting toys, activities, and positions to promote optimal play opportunities.

STAGES OF PLAY

A child's style of play goes through predictable stages during the preschool years. These stages include

- Exploratory play: Manipulating toys in an infantile way, mostly in order to experience new sights, sounds, tastes, and textures
- Independent play: Playing alone, using toys in a functional way, and not paying attention to other children
- Parallel play: Playing alongside other children, using similar toys but not sharing them
- Associative play: Playing alongside other children, sharing toys
- Cooperative play: Playing with others in an organized way with a common goal; role-playing and imaginative games emerge

DESIGNING PLAY ACTIVITIES
FOR A CHILD WITH MOTOR IMPAIRMENTS

The amount of creativity required for developing play activities for children with motor impairments increases with the severity of the motor difficulties. The greatest challenge is helping children play at a level commensurate with their cognitive capabilities. To design appropriate play activities, four questions need to be addressed: What is the stage of the child's play? What are the best positions to promote play? What are the motor capabilities of the child? What can be done with toys?

What is the stage of the child's play?

For children who have strong verbal skills or have adequate motor skills, it is easy to determine the stage. If the child does not talk and has poor motor skills, use trial and error to estimate the level of play. Observe spontaneous play, then provide assistance for more mature play. Does the child show enjoyment and seem to want more?

What are the best positions to promote play?

Place the child in several different positions to see which ones are easiest for the child. Try sitting, sidelying, semi-reclining, standing in a prone or supine stander, and lying on the stomach over a wedge. Vary the position of the toys in each position. Use trial and error to determine functional play positions. Allow plenty of time for the observation, and watch to see where the child has the best freedom of movement, accuracy, and endurance. Strive to identify several play situations with a variety of games.

What are the motor capabilities of the child?

Successful play depends on designing activities to match the child's motor abilities. Important areas to look at include

- Head control: Can the child keep head upright and turn from side to side without losing balance? When lying on the back, can the child maintain his or her head in midline while raising arms and bringing them together in midline?

- Eye control: Can the child look straight ahead, up, down, sideways? Are eye movements independent of head movements?

- Trunk control: Can the child sit up straight with the hands free for play?

- Arm control: Can the child reach in different directions and reach overhead? Is the child's trunk stable when he or she is reaching? Can the child use both arms at the same time?

- Hand control: Can the child swipe with a closed fist? Can the child hold on to an object and maintain grasp as the arm is moved? Can the child use fingers to pick up, push, and poke? Can the child use both hands at the same time?

- Leg control: Can the child bear weight on the legs, either independently or with support?

- Mobility: Can the child change position to reach new toys or add variety to an activity?

What can be done with toys?

The characteristics of toys should match the developmental play level and motor characteristics of the child. Toys can offer different combinations of sensations and can provide opportunity for manipulation, cause and effect, functional relationships, construction/destruction, and social interaction. Different toys require a range of motor skills depending on size, weight, ease of manipulation, and possibility of adaptation. All toys must be safe and well-constructed.

Many commercially available toys and materials can be used for children with special needs. There are also many ways to adapt toys to meet the specific needs of a child. Occupational and physical therapists routinely assist parents and teachers in adapting toys and activities. Some common techniques include

- Placing rubber shelf liner or Dycem mats under objects so they won't slip

- Devising ways of keeping toys in a child's hand (e.g., using gloves or cuffs with a piece of Velcro sewn on, attaching Velcro to the toys, attaching large handles to the toys)

- Contructing eye-gaze charts so a child can indicate choices for play

- Using switches to activate toys

PLAY WITH OTHER CHILDREN

Play with other children is particularly difficult for a child with significant motor impairments, especially if the motor impairment affects speech. As much as possible, provide the child with a means of communication that can be used in play. Although there are no magic solutions, strive to teach the child to take turns, win and lose, negotiate, and share, both at home with siblings and in the classroom with other children. Enlist the help of teachers to involve the child in group activities, promote friendships, and encourage classmates see the child as a same-age peer and not as the "baby."

CASE STUDY: TOSHA

Tosha is a 3-year-old girl who is at the stage of independent play but is starting to engage in parallel play. Most of her play has been with simple cause–effect objects, such as rattles and pop-up toys. Because of complex medical problems, she has been cared for at home all of her life with one-to-one adult attention. Tosha's health has improved, and she has just started preschool. She is interested in the other children but interacts with them only minimally. Physically, she shows diffuse muscle weakness. Her head and eye control are good. Her trunk is weak, and she sits with her trunk curved forward unless it is supported from behind. Tosha can use both arms to reach, but she uses the left more than the right. She can grasp medium-size objects with her hands, pick up small objects using her thumb against the side of her index finger, and point with her left hand. She also can stand with support and commando crawl.

Play Activities

Tosha's parents and teachers agreed that it was important for her to develop independent and parallel play. Together, they designed play activities that would help Tosha develop her existing language and motor skills while providing support for her weak trunk. They also wanted activities that could be used both at home and at school. Their ideas included the following:

1. Place Tosha in an adapted chair that holds her back straight and has a tray. Give her a baby doll with accessories and show her how to hug the baby, point out body parts, and feed the baby a bottle. Then, introduce activities that require more finger dexterity, such as taking off the baby's diaper, pulling off the baby's clothes, and wrapping the baby in a blanket. From time to time, bring over another child who also has a baby doll and help them play side by side while doing similar activities.

2. Place Tosha sitting with her back against the wall. Let her choose from a variety of interactive books such as flap books or board books with small holes for finger poking. Go through the books with Tosha, encouraging her to point with both index fingers, turn the pages, and manipulate the pages. From time to time, bring over another child to read books. Let them take turns with books and watch each other look at the books.

3. Support Tosha in standing at the kitchen center. Help her explore the materials and do pretend cooking. Gradually introduce other children into this activity and help them cook together, sharing equipment.

As Tosha's enjoyment of these activities increases, new and more challenging games will be gradually introduced. At home, Tosha's parents will incorporate new skills into daily routines. At school, Tosha will be supported in participation in classroom activities and developing relationships with special friends.

Appendix D
Object Boards
as Aids for Teaching Children
with Severe Motor Impairments

Some children with severe motor impairments may be unable to indicate their needs or to demonstrate their knowledge through reaching, pointing, or vocalizing in ways that infants and toddlers typically do. For months, or even years, eye gaze may be their primary means of communication. They may be able to answer the questions, "Where's Mama?" or "Where's your shoe?" by looking toward the correct location, or respond to the question, "What do you want?" by looking at either the glass of juice or the piece of bread held up in front of them.

The usefulness of eye gaze as a communication symbol is dependent on the ability of another person to "read" the gaze. This becomes increasingly difficult as the number of choices is expanded. Teaching a child with severe motor impairments to gaze in a precise manner so that others can readily determine where the gaze is directed is an important aspect of intervention.

Object boards are an effective way to teach a child precision in eye gaze while also teaching other information. A piece of Plexiglas, approximately 25 inches by 25 inches with a 4-inch by 6-inch window cut out of the center, makes a useful board. Pieces of Velcro can be attached to the board and to objects so that the objects can be mounted on the board and changed easily. Common arrangements that facilitate "reading" up to four choices are pictured on the next page. The adult positions him- or herself behind the board, looking at the child through the center window. He or she encourages the child to look at all of the things on the board and then says, "Look at me." When the child looks at the adult, the adult asks a question (e.g., "Where is the ball?") and observes where the child looks.

In the case of teaching items that involve looking at the correct place for an object after seeing it covered in one of three places, a handkerchief can be attached to the top of each of the three Velcro strips on the board and the object hidden as described in the item. The object is left under one cover by attaching it to the remainder of the Velcro under the handkerchief.

The object board also can be used for sorting tasks. For example, a red box and a green box can be attached to two of the Velcro strips. After demonstrating that red forms go in the red box and green forms in the green box, the adult holds up a red form and asks, "Where does this one go?" Shapes can be sorted the same way, having a simple shape drawn on the side of each box.

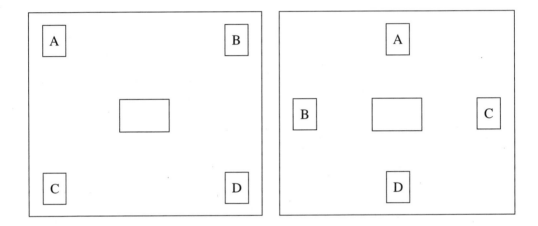

Appendix E
Motor Milestones
in Infant Development

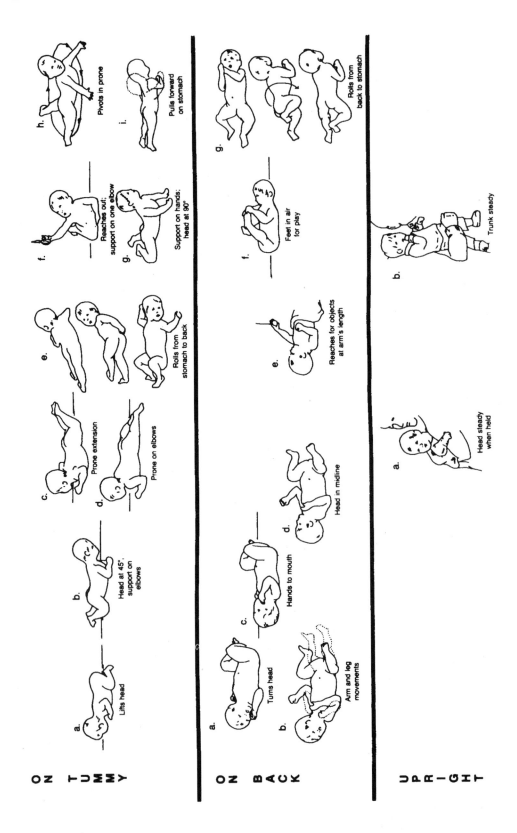

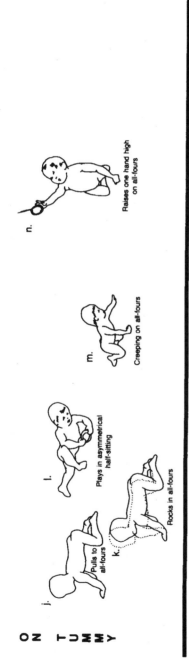

ON TUMMY

j. Pulls to all-fours

k. Rocks in all-fours

l. Plays in asymmetrical half-sitting

m. Creeping on all-fours

n. Raises one hand high on all-fours

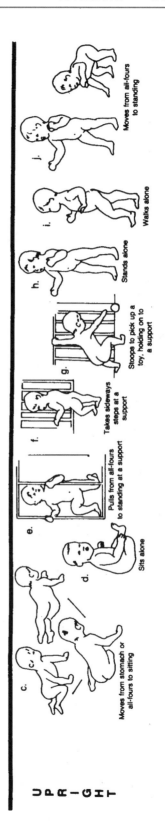

UPRIGHT

c. Moves from stomach or all-fours to sitting

d. Sits alone

e. Pulls from all-fours to standing at a support

f. Takes sideways steps at a support

g. Stoops to pick up a toy, holding on to a support

h. Stands alone

i. Walks alone

j. Moves from all-fours to standing

Index